Contemporary Christian Authors

Lives and Works

Janice DeLong
Rachel Schwedt

The Scarecrow Press, Inc.
Lanham, Maryland, and London
2000

SCARECROW PRESS, INC.

Published in the United States of America
by Scarecrow Press, Inc.
4720 Boston Way
Lanham, Maryland 20706
www.scarecrowpress.com

4 Pleydell Gardens, Folkestone
Kent CT20 2DN, England

British Library Cataloguing in Publication Information Available

Library of Congress Cataloging-in-Publication Data

DeLong, Janice, 1943–
Contemporary Christian authors : lives and works / Janice DeLong, Rachel Schwedt.
p. cm.
Includes bibliographical references and index.
ISBN 0-8108-3688-2 (alk. paper)
1. Christian fiction, American—Bio-bibliography Dictionaries. 2. Novelists, American—20th century—Biography Dictionaries. I. Schwedt, Rachel E., 1944– . II. Title.
PS374.C48D45 2000 99-41563
810.9'3823—dc21 CIP
[B]

∞™ The paper used in this publication meets the minimum requirements of American National Standard for Information Sciences—Permanence of Paper for Printed Library Materials, ANSI/NISO Z39.48–1992.
Manufactured in the United States of America.

Contents

Acknowledgments

A number of special people contributed to this pleasant piece of work. We would like to recognize Peggy Pickering for research we used from *Biographies of Christian Authors Who Write for Young Readers* (vol. 2, 1995). From this we gathered interesting facts about the childhoods of Barbara Davoll and Peter Reese Doyle. Student assistants Esther Alcindor, Angie Kraje, Kari Carlisle, Kara DeLong, and Shelli Warner gave hours of invaluable service as they typed, copied, edited, and ran errands. Their organizational and computer skills allowed us the time needed to focus on assembling the mass of information we received. Reviewer Dave Barnett and student reviewers Sarah Barnett, Rachel Hassenpflug, Mark Jones, Timothy Lai, Sarah E. Meyer, Trevor Raspberry, Stacie Roy, Joshua Stone, Stuart Smith, Janelle Vaughan, and Jena West provided fresh insight by their additions.

Our tribute goes to the authors who took time from their busy schedules to write, e-mail, talk on the phone, or send audiotapes. We pray that they will be blessed for their contribution to this work.

Finally, we would like to extend appreciation to our families for their encouragement and interest. To our husbands, Ron and Robert, who helped with the photography, took us out to eat, and sent clothes to the laundry so that we could have more time to read, research, and spend at the computer, we say, "Thank you." We certainly could not have survived without your patience, understanding, and help. To our children, Julie, Alan, Beth, Mike, Lynne, and Kara, your simply asking, "How's the book going?" let us know that you cared. Bless you.

Introduction

Since creation, mankind has enjoyed a good story. The Bible sets the tone in the way it presents truth through the real stories of the Old Testament. Jesus continues this approach as he teaches through parables in the New Testament. Like those parables, tales woven by modern-day writers present examples of life, death, loyalty, courage, and victory over adversity. The principles they teach are illustrated through the lives of the characters they create. Well-written fiction can be a powerful vehicle for truth, clarifying life situations and putting them into clearer focus. Stories touch the heart and mind in ways that a simple statement of fact cannot do. As readers watch and identify with a character's struggles, pain, and growth, reading can become a regenerative process.

When asked why they chose fiction as their vehicle of expression, the authors profiled in this book acknowledged the power of the medium in various ways. Randall Arthur stated, "Mankind, since the beginning, has unabatedly enjoyed good stories and always will." Jack Cavanaugh shared, "By transporting my readers back to another day and age, I hope that they will realize we are not alone in our struggles." Paul McCusker revealed, "I hope my writing tells a good story with insights into our human condition." Robin Gunn summed up the universal importance of fiction when she said, "Stories are the common ground of all peoples of all nations."

George MacDonald, writing in the late 1800s, Grace Livingston Hill and Charles Sheldon in the early 1900s, and C. S. Lewis in the mid-1900s were pioneers in the field of inspirational fiction, but the genre remained nearly virgin territory until the early 1980s, when Janette Oke and Frank Peretti seeded and watered the ground with their vastly different novels. Now we are reaping the harvest. While Oke and Peretti remain on the best-seller lists, dozens of writers currently share the foundational principles of their lives through created story. Finally, it appears that Christian fiction is coming of age.

Yet it seems that many avid readers of spiritual nonfiction books are unaware of the power and scope of inspirational fiction. Some might have read one or two traditional titles but have not tapped into the rich source of entertainment, enrichment, and encouragement created by the contemporary pen. Every year thousands of inspirational fiction books are sold, with fresh faces coming to the market each season. It is the purpose of this book to introduce novice readers to the endless plots and themes found on the pages of inspirational novels and to bring new names to the reading shelves of those who are longtime fans of Christian fiction.

Contemporary Christian Authors focuses on story makers who have achieved a wide following through at least one outstanding contribution to the market, although most have penned numerous offerings. Some are recognized in more than one genre, and many publish across age levels. All featured authors are living at the time of our writing. Writers included employ a wide variety of approaches to inspirational novels. They encompass styles as comfortable as that used by Lori Wick to that as disquieting as that of James Byron Huggins. Some console with glimpses of close family living; others alarm with unsettling views of ethical dilemmas facing society. However, one common thread running throughout the works of all the writers featured in this book is the commitment to a philosophy based on traditional values and a Christian worldview.

Types of writing featured in this book span the gamut of the broad term "fiction," whether they are problem novels whose characters face conflicts unique to this generation (Harry Kraus and Beverly Bush Smith) or age-old conflicts expressed in picturesque historical fiction (T. Davis Bunn and Lynn Morris). There are mysteries with appeal for both adults (Terri Blackstock and Doris Elaine Fell) and children (Dave Gustaveson). Adventure stories appear that are set in one's own backyard (Paul McCusker and Lee Roddy) or in mystical countries across the sea (Linda Chaikin). Fantasy works range from those lauding the courage of mice (Barabara Davoll) to those in which characters battle to save civilization from evil forces (John White). Other categories are westerns (Judith Pella and Stephen Bly) and humor (William Kritlow and Bill Myers). Multicultural literature includes books introducing young adults to what life is like in America for cultural groups such as the Amish (Mary Borntrager) and those set in countries as far away as Australia (Sandy Dengler). Although most of these categories are common to both secular and Christian publishing, the areas of spiritual warfare (Will Cunningham) and prophecy (Jerry Jenkins) are unique to the religious community. Whatever the style, inspirational fiction has the distinction of including spiritual principles to guide and strengthen the reader's daily life.

Each writer's entry reflects the amount of information supplied in response to the research questionnaire. The format of the final survey requested photographs and information covering specific details, such as date of birth and educational background, as well as more esoteric issues, such as personal goals for writing and predictions regarding the future of Christian fiction. Some authors chose to reveal much about themselves, whereas others chose to be very concise. Biographical information presented is directly quoted or is a restatement of comments of the authors; however, evaluative observations express the views of the compilers based on their own research.

Individual entries begin with a brief introduction to the writer as a person and are followed by the "Professional" section, listing education completed, career experiences, awards won, and memberships maintained. A comprehensive inventory of the author's published works arranged by target audience and genre makes up the "Publications" section. An expanded biographical narrative in the "Personal" section provides insight into each person's research techniques and the literary elements emphasized in his or her writing. Authors reveal influences, both literary and personal, that have motivated and inspired them. They further share goals they hope to achieve for themselves and their readers, and venture predictions regarding the future of Christian fiction.

Finally, the "Summary" section highlights at least one title that represents the author's style with a brief synopsis. More than one annotation is given for those who have written multiple series, who have penned works demonstrating a wide range of creativity, or who have worked both alone and with other writing partners. To give authentic reactions to works aimed at a juvenile audience, reviews were solicited from young readers. On occasion, authors have provided personal annotations of their works that are included to reveal the purpose, style, and richness of the writer's language.

The research process for this work involved two of the most difficult aspects of writing: choosing subjects and creating a viable questionnaire. The authors we selected have written beloved books and have taken an innovative approach to their subject, and they always tell a good story. We culled names from booksellers' reviews, best-seller lists (both printed and electronic), word-of-mouth recommendations, and personal favorites. We made no attempt to select authors or contributors on the basis of doctrinal positions. More than a hundred authors received invitations to participate in this project. Some chose not to respond, whereas others felt that writers should retain a sort of mystery about themselves or wished to protect their privacy and so stated that they did not want to be a part of the work. Thus, if a favorite is not found, perhaps the author chose not to participate.

Celebrity always carries with it mystique, yet participating authors have chosen to reveal an intimate side, allowing readers to become better acquainted with them. Sometimes they share a smile, sometimes a tear, but always they convey a passionate belief in creating stories to nurture and inform. It is our belief that readers of inspirational fiction will enjoy these personal visits afforded by *Contemporary Christian Authors.*

Randy Alcorn

Writing is one more facet of an already extensive ministry for Randy Alcorn. As founder and director of Eternal Perspectives Ministries (EPM), his life is devoted to "teaching biblical truth and morality and drawing attention to the needs of the 'un' people for whom Christ died—unreached, unfed, unborn and unsupported, including women exploited by abortion." His life emphasis is on communicating the importance of using "time, money, possessions and opportunities" to meet the needs of others while "analyzing, teaching, and applying the moral, social, and relational implications of Christian truth in the current age."

Alcorn lives in Oregon with his wife and daughters, from whom he receives much encouragement for his writing efforts. Nancy, his wife, sacrifices their time together to allow him the time he needs to write. His daughters not only read their father's books but also share them with friends, whose names or nicknames have been used by the author as characters or street names in his books. In rare moments of relaxation, he enjoys reading, snorkeling, playing tennis, and traveling internationally with his family.

PROFESSIONAL

Education

M.A.B.S., Western Baptist Seminary; Th.B., Multnomah Bible College

Career

1976–1990, pastor, Good Shepherd Community Church; teacher and conference speaker; part-time faculty, Western Baptist Seminary and Multnomah Bible College; founder and director, Eternal Perspectives Ministries; publisher, *Eternal Perspectives Journal*; guest on radio and television; author

Awards

Gold Medallion Finalist, *Pro-Life Answers to Pro-Choice Arguments,* 1992; Book of the Year, Italy, International Category, Tito Casini, 1996

PUBLICATIONS

Adult Fiction

Deadline, 1994
Dominion, 1996
Edge of Eternity, 1998
Lord Foulgrin's Letters, 2000

Adult Nonfiction

Christians in the Wake of the Sexual Revolution, 1985
Women under Stress: Preserving Your Sanity, 1986
Sexual Temptation, 1989
Is Rescuing Right?: Breaking the Law to Save the Unborn, 1990
Pro-Life Answers to Pro-Choice Arguments, 1992
Does the Birth Control Pill Cause Abortions?, 1998
In Light of Eternity: Perspectives on Heaven, 1999

Articles

Numerous articles published in *Discipleship Journal, Moody, Leadership, New Man,* and *The Christian Reader*

PERSONAL

One strong motivation that compels Randy Alcorn to write is his desire to communicate truth. He wants to accomplish something that will count toward eternity. He began writing nonfiction articles and books but made the choice to move to fiction to appeal to a broader audience. He wanted to reach those who would not pick up an issue-oriented book—those who wanted a story.

Alcorn likens his approach to the Trojan horse effect. Although readers are enjoying the story, it is "reflecting truth in a disarming way." He tries to put this in an eternal or otherworldly perspective. For Alcorn, fiction "casts a wider net."

Whereas some authors research only when they need specific information, Alcorn does not wait for the need to arise. His approach is to use exhaustive information-gathering methods. "When you have an idea, you want to research it thoroughly before starting." Preparing to write *Dominion,* which is set in an inner-city location, he "read books, watched videos, talked with detectives, rode along with police, and took part in investigations of drive-by shootings. . . . It is important that details of character and setting are accurate. With errors, you lose your readers. In reality, the reader understands that your story is not true, but in essence they don't. When they see an error, they *know* it is not true."

To accurately portray the main character in *Dominion,* who writes a sports column for a local newspaper, Alcorn visited several newspapers and talked with journalists from various cities. To portray Obadiah Abernathy—an elderly black man who played baseball in the African-American leagues—he read, talked with former players, and watched videos about the teams. Even though Obadiah was a minor character, Alcorn felt that the research he did was important. "The more I research, the more I feel I am accurate and bring depth to my characterizations. . . . I believe in the iceberg principle. For the tip to show, there must be a mass of material underneath (below the surface). Then characters will have depth. They will not be cardboard characters that disappear when they turn sideways. This tends to be a weakness in fiction. Characters are built to serve the plot. If the reader doesn't care enough about a character to believe he could be real, he won't really care about what happens to him."

Some characters who Alcorn creates are given the names of people he knows, but "their personalities don't always fit." He weaves character qualities of various people together, even using some of his own habits and idiosyncrasies. "A lot of me comes out in my novels, but not usually in one character."

Much of Alcorn's work is done in a home office attached to his garage. He does not have a scheduled time of day to work but tends to work toward deadlines. He "knows about how much needs to be done per week." He will often take his laptop computer to a library to work, but for much of his research he prefers to purchase books that would be useful instead of borrowing them. Periodically, he will take "two- to five-day writing retreats at a beach cabin on the Oregon coast. It is isolated. I can get huge amounts done away from the telephone, e-mail, and so on."

The audience whom Alcorn addresses varies with his books. His nonfiction volumes target "hungry, serious, open Christians who want to be challenged." His fiction reaches beyond to those who want to be entertained. "If you want to be entertained, do it with a good story, one that will enrich and deepen your understanding." He has also received a very positive response from the non-Christian community. Some who had taken opposing positions on issues have written the author to share how they had been persuaded to agree with his approach by watching his characters find things that either worked or did not work for them.

When asked who has most influenced his writing, Alcorn names three writers whom he respects for their "commitment, their intellect, and the moral and ethical dimension of their works": A. W. Tozer and Francis Schaeffer, who have greatly influenced his theology, and C. S. Lewis, who has greatly influenced his fiction. He feels that the thoughts of these men are reflected in everything that he writes.

Alcorn's personal goal for his writing is to glorify God. His spiritual beliefs permeate his writing. "Not every paragraph is laced with Bible teaching, but every paragraph is there because it contributes to a whole that will glorify God. . . . At the end of my life, whether it is tomorrow or forty years from now, I want to look back and believe that I have made a difference in people's lives."

For his readers, Alcorn hopes that "they would truly be changed whether in a small way or a huge way." He has received letters from some who have come to a knowledge of God after reading *Deadline*. Others have written that the racial themes in *Dominion* opened their eyes to issues they had never dealt with. These responses bring pleasure, for Alcorn wants his readers "to be entertained, but to walk away different." He also hopes to encourage his readers to take an eternal perspective on life, to see beyond the moment, accepting the stresses and difficulties of life as God's refining process. Likening life to a tapestry, he states that most of people's lives are spent looking at the underside of the cloth. He tries to take them above to see their lives as a beautiful, organized, and purposeful work of art that God is creating. He attempts to encourage readers to live beyond the present, "not sacrificing the eternal on the altar of the immediate."

Alcorn sees both positive and negative in the present field of Christian fiction, with more people undertaking the effort to produce in the genre. "When Frank Peretti broke through, it exploded." Although fiction had been popular in the secular field for a long time, it was sparse in Christian publishing. "For myself, I saw fiction as the opposite of truth. Finally, I saw that it could be true and effective. . . . Often it can cut to the truth more effectively than nonfiction. In Luke 15, the story of the prodigal son most clearly captures the imagination regarding God's grace."

Alcorn is concerned about the quality of some of the materials currently being published. "Secular publishers already had a full plate. Editors could recognize bad fiction. Christian publishers did not have one hundred others to compare to. They lowered the bar to meet the market demand. . . . Publishers have used writers almost like buying a lottery ticket, hoping that one will be the next Frank Peretti. There has not been a clear level of discernment." Despite these drawbacks, the author is "guardedly optimistic . . . hoping that the good stuff will rise to the top. . . . There is more good writing than five years ago, but readers are trying to find and access the good which is buried under a sea of the mediocre."

Alcorn sees the large number of wholesale titles that are available compared to the small size of most Christian bookstores as one factor working against the success of any particular fiction title. Most stores simply do not have enough display area to do the genre justice. "It is overwhelming walking around the Christian Booksellers Association, seeing booths having an enormous selection of titles available. . . . You could walk all day and not see most of the books there." In another way, he sees this as a responsibility of the publishers to be more selective in what they publish.

Alcorn is deeply appreciative of readers who have written or called and who have approached him when he speaks. "When I write a book every other year, it is not like preaching a sermon, where feedback is received after one week of work. From the time research begins, to the production of a hardcover, is a long time. It's like building a house that no one is permitted to see. It's a strange, lonely feeling. What keeps me going on a current book is the letters and e-mail which come saying how my books have affected lives."

SUMMARY: *DEADLINE*

Looking forward to a Sunday afternoon spent with Finney and Doc, two men who have been his friends since childhood, Jake Woods is unprepared for the tragic accident that takes Finney's and Doc's lives. Escaping with only minor injuries, Jake is left behind to unravel the mysterious circumstances surrounding the incident. The clues become more complex and dangerous as he discovers much about Doc's medical practices that he did not know.

Confronting the issues raised by his investigation, Jake is forced to examine his own beliefs and the result of the choices he has made throughout his life. Watching from heaven, Finney continues to pray for Jake as Jake searches for answers not only to the death of his friends but also to the remainder of his life on earth. As the dual story line unfolds on earth and in heaven, Alcorn uses "sanctified imagination" based on solid biblical research to create for the reader a picture of what heaven might be like.

Randall Arthur (Dodd)

Randall Arthur was born on December 12, 1953, to Flora Dodd, a homemaker, and Toy Dodd, a railroad worker in Atlanta, Georgia. He received his ordination in 1975. He and his wife, Sherri, have three children. The Dodds have served as church planters in Europe since 1976.

Arthur did not grow up in a home "where literature was read aloud or even emphasized," so he has "no childhood memories of any particularly outstanding books." Thus, his own books have not risen out of an ambition to write novels but "out of a therapeutic need to put into writing the things regarding Christian legalism that I (as legalist) was feeling, thinking, and learning while living in Europe as the founder and pastor of a multinational church."

Being "an adventurer at heart," Arthur considers Christian fiction a natural vehicle to present his heart in writing. This adventurous spirit shows in his choice of hobbies, which include mountain climbing, motorcycling, and scuba diving.

PROFESSIONAL

Education

Th.B., Tennessee Temple University

Career
Church planter and pastor in Europe since 1975

PUBLICATIONS

Adult Fiction

Wisdom Hunter, 1991
Jordan's Crossing, 1993
Betrayal, 1999

PERSONAL

Randall Arthur shares, "When I was living and working in Oslo, Norway, I read an unpublished novel written by a young American man my own age who resided in my neighborhood . . . his novel—several hundred typewritten pages contained loosely in a small cardboard box—held me spellbound. At that time I had already been toying for several weeks with the idea of attempting to write a novel myself. Reading this young man's work and thinking 'If he can do it, I can do it' was what motivated me to pick up a pen and begin my own project. This was in the fall of 1984.

"I wrote consistently for six months. After completing one-third of my story (216 typewritten pages, double spaced), I tabled the project. Personal struggles in my life were draining me emotionally, physically, and mentally and took away my will to write anymore. Approximately six months later, when I returned to the States for a period of furlough, I unpacked the partial manuscript. I was curious, in the event that I might someday be compelled to finish the project, to find out if the 216 pages I had already written were deemed by others to be readable and worthwhile." When each of the three or four people Arthur asked to read his manuscript returned it after reading less than twenty or thirty pages, he decided that "the manuscript had failed miserably to interest any of them."

Arthur's next step was to approach a published author who lived in his community about reading his work and giving a truthful critique. She gave him a typed list of what she claimed were necessary elements to use in building a successful novel along with the advice to scrap everything and start over. Showing incredible perseverance, Arthur did just that. A year and a half later, after returning to Europe, he laid out the typed list along with his manuscript and began again at page one. Employing the help of test readers, he wrote and rewrote the first chapter until the readers said, "Where's chapter two?" Working his way through the next nine chapters following this procedure, Arthur established a style and pace that his readers enjoyed. "And for the next two years, as I finished the book, I abstained totally from reading any other literature except for the Scriptures. As a vulnerable first-time writer, I simply did not want my newly found and painfully-worked-for rhythm to be abruptly influenced and altered by the writing styles of other authors.

"Before I commence writing page one of my first draft, I establish my story line from beginning to end. Once the entire story is cemented in my mind, I make a mental note of the elements of the story which will require research. . . . I mostly do my research on a when-I-need-to-know basis. The story line, of course, tells me *when* I need to know. At that point, I refer to whatever resources are available—the phone, encyclopedias, people in positions of experience and authority, and so on.

"My procedure for most days, is as follows: I first write three or four paragraphs by hand. This initial handwriting, however, is almost never done in my office. It is usually done throughout the day as I move about in my pastoral duties—while waiting in the car, sitting at a restaurant for lunch or dinner, and/or traveling by subway. I continue to rework the handwritten paragraphs until I'm satisfied with their quality. At that point (normally in the early evening) I type them into my computer, save them on the hard drive, and make a printout. This piecemeal type of writing is done five to six days a week."

Although Arthur's writing style has been influenced by secular novelists such as Morris West and Ken Follett, he says that his writing "has progressively been shaped more by the help and insights of an editor friend than by prolific reading." The substance of his writing has been influenced more "by real-life experiences than by ideas gleaned from other books.

"My plots are primarily theme driven; secondarily action driven. The major themes have thus far been taken from my own life and my own personal experiences and observations. As a young Christian, raised in an environment of hard-core religious legalism, I was trained by dictatorial-type church leaders. And subsequently, I became such a leader.

"The heart-and-mind journey of Jason Faircloth, the major character of my first book, mirrors my own personal pilgrimage as I eventually became disillusioned with my denomination and swung painfully out of control from the far right to the far left. . . . I write not as an authority on the Church or on the Christian life but rather as a student who has learned from his personal failures and as an insider who is familiar with the many victims left in the wake of religious legalism.

"Specifically, I envision my targeted audience to be those who—as perpetrators, victims, or observers—can relate personally to my chosen themes. Generally, however, I would like for any adult regardless of their faith, background, or experiences in life to be able to pick up one of my novels and be captured, entertained, and challenged by what they are reading.

"My spiritual beliefs are the backbone of my writing. My spiritual experiences then add the flesh and blood. One of my main goals is to take some of the abstract thoughts and feelings which are common to disillusioned, questioning, and struggling Christians and sculpture them—using words as the raw material—into clear and recognizable insights. I want my readers to be emotionally and spiritually refreshed, thoughtfully provoked to analyze their belief systems, and behaviorally challenged.

"My first book, when it was published, proved to be too controversial for my denomination. Upon reading *Wisdom Hunter,* the president of the mission agency with which I had served for seventeen years fired me literally overnight. Within a matter of weeks, nearly all of my sponsoring churches reacted with equal offense, quickly severing their relationship with me. Consequently, I lost nearly my entire network of lifelong constituents and over sixty-five percent of my income. I was thirty-eight years old.

"Starting over in life was not easy, but I was left without any other viable options. As difficult as it was, however, the new beginning proved to be a major stepping stone. Not only did I find a new and healthier direction as a pastor, but I was also launched into a secondary career as a successful novelist. I am now working on my third novel, with the first two currently being translated into several foreign languages. The transition also brought me into contact with a whole new network of friends, the most wonderful and understanding friends I have ever known."

Testimonials from around the world have confirmed for Arthur that "Christian fiction has the ability to make a positive impact on people's lives and thinking readers." When asked about his view regarding the future of this genre, he had this to say: "Mankind, since the beginning, has unabatedly enjoyed good stories—and always will. As long as quality stories are created, there will be a market for them, either on a mass scale through the publishing industry or on a small scale from person to person."

Arthur does not yet have a long list of titles to his credit, but the books that he has written have the potential to greatly affect the thought patterns of those who call themselves Christian.

SUMMARY: *WISDOM HUNTER*

Jason Faircloth, given the nickname "The General" by his congregation, is greatly respected and strongly supported by those in his church who share his stringent legalistic views. Those who do not agree with his methods have no choice but to leave the church. Hannah, his daughter, is one of those who chooses to leave—running away during her junior year in high school to escape her father's heavy hand of control. When word comes to the devastated parents that Hannah has died in childbirth, Jason's wife, Lorene, can no longer sustain her own will to live.

Crushed and disillusioned by these overwhelming events, Jason resigns his position as pastor and begins a hunt for his granddaughter that takes him through many countries. As his search stretches out from months to years, Jason comes to terms with his failures and becomes a "wisdom hunter," reaching out to find the reality of a God whom he had previously kept in such a very small box of rules and regulations.

Through the character of Jason Faircloth, Arthur successfully embodies his own search for a true living God—one that is undistorted by cultural bias. So successful is Arthur's portrayal that readers are made to feel the frustration and pain of loss and are drawn into this desperate search for truth.

Lynn Austin

A full-time freelance writer and speaker, Lynn Austin attended Hope College and received her B.A. degree from Southern Connecticut State University. With her husband, Ken, Austin has lived and worked in Bogota, Columbia; Ontario and Manitoba, Canada; and several cities throughout the United States. She is presently on the editorial board of *Profile,* the journal of the Chicago Women's Conference. Her husband is a professor at Trinity Christian College. They live in Illinois with their three children.

The thorough knowledge of biblical history that Austin displays in her novels stems from graduate work in biblical backgrounds and archaeology that she completed at Southwestern Theological Seminary. She also was fortunate to spend the summer of 1989 in Israel participating in an archaeological dig at the biblical city of Timnah. In addition to her biblical novels, Austin is a frequent contributor of articles to Christian periodicals.

PROFESSIONAL

Education

Graduate work, Southwestern Theological Seminary; B.A., Southern Connecticut State University; three years, Hope College

Career

Editorial board, *Profile,* the journal of the Chicago Women's Conference; contributing editor, *The Christian Reader;* freelance writer and speaker

Awards

New Writer of the Year, Moody Write-to-Publish Conference, 1993; Writer of the Year, Wheaton College Write-to-Publish Conference, 1996

PUBLICATIONS

Adult Fiction

Fly Away, 1997
Chronicles of the King Series
  The Lord Is My Strength, 1995
  The Lord Is My Song, 1996
  The Lord Is My Salvation, 1996
  My Father's God, 1997
  Among the Gods, 1998
  Eve's Daughter, 1999

Articles

Numerous articles in *The Lookout, Teen Power, Women Alive!, Christian Educator's Journal, Standard, LIVE, Profile, Discipleship Journal, Moody Magazine, Christian Reader, Parents of Teenagers,* and *Teachers in Focus*

PERSONAL

My love of reading initiated my interest in writing. I enjoy reading all types and genres of books and usually read one to two a week. I am especially intrigued by a good story, well told. When I found that I was constantly creating stories in my head, I decided to try it on paper. I chose to write Christian fiction because of my desire to use my talents to glorify God. My Christian worldview is going to permeate everything I write, making it "Christian" fiction whether I consciously choose it or not.

I began writing during my children's naptime when they were preschoolers, then learned to set up my portable typewriter wherever the kids were playing and write in the midst of interruptions and chaos. Today those children are teenagers, and I write full-time, from 8 A.M. to 4 P.M. Monday through

Friday (and sometimes Saturdays and evenings when I have an approaching deadline). Although I now use a computer, my "office" is in our living room, where I still write in the midst of interruptions and chaos.

More than any other person, my husband, Ken, has inspired, encouraged and motivated me to write. Long before I ever published a single article, he believed that my Chronicles of the King Series would one day be published, and he wouldn't let me quit even when I was discouraged. I've lost track of the many hours he's spent babysitting and the countless meals he has cooked so that I could write, and I'm grateful that he is still my biggest fan.

My research process is extensive. As a writer of historical fiction, I find that research consumes a huge portion of my time—but it is a process I thoroughly enjoy. I've always loved history, particularly Old Testament history. To research my five-book series, Chronicles of the King, I studied biblical backgrounds and archaeology in Israel, participating in an archaeological dig during the summer of 1989. This provided me with inspiration as well as the necessary background information for everyday life in ancient times. I've also extensively researched the Jewish religion in order to accurately portray all aspects of Old Testament faith.

While my primary source of information is always the Bible, other resources I've used include *Biblical Archaeology Review,* the Talmud, Assyrian records, the Greek historian Herodotus, and the Jewish historian Josephus. I complete most of my research before beginning each novel but look up more information as needed once I begin.

When plotting my books, I strive to maintain an even balance between action, character, and theme. In creating books that the reader "can't put down," action plays a major part, but the source of that action and conflict always arises from the character's own drives and flaws. I try to create three-dimensional characters that readers can identify with and learn from as they grow and change. Each book also has a definite theme (unforgiveness, pride, etc.) that I try to weave into the story line. This theme is a source of conflict for my characters and is usually most clearly revealed during the climax and resolution of the book.

None of my characters are based on people that I know, but many of their situations and their reactions to those situations are based on real-life people and events. For example, the heroine in *The Lord Is My Song* struggles with infertility; her emotions are based on my own experience as I struggled for nearly eight years to conceive. In *Among the Gods,* a father deals with the heartache of a rebellious son; I prayed with close friends of mine as they dealt with a similar problem. . . . The recurring theme in each of my books is the greatness of God and His infinite love. My goal is to weave God into the story in such a way that He becomes the main character of each book, actively involved in the other characters' lives and revealing some aspect of His awesome nature to them—and to the reader.

I have always been a very eclectic reader, enjoying both fiction and nonfiction—everything from Shakespeare and the classics to biographies, mysteries, and suspense novels. Over the years, I've developed a mental image of the "ideal" book: It makes you laugh and cry and think; you can't put it down; the characters become old friends that stay with you after you've finished it; and most of all, it glorifies God. This "ideal" shapes my writing today. More than any other book, however, the Bible has influenced my writing (and me).

My spiritual beliefs strongly influence and affect my writing. I need to keep a close, personal walk with God, continuing to grow and learn every day because my writing will only attain a spiritual depth that I personally have attained. I am on a lifelong spiritual pilgrimage, seeking a deeper relationship with God, as are my characters. . . . One of my personal goals is to learn to yield more and more to the Holy Spirit as I write. I'd like to allow the trials and joys of writing to draw me closer to God as I learn to depend on Him.

I write primarily to inspire my fellow adult Christian readers, both men and women. I have learned, however, that at least one Christian school has implemented my books into their middle-school curriculum and that non-Christians have also enjoyed and benefited from my books. The oldest reader I have met is ninety-six, the youngest is twelve. My goals for my readers include helping them to see God in a different way, to expand their thinking about spiritual matters and give them a hunger for a deeper relationship with God. Another goal is to draw readers to the Word of God where God reveals Himself. As I strive to bring the Old Testament to life, I'd like readers to see its characters not as plastic saints but as struggling human beings, just like us, and recognize that the Bible has relevance today. . . . My love of the Old Testament and its people has influenced my writing the most. Bible characters and their stories have always come alive for me, and when I realized that this wasn't true for most people—that many Christians found the Old Testament difficult to understand—it became my desire to bring its pages to life for my readers.

Many Christians I know never read Christian novels because much of the fiction that has been published has been a disappointment to them. They are avid readers but prefer the quality, variety, and intellectual stimulation of secular books. In order for Christian fiction to avoid stagnation and to see future growth, publishers are going to have to offer higher quality and a greater variety of books to draw these readers back.

SUMMARY: *THE LORD IS MY SALVATION* (CHRONICLES OF THE KING SERIES)

Having given his life to restoring the worship of God to his people, King Hezekiah is shattered to find his barren wife, Hephzibah, giving homage to Asherah, the goddess of fertility. As rage takes control, he destroys the shrine, but in so doing he starts a fire that burns him severely. Hovering between life and death, Hezekiah cries out to the Lord for healing and salvation. As God grants his wish to recover, he finds himself in battle against those who would destroy the kingdom of Israel from within and without. But perhaps the strongest foe he must face is the bitterness against his beautiful wife that has gripped his heart and torments his mind. Will he find the grace to forgive?

Terri Blackstock

Born on December 7, 1957, in Belleville, Illinois, Terri Blackstock is the daughter of Jo An Weathersby and Colonel O. L. Ward Jr., an airline pilot and retired Air Force colonel. She and her husband, Ken, now live in Mississippi and are the parents of three children.

Writing since she was twelve years old, Blackstock published her first poem, about Vietnam, in her local newspaper. From that point on she planned to be a writer. She sold her first novel to Silhouette Books in 1983 under the name Terri Herrington. Other books were sold to Dell Publishers and Harlequin Books under the name Tracy Hughes. When Blackstock decided to switch publishers, genres, and pen names in 1994, she had three and a half million books in print worldwide.

PROFESSIONAL

Education

B.A. in English, Northeast Louisiana University (graduated magna cum laude)

Career

Guest on *The 700 Club,* fall 1996; guest on the ACTS Network; interviewed for the publications *Christian Retailing* and *Homelife*

Awards

Gold Medallion Award, Romance Writers of America, 1987; Lifetime Achievement Award, *Romance Times* magazine, 1989

PUBLICATIONS

Sun Coast Chronicles Series
- *Evidence of Mercy,* 1995
- *Justifiable Means,* 1996
- *Ulterior Motives,* 1996
- *Presumption of Guilt,* 1997

Second Chances Series
- *Never Again Good-Bye,* 1996
- *When Dreams Cross,* 1997
- *Blind Trust,* 1998
- *Broken Wings,* 1998

Newpointe 911 Series
- *Private Justice,* 1998
- *Shadow of Doubt,* 1998
- *Word of Honor,* 1999

Coauthored with Beverly LaHaye

Seasons under Heaven, 1999

PERSONAL

The year 1994 marked an important change for Terri Blackstock. She ended her career in romance writing and turned to suspense. "I found that those were the books I most liked to read. I loved the idea of the ticking bomb and ordinary people in jeopardy. I decided that I wanted to write those types of stories instead." Another decision influenced her change. Because of her renewed interest in spiritual things, she "wanted to be able to tell the truth in [her] stories and not just be politically correct. It doesn't matter how many readers I have if I can't tell them what I know about the roots of their problems and the solutions that have literally saved my own life. . . . I wanted to glorify God and point people to Him with everything I wrote. I also wanted to speak to Christians about forsaking their first love, being lukewarm, making wrong choices, God's provision for their mistakes, and so on. These are all things I've had to learn the hard way, and I'd like to pass them on to my readers now."

Blackstock often interviews people personally and uses the Internet for research. "And I read biographies to get ideas about subjects. For example, when I wrote a book about an automobile mogul, I read about Iacocca. When I wrote about rich people, I read about Trump or the Helmsleys. When I dealt with a paraplegic, I read books by famous people who'd had back injuries and so on."

Blackstock sees as her audience anyone who likes to read suspense or romance. Her settings tend to be fictionalized, so she does not "feel bound by reality." Rather than being based on people she knows, her characters are "really more like compilations of people I know. My husband's sense of humor often winds up coming out of my characters, though." If there is one recurring theme in her books, it is "God's provision for our worst mistakes and our worst weaknesses."

When asked who has most influenced her writing she replied, "Everything I read influences my writing. My biggest influence, however, is the Bible. Whenever I'm deeply convicted, I start thinking of plots to illustrate that conviction. Jesus did it first with his parables. If my parables can have even a fraction of the impact that Jesus' did, I'll be a success."

Blackstock's goal for herself is to "somehow change the lives of my readers for the better and be obedient to God's will in my life." She wants her readers "to think and take hard looks at themselves. They don't have to agree with my theology, but if I make them think about their own, I've reached my goal."

As to the future of Christian fiction, Blackstock believes "that over the next few years we will see Christian fiction catching up with secular fiction, and the Christian best-seller list will look more like the secular best-seller list. The difference will be that readers—Christian and non-Christian alike—will know that they can buy our books and not be offended by gratuitous sex and violence or profanity. I'm excited about what God is doing in this area."

SUMMARY: *EVIDENCE OF MERCY* (SUN COAST CHRONICLES SERIES)

Evidence of Mercy was released in October 1995 under the author's real name. "This suspense novel tells the story of Lynda Barrett, a young lawyer who can no longer afford to keep her beloved plane, due to her debts from her father's illness. When she takes a potential buyer up for a test flight, she finds that her plane has been sabotaged. The flight ends in disaster—hurling them into a terrifying sequence of events. Through it all, one thing becomes clear: someone will not be satisfied until Lynda is dead. This novel takes the reader on a suspense-filled flight into a world where the dark side of human

Just Because They've Left Doesn't Mean They're Gone: How to Love and Support Your Adult Children, 1993
The Surprising Side of Grace: Appreciating God's Loving Anger, 1994
Once a Parent, Always a Parent, 1999

Articles

Hundreds of articles and short stories published in over 100 periodicals

Reprints

Many of Bly's books have been reprinted in foreign languages, and a number have large-print editions available.

PERSONAL

Stephen Bly first became interested in writing "in 1976 (at the age of 34), when my wife actively began to submit some of my writings to various publications. She is the one who initiated my writing and followed through until I was published. I would never have written anything without her encouragement and help. She is a very fine writer herself.

"Christian fiction gives me an avenue to be creative and to encourage people to seek after and hold on to a Christian worldview. I have found that more people, and often a different group of people, are reached with fiction. A fiction book can be aimed at a much wider audience that a nonfiction book.

"[My] research includes reading contemporary historical accounts of the era about which I am writing. It includes on-site research at all the places mentioned in my book. It also includes serious lexicographical studies to ensure the vocabularies and dialects are authentic. Plus, I research the details of the protagonists' lives. For instance, I own the guns that my western heroes use and have shot them myself so as to accurately portray the scenes."

Bly sees his audiences as spanning from "junior high to senior citizen . . . both male and female. From the letters I receive, I know my books are cross-generational [and are] read by men and women.

"My writing is heavy on dialogue and action. . . informal, yet intelligent . . . challenging readers' minds . . . and touching their emotions (at least this is my goal). Most of my plots are action/character driven. My heroes cannot really be separated from their action." His choice of setting is normally in the western United States because that is the area he is "most familiar with on a personal basis and the area I'm most interested in." However, he will set scenes wherever the story demands. For example, in the Austin-Stoner Files series, action takes place in New York City. As a demonstration of his dedication to accuracy, Bly states, "I research every location I use.

"My historical fiction is most influenced by my desire to present life in the Old West as accurate to the times. So the old journals, biographies, and historical accounts greatly affect how I tell a story. I really don't try to style myself after any particular author but undoubtedly was influenced by the fiction I enjoyed in my earlier years (Hemingway, Steinbeck, Faulkner, Saroyan as well as Louis L'Amour, Zane Grey, Luke Short . . . and now Elmer Keaton, and others).

"My protagonists are most often based on my own personal experiences. Other characters are many times patterned on people I have met . . . or read about. Example? Without thinking about it, I named my hero in one western series Stuart Brannon. His initials, S. B. . . . are the same as mine. He does act a lot like me. Also, in the Hidden West series (which I am writing with my wife) the protagonists are a husband-and-wife team. Autobiographical? Yep. If I have a recurring theme, it is that God wants to rule in every area of my protagonist's life and that he/she must come to a decision to allow Him to be Lord."

The personal goal that Bly hopes to achieve through his writing is "to demonstrate that a committed Christian can write quality fiction equal to that of any other writer in the country and still hold on to biblical standards." He hopes that his readers "have fun and enjoy the work . . . and in the process be encouraged and/or challenged in their life of faith."

In regard to the future of Christian fiction, Bly believes that "the market for quality Christian fiction will remain strong, but many publishers and writers will fall away as the market is glutted."

SUMMARY: *THE LOST MANUSCRIPT OF MARTIN TAYLOR HARRISON* (THE AUSTIN-STONER FILES SERIES)

As a successful editor at the firm of Atlantic-Hampton Publishing Company, Lynda Austin's life is well ordered and predictable, a state that is quickly changed by the appearance of one eccentric old man who calls himself Fondue. Claiming to have in his possession a copy of a previously unpublished novel by Martin Taylor Harrison, one of Atlantic-Hampton's most popular authors, he puts the office into turmoil. Harrison has been missing and presumed dead for many years. Before he can collect on his treasure, Fondue is killed in a freak accident and his copy of the manuscript destroyed. Not wanting to publish a possible fake and afraid of the change of philosophy expressed in this third work, the firm takes advantage of the man's death and decides not to pursue searching for the original manuscript.

Angered at their refusal and driven to find the truth about Harrison's philosophical turnabout, Lynda uses vacation time to hunt for the original work and to attempt to prove its authenticity. Guided through the Arizona desert by cowboy Brady Stoner, she finds more adventure and excitement in this wild country than she has ever known. She finds herself seeking not only for a lost manuscript but also for a new direction for her life—one that might include spending a lot more time with the surprising Brady Stoner.

TREACHERY AT THE RIVER CANYON **(THE LEWIS AND CLARK SQUAD SERIES)**

Cody Clark is disgruntled at having to ride his mountain bike eight miles into the Salmon River Canyon to check on the elderly and reclusive Chad Levine. He is further dismayed and alarmed when someone driving the old man's pickup attempts to run him off the road. The mystery escalates as Cody and his friends on the Lewis and Clark squad attempt to discover who broke into Mr. Levine's home and into the tepee, where their friend Feather lived with her mother. Working together to solve these mysterious events, the squad is drawn into danger and into a stronger commitment to one another.

Mary Borntrager

When the farming family of Noah and Martha Christner welcomed the birth of infant Mary on March 27, 1921, they probably could not have predicted that she would become an award-winning author. Yet it was their own background, as well as the spiritual and cultural environment that they nurtured, that inspired their daughter to write. Today, as a widow and mother of four, Mary Borntrager states that it was motherhood that motivated her to record stories that she remembered and so to preserve the rich heritage of the Amish for her children and those to follow.

PROFESSIONAL

Education
Certificate in youth social work and child care; eighth-grade certificate

Career
Youth social worker, twelve years; elementary teacher, seven years

Awards
Angel Award of Excellence, *Ellie,* 1989

Memberships
Past member of Ohioana Library, Columbus, Ohio

PUBLICATIONS

Ellie's People Series
Ellie, 1988
Rebecca, 1989
Rachel, 1990
Daniel, 1991
Reuben, 1992
Andy, 1993
Sarah, 1994
Polly, 1995
Mandy, 1996
Annie, 1997

PERSONAL

Mary Borntrager states that her motivation to write about the Amish came as a result of her desire to make the Amish culture known to her children and grandchildren. Her daughter Kathryn has been a significant influence on Borntrager's career. Describing her research process as very personal, she simply says, "I lived it." Not only is her information source close to her heart, but the very act of writing seems to be almost an extension of her being because she does not use a typewriter or a word processor but writes all her books out with pen and in the same room in her house. Such a method perhaps contributes to the warmth and the family atmosphere of her series.

It is not surprising that Borntrager grew up in a Christian Amish home, since this is the foundation of all her books. If her characters seem as real as life itself, it is because she patterns her creations from childhood experiences. The popularity of *Ellie,* her first novel, inspired her to continue the series and delve more deeply into the daily lives of her earliest acquaintances, revealing to those who are not Amish that many of the problems faced in that community are not unique to the culture but rather are universal to the human experience.

Books that have influenced her writing are the Bible as an adult and the Little House on the Prairie series as a child. She finds in both principles that promote "good, clean living," ideals that govern her own works.

Borntrager states that her goal for her writing is to create an appetite for "worthwhile reading. . . . I believe there is a desire among many youth and children for Christian fiction because so much of the mail I receive shows it to be so. If it is made available, I believe it will be read."

SUMMARY: *REUBEN* (ELLIE'S PEOPLE SERIES)

Although life in the large Amish household might seem simple to the outsider, it often is not, as is demonstrated by the Weaver family. Reuben, the oldest son, grows from a fifth-grader to young manhood in this story. Peer pressure, a powerful desire for acceptance, and a supersensitive conscience create frequent conflicts as he moves toward maturity. His nemesis, Wally Chupp, seems to delight in daring Reuben to do forbidden things and then refusing to acknowledge his part in whatever mayhem follows.

For a lively, affectionate view of Amish life, the reader is invited into the home, the school, and the church and to social functions, such as singings and horse sales. Borntrager makes the visit more realistic by spicing her dialogue with words or phrases used in daily Amish conversation, accompanied by the English translation in parentheses. Having met Reuben, one might want to read about both his ancestors and his descendants in the Ellie's People series.

Shirley Brinkerhoff

"A day is wasted if I can't spend some time outside," Shirley Brinkerhoff observes. This love of nature and its rejuvenating power is a legacy passed on to her by her parents, from whom she also inherited a voracious appetite for reading and a love of music. She relates that her parents valued reading so far beyond watching television that when their daughter was ten, they chose to get rid of the set. Reading and playing the piano became the main forms of entertainment for her family. Creativity and an appreciation for the environment have shaped her career, and Brinkerhoff pays tribute to the lifelong influence of both her parents.

Born in Glen Willard, Pennsylvania, Brinkerhoff currently resides in Clarks Summit, Pennsylvania. She has three children: Marcus, a university student; Melanie Brinkerhoff Brock, also a university student; and Ryan, who is seven and an elementary school student.

PROFESSIONAL

Education

Masters degree in music, Western University (Michigan); bachelors degree in music, Grand Rapids Baptist College (now Cornerstone College) (graduated summa cum laude)

Career

Stay-at-home mom; retail sales; secretary; assistant to husband in youth work and music; piano instructor; piano accompanist and classical duo performer; college adjunct faculty in music; staff writer for a Christian school and college; freelance writer, editor, and publicist

Memberships

Writers Information Network

Awards

Most Promising New Writer Award, Sandy Cove Writers Conference, 1994; Carole Gift Page Award, Mount Hermon Christian Writers Conference, 1996; Joy Publishing Award, Mount Hermon Christian Writers Conference, 1996; Writer of the Year, Greater Philadelphia Christian Writers Conference, 1997

PUBLICATIONS

Adult Fiction

Numerous short stories

Juvenile Fiction

Numerous short stories
Nikki Sheridan Series
Choice Summer, 1996
Mysterious Love, 1996
Narrow Walk, 1997
Balancing Act, 1998

Adult Nonfiction

Numerous devotionals
Newspaper articles and interviews

Juvenile Nonfiction

Numerous devotionals

PERSONAL

When Shirley Brinkerhoff shares that "reading is as natural to me as breathing," she is giving a glimpse into her lifelong love affair with the printed word.

As a child she remembers that books were "highly respected" and that her parents were enthusiastic readers—to their children, for pleasure, and for information. Brinkerhoff reveals that she was an omnivorous reader as a child, "reading everything—not just those pieces that today would be considered quality literature. As a result, it was a presupposition that the most valuable thing one could do is to create a book." By the time she was twenty-four, Shirley was a published author, and has continued to write since that time.

When asked why she chose Christian fiction, Brinkerhoff gave a dual response to the classification. First, "I write fiction because I think I can express far more truth in story than any other way. I think in story; I learn in story." Second, in responding to the Christian aspect, she asks, "What else is there? It is not what I consciously chose. To me, all writing is a by-product of who you are. Christian fiction is simply a natural, unintentional by-product of that intimate relationship with God that renews the mind."

Brinkerhoff sums up her research process in two powerful words: "I live." To illustrate, she gives as an example her longtime involvement with the pro-life movement prior to writing the Nikki Sheridan books, which deal with decisions related to teen pregnancy. She relates that the initial seed for this series was sown as she lay in a hospital bed. Her roommate was an expectant mother who was awaiting an abortion procedure the following morning. The anguish experienced by this woman so touched Brinkerhoff that she felt compelled to share the pain in story form so that others would be aware of the emotional trauma resulting from such a loss. Years later she created Nikki. Other resources that helped her prepare for this young-adult series included interviews with adoptive parents and adoption lawyers, which adds to the authenticity and balance of her information. Whenever possible, her modus operandi involves hands-on, or face-to-face, fact-finding. Her credo, "Be true to what is," speaks to readers across generational gaps. Although her current writing is focused on an adolescent audience, she has also received letters of appreciation from parents and grandparents. She shares that one set of grandparents, after reading the Nikki series to each other, had written to congratulate her on its content.

Professionally, Brinkerhoff has words of gratitude for the many mentors she has met at writers' conferences, such as those held at Mt. Hermon and Sandy Cove. She relates that her first conference experience came quite "by accident," or by Providence. She received information for registration by "mistake," but then she felt that "God told me I needed to go there. I had no money to go, but through a scholarship I attended the Mt. Hermon Writers Conference in California. Carole Gift Page was my first teacher and was a great encouragement. Then a comical set of circumstances landed my manuscript in the hands of Robin Jones Gunn, who recommended my work to Focus on the Family [which became her publisher]."

In describing her current series, Brinkerhoff categorizes her books, without hesitation, as "totally character driven." Readers would agree that Nikki and her friends are so realistically drawn that one walking on the sand dunes at Lake Michigan would almost expect to find them there. Yet her characters are completely Brinkerhoff's original creations. She might employ temperaments, personal aspects, or some facet of appearance from various individuals, but she does not base any of her characters totally on any one person.

The recurring theme that Brinkerhoff intends to reveal is that "all human life is interrelated. No one belongs to him- or herself. We belong to one another, which is an outgrowth of belonging to God. Living is laying down our lives for one another. As Christ set the example in His sacrifice for us, so we share in mutual self-sacrifice for one another."

When asked about the influence of other authors on her writing, Brinkerhoff pays tribute to the competent Christian authors who have taught at conferences. However, she credits much of her interest in writing to those books she has read and writers she has admired since childhood. Having been a lifelong reader, she gratefully remembers the writers of children's books and lists Richard Peck, Lois Lowry, Katherine Paterson, Zilpha Keatley Snyder, Madeleine L'Engle's earlier works, E. Nesbit, and Virginia Stem Owens. As an adult, she recognizes especially Phillip Yancey, Dorothy Sayers, Karen Mains, Edith and Francis Schaffer, and Corrie Ten Boom. She shares that her love of reading and writing have been inspired by "everything that C. S. Lewis has written" as well as J. R. R Tolkien's Lord of the Rings trilogy.

When asked to consider how her spiritual beliefs have shaped her writing, Brinkerhoff replied, "My beliefs are who I am. What I believe is the most real, most bedrock thing in my life. They make me who I am. Writing is a by-product of who I am."

Just as faith shapes Brinkerhoff's writing, it is reflected in her personal goal for her product. She has no personal goals for herself. She relates that when she was recovering from cancer and was walking among the dunes at Lake Michigan, she held the following communication with her Lord: "Well, it looks like I'm going to recover. What do you want me to do now ?" God told her that He wanted her to write first about what she had learned about the affect of abortion on women—thus the birth of Nikki Sheridan. Of the future, Brinkerhoff reveals, "The only thing that I really hope to achieve is to be totally obedient to the Father each day, impacting people as He leads. On the dunes, that is what He told me to do. Tomorrow, He may tell me to do something else."

Although Brinkerhoff might have no personal aspirations, she does have a goal for her readers. She would hope "that there would be a sense of holiness as they read my work. That they would come in contact with a transcendent God, even though the full effect might be delayed. It's like dropping a pebble in the pond—sometimes it may take years to culminate, but the ripples are there and set in motion."

When asked for her view regarding the future of Christian fiction, Brinkerhoff responded, "I would hope for a synthesis, a fusion of (1) presenting a transcendent God with (2) enough appeal to the people of our culture while (3) maintaining the highest possible literary standards with artistic integrity." As her readers would attest, Brinkerhoff has set the example for the writing of the future, and they look forward with anticipation to all that she has yet to produce.

SUMMARY: *CHOICE SUMMER* (NIKKI SHERIDAN SERIES)

When sixteen-year-old Nikki Sheridan is invited to go to the Junior-Senior Banquet by T. J., a longtime crush, she little realizes that before the evening is over she will have experienced her first sexual intimacy and become pregnant. T. J. will leave the festivities too drunk to drive, and Nikki, being stranded, will have to walk home, her life altered forever.

It is later—on the lonely drive from her home in Ohio to spend the summer with her beloved grandparents on the shores of Lake Michigan—that Nikki stops at a clinic and has her fears confirmed. The constant morning sickness has been a warning, and when the test results are returned, Nikki is informed that she is pregnant. The nurse also attempts to ease the shock by telling her that terminating a pregnancy is a fairly common practice and not a difficult process to manage.

As the story progresses, Brinkerhoff takes the reader through the discomfort, embarrassment, lying, and finally disclosure and decision making that is demanded by teen pregnancy. She skillfully interweaves relationships across generations and with peers. The satisfying conclusion is both realistic and rewarding, leaving the reader with a desire to reach for the next volume of the series.

Information is supplied at the end of this book about abortion alternatives, and an address is given for the Crisis Pregnancy Ministry, sponsored by Focus on the Family.

MYSTERIOUS LOVE (NIKKI SHERIDAN SERIES)

Nikki has made the decision that she felt was best for herself and for her baby. She is attempting to deal with the trauma of her loss by keeping a journal of letters to her child. She has made a home with her grandparents where she is helping her grandmother become rehabilitated following a stroke. Her circle of friends has broadened to include Keesha, a schoolmate who is expecting her first child, and Chad who is handsome, talented, and very attentive to Nikki.

As the story progresses, Nikki battles with ambivalent feelings related to giving up her son, made even more difficult as she assists Keesha in surviving her difficult childbirth. She also discovers, through a near tragedy, the real reason for Chad's determination to date her. As if these experiences were not enough of an emotional exercise, Nikki uncovers her mother's old journal, which reveals family secrets and the mysterious love that has held them all together.

Brinkerhoff has done a masterful job of telling Nikki's story with realism and compassion. She is never judgmental or sentimental, yet all who read this story will have no question regarding the agony of deciding what to do about an unwanted pregnancy.

T. Davis Bunn

As a child, T. Davis Bunn states that he used to "eat books." There were weeks when I read a book a day." As an adult, he is just as involved with books, adding his own stories to the world's storehouse of good literature. Among Christian fiction writers, there are few who write successfully in so many genres. His titles span the range from romance to modern fantasy and from children's stories to those for an adult audience. Supporting him in this venture is his wife, Isabella, whom Bunn credits with being the greatest influence on his writing. "She helps with editing and the commercial side. She writes the flap and back cover. She gets them out the door."

Although born in Raleigh, North Carolina, Bunn has spent much of his adult life abroad. After completing work in psychology and economics at Wake Forest University, he became involved in an international management company based in Germany. Fluent in three languages, Bunn was recognized as a consultant and lecturer in the area of international finance, traveling to as many as three countries a week for business and speaking engagements. In 1991 he left this position to pursue a full-time writing career. His wife's pursuit of a degree in theology at Oxford University now has the couple residing in England.

PROFESSIONAL

Education
M.S. in international finance and economics, Gresham Institute, London; B.A. in economics, Wake Forest University (graduated cum laude)

Career
International businessman residing and working in Europe and Africa; full-time author (since 1992); novelist in residence at Oxford University

PUBLICATIONS

Adult Fiction

The Presence, 1990
Promises to Keep, 1991
The Maestro, 1991
The Quilt, 1993
The Gift, 1994
Riders of the Pale Horse, 1994
The Messenger, 1995
The Music Box, 1996
Dangerous Devices, 1996
To the Ends of the Earth, 1996
Tidings of Comfort and Joy, 1997
One False Move, 1997
The Warning, 1998
Priceless Collection Series
  Florian's Gate, 1992
  The Amber Room, 1992
  Winter Palace, 1993
  One Shenandoah Winter, 1998
  The Ultimatum, 1999
Rendezvous with Destiny Series
  Rhineland Inheritance, 1993
  Gibraltar Passage, 1994
  Sahara Crosswind, 1994
  Istanbul Express, 1995
  Berlin Encounter, 1995
  In the Shadow of Victory, 1998
  A Passage through Darkness, 1999

Coauthored with Janette Oke

Return to Harmony, 1997
Another Homecoming, 1997
Tomorrow's Dream, 1998
The Meeting Place, 1999

Juvenile Fiction

Light and Shadow, 1995
Princess Bella and the Red Velvet Hat, 1998

Written under the Pseudonym of Thomas Locke

Thomas Locke Mystery Series
Delta Factor, 1994
Omega Network, 1995
Spectrum Chronicles Series
Light Weaver, 1997
Dream Voyager, 1997
Path Finder, 1997
Heart Chaser, 1997

PERSONAL

When T. Davis Bunn became a Christian at age twenty-four, he discovered that God had more for him than a new faith. He had a whole fresh direction and calling for his life. Before accepting Christ, Bunn feels that he was unable to see his natural calling. He compares his situation to that of Moses, who was chosen despite a cleft palate and the painful shyness that made it difficult to do what God asked him to do. In like manner, Bunn feels that he was chosen to write not for his own natural ability but because "God chooses people who in their own weakness must rely on Him." Once he responded to this call, success did not come quickly. He wrote nine books while maintaining his business career. *The Presence,* his first book accepted for publication, was his seventh attempt at writing novels.

Bunn shares that he has "always had lots of ideas for stories, and I love the search, the structuring. I enjoy putting together people, places, and plot . . . watching in my mind how it all comes together." All his adult life, Bunn has been a traveler, but today his travel is a part of the research necessary to build a background for his novels. Now he will stay in one place "long enough to feel that the place lives in me."

The audience that Bunn has in mind when he writes depends on the book. "My first children's book was written for my two youngest nieces who were two and four years old. *Tidings of Comfort and Joy,* a historical romance about Christmas, was written for my sister, who loves women's stories where everything works out at the end. I am always sensitive to the reader. That is what drives me. When I write, I choose in my mind someone I want to make cry."

When asked whether he had a favorite book among those he has written, Bunn replied, "No, they are written for other people." Stating that he would like to go back and rewrite sections of some titles, he likens them to children. "They are all favorites in one way or another. We love them each for who they are. A book is only half done when unpublished. The other half is getting it out there for people to enjoy. Once they are out there, however, they must stand on their own two feet."

Few authors write in as many styles as Bunn. To spur this ability, he reads a great deal in various genres. "If a writer is comfortable with one or two genres which come naturally, that's alright, but if someone wants to grow, they must search. They have to understand what is going on in the world of art and culture. They must understand how characters are built. They must learn how to establish flow. Setting, flow, tone, and pace are individual things. Learning to flow in a different direction, the way you want to grow, takes effort. Other genres prepare you for what you are doing. You don't always know if it will work when you've never done it before." Writing the monumental epic *To the Ends of the Earth* was one of those growing experiences, as was his fantasy series for young adults published under the pseudonym of Thomas Locke.

Character development is an exercise of personal involvement for Bunn. "There must be poignancy in stories when creating characters. People are shaped by a hard life. I work at the difficult task of [showing] the good in people even though they are having a bad day or doing bad things. The emotions must be real. They must be true. That doesn't mean you have experienced that particular thing, but you are drawing on an honest experience that happened to you or to someone you love deeply. This was the essence of Christ's love—taking on someone else's burden as your own. It is a difficult lesson that we must learn over and over. This dependency comes from lessons that are not of our own making. Authors must see the world through others' eyes and not lock themselves in a writer's garret. They must involve themselves in the world."

When people read his books, Bunn desires for them "a point of illumination. I hope that when the reader closes the book, the heart stays awake—the heart stays open." Surprised by the unexpected way his books touch people, he loves getting letters from his readers. "As others share with me how my books have impacted their lives, I am in turn touched by their stories."

In Bunn's eyes, there is an important separation between Christian fiction and mainstream literature. "Authors have an opportunity to give more than just a good read. They can challenge, comfort, make a plea for forgiveness, call the reader to love or understanding. There must be something that ties to God's message. The reader should be able to find some small facet of God's call or God's heart in the heart of the story."

Bunn remembers that when he was in his twenties, contemporary Christian music was in its infancy. The major artists were just beginning their careers. A musician himself, he feels that living with contemporary Christian music has shaped much of his life. Extensive ministry has come to him in this way. With Christian fiction now in its adolescence, he believes that it has a similar opportunity to touch the hearts and minds of those who read.

SUMMARY: *THE PRESENCE*

This first published novel of Bunn's is much more than a political thriller. Following the career of T. J. Case, lawyer and politician, it combines compelling suspense and gripping emotion. After taking a stand for righteousness causes him to lose a reelection bid in his home state of North Carolina, T. J. follows God's leading to move to the nation's capital. There doors open for him that he never could have expected, and he finds himself thrust into the center of the American political scene. In his new position, God gives Case messages for those around him that cut through partisan interests to the core issues of corruption and greed. Although many are drawn to his life, others are alarmed and angered by the convicting power of his words. Despite the danger, T. J. experiences peace, knowing that he is walking by the divine direction of God even if obedience costs him the ultimate sacrifice. *The Presence* demonstrates God's ability to penetrate the most powerful strongholds, while T. J.'s example of strength and obedience stirs the hearts of readers seeking to hear God's voice.

FLORIAN'S GATE (PRICELESS COLLECTION SERIES), REVIEWED BY DAVE BARNETT

Tired of the corporate world, Jeffrey Sinclair accepts the invitation of his uncle, Alexander Kantor, to join him in the operation of his store in London known for its stock of priceless antiques. As Jeffrey proves his honesty and his ability to learn, he gains Alexander's trust and begins to penetrate the veil of mystery that his uncle has always drawn around himself.

Accompanying Alexander on a buying trip to eastern Europe, Jeffrey is immersed in a world of intrigue as he travels through nations savoring their first taste of freedom following the demise of Communism—nations that at the same time are struggling with deep economic problems left behind by years of exploitation. It is this desperate poverty, forcing many to part with family treasures and hoarded pieces, that he discovers to be the source for the exquisite antiques that find their way to Alexander's store.

As Alexander's health deteriorates, Jeffrey finds himself traveling across Poland as his uncle's agent, accompanied on occasion by the beautiful and mysterious Katya. It is on these journeys that Jeffrey finds the chaos of the country mirrored in his own soul as he wrestles with issues of faith and of love. It is also on these trips that he is able to see the hand of his Heavenly Father, consistently and gently working to bring him to the place of true peace and contentment.

TO THE ENDS OF THE EARTH

By A.D. 338, the center of the Roman Empire had moved from Rome to the city of Constantinople. With the death of Emperor Constantine, his three sons struggle for control of the vast empire, pulling troops away from outlying districts to strengthen their own positions. Confusion reigns and corruption is rampant as those with political ambition take advantage of the lack of central leadership.

Sent from the North African estate that his father manages for a Roman consul to find a way to preserve the family's fortune in these troubled times, Travis, son of Cletus, is thrust into a world where hunger for wealth and power drive men to acts of ruthlessness and evil.

Stopping in Carthage, Travis soon finds his life entwined with Hannibal Mago, a merchant and respected elder of the local Christian church, a man known for his honesty and fairness. Asked by his bishop to spy out possible heresy in the church at Constantinople, Hannibal agrees to join Travis on his journey, taking his beautiful daughter Lydia to help unravel the intrigue that he so despises. Drawn to Lydia by a love forbidden by her faith, Travis searches for a true foundation for his life amidst the chaos of political intrigue and religious conflict.

Bunn's extended study of the Byzantine period has produced a novel not only strong in historical fact but also rich in human detail. His descriptive phrases engage his readers and place them in the midst of the heat and dust and noise of the marketplace. The author's thorough research into the development of the early Christian church as it struggled against the prevailing climate of paganism makes the story forceful and believable. Once again Bunn has proven himself a master at engaging the heart as well as the mind.

THE MESSENGER

Sent to earth for the first time on what should be a rather simple assignment, the angel Ariel finds herself in an area where poverty and crime flourish. She is overwhelmed by the contrast between the beauty that God has created and the sadness and dark anger that overlays it all. Naive to the ways of the world, Ariel becomes entangled with Manny, a street-smart pickpocket who steals the card she was given as a pass to return home.

Unnerved by the purity and compelling love that stream from his "pigeon's" eyes, Manny finds his heart exposed and feels a yearning toward a life that he never thought possible. Caught in his desire to maintain the stubborn independence that has kept him alive this far, Manny is drawn by two unseen and opposing forces. As the tension escalates, Manny realizes that the choice he makes will have profound consequences. Ariel discovers that she must learn to apply the lessons of faith and prayer that she has learned on earth.

RETURN TO HARMONY

In a novel designed to tug at the heart, Bunn joins his descriptive talent with Janette Oke's ability to draw a story out of the ordinary details of life. Together they have created a story of two girls growing up in the small town of Harmony, North Carolina.

Bethan, a quiet, young girl, has ambitions centered on home and family, while Jodie, gifted in science, has dreams of college and a career in biochemistry—no small ambition for a girl in 1915. Together they share the joys and trials of growing up, until tragedy strikes Jodie's family. Unable to stand the crushing grief of her mother's death and her father's consequent retreat from life, Jodie's faith in God begins to crumble.

Aware of the effects of her friend's growing bitterness, Bethan discourages a budding love between Jodie and her brother Dylan. Angry at what she sees as betrayal, Jodie dissolves their relationship. Winning a scholarship to college, she leaves Harmony, her faith, and her friendship behind. The prayers of Bethan continue even in her friend's absence, and as circumstances dictate Jodie's return, the girls have the opportunity to rebuild the love that seemed to be lost forever.

LIGHT WEAVER (SPECTRUM CHRONICLES SERIES)

Falling into a deep sleep after being injured in an accident, Dan finds himself transported to the fantasy world of Borderlands, where evil forces gather for conquest. Inspired by the beautiful Bliss and strengthened by the *Book of Light,* this young man who has always thought of himself as boringly normal finds courage to join the battle.

Hovering in and out of slumber, Dan moves back and forth between the two worlds, finding an uncanny resemblance between the doctors and the nurses in one and the characters whom he meets in the other.

In this tale designed for the younger person, Bunn has created a story strong in imagery without losing its entertainment appeal. He spices his dialogue with a delightful sense of humor displayed in both animals and humans.

Melody Carlson

A degree in child development, a subsequent career as a preschool teacher, and a senior editorial position with Multnomah Publishing have provided Melody Carlson's expertise in her current career. Out of her years of experience, she creates a wide range of books that touch adults, teens, children, and even babies.

Carlson's husband, Christopher, is a general contractor. She credits her husband with being a great encouragement to her and supporting her writing "before it was profitable." Living in Sisters, Oregon, with their teenage sons, Gabe and Luke, the Carlsons enjoy the "beautiful Cascades" by boating, hiking, and skiing.

PROFESSIONAL

Education
Associate of science degree in early childhood education and child development

Career
Editor/author; preschool teacher

Awards
Children's Best Seller List, Christian Booksellers Association, *Benjamin's Box,* May 1997; Children's Best Seller List, Evangelical Christian Publisher's

Association, Number One, *Benjamin's Box,* May 1997; nominated for WOW Award, INSP Children's Inspirational Product, *Benjamin's Box,* 1998; Finalist, Rita Award, *Homeward,* 1998

PUBLICATIONS

Adult Fiction

Wise Man's House, 1997
Homeward, 1997
Heartland Skies, 1998
Shades of Light, 1998
Awakening Heart, 1998
A Place to Come Home To, 1999

Juvenile Fiction

Jessica (contemporary), 1996
Benjamin's Box, 1997
Tupsu, 1997
The Sea Hag's Treasure, 1997
The Christmas Treasure Hunt, 1998
A Battle of the Weeds, 1998
A Tale of Two Houses, 1998
What Nick and Holly Found in Grandpa's Attic, 1998
The Other Brother, 1999
The Wonder of Christmas: A Family Advent Journey, 1999
Allison Chronicles (historical)
  On Hope's Wings, 1998
  Cherished Wish, 1998
  Autumn Secrets, 1998
  Dreams of Promise, 1999
Fruit Troops (board books)
  Anna Apple, 1997
  Blackberry Bart, 1997
  Gladys Grape, 1997
  Lyle Lemon, 1997
  Peachy Pete, 1997
  Penny Pear, 1997
  Pineapple Paul, 1997
  Strawberry Sam, 1997

Tammy Tangerine, 1997
War of the Weeds, 1997
Story Pockets (board books)
Jonah and the Big Fish, 1997
Moses in the Bulrushes, 1997
Noah and the Ark, 1997
Daniel and the Lions' Den, 1997
God Is Here Series
God Lives in My House, 1999
I Can Count on God, 1999

Adult Nonfiction

How to Start a Quality Child Care Business in Your Home, 1995

Juvenile Nonfiction

His (and Her) First Bible (baby Bible book), 1997
Gold 'n' Honey Bible (children's picture Bible), 1997
My First Bible Brain Quest (three- to five-year-olds), 1997
The Ark That Noah Built (picture book with audio), 1997
The Greatest Gift (Christmas book), 1997
The Lullaby Bible, 1998
King of the Stable, 1998
The Lost Lamb, 1999

PERSONAL

Melody Carlson reports that although she has always loved to write, she did not consider it seriously until around 1990. As may be seen by a brief scan of copyright dates, both she and her publishers have made up for lost time.

Following the example of the master teacher, Carlson reveals that she chose the medium of fiction to instruct in some of life's most difficult lessons. She reminds us that "Jesus taught through stories." However, her method of delivery is different from His since she uses a laptop computer to record her creations.

Research for Carlson takes a minimum of her writing schedule. She does "little research" for her contemporary novels, unless her own outdoor pursuits are considered. For her historical works, she uses many resources, including relatives who supply her with personal anecdotes.

Carlson sees her audience as including children, teens, and women, with her characters being the most significant literary element for readers of all ages. She describes those memorable folks who breathe life into her novels as "composites of people I've known . . . and a lot of imagination all mixed together like a secret recipe."

In crediting those individuals and books who have given her inspiration, Carlson makes reference to an "excellent critique group who were very helpful." (Some members of that writers' circle—Doris Elaine Fell, Ethel Herr, and Carole Gift Page—are included in this book.) Other authors who have contributed to Carlson's background knowledge vary widely, from the nineteenth-century George MacDonald to the contemporary Rosamund Pilcher. She also lists Robert Frost, L. M. Montgomery, and Madeleine L'Engle.

For her personal source of inspiration, Carlson shares that she prays about what she writes and that she desires "God's love and grace to shine through" her books. It is her goal that her readers will have come to a greater self-knowledge and a greater understanding of God when they close the last page of each of her books.

Regarding the future of Christian fiction, Carlson sees this division of inspirational writing as becoming increasingly popular as readers discover its unique ministry to the complex problems faced in contemporary life.

SUMMARY: *HOMEWARD*

Heart-weary and in recovery from a failed romance, Meg Lancaster takes time from her executive life to return to the small town of her childhood with the goal of making peace with her past, her free-spirited mother, and her sharp-tongued grandmother. As she walks familiar paths, bittersweet memories of her warmhearted, hard-working grandfather and the happy hours they shared in his cranberry bogs assail Meg. She is first chagrined and later charged into action at the sight of the overgrown morass where once blossomed the prolific crimson fruit so vital to the existence of her beloved grandparent.

A restored relationship with her sister Erin, accompanied by the warmth of her entire household, provides an anchor for Meg as she steps into greater storms than she could have imagined. Restoration of the bogs to profitable production by the uprooting of tenacious weeds that have grown strong through neglect serves as a physical symbol of dark family secrets, long hidden, that she also uncovers. With renewed faith, Meg struggles to maintain the heritage of the bogs while gaining an understanding of three generations of Lancaster women, and the grace to forgive is born.

This novel is a must for those who grew up in dysfunctional families, especially if time or tragedy prevents complete reconciliation.

WISE MAN'S HOUSE

When Kestra McKenzie is widowed, she is too young to simply live off her wealthy husband's insurance, yet she is unprepared for a profession. In loneliness and confusion, she returns to her mother's grave in search of security and to her hometown in search of herself.

While visiting her past, she stops to relive childhood dreams of owning the large, old house with its foundation built on the rugged rocks of the coast. As a little girl, she had secretly pretended to be the owner of the house and had even named it The Wise Man's House because it was built on rocks. Since no one is living in the neglected dwelling, she takes the liberty of exploring the house and grounds. That decision to investigate becomes the turning point in her life.

Kestra exhibits courage, wisdom, determination, and creativity in picking up the pieces of her life and beginning anew. This time she fulfills her own long-neglected dreams, not those dictated by someone whom she is trying to please. This time she finds herself to be a whole person, not simply a shadow of someone she views as having more worth than she.

Carlson has focused on issues of faith, self-perception, and the rewards of achieving a goal through hard work. This novel provides the encouragement needed by so many contemporary young women who find themselves alone and seemingly unequipped to face the future.

JESSICA

Jessica Johnson, age sixteen, longs to find broader horizons than those offered by her Kansas family farm. When she meets Barry Bartowski, guitar player, waiter, and dramatic reader, at a new coffeehouse, she feels that she has found a kindred spirit.

Warned by her brothers that Barry is not worthy of her attention, Jessica becomes only more determined to spend time with him. When she buys counterculture clothes and drastically cuts and bleaches her beautiful hair, her family becomes alarmed and attempts to thwart any association between Jessica and Barry. When she rebels against house rules to be with him anyway, Jessica makes a startling discovery that almost destroys her life.

Carlson has created realistic characters with believable dialogue. Jessica's responses to the attention she receives from the forbidden man and her efforts to solve problems on her own will ring true for many teenage girls. This fast-paced yet introspective little novel touches on the issue of adoption as well as on the teen subculture of rebellion, drugs, alcohol, and premarital sex without being "preachy" or embarrassing the reader. For both adults and adolescents, it will also whet the appetite for more Carlson books.

Jack Cavanaugh

Jack Cavanaugh was born in Youngstown, Ohio, on March 22, 1952. He is the son of William and Marjorie Cavanaugh. His wife, Marlene, is a teacher's aide in special education classes. (Note his affectionate dedication to her in *The Patriots*.) They are the parents of Elizabeth Ann, Keri Marie, and Samuel Brand.

Cavanaugh recalls that he was inspired to write by a seminary professor's challenge: "Men, if you want to expand your ministry, even beyond your own lifetime, write." Believing that the printed word can be a "powerful tool of communication through which Christian values and perspectives can be conveyed," the Reverend Cavanaugh chose to become writer Cavanaugh.

PROFESSIONAL

Education

M.Div., Southwestern Baptist Theological Seminary; B.A., Grand Canyon College; Granite Hills High School, El Cajon, California

Career

Managing editor, Christian Ed Publishers, San Diego, California, 1990–1993; pastor, First Baptist College Grove; First Baptist Imperial Beach, San Diego, California, 1978–1990

Awards

Gold Medallion Finalist, Evangelical Christian Publishers Association, *The Puritans,* 1994; Best Historical Fiction, San Diego Book Awards (secular), *The Puritans,* 1994; Writer of the Year, San Diego Christian Writers Guild, 1994; Book of the Year, San Diego Christian Writers Guild, *The Puritans,* 1994; Book of the Year, San Diego Christian Writers Guild, *The Patriots,* 1995

PUBLICATIONS

Adult Fiction

American Family Portrait Series
The Puritans, 1994
The Colonists, 1995
The Patriots, 1995
The Adversaries, 1996
The Pioneers, 1996
The Allies, 1997
The Victors, 1998
The Peacemakers, 1998
African Covenant Series
The Pride and the Passion, 1996
Quest for the Promised Land, 1997
Book of Books Series
Glimpses of Truth, 1999

PERSONAL

As a writer of historical fiction, Jack Cavanaugh underscores the importance of research to the accuracy of the written piece. Fifty percent of his 7:30 A.M. to 11:00 P.M. workday is spent searching for the facts and feelings that lend the authenticity characterizing his work. Utilizing current technology, he relies on the Internet and his computer's database to bring ages past right to his fingertips.

In addressing the literary elements of his writing style, Cavanaugh reports that the recurring theme throughout his books, as well as in his life, is that "God's ways are always best." As he sets about to weave a story through a given historical period, with the previously stated theme as the connecting thread, he also designs memorable characters. He has chosen the family-tree motif to connect generations of characters who have struggled with their environment, their faith, each other, and themselves. Yet victory is always achieved and is realistically depicted.

Background for Cavanaugh's writing approach comes from being an avid reader and having an appetite for excellence in achievement. He relates that when a novel is a best-seller, he wants to know why it has arrived at such status, and therefore he seeks out award winners to read. Balancing contemporary and classic works gives him a variety of masters in the trade by which to evaluate his own compositions. Specifically, he cites as favorites examples from such diverse genres as *Once and Future King* (T. H. White), *The Caine Mutiny* and *Winds of War* (Herman Wouk), and *The Martian Chronicles* (Ray Bradbury). The Bible, of course, takes precedence over all in both reading and memorizing.

Cavanaugh states that it is his evangelical Christian beliefs that prompt him to write. He sees writing as a refinement and an expansion of his previous role as pastor. It is his goal to have his readers understand that they are not alone in the struggle to live holy lives. "Millions of Christians have gone before us. They faced the same trials and temptations we face. And it is my prayer that, by their example, we will be inspired to leave a Christian legacy that is as inspiring as theirs."

His hope for the future of inspirational fiction is that one day Christian novelists will be "producing works of such great value that the world will no longer be able to ignore them or their message." Cavanaugh is certainly making a significant contribution to achieving that goal with his authentic settings, artfully created conflicts, and memorable characters.

SUMMARY: AMERICAN FAMILY PORTRAIT SERIES

The American Family Portrait series covers the time period from 1630 to World War II, chronicling the struggles, survival, and victories of the Morgan family as traced from England and the settling of the New World through both world wars. The following is a summary of the award-winning volume 1, *The Puritans*.

The pageantry and corruption of seventeenth-century England form the background for this story of intrigue, betrayal, adventure, and courage. Young Andrew Morgan, wealthy, selfish, and hungry for fame, becomes an unwitting pawn for ruthless Bishop Laud as the powerful churchman seeks to hunt down all Puritans. Always looking for adventure, Andrew is easy prey for Laud when he is convinced that the famous cleric is on God's side and that those who differ with him are the instruments of Satan.

Setting out to become a spy to infiltrate the heretics, Andrew uses the King James Version of the Bible to send messages back to the bishop. After a few less-than-stellar attempts at religious espionage, the knight (as he sees himself) is successful in bringing about the arrest and conviction of a young couple whose beliefs he had pretended to share. Andrew chooses not to think of their sure punishment. After all, he is a soldier in a holy war, and there are bound to be casualties.

Quickly, without a backward glance, he moves on to his next mission in a small English village. It is in that little town, which is sustained only by the wool trade and Christian love, that Andrew's ideals of personal success and true spiritual victory collide when he is defended, befriended, and housed by the man whom he has come to betray.

Cavanaugh gives Andrew Morgan credibility by creating a thoroughly human villain-hero. When the reader first meets him, Andrew is a bumbling yet daring teenager with stars of valor blinding him to the mundane realities of daily life. It is precisely his ambition to do wondrous deeds and his desire to become a hero that lead him down a decadent, deceitful path—trusting in the one man whom he should have been able to rely on but could not.

While introducing Andrew and his fellow cast members, Cavanaugh also devises a page-turning plot that defies predictability as it draws to the dramatic conclusion. Historically supported in the epilogue, this novel is certain to paint in glowing color facts and faces that might seem bland or dull in textbooks and to revitalize pride in the spiritual heroes who settled America and preserved Christianity at great peril.

Linda Lee Chaikin

Linda Lee Chaikin, born to Harry and Mae Kinley of Elsinore, California, was one of ten children. Frequent childhood illness gave her the opportunity to read a great deal, initiating her interest in writing. A graduate of Multnomah Bible School, Linda now lives in California with her husband, Steve, an electrical engineer. Her hobbies include history and hiking in the High Sierras.

PROFESSIONAL

Education
Graduate degree, Multnomah Bible College

Awards
Silver Angel Award for Fiction, Excellence in Media, 1995

PUBLICATIONS

Adult Fiction

The Everlasting Flame, 1995
Endangered!, 1997
Day to Remember Series
Monday's Child, 1999

Trade Winds Series
  Silver Dreams, 1998
  Captive Heart, 1998
  Island Bride, 1999
Jewel of the Pacific Series
  For Whom the Stars Shine, 1999
Heart of India Series
  Silk, 1993
  Under Eastern Stars, 1993
  Kingscote, 1994
Buccaneer Series
  Port Royal, 1995
  The Pirate and His Lady, 1997
  Jamaican Sunset, 1997
Great Northwest Series
  Empire Builders, 1994
  Winds of Allegiance, 1996
Royal Pavilion Series
  Swords and Scimitars, 1996
  Golden Palaces, 1996
  Behind the Veil, 1998
Lions of the Desert Series
  Arabian Winds, 1997
  Lions of the Desert, 1997
  Valiant Hearts, 1998

PERSONAL

Working at a word processor seven hours a day, five days a week, makes writing a full-time occupation for Linda Lee Chaikin, although she sees it as more than a job. "All of my heroines are interested in serving Christ. This is my heart, too." In fact, her series have been influenced by such giants of Christendom as William Carey (The Heart of India series) and Oswald Chambers (*Arabian Winds* and *Lions of the Desert*).

When asked how her own personal reading has shaped her writing, Chaikin replied, "I don't like many of the Godless books that are out so I write my own." Her favorite childhood books were listed as the Bible and the Nancy Drew mysteries. Reflecting this same interest in both sacred literature and mystery writing, persons mentioned as the most influential to her own writing were C. S. Lewis, J. R. R. Tolkien, and Dr. J. V. McGee.

Full of suspenseful, heart-stopping action, Chaikin's story lines do not neglect the development of her characters. She presents well-rounded characters who struggle with pride, fear, and learning to trust themselves and their God in the face of impossible odds. Placed in exotic settings (e.g., *Arabian Winds,* Heart of India series), her characters face challenging situations such as losing a child, choosing between suitors who offer vastly different futures, discerning the true motives of those who appear to be acting for their good, and coping with the serious illness of a family member.

To make the dangerous and romantic adventures of her heroines believable, Chaikin must do "deep research," which she says she enjoys. Her series have required the study of widely disparate situations, such as India during the era of British colonization, the Northwest Territory of the United States during the 1800s, mysterious Constantinople at the time of the Crusades, and the Arabian desert just prior to the outbreak of World War I.

Writing for "women of all ages," Chaikin desires to build up her readers in their faith. Themes that recur in many of her works emphasize the importance of missions and a dedication to God that forms the basis for all of life's decisions.

Chaikin's basic motivation to write Christian fiction is "to honor the name above all names: Jesus." In regard to the future of this genre, she states that "the opportunity to honor God is there as an open door."

SUMMARY: *SILK* (HEART OF INDIA SERIES)

As heiress to Kingscote, her family's silk plantation in northern India, Coral Kendall faces stiff opposition from Britishers and Indians alike when she decides to adopt a young orphaned boy of the "Untouchable" caste. When the child is abducted and reported to be dead, Coral is in despair until discrepancies in reports of the event lead her to believe that the boy is still alive and that he might in truth be the son of a maharaja. Seeking an ally to aid in searching for her son, Gem, Coral turns to the brash and darkly handsome Jace Buckley for help.

When her father is called away by military duty and her mother falls dangerously ill, Coral finds herself entrusted to the care of the enigmatic Sir Hugo Roxbury and pursued by his adopted son, Dr. Ethan Boswell. As Sir Hugo's schemes to take control of Kingscote become apparent and his search for wealth and power threatens to destroy her family's possessions and their very lives, Coral must learn to depend on her God for comfort and protection. Danger stalks on every side as she seeks to recover her abducted son and to protect her family's interests within the context of the racial, religious, and political conflicts of eighteenth-century India.

The Heart of India series displays the effectiveness of Chaikin's ability to do "deep research." In it she introduces the reader to the geography and political intrigue of India, showing in an effective and historically accurate way how these elements affected the lives of that country's inhabitants. The numerous twists of plot stretch the imagination, while the action draws readers in and makes them willing participants in the spinning of the tale.

Neva Coyle

If one is an aspiring writer and is looking for an author to help handle the personal trauma of dealing with rejection letters, Neva Coyle is not the writer to seek out. It is not that she is not a sympathetic person; it is just that in nineteen years of being in print, she has received only one of those dreaded pieces of mail, and then she "simply submitted" her idea to another publisher who accepted it and asked for three more of the same kind. Since that time, Coyle has written more than thirty books, both fiction and nonfiction, and enjoys speaking at women's conferences, retreats, and writers' conferences, an opportunity that has resulted from her success.

Married for thirty-six years to Lee Coyle, whom she says she spoils, Coyle lives in Oakhurst, California. She and her husband are the parents of three: Rhonda Ikes, Sandra Apodaca, and Dan Coyle. They also have six grandchildren and a cat.

Coyle ranks the best, the worst, and the most difficult aspects of being a writer as follows: "The most wonderful thing about being a writer is the day a new book comes out. Also quite wonderful is the opportunity writing gives me to speak and make personal appearances. I meet delightful people, and my publishers treat me very well. The hardest part . . . is getting started. I have to have a great deal of self-discipline, and so I rent a small office just to have a place to go to work each day. The thing I like the least . . . is that I get paid only twice a year. It's hard to budget that far in advance."

In her spare time, Coyle is involved in church activities, such as prayer ministries, teaching adult Sunday School classes, and Bible studies, where she got her start as an author. Her hobbies include rubber-stamping and making pop-up greeting cards. Her least favorite thing to do is housework.

PROFESSIONAL

Education
Crafton Hills Community College, Yuciapa, California; credentialed in specialized ministries with the Assemblies of God; Berean School of the Bible, Springfield, Missouri; Lakewood Community College, St. Paul, Minnesota; Rasmussen Business College, St. Paul, Minnesota

Career
Retail management

Memberships
Assemblies of God, minister

PUBLICATIONS

Adult Fiction

Cari's Secret, 1994
Jen's Pride and Joy, 1995
Megan's Promise, 1995
Sharon's Hope, 1996
Summerwind Books
  A Door of Hope, 1995
  Inside the Privet Hedge, 1996
  Close to a Father's Heart, 1996

Adult Nonfiction

Free to Be Thin, 1979
Living Free, 1981
Free to Be Thin Study Guide, 1982
The Free to Be Thin Cookbook, 1982
Free to Be Thin Daily Planner, 1983
There's More to Being Thin Than Being Thin, 1984
A Woman of Strength, 1985

Slimming Down and Growing Up, 1985
Perseverance for People under Pressure, 1986
Getting Your Family on Your Side, 1987
Free to Dream, 1990
Overcoming the Diet Dilemma, 1991
The All New Free to Be Thin Lifestyle Plan, 1993
The All New Free to Be Thin Book, with Marie Chapian, 1993
Living by Chance or by Choice, 1995
Loved on a Grander Scale, 1998

Devotion and Personal Study

Daily Thoughts on Living Free, 1982
A New Heart, a New Start, 1992
Making Sense of Pain and Suffering, 1992
Learning to Know God, 1993
Meeting the Challenges of Change, 1993
When Life Takes More Than It Gives, 1996
Answering God's Call to Quiet, 1997
Why Do I Feel So Alone?, 1999
What Does God Want Anyway?, 1999

PERSONAL

Neva Coyle's professional career began when a writer, attending a Bible study that she was teaching, asked whether she had ever considered putting her instructional material into printed form. "It was a great opportunity for me to work alongside a published author and learn how a book is researched, planned, outlined, written, revised, edited, and finally published." When the publisher asked her to do more on her own, Coyle was on her way. She views *Free to Be Thin* as her best-known book, having sold almost two million copies and having been translated into six languages.

For Coyle, entrance into the world of fiction writing came much later. That genre was a bit more difficult to launch. "Because of the no-nonsense seriousness of my nonfiction, I had a hard time convincing my publisher that I was serious about writing fiction." Coyle's fiction also deals with serious issues, such as spousal abuse—verbal and physical, rape, stalking, the pain of being unequally yoked in marriage, and other topics that Christians as well as those yet-to-be Christians confront in contemporary society. As can be noted by her titles, Coyle offers hope in each situation when right choices are made by her characters.

In describing the process of writing, Coyle reports that her research is "lengthy, detailed, and all consuming." She utilizes print and electronic media, spending time in libraries, in used bookstores, and on the Internet. One unique source of information that she finds especially intriguing is the picture book, stating that she "loves to find picture books of my eras." Her schedule is much like that of the proverbial office worker. "I write during the daytime business hours in a small two-room writing studio located in an office building in the small town where I live. I go to work each morning and take a lunch break, then go home each evening, just like other working people do. I find that keeping a regular schedule helps me to meet deadlines and plan outside activities, and it adds a certain seriousness to my working."

A list of those who have been most influential in Coyle's writing would show her family to be first. A finely crafted literary heritage resides in both her mother and her father. She shares that her father was "a storyteller/preacher" and that her mother wrote both poetry and short stories. It would seem that it is almost an obligation to create stories with such a background. Others who have inspired her writing are Catherine Marshall, Janette Oke, and Lori Wick, all contributors to the field of inspirational fiction.

In considering the literary elements found in her work, Coyle states that her plots are character driven and that her characters are original creations. However, "if I am completely honest, I'm sure they are composites of my friends, family, and even myself." The intended recurring theme in her novels is the profound influence of older Christian women on her main characters. "I use romance for tension and always show my main character solving a personal/spiritual dilemma by ultimately choosing morality and right."

Coyle gives tribute to her editors as those who have had a major role in shaping her as an author. "They encourage me to be the best, to dig a little deeper, and to find the courage to become as transparent as I possibly can. This has always proven to be the best advice. My nonfiction has been influenced by my step into fiction. As I have learned to set scenes, write dialogue, and so on, my nonfiction has become much more readable and lively. . . . I am a voracious reader and book collector. My living-room walls are lined with bookcases, as is my office. Good form, cohesive thought, argument, and skill have come through as I have learned to appreciate good writing in others and have challenged myself to grow as well."

SUMMARY: *SHARON'S HOPE*

At twenty-six years old, Sharon Potter is the survivor of a bitter divorce. She is bravely tackling the job of reconnecting the broken pieces of her life. Trying to forget the years spent with her abusive husband, Sharon is attempting to create a pleasant haven of security for her son and daughter. Without the gracious support of her Uncle Mac and his autumn-of-life wife, Meg, Sharon would find being a single parent almost overwhelming. Mac and Meg, however, have provided her with a small house, the safety of family, and an opportunity to work—both on their egg farm and in her own small pottery workshop.

Contentment, it seems, will be the best emotion that life can offer her—until Mac's stepson, Kenneth, returns home on leave from Vietnam. As Kenneth tries to establish a friendship, Sharon retreats. When he asks her whether she is happy, she is brought to the realization that her ex-husband had convinced her that she did not deserve happiness. It is Kenneth's desire to change that perception and to share the joy of life with Sharon and her children.

Sharon finds that trusting in the love of a man is more than she is capable of accomplishing, even when her children readily accept "Kenny," as they prefer to call him. When both Sharon's mother and Uncle Mac voice opposition to the union, she seems resigned to remain single.

Coyle has captured well the posttrauma emotions of an abused wife and her children. She demonstrates to her readers that even though the grace of God is *extended* to meet all needs, *receiving* it requires trust and that betrayal by a husband and father makes such trust nearly impossible to experience. This is a significant work that should be read by anyone who has been through an abusive relationship or by those who minister through marriage counseling.

Donna Fletcher Crow

At first glance, it might seem that Donna Fletcher Crow has had rather limited horizons in the first fifty-some years of her life. Born to Leonard and Reta Fletcher in Nampa, Idaho, she later married Stanley Crow, became the mother of four children, and settled down in Boise, less than fifty miles from her birthplace. The "settled down" is a bit deceptive, however. When one considers her careers, which include high school drama, English, and journalism teacher and her move to college instructor and later to nationally known author, there is obviously some vocational mobility. Further research reveals speaking engagements, taking her from Maine to California and from Florida to Washington, with periodic research ventures to the British Isles. It is clear that Crow has traveled far, both professionally and geographically, while maintaining roots in her native soil.

PROFESSIONAL

Education

B.A. in languages and literature, Northwest Nazarene College (graduated summa cum laude); European Study Tour; Pasadena College; Nampa (Idaho) High School (salutatorian)

Career

Teaching experience: Northwest Nazarene College, 1988; numerous seminars taught across the country, 1986–1997; Boise (Idaho) High School,

1967–1968; Lexington (Maine) Christian Academy, 1965–1966; Nampa (Idaho) High School, 1963–1964 (part time)

Awards

First Place Historical Fiction, Idaho Press Women, *The Fields of Bannockburn,* 1997; *Contemporary Authors,* New Revision Series, 1996; Professional Achievement Award, Northwest Nazarene College, 1994; First Place Historical Fiction, National Federation of Press Women, *Glastonbury,* 1993; Award of Merit, Juvenile Books, Idaho Press Women, 1990; Pacesetter Award, Mount Hermon Christian Writers Conference, 1990; Outstanding Historical Fiction, Idaho Press Women, National Federation of Press Women, 1989; *Something about the Author,* 1989; *Notable American Women,* first illustrated edition, 1988; Idaho Writer of the Year, 1988; *Who's Who of American Women,* fourteenth edition; *The World's Who's Who of Women,* eighth and tenth editions; *Who's Who in U.S. Writers, Editors and Poets,* third edition; *International Authors and Writers Who's Who,* eleventh and twelfth editions; Biography International, 1986; Best Inspirational Novel, Finalist, Romance Writers of America, 1985; Writer of the Year, Mount Hermon Writers Conference, 1983; *Contemporary Authors,* 1983; *Dictionary of International Biography,* twenty-first edition; *Five Thousand Personalities of the World,* second edition; *Personalities of America,* fifth edition; Outstanding Young Women of America, 1972; *Who's Who in American Colleges and Universities,* 1964

Memberships

Arts Centre Group, United Kingdom, 1994 to present; Writer's Information Network, 1988 to present; Idaho Press Women, 1987 to present; National Federation of Press Women, 1987 to present; Inklings II, Toccoa Falls College, 1996; National League of American Pen Women, 1988–1995; Idaho Writers' League, 1985–1992; Romance Writers of America, 1982–1993

PUBLICATIONS

Adult Fiction

Epic Novels

The Castle of Dreams, 1992
Glastonbury: The Novel of Christian England, 1992
The Fields of Bannockburn, 1996
Encounter the Light, 1997
The Banks of the Boyne: The Generations of Northern Ireland, 1998

Where Love Calls, 1998
In the Presence of the Holy, 1999
Above All Else, 1999
Virtuous Heart Series
All Things New, 1997
Roses in Autumn, 1998
Daughters of Courage Series
Kathryn: Days of Struggle and Triumph, 1992
Elizabeth: Days of Loss and Hope, 1993
Stephanie: Days of Turmoil and Peace, 1993
Lord Danvers Mysteries
A Most Inconvenient Death, 1993
Grave Matters, 1994
To Dust You Shall Return, 1995
The Cambridge Chronicles
A Gentle Calling, 1987 (large print, 1997)
To Be Worthy, 1994
Where Love Begins, 1994
Treasures of the Heart, 1994 (large print, 1997)
Love Embraces Destiny, 1999
Serenade Romances Series
Greengold Autumn, 1984
The Desires of Your Heart, 1985
Love Unmerited, 1986

Juvenile Fiction

Choose Your Own Adventure Series
The Evil Plot of Dr. Zarnof, 1983
Professor Q's Mysterious Machine, 1983
Mr. Zanthu's Golden Scheme, 1985
General Kempthorne's Victory Tour, 1987

Adult Nonfiction

Recipes for the Protein Diet, 1972
The Frantic Mother Cookbook, 1982
Mountain Tops (contributor), 1983
The Church Kitchen Handbook, 1985
The Zondervan Family Cookbook, 1988
A Moment a Day (contributor), 1988
Seasons of Prayer: Discovering the Depths of the Christian Calendar through Classical Prayers, 2000

Screenplays

The Caravan Connection, 1985
Wilberforce, Light to a Nation (collaboration with Gwen Mansfield), 1986

Plays

An Upper Room Experience, 1983
A Rumor of Resurrection, 1985
Puppet Programs, 1985
Because You Ask Not, 1986
Called unto Holiness, 1987
That Was Then, 1987
The Case of the Mysterious Parables, 1989

Poetry

The St. Michael's Cycle (ten villanelles on the liturgical year, arranged for choir and orchestra by C. Griffith Bratt, No. 1, "Christmas Midnight," performed Christmas Eve 1997)

Articles

Published in the following publications: *Virtue, Family Life Today, Plastercraft, Living with Children, Arkenstone, The Preacher's Magazine, Modern Liturgy, The Hearld of Holiness, The Christian Writer, Come Ye Apart, Fiction Writer's Monthly, Writer's Inspirational Market News, Fiction Writers' Magazine, Rave Reviews, Romance Writers' Report, The Pen Women, Washington Kaleidoscope,* and *The Lookout*

Ghostwriting

Love Hunger, Dr. Frank Minirith, Dr. Paul Meier, Dr. Robert Hemfelt, and Dr. Sharon Sneed, 1990, Number One "Bookstore Journal" best-seller list, CBA Gold Medallion winner
Filling the Holes in Our Souls: Caring Groups That Build Lasting Relationships, Dr. Paul Meier and Dr. Allan Doran, 1992

PERSONAL

Donna Fletcher Crow states that although she has always had a passion for writing, an equally important component of her career is that she is an avid reader. At her writers' conferences, she emphasizes, "Read, read, read. Stock the shelves of your mind. You can't take something out of the refrigerator that you didn't put in first. Read the classics. You may never write as well as you read, but you put an automatic limit on the level of your excellence by the level of your reading."

When asked why she chose Christian fiction as her genre, Crow responded, "I write truth. Christianity is True. One can only write from their own perspective. To write from any other perspective would be to lie."

Describing herself as one who loves research and yet as one who is "low-tech," Crow begins her investigative process by reading general background from anything that she finds interesting. Then, when an idea strikes a spark, she focuses on creating her story. Historical events, themes, historical characters, fictional characters, lifestyles, food, fashions, or mind-sets of the period soon become grist for her writer's mill. Since many of Crow's novels take place in the British Isles, she must be certain that her setting and characters accurately portray that life and land. Fortunately, her exploration can take a proactive approach. Describing the next step, she reports, "When I've done all I can do on this side of the Atlantic (thank God for interlibrary loan service!), I then spend a month or two in Great Britain researching on site. I go over every two or three years, depending on my writing schedule. The greatest joys are the wonderful friends I've made in the UK and the fact that I've been able to take some of my family with me on each trip."

The actual creating of a story, here in the United States, follows a writing schedule much like that of the workday of her readers. In the office by 9:00 A.M., Crow works until 3:00 P.M., when her children come home from school. She says that when they arrive, she stops, "even midsentence," and puts on the tea kettle. Such organization, self-discipline, and devotion to her family have certainly paid dividends, as her numerous works bear witness.

Crow has an international goal: to encourage Christians on both sides of the Atlantic. She desires to give those of our motherland a "sense of the deep and very special Christian heritage of their nation" and to see "spiritual renewal in that land." However, she has not only the broader, nationwide view in mind but also the individual reader and especially the authority on the particular topic about which she is currently writing. That one provides a special kind of motivation for her. "Feeling that I have an expert looking over my shoulders urges me on to strive for ever greater accuracy of detail and expression."

Crow describes her style as theme based, with grace being the emerging, consistent thought. She says that her goal as a writer is "to give the most accurate picture possible of the people, times, and events I write about; to put my reader in the scene with a well-developed background; and to let my reader experience the events through the mind of my viewpoint character." Part of the acclaim that she has received as a writer rests, no doubt, on the fact that she strives for historical accuracy in both setting and character that her travel and on-site observations support. Crow also consults authentic biographical and historically accurate sources to round out her own picture before sharing with her readers. She creates fictional characters from a composite of physical and psychological traits drawn from people whom she knows or from her observations about human nature in general. She cites Gareth, the hero of her two epic novels, *The Fields of Bannockburn* and *The Banks of the Boyne,* as a case in point. "He is based on the delightful Scottish gentleman who escorted me through the Highlands and the Hebrides." She pays tribute to this guide through her dedication in *The Fields of Bannockburn.*

Crow lists a number of other people and resources as significant to her writing success. She states that her husband "has been a constant support, encourager and prayer partner." Elaine Colvin directed her to professional writing and helped "launch" her career, Lee Roddy instructed her in the establishment of conflict in plot construction, and Lois T. Henderson was her mentor when she was just beginning to write. Crow wishes to acknowledge each of their contributions and quotes Henderson's philosophy regarding theme: "For every book you write, you will have a theme. But as you write, you will see that you also develop a theme in the total body of your work." She says that she often remembers that theory as she writes and that "no matter what I think my theme is, I always wind up writing about grace."

Crow's love of the past and the people breathing life into it in the lands of Great Britain and her "passion to see revival there" are the strongest influences in her writing. "Even the Daughters of Courage, my Idaho pioneer series, gets lots of Scottish history into it." Perhaps it was the requirement of her tenth-grade English teacher that set her on the path that she still follows today. That teacher set a high standard for her in requiring that she write a book report on *Wuthering Heights*. "I have hardly read anything but English literature since then. Jane Austen is my great literary love. Georgette Heyer had the most direct influence on my writing. I wrote my first novel as a direct reaction to her Regency romances. Delightful tales though they are, they are so totally secular. One would think all the churches in England to be boarded up. I knew that, in fact, that period was the beginning of the great Evangelical fervor. I wrote *Brandley's Search* (reissued as *Where Love Begins*) to set the record straight."

Crow reminisces that her mother's reading aloud to her created a love for the printed word. She recalls especially *Bambi, Hans Brinker, Heidi, Girl of the Limberlost,* and *A Child's Garden of Verses* and is sure that the King Arthur stories "must have been in there some place" because her very first creative composition in third grade dealt with the demise of the dragon at the hand of Sir Lancelot. She remembers that she was "totally amazed that none of the other children wrote about knights and dragons" since she thought that those were the only tales worth telling. Donna Fletcher Crow fans may recognize the little-girl-come-to-fruition-as-writer in the epic novel *Glastonbury,* which also includes elements of the Arthurian legend.

Crow states that her writing style has often been described as "very optimistic, very sunny." She believes that her Wesleyan-Holiness theology is a strong factor in that approach since it focuses on "the restoration of the image of God in the believer and the believer's complete submission to the will of God." She follows this tenet as she states, "My goal in my writing, as in everything else in my life, is to do God's will." Her goals for her readers are to "gain a sense of God's moving through history and apply the truths of the past to today. I write history, but I'm talking about today."

When asked about the future of Christian fiction, Crow places the responsibility on herself and her fellow authors. "If we cater to the shallow tastes of the popular market, we will remain on the fringes of the literary world. If we push on for true literary excellence in proclaiming God's truth, we can restore writing to what it was in the days of Spenser, Milton, and Bunyan when Christians were the ones producing the greatest literature."

SUMMARY: *THE FIELDS OF BANNOCKBURN*

Using the vehicle of the traditional Highland storyteller sharing with his contemporary audience the courage that created the wild and restless land, Crow unfolds the Christian history of Scotland. Readers relive the birth of the steadfast, hearty nation through the words and music of Hamish MacBain, a modern bard, but learn from the perspective of American tourist Mary Hamilton.

Along with her degree, college graduation has granted Mary two gifts: a monthlong visit to her cousin in Scotland provided by her parents and an engagement ring presented by successful Harvard graduate Michael Warden. Mary has come to this ancient British Isle to seek her roots and perhaps find answers to who she is and who she wants to be and to decide whether she wants to marry Michael.

Mary's search for identity is the connecting thread between each book in this epic work. Yet the reader also becomes intrigued with the passage of Scotland from its ancient pagan rites and inauspicious beginnings to the victorious stand for independence championed by Robert the Bruce on the fields of Bannockburn. As Hamish recounts the tales of St. Columba, Kenneth MacAlpin, St. Margaret, and William Wallace, Mary falls in love with the lore that is the land, and the reader is swept right along.

Research as detailed and intricate as the manuscripts of ancient monks reveals the influence of Christianity in unified patriotism, peasant loyalty, and royal leadership. Crow has impressive documentation for each chapter, yet it is the heart that holds the reader. As the 700-plus pages are drawing to a close, one is tempted to plan to begin again. So personal has this history become that as the last leaves turn, one is almost certain that somewhere in the background there is the echo of a bagpipe and the whispered prayer of a saint.

Will Cunningham

Will Cunningham was born to Dr. Bill Cunningham, an ophthalmologist, and his wife, Jean, a homemaker, on July 31, 1959, in Arcadia, California. He and his wife, Cindy, are the parents of two sons, Wesley and Peter. In his spare time, Cunningham enjoys fishing, basketball, and playing guitar.

PROFESSIONAL

Education
M.A. in counseling, Denver Seminary; B.A. in English literature, Oklahoma State University

Career
Twenty years in youth ministry; twelve years in marriage and family counseling

Memberships
Christian Association of Psychological Studies

PUBLICATIONS

Adult Fiction

It Happened at the Sunset Grille, 1993
Letters from the Other Side, 1995

Adult Nonfiction

How to Enjoy a Family Fight, 1988

Work in Progress

Faith of the Fathers

SUMMARY: *IT HAPPENED AT THE SUNSET GRILLE*

As the economy of the farming community of Ellenbach begins to decline, it seems that fate has smiled on the inhabitants when strangers roll into town on tractor trailers and in an amazingly short time have erected a new restaurant. Advertisements read, "The Sunset Grille, Fine Steaks, Spirits, and Live Entertainment." Anonymity surrounds the owner and his employees, but the manager exhibits a welcoming manner and insists that he be informally called "Billy Bob."

Within a short time, the eating establishment is thriving, and, since grain-fed beef is bought from the local farmers, the economy is thriving as well. Those who frequent the lower floor of the place never discuss openly exactly what live entertainment is provided, but everyone knows that lust is the food for that economy.

Although Pastor Larry Ravelle is troubled by the reported activities of the establishment, it is not until the rape and murder of an innocent seventeen-year-old that he begins to marshal his forces to attack this financial stronghold of the community. Supported by only a faithful few of his friends and congregation, he sets out to have the business closed. Little does the well-meaning minister know what sinister sins will be revealed before the struggle reaches its climax.

Cunningham uses as narrator the first-person voice of Skandalon, a Trial (what we humans would call an angel), to reveal what is witnessed only by the spirit world. The battle rages between good and evil as the minister wrestles with his own temptations and dark secrets. Skandalon is opposed by Dias, a Way (of escape), who protects, guards, and defends but does not make choices for Ravelle. Pitch and Stool, emissaries from Hell, employ physical, emotional, and psychological weapons to confound, confuse, damage, and attempt to destroy him.

Written with the page-turning style of a mystery, this gripping novel leads readers into the profound revelation that in spiritual warfare there exists the absolute necessity of having Trials, but there is also hope, provided by Ways of Escape. Humor and a surprise ending lighten the compelling story without diminishing the power of its message.

W. E. (Wally) Davis

Born in Sioux Falls, South Dakota, on September 11, 1951, W. E. Davis grew up in southern California. He still lives in California with his wife, Marcie, and their children. For entertainment, he enjoys playing the guitar, painting, and drawing cartoons.

PROFESSIONAL

Education
B.S., California State Polytechnic University

Career
Law enforcement, twenty-two years; deputy sheriff; cartoonist, five published cartoon books for law enforcement

PUBLICATIONS

Adult Fiction

Gil Beckman Mysteries Series
Suspended Animation, 1994

Black Dragon, 1995
Victim of Circumstance, 1996
Drastic Park, 1997
Valley of the Peacemaker Series
The Gathering Storm, 1996
The Proving Ground, 1996
The Refining Fire, 1997

PERSONAL

I've always been interested in writing, as far back as I can remember. I had two big interests as a child . . . drawing and writing. But I was practical and never thought I could make a living at either, so I concentrated on practical stuff and left the art and writing as hobbies, until about seven years ago, when I was bedridden after surgery. [At that time] I began a historical novel on the real gold camp of Bodie, California. It took off from there. I thought I'd have a better shot at making it in the Christian marketplace. . . . Besides, being a Christian, with "talent on loan from God," it seemed appropriate to use it for Him.

I go where the action takes place as much as possible when preparing to write a story. Sometimes the locale gives me ideas for the plot. I don't write about Australia or the Mideast because I doubt I'll ever make it there. Besides, it's so much more interesting and accurate to describe what I can see and smell and feel for myself. After I moved to Washington's Olympic peninsula, I wrote a mystery that takes place there, based on real topography and history. For a mountain-climbing sequence I went climbing with my daredevil son . . . free climbing (no ropes) up nearly vertical cliffs. How can I write honestly about the sensations if I don't experience them?

My western series takes place in Bodie, which is now a well-preserved ghost town. There are no accommodations, no stores, no gas, nothing but what's left of the town. And there are rangers there to make sure it stays that way. But they let me spend the night in one of the primitive buildings (the town is closed to the public from 6 P.M. to 9 A.M.), so I could experience dusk and dawn and the cutting cold of night at 9,000 feet in October. That makes me a minority of one. Also, I have a leg up on most mystery writers: I've been a law enforcement officer for twenty-two years (still am, actually). That gives me bit of inside information other writers have to work at acquiring.

My audience is anyone who reads and likes my books. I gear them primarily for high school and above, but even some fifth- and sixth-graders have read my books. I try to make them interesting to both men and women. There's action and romance. And I try to keep the big words out (twenty-plus years of writing police reports has given me plenty of experience keeping it simple). The reality is, women buy eighty percent of the Christian fiction. But sometimes they buy it for their husbands. I'd like more men to read.

I don't know that I even have a style. I just try to write a complete sentence, then a complete thought, make it grammatically correct and interesting, and in the process tell the story I have in mind. The result is what you might call my style. I don't use a lot of metaphors, and I've been told I pack a lot of substance into a small space. Some writers tell you the same thing three or four times before they go on. I've been criticized for being too brief. One publisher said, "Nice proposal." I said, "That was the whole novel." But I'm learning to wax poetic.

Not having taken any writing courses, I couldn't tell you if my plots are action, character, or theme driven. Sometimes I start with a plot, sometimes with an interesting character that I place in a situation just to see what happens. Other times I want to tell about a place, or a historical event, and develop characters and a plot to make it happen. Or I might have a scriptural principle I want to illustrate. In the end, all I want to do is tell a compelling story to entertain myself, and maybe someone else if I can sell it.

A recurring theme in my work is failure. People are imperfect, after all, and need God. My main protagonist in the westerns gets by by the skin of his teeth time after time. He learns but, like the donkey following the carrot, can't ever seem to get a grip on things completely. Of course, what he can do at the end of the series would have killed him at the beginning. It's that way with life. As we learn, we grow stronger, and God gives us more challenging hurdles. "As thy day, so shall thy strength be."

My characters are almost always based on people I know, though hardly ever in total. Many of my characters are based on facets of myself and my life, others on co-workers or people I know or have read about. Let's face it: It's easier to model from life than from imagination. Artists use models; so do writers. If I have a personality developed but don't know what the character looks like, I just pick someone out of a crowd who I think looks like my character and describe that person. One thing I try not to do is make it too obvious who I'm modeling a character after, especially if the character has negative qualities. Never is one of my characters wholly a single person. In real life, people are much more complex than characters in a novel. I deal in generalities, or types, with some details thrown in. If I do base a character or a circumstance on someone close to me, I get their permission. And I once used a friend's first name for a minor character based on them, also with permission—kind of my way of saying thank you for their friendship. But this is the exception rather than the rule. In my first novel, *Suspended Animation,* both the protagonist who solves the mystery and the murder victim are based in part on myself and my experience at a well-known theme park where I worked for a time.

I read a lot, especially if I'm stuck, just to prime the pump, as it were. But no single writer has influenced me . . . inspired me. Yes, I have many favorites. Bill Pronzini is one. Louis L'Amour [is another]. But I'm inspired in reverse, I guess you could say, by other writers. Zane Grey is too wordy, spends too much time explaining and describing characters' emotions and not enough time describing action. Some of Agatha Christie's and Clive Cussler's plots are contrived. Improbable I can handle. Impossible is another matter. Ignoring the laws of physics or historical reality ruins a book for me. You have to be able to say, "You know, it could have happened like that" when you're done reading it. (If you saw *Star Wars* and *Star Trek* for that matter, you'll remember that they hyperdrive through the stars as though they were just points of light rather than the great balls of fire they are. I don't recall seeing such stars in photos of space shuttle action. And isn't space a vacuum? Would there be any noise from an explosion?) Did I digress too much? No, there is no writer I can point to as influencing me. I read what I need to read to prepare me to write what I'm going to write. I think my sense of humor, which is generally sarcastic with a bit of irony thrown in, was largely developed by *MAD* magazine.

I don't have any goals [for my writing] because I don't have any control over what gets published. I just write, and if I sell something, great. I want to be well known, sure. Well read would probably be more accurate, but I want to do what God wants me to do. Right now He has given me the desire to write and granted it by allowing me to be published. Beyond that, I don't know. I'll just keep plugging away until it becomes clear I'm wasting my time. I would love to make my living writing, but that is not a goal. I aspire to it, hope for it, but pray for God's will. I don't expect it but will take it if God chooses to bless me that way. I like my job (are you kidding? I get to drive a cop car through some of the most beautiful scenery on earth and get to wear a cowboy hat while I do it!), and I can't see leaving it any time soon. Of course, if one of my books goes platinum, I'll consider it. The fact is, even working full time I write quickly enough to keep with my deadlines (270,000 words, about 900 pages in printed form last year).

I want my readers to enjoy what I write and want to read more. I don't expect to influence their lives, or save them from suicide, or set them on the path to a new and better life. That's between them and God, and if God uses me, that's wonderful. But I can't have a goal in that regard. I write, God uses it as He wills. It's the same for those in the ministry. Preachers preach, God gives the increase. In fact, I view my writing as a ministry. It is His to use as He will, mine is to be faithful.

I have no clue as to the future of "Christian fiction." It seems to have increased many times over in the past few years and is now peaking. Will there be a decline, or will it level off? I have no clue, and if I did, there'd be no way to tell. What's going to be the next best-seller? Who can tell? Frank Peretti's *This Present Darkness* was rejected many times over before it was published, and now it's sold over two million.

There is a trend these days that I believe is muddying the waters: ghost-written novels by "famous" Christians. These novels, written by an anonymous person but bearing the name of a famous person, are outselling just about everything else. What's the problem? It's an ethics question. While purporting to have written a novel when in fact perhaps all they did is get the idea is deceiving the buying public. . . . To me it's compromise at the least, lying at the worst. Isn't it the same as having your classmate do your homework or copying the test answers from their paper? We have a standard to uphold. . . . I am proud to say my publisher refuses to do ghost-written books.

Frankly, I like to see Christian fiction continue to expand. We have enough self-help books, thank you. It's almost to the point of being ridiculous. But the buying public will dictate what happens. I'm excited and apprehensive at the same time, as are most of the publishers, I would imagine. Of course, we can all hope that Christ will return soon, which will make all the speculation rather pointless.

SUMMARY: *BLACK DRAGON* (GIL BECKMAN MYSTERY SERIES)

Gil Beckman works on the security force of a California theme park that is opening several new state-of-the-art attractions. These rides have drawn the attraction of Japanese businessman Keini Hiromoto. Hiromoto plans to visit the park to judge the feasibility of building similar rides for his own park in Japan, and it is Gil's job to protect the businessman's safety while on the grounds. When a sabotage attempt is made on the giant roller coaster, The Dragon, Gil's job of keeping Hiromoto alive becomes more complex. The saboteur's trail of clues leads Gil to Manzanar, a museum on the site of the former internment camp for Japanese-Americans during World War II. As Gil's investigation uncovers secrets surrounding others' lives, his own areas of insecurity and his need for growth are clearly revealed.

Davis's Gil Beckman mysteries are full of action and suspense. Although the author's main emphasis is not on character development, his hero displays courage, ingenuity, and the willingness to learn from his experiences.

Barbara Davoll

Being a World War II baby might have influenced the entire life and career of at least one little girl. Born on August 15, 1939, Barbara Hardman soon moved with her mother to live on her grandparents' farm while her father went off to fight in the service of his country. Because her grandfather was a veterinarian who constantly housed convalescing animals, Barbara's love of the small, helpless farm creatures developed early. She states that she "assisted" her grandfather by carrying the little patients from place to place in her small wagon. She sometimes developed close attachments with the injured and was sad to see them returned to their owners after they had recovered. Such personal early experiences with farm animals might have been God's way of sparking Barbara's interest in other creatures that resulted in the Christopher Churchmouse and the Molehole Mysteries series, which launched Barbara Hardman Davoll into her very successful writing career. Her interest in writing was initiated when she taught kindergarten in a Christian school where she realized that there was a great need for "quality-building books that would not only entertain but teach the Word of God."

Barbara is married to V. Roy Davoll, with whom she travels as they share in a variety of evangelistic ministries. They are the parents of Jeffrey Jon Davoll and Lisa Renee Davoll Walsh.

PROFESSIONAL

Education
Morris Harvey College; Tennessee Temple University; Moody Bible Institute

Career
Author; youth pastor's wife; kindergarten teacher; staff pianist, Children's Bible Hour

Awards
Finalist, Gold Medallion Award, Christopher Churchmouse series, 1988; C. S. Lewis Award for Best Series, Christopher Churchmouse series, 1991; Finalist, Gold Medallion Award, Molehole Mystery series, 1993; Finalist, Gold Medallion Award, Tales from Schroon Lake series, 1997

Hobbies
Church organist and pianist; dramatic coach for Word of Life Institute for nineteen years

PUBLICATIONS

Although most other works in this book are listed only by title and year of publication, it seemed that a note regarding theme or character quality expressed would be more beneficial to readers of Davoll's books.

Christopher Churchmouse Classics (primary series, ages four to nine years)
Saved by the Bell (anger), 1988
The White Trail (stealing), 1988
A Sunday Surprise (behavior in church), 1988
The Potluck Supper (sharing and greed), 1988
A Load of Trouble (deceit), 1988
Rainy Day Rescue (obedience), 1988
A Pack of Lies (lying), 1989
A Sticky Mystery (jealousy), 1989
A Shiny Red Sled (quarreling), 1989
A Short Tail (appearance), 1989
A Flood of Friends (friendship), 1990
Tattletale Tongue (tattling), 1990
Christopher Churchmouse Classic Treasury, 1992
Christopher Churchmouse Birthday Collection, 1993
The Camping Caper (mercy), 1993

Grandpa's Secret (wisdom), 1993
A Churchmouse Birthday (kindness), 1994
A Churchmouse Christmas (nativity and salvation), 1994
A Churchmouse Musical Book, 1992

Little Churchmouse Library (board books, ages six months to four years)
My Home and Family, 1996
My World, 1996
My Church, 1996
My Helpers, 1996
My Grandparents, 1996
My Friends, 1996

Tales from Schroon Lake, featuring Bucky Beaver (primary age)
Hobo Holiday, 1996
The Problem with Prickles, 1996
A Visit from Rudy Beaver, 1996
Fire in the Bramblewood, 1996

Molehole Mystery Series (middler to junior, ages seven to twelve)
Dusty Mole—Private Eye (right choices), 1992
Secret at Mossy Roots Mansion (getting along), 1992
The Gypsies' Secret (family values), 1992
Foul Play at Moler Park (sportsmanship), 1993
The Upstairs Connection (care of our world), 1993
The Hare-Brained Habit (good use of time), 1994

PERSONAL

As a young child, Barbara Davoll began piano lessons, and by the age of ten she was traveling with her parents as an accompanist for their quartet. She also developed an interest in singing and drama and remembers with enthusiasm acting in her senior high school play.

After high school, Davoll attended both Moody Bible Institute and Tennessee Temple University. At Moody she met her husband, Roy. They are currently in their twenty-third year as children's representatives and evangelists, serving at home and abroad with Word of Life International, living at Schroon Lake, New York. Davoll served for nineteen years as drama coach for the Word of Life Bible Institute, directing the dramatic musicals, and recently has retired from this phase of ministry.

A landmark year for Davoll was 1978. She wrote her first children's musical, *The Little Bell That Couldn't Stop Ringing,* and began writing her first book of the Christopher Churchmouse series. After ten years and nineteen rejections, that book was published in 1988. The rejections, acceptance, and subsequent success that Davoll experienced could serve as inspiration for any beginning writer.

Currently, books in the Christopher Churchmouse series can be enjoyed in three formats: in books, on audiotape in both song and story, and on video. Children can also meet Christopher through a game, a calendar, greeting cards, a doll, and a dollhouse, and a CD-ROM is on the way. In addition, the Christopher Churchmouse series has been translated into eight languages.

In 1990 other small animals contributed to Davoll's status as an author. Designed as chapter books, the Molehole Mysteries series features Dusty and Musty Mole and other members of the Molehole Mystery Club. This series gives older children food for thought through the antics of woodland creatures who face problems much like those of their readers. Each book includes a card that can be mailed in to gain membership into the Molehole Mystery Club.

Davoll and her husband travel as an evangelistic team. They have ministered in the Ukraine, Romania, the Czech Republic, Poland, Russia, the Philippines, Holland, Hawaii, and Hungary. In the United States, Davoll, her husband, and Christopher Churchmouse maintain a busy schedule visiting churches and Christian schools.

Davoll describes her writing process as beginning with the Bible. "Every story which I have written illustrates a particular scriptural truth. I prefer to do it this way rather than to write the story first and fit a scripture to it. As I meditate on the Word of God, the Lord brings to mind plots and ways I can illustrate this to little ones. Further research takes me to the library to find out real-life traits about the animal; to beaver ponds, where I have sat waiting amidst the mosquitoes for a coveted glimpse of a little beaver; or to a field to follow the trail of a mole. Exciting research process!"

Davoll's writing procedures are governed by her location and her travel schedule. Most often she uses a word processor in her office at home, and she says that her window looks out over the Adirondacks and is "always an inspiration." However, as might be imagined, the demands of evangelism create the need of frequent mobility, and she adapts by using a laptop computer in her van, in airports, and in motels. Through these varied exposures, she gains insights that she records in her prayer journal, making observations and notations that fuel future plots.

In describing her work, Davoll states that her target audience is children of primary and junior age, but that she would like to write for teens in the future. She sees her plots as action driven, but the characters whom she has developed for each of her series are also central to the story. Her recurring theme is that of character building, which she strives to do without being "preachy." It is her desire that the young reader discover truths for him- or herself rather than feeling that her book is just another sermon.

Influences in Davoll's life as an author include her "greatest encourager," her husband, Roy Davoll, and Dr. Warren Wiersbe, who has been a "great friend and mentor. . . . Dr. Wiersbe has encouraged and motivated me, and we share an interest in old and rare books." She also has a "voracious" appetite for the Word of God and for reading other fine literature. "The Word of God is more than my 'necessary food.'" Her personal practice includes reading two or three different books at the same time, her preferences being history and English literature.

Davoll says that her personal goal for writing is to "make a difference in the lives of children and be the means of bringing them to Jesus Christ."

When asked to express her view regarding the future of Christian fiction, Davoll responded, "I am very distressed in seeing the development of books for children such as the those dealing with horror, the occult, and New Age making such inroads. I feel for the children of our country whose lives are polluted by the media and the printed page. We have come so far in this country that in the name of censorship we allow the fundamentals upon which this country was founded to be destroyed by what we watch and read. I am encouraged when I see fine works such as Jane Austen's books *Pride and Prejudice* and *Emma* receive new acclaim in literature and films and pray that we can see a return to wholesome family values."

SUMMARY: *RAINY DAY RESCUE* (CHRISTOPHER CHURCHMOUSE SERIES)

When Christopher gets restless from playing inside on a rainy day, his mother suggests that he go out and jump in puddles because the rain is not falling very hard. Mother Mouse warns her little son to stay out of the storm sewer because it is dangerous. Naturally, Christopher and his cousin Ted find themselves tempting fate by playing too near the forbidden spot and are swept into the drain.

Wet and frightened, they land safely but are soon discovered and threatened by a pack of sewer rats. The mice are helpless, but a friend who has been watching rescues them. Christopher and Ted learn that being obedient is safer and not nearly as scary as being disobedient.

Charming illustrations by Dennis Hockerman round out the characters of Christopher, Ted, and even the sewer rats. The combination of lovingly drawn figures and a plot pitting small animals against larger, more powerful forces make this small volume a winner with children. Questions for discussion at the end of the story provide an added dimension that parents appreciated. It is Davoll's goal that the story be enjoyed by both children and parents.

THE GYPSIES' SECRET (MOLEHOLE MYSTERIES SERIES)

When Murdoch Mole, Esquire, visits Dusty Mole, junior detective agent, and requires his services to find a missing son, he gets more than he had expected. Mr. Murdoch is a wealthy businessman, and his wife is usually busy with her social obligations, but when their only son, Millard, disappears, their lives are changed forever.

Dusty and Musty Mole, twin agents, set out to find the missing boy and learn much about the inner workings of his family in the process. The twins come away from the case grateful for their parents and their humble home, with its security and love. They also gain a new member in their Molehole Mystery Club.

Special features in this series include a map of Molesbury, R.F.D., complete with tunnel streets connecting places of interest in the story. At the end of each book is an application form that a child can mail in to join the Mystery Club. An Underground "Dig-tionary" gives interesting facts about some facet of life below the earth's surface. Dennis Hockerman's endearing illustrations give complete personality to Davoll's creations.

Sandy Dengler

If varied interests and a spirit of adventure are important ingredients in becoming a good writer, Sandy Dengler must rank near the top of her field. Born to Walter and Alyce Hance in June 1939, Dengler spent her childhood in Newark, Ohio, where her father supported his family as a businessman. However, in the spring of 1961, never having been west of Chicago, she went to west Texas "and spent three weeks in the backcountry on a leased horse." This experience was just an introduction to that part of the country for the author since much of her married life was spent in the western half of the United States. Working for the National Park Service for many years, Dengler's husband, Bill, was given responsibilities in one park after another. They lived and raised their daughters, Alyce and Mary, in Grand Canyon National Park, Saguaro National Monument, Death Valley National Monument, Joshua Tree National Monument, Acadia National Park, Yosemite National Park, and Mount Rainier National Park. Sandy can boast of hiking barefoot to the bottom of the Grand Canyon. She says that her feet "came out fine, but my legs were so sore I descended staircases backward for two weeks."

PROFESSIONAL

Education

M.S., Arizona State University; B.S., Bowling Green State University

Career

Carhop, root beer stand; research chemist, Bowling Green State University special project; chicken plucker in poultry factory; research assistant, Poisonous Animals Research Lab; substitute teacher; naturalist, Acadia National Park; wrangler, Camp Wawona; wrangler, Mount Rainier National Park; emergency medical technician

Memberships

Mystery Writers of America; Romance Writers of America; Sisters in Crime

Awards

Best Traditional Romance, Romance Writers of America, *Opal Fire,* 1986

Hobbies

Needlework: embroidery, crocheting, knitting, sewing, quilting; sports: skiing (cross-country and downhill), horseback riding, canoeing, hiking, camping, birding; miniatures: dollhouses and ship modeling; gardening: vegetables, flowers, landscaping, bonsai; fine arts: watercolor, sketching, oils, pencil, acrylic

PUBLICATIONS

Juvenile Fiction

Summer of the Wild Pig, 1979
Melon Hound, 1980
The Horse Who Loved Picnics, 1980
The Arizona Longhorn Adventure, 1980
Rescue in the Desert, 1981
Mystery at McGehan Ranch, 1982
Socorro Island Treasure, 1983
Chain Five Mystery, 1984

Adult Fiction

Summer Snow, 1984
Song of the Nereids, 1984
Opal Fire, 1986
To Die in the Queen of Cities, 1986
Hyaenas, 1998
Serenade/Saga Books
  Winterspring, 1985

This Rolling Land, 1986
Jungle Gold, 1987
A Jack Prester Mystery
Death Valley, 1993
A Model Murder, 1993
Murder on the Mount, 1994
The Quick and the Dead, 1995
Mirage Mysteries
Cat Killer, 1993
Mouse Trapped, 1993
Last Dinosaur, 1993
Gila Monster, 1994
Heroes of the Misty Isles Series
Dublin Crossing, 1993
The Shamrock Shore, 1994
Emerald Sea, 1994
King of the Stars, 1995
Australian Destiny Series
Code of Honor, 1988
Power of Pinjarra, 1989
Taste of Victory, 1989
East of Outback, 1990

Juvenile Nonfiction

Beasts of the Field (puzzles), 1979
Birds of the Air (puzzles), 1979
Man and Beast Together (puzzles), 1981

Adult Nonfiction

"Barn Social" (article in the *Mariposa Gazette*), 1978
Yosemite's Marvelous Creatures, 1979
Ge*tting into the Bible* (adult guide), 1979
The Headache Book (with Frank Minirth), 1995
Where Was God at 9:02 A.M.? (with Robin Jones), 1995
Eighteen nonfiction "ghosts" for Thomas Nelson

Adult Biography

Fanny Crosby, 1985
John Bunyan, 1986
D. L. Moody, 1987

Susanna Wesley, 1987
Smokey: A Simple Country Bear Who Made Good, 1987
Florence Nightingale, 1988

PERSONAL

For Sandy Dengler, writing is her job. With the exception of the first phase of her husband's retirement, when she spent only three to four hours a day at the keyboard, she gives eight hours a day to her craft. Writing in an office in their home, Dengler states that she tried WordPerfect 6.0 but hated it and so switched to WordPerfect 5.1. "Rather a Luddite attitude really," she admits.

Dengler never bases characters "closely on real people. That's the quickest way in the world to get written out of their will. But nearly all characters are composites of real people." Despite this, "there are at least three rangers in the National Park Service who are certain my Jack Prester is based on them. Just about all my readers who know me will approach me and mutter conspiratorially, 'Is [this character so-and-so]?' It's fun."

Dengler maintains that she does not have any goals for her writing. "My goals could never anticipate or match what God actually provides for me. Example: When I was growing up in rural Ohio, I yearned to be a paleontologist. But Ohio farm girls in the 50s did not dare to dream of Ph.D.s or an exotic career like that. Just getting my masters in zoology was unusual. Half a century later in Oklahoma, a state I never dreamt I'd end up in, I answered a piece in the local paper asking for volunteers to help with exhibits for the state-of-the-art natural history museum now under construction. I am now making a significant contribution to the vertebrate paleontology section of one of the nation's premier new museums, working with dinosaurs and other fossil creatures. It's a dream come true in every sense of the word. No way could I have engineered that on my own. God can't drive a parked car. You get it moving and let Him decide where to take it."

SUMMARY: *EAST OF OUTBACK* (AUSTRALIAN DESTINY SERIES)

Set against the vast open spaces of the outback, Dengler's Australian Destiny series follows the fortunes of Cole Sloan and his family as they struggle with the harsh forces of nature, with strained family relationships and with God.

Angered by what he feels is unjust disapproval by his father, Cole's sixteen-year-old son, Colin, sets out on his own, leaving his family torn apart by his rebellious behavior. Mourning the loss of her brother and deeply concerned for his welfare, twelve-year-old Hannah determines to follow after and to find him. Grateful for her love but unready for the responsibility of her care, Colin determines to send her home. The fortunes of the children rise and fall as they work their way across the outback attempting to pay their way and to raise money for Hannah's return trip home. Searching desperately for his children, Cole comes to a deeper awareness of the strengths of his son and to a new understanding of his role as a father.

SOCORRO ISLAND TREASURE

Set in the Old West at the time of stagecoaches and clipper ships, *Socorro Island Treasure* is an adventure story that young adolescents will enjoy. Looking for extra cash, Chet, David, and Wahoo, three young cowboys from Arizona, answer an ad for detectives that has been placed in the local newspaper by a Miss Susan Gleason. Miss Gleason maintains that she needs someone to find her father, who had disappeared several days before. Following the trail of clues all the way from Arizona to the port city of San Diego, the boys find nothing but trouble for themselves. Chet is shanghaied by the crew of the *Orca,* while David narrowly escapes the same fate through the last-minute intervention of the friendly Captain Wheeling. As it begins to appear that Miss Gleason's father might be on the same ship as the one that kidnapped Chet, Captain Wheeling agrees to help recover the men. He has his own score to settle with the captain and crew of the *Orca.* Suddenly, these young cowboys from Arizona find themselves aboard a ship in the Pacific Ocean, searching for pirates, kidnapped people, and buried treasure.

Peter Reese Doyle

Perhaps having been born into the family of a Navy admiral instilled a fascination with travel and adventure that led Peter Reese Doyle to write stories with exotic settings. Perhaps it was his experience as a missionary in West Africa. However, Doyle states that he began to put his creations on paper because his daughter, Susan, begged him to write the stories he had already related to entertain her and her brother, Jonathan.

PROFESSIONAL

Education
Th.D., Trinity Theological Seminary; M.Div., Seabury-Western Theological Seminary; B.A., Washington and Lee University

Career
Teacher of theology in Africa, Kentucky, and Alabama; pastor; missionary in West Africa

PUBLICATIONS

Juvenile Fiction

A Daring Adventure Series
Trapped in Pharaoh's Tomb, 1993

Stalked in the Catacombs, 1993
Ambushed in Africa, 1994
Surrounded by Crossfire, 1994
Hot Pursuit on the High Seas, 1994
Hunted along the Rhine, 1994
Launched from the Castle, 1995
Escape from Black Forest, 1995
Kidnapped in Rome, 1996
Lost in the Secret Cave, 1996
Chased by the Jewel Thieves, 1997

Drums of War Series
Independence, 1998
Drums of War, 1999

PERSONAL

Peter Reese Doyle and his wife, Sally Ann, are the parents of two children, Jonathan and Susan. It was as a father sharing his creative imagination with his children that Doyle first began telling his stories. Later, Susan prevailed on the grandfather's instinct and persuaded him to put his adventures on paper for her children. Now Pastor Doyle says that he writes for the children in his congregation as well and takes unpublished pages to get their approval before submitting the manuscript to press. He confesses that he would write for that audience whether or not he was being published.

Doyle states that he writes Christian fiction "to communicate biblical principles of character: to show boys being raised to honor, respect, and defend women and girls; to show girls being raised to be competent and responsible women who are not ashamed of their God-given feminine nature. I wanted to portray families who raise their children to love God and trust His Word, pray to Him and look to Him for guidance and strength, obey His commands and walk in integrity and purity, honor and respect people of other races and cultures, appreciate the marvels of God's great creation and the many places of interest in it, and show the pleasures and benefits that can come from studying foreign languages and learning the history of other peoples. God's Kingdom is a great deal larger than church, and Christians have a major role to play in serving the Creator in every area of life on this earth."

Although his first books for young adults, the Daring Adventure series, have been advertised as being for readers from nine to sixteen years of age, they reach a broader range. "Younger as well as older people correspond with me about them—including parents. This is a wider span of reader interest than the editors and I had at first thought we'd reach. I am particularly interested in these books coming into the hands of non-Christians also, so that boys and girls who don't normally have access to Christian literature might be given honorable examples to emulate and, hopefully, an interest in the God my characters know and serve."

When asked to describe his approach to plot, theme, characters, and setting, Doyle replied, "My style of writing would be characterized, I believe, as that of fast-paced action. . . . The invention of plots . . . is a lot of fun, as is the depiction of action." He notes obedience, protection of the home, and character building to be three of the most frequently emphasized themes running through his work. "Character is key to success in life: Obedience to God's principles produces boys and girls of integrity, discipline, courage, and responsibility, who are able to work together to face trials and surmount difficulties." Some of the characters whom he chooses to play out these roles are "absolutely fictional," but others are based on people he knows. Doyle pays tribute to his son as he reveals that Jonathan is "the basis for the traits of integrity, humor, learning, discipline, and kindliness" on which the characters of two of his protagonists are built. Some of his other models are "drawn from personal friends." Visiting Germany provided authentic locales for three of the novels that Doyle has written. For background information in other works, he consults guidebooks and a variety of sources that provide a sense of setting.

Authors who can be listed as favorites of Doyle's include an interesting mix. He shares that his writing has been influenced by Alistair MacLain, Helen MacInnes, Louis L'Amour, Rafael Sabatini, C. S. Forester, J. R. R. Tolkien, and Robert W. Service. As a family, the Doyles have collectively enjoyed P. G. Wodehouse and James Herriot.

When asked about future goals, Doyle states that he wants to reach children and their parents with the principles previously mentioned. He states his objectives this way: "to show the responsibility of Christians to train their children to cope in a great but dangerous world, to show the continual struggle to maintain free societies against the incessant onslaught of totalitarian forces and/or criminal interests.

"In the Independence Series . . . I hope to show the great biblical principles of responsible government under God's law, responsible citizens active in local government and affairs, governmental figures held in tight check by citizens and Constitution, and families who train their children for those responsibilities which God's Word requires and which human history demonstrates are essential to sound society and genuine liberty."

SUMMARY: *STALKED IN THE CATACOMBS* (A DARING ADVENTURE SERIES)

Mark and Penny Daring, with their friend David, are on the trail of adventure in Paris. While vacationing and sightseeing, they have also accepted the task of transporting photographs of ancient manuscripts of great value from the Louvre to Mr. Daring's office to be used in archaeological research. However, there are others who would use this recent discovery for personal gain.

Their constant archenemies, Hoffman and his henchmen, set in motion a virtually foolproof plan to steal the valuable information. Foiled by Russian wolfhounds out for a stroll, a rolling tomato cart, and a nun who means business, the determined thieves set out to kidnap Penny and hold her hostage until they get the photographs.

Nearly breakneck-speed action adds spice to the historic and cultural facts providing the core of the story for a delightful blend in this young-adult novel. Penny, David, and Mark are courageous, resourceful, and believable as a team of Christian teens having both fun and adventure in an exotic setting. There is also tantalizing foreshadowing in the final pages of this book leading to the mystery and intrigue to come in the next volume of the Daring Adventure series.

Robert Elmer

Robert Elmer was born to Knud and Evy Elmer on January 17, 1958, in Berkeley, California. His father, employed in hospital management, and his mother, a homemaker, are now both retired. Elmer lives with his wife, Ronda, and his three children: Kai Loren, Danica Elise, and Stefan Peter. When he is not working at the advertising agency where he is employed or writing books for children, Elmer enjoys sailing, traveling, camping, and spending time with his family.

PROFESSIONAL

Education

B.A. in communications, Simpson College, San Francisco; postgraduate program in elementary education, St. Mary's College, Moraga, California; journalism classes, University of California, Berkeley; Ygnacio Valley High School

Career

Freelance writer; public relations/admissions work, Simpson College; assistant pastor, Olympia, Washington; reporter and editor, community newspapers; copywriter, advertising agency

Memberships
American Christian Writers

PUBLICATIONS

Juvenile Fiction

The Young Underground Series
- *A Way through the Sea,* 1994
- *Beyond the River,* 1994
- *Into the Flames,* 1995
- *Far from the Storm,* 1995
- *Chasing the Wind,* 1996
- *A Light in the Castle,* 1996
- *Follow the Star,* 1997
- *Touch the Sky,* 1997

Adventures Down Under Series
- *Escape to Murray River,* 1997
- *Captive at Kangaroo Springs,* 1997
- *Rescue at Boomerang Bend,* 1998
- *Dingo Creek Challenge,* 1998
- *Race to Wallaby Bay,* 1998
- *Firestorm at Kookaburra Station,* 1999
- *Koala Beach Outbreak,* 1999
- *Panic at Emu Flat,* 1999

Adult Nonfiction

Hundreds of newspaper articles published during years as a reporter and editor

PERSONAL

Robert Elmer shares, "For as long as I can remember, I've always loved writing. When I was in grade school, I created a family newspaper [and] wrote essays for fun. In high school, I took every writing class available. My parents, both from Denmark, passed along to me a love of language and books. Writing naturally came from that kind of environment." Later in life, Elmer credits his children with providing "the impetus to begin writing. Overall, though, I would have to say that my wife continues as the greatest encourager of my writing."

Indicating what books might have inspired his own love of reading and writing, Elmer answered, "My childhood favorites were many of the 'boy' books popular in the '60s, books like *Homer Price* or *Henry Reed*. Robert McCloskey was probably my favorite author, followed by Beverly Cleary. I enjoyed action and adventure series like the Hardy Boys and Sandy Steele." When asked who he sees as his audience, Elmer replied, "Mostly children eight through about thirteen, as well as their parents and grandparents.

"Usually, I write in the early mornings, before my wife and three kids are up. With an increasing number of books, however, I've also scaled back my 'daytime job' as a writer at an advertising agency. Now I work Mondays, Fridays, and part of Saturday writing.

"I enjoy writing so much that sometimes it really doesn't seem like work. (Other times I'm reminded that, yes, it really is!) Personally, I'd like to be able to support my family to a growing extent on writing and a writing-related ministry to children and their families. I'd also like to continually improve as a writer displaying originality, creativity, and craftsmanship. I have a long way to go.

"Perhaps [the person who has most influenced my writing] was the man who gave me my first writing job out of college. He developed a 'Clear Writing' seminar, and his succinct, to-the-point prose—as well as his overall writing philosophy—did influence me greatly. I worked with him on a number of freelance writing and editing assignments. I enjoy reading tightly written, quality magazine nonfiction, the kind found in magazines like *National Geographic*. That's given me a sense of short story in everything I write, where every word counts and each paragraph must flow out of the previous one. I strive for an economy of words and try to 'sculpt' my writing.

"The Young Underground series is inspired by family stories from World War II. I've done extensive reading, then personal interviews, then more reading. Whenever appropriate, I've used local resources, like going out to a sheep ranch to collect authentic details for one section in book 2 of the series (set on a sheep ranch). The Adventures Down Under, set in Australia during the 1860s, is only a little different. I've worked with Australian historians and advisers over the Internet [and I've] immersed myself in books on Australia."

Elmer sees his books as "essentially action driven, as this is the kind of format I've chosen to appeal to a mix of boys and girls. Characters are developed within the context of the action, and each book contains a biblical theme as well—though that's not always completely evident to the reader until after they've read the entire book. I try to have the characters grow in a distinct way, learning the power of forgiveness, for example, or the importance of prayer. The main characters are usually flawed people in need of growing (just like the rest of us!). Although I sometimes name minor characters after family members, they're seldom based on real people. In most cases, they're an amalgamation of character traits. The main character in the Young Underground series displayed a lot of my own character traits as a boy. Besides that I like to show that the Lord is not removed from our everyday lives. When I write, I try to infuse the characters' beliefs in a natural way. If a character is not a believer, I try to describe their life in a natural way as well but without the benefit of faith. My beliefs influence my writing to the extent that I want to portray living, victorious faith. I want to show faith in action as a completely natural way."

Elmer has several goals in mind for his readers as they are exposed to his work. "I want them to understand other times and places, put themselves in the shoes of people who are not like them at all. I want them to understand the world as it ought to be, or as it was. I want to model ways of thinking that are no longer portrayed on television. I want them to understand how faith works in everyday life, to come to know the Lord. I want them to vicariously live the experience of kids with whole families, of kids who grow as Christians. I want them to enjoy reading wholesome fiction that doesn't stoop to horror or gross situations to be interesting. I want them to connect with their past and understand the common ground they share with other cultures. I could go on. . . . By the way, as a child I don't recall ever reading a good novel with a Christian message. If I had, it might have changed my life, and I might have come to know the Lord at an earlier age."

Elmer has chosen to write fiction from a Christian point of view "because . . . I can't separate my faith from the bigger issues of life. For me, faith has to be a part of great literature." In regard to the future of Christian fiction, Elmer replied, "Oh, we have a long way to go! I'd like to see Christian fiction lead the way through the dark days of television illiteracy to open up new, creative avenues of fiction. Christian fiction ought to be a leader in excellent new reading experiences for young (and older) audiences. I can't predict the future of Christian fiction, but the door is wide open!"

SUMMARY: *BEYOND THE RIVER* (YOUNG UNDERGROUND SERIES)

The promise of a peaceful summer is broken for Peter and Elise on the day of their arrival at their Uncle Harald's farm on the west coast of Denmark during World War II. Seeing a British plane shot down near the farm, the twins and their cousins scramble to help the pilot out of the wreckage, only to find that he has already escaped. As German patrols increase and their invasion into the lives of the townspeople intensifies, the children search diligently for the injured man. They know that they must find him before the soldiers do if they are to save his life and effect his return to England. The children come to realize the personal price that must be paid to help another and to fight for their own freedom.

Drawing on his own heritage and the stories passed down by his parents and grandparents, Elmer has created the Young Underground series for children in the middle grades. Both boys and girls enjoy these historical adventures set in Scandinavia during World War II.

ESCAPE TO MURRAY RIVER (ADVENTURES DOWN UNDER SERIES), SUMMARY BY THE AUTHOR

In *Escape to Murray River,* twelve-year-old Patrick McWaid's world is turned upside-down when his father is framed for a crime and sent on the last prison ship to Australia in 1867. Desperate to keep the family together, the McWaids decide to find passage on another ship headed "down under." But leaving Dublin, Ireland, means leaving the only home they've ever known. And what will they do when they reach Australia?

Then Patrick learns that his grandfather was sent to Australia thirty years before. No one has heard from him in years, but perhaps the senior McWaid might help them—if they can only find him. Their hopes high, Patrick and his family set sail. What kind of new life will they find?

CAPTIVE AT KANGAROO SPRINGS (ADVENTURES DOWN UNDER SERIES), SUMMARY BY THE AUTHOR

In *Captive at Kangaroo Springs,* Patrick McWaid and his family have safely reached Echuca, Victoria, where they hope to find his missing father, who was sent to Australia on a prison ship. But there's a reward out for the capture of escaped prisoner John McWaid, and some of the worried townspeople are forming a search party—with dogs!

When Conrad Burke, Mr. McWaid's old enemy, shows up, Patrick knows that his father is in even greater danger. Hoping to hide from unfriendly eyes, Mrs. McWaid quickly accepts an offer to let the family use a shanty outside of town until things quiet down. But they've barely settled in before a gang of bushrangers, or outlaws, takes them hostage. Can Patrick find a way to rescue his family?

Doris Elaine Fell

Born in New Jersey and currently residing in California, with intermittent stops in Mexico, Guatemala, Switzerland, and the Philippines, Doris Elaine Fell writes authentically of settings both exotic and familiar. With careers as diverse as her travels, Fell brings to her writing firsthand experience as a teacher, missionary, nurse, and author. Even in her childhood dreams of becoming a writer, it is unlikely that she would have envisioned one day being published in both English and German, writing for both the inspirational and the secular market, and being recognized as both an author and an editor. Yet these are her accomplishments today.

Fell lists a wide variety of leisure activities, including "writing, reading, and listening to books on tape"; editing, especially "editing marathons" with friend Carole Gift Page; traveling; collecting "huggable, loveable teddy bears"; visiting the elderly in nursing homes with her teddy bear ministry; and "'spoiling' great-nephews Ryan and Jesse and great-niece Hannah Marie."

PROFESSIONAL

Education

R.N. and B.S. in nursing, Columbia University/Columbia-Presbyterian Medical Center; journalism and graduate class, Multnomah Bible College; fifth-year teaching credentials and graduate studies, University of Washington; B.A. in education, Seattle Pacific University

Awards

Writer of the Year, Mount Hermon Christian Writers Conference, 1997; nursing honorary society

Career

Author; freelance editor; caregiver for mother, six years; registered nurse, pediatrics and family medicine; editorial assistant; missionary teacher, Wycliffe Bible Translators (Philippines); elementary school teacher

Memberships

National Writers Association; National Writers Association/Southern California Chapter; Romance Writers of America; National League of American Pen Women

PUBLICATIONS

Adult Fiction

Blue Mist on the Danube, 1999
Summer Is Coming, 1999
Seasons of Intrigue Series
  Always in September, 1994 (large print, 1998)
  Before Winter Comes, 1994 (large print, 1998)
  April Is Forever, 1995 (large print, 1998)
  The Twelfth Rose of Spring, 1995 (large print, 1998)
  To Catch the Summer Wind, 1996
  The Race for Autumn's Glory, 1997

Coauthored with Carole Gift Page

Mist over Morro Bay Series (Harvest House)
  Mist over Morro Bay, 1985
  Secret of the East Wind, 1986
  Storm Clouds over Paradise, 1986
  Beyond the Windswept Sea, 1987

Foreign Translation, German (Franke)

Schatten im September (*Shadows in September*), 1996

Adult Nonfiction

Lady of the Tboli, 1979
Give Me This Mountain, 1975

Articles and Short Stories

Fell writes for both secular and inspirational publishers. The following are examples of her work appearing in the books listed:
"Midnight Vigil," in *Sing a New Song,* compiled by Mary Beckwith (Evergreen Publications), 1991
"Mom and the Talking Bears," in *Mom in the Heart,* compiled by Joe Wheeler (Tyndale Publishers), 1997

Works in Progress

Jade (romance), Steeple Hill, to be released in 1999. Ever the busy author, Fell reports that she has "thirteen proposals in synopsis and first-chapter stage, including several series ideas and one nonfiction manuscript. . . . My 'heart book' is the nonfiction manuscript based on my journey with the Mom of the talking bears." Dealing with such a pertinent and personal topic, this labor of love will surely touch the hearts of thousands of readers as well.

PERSONAL

Doris Elaine Fell states that her interest in writing was initiated by "books, books, books! People, people, people! Authors, authors, authors! (1) I had a mother who loved poetry and dabbled at writing it. (2) Books were placed in my hand as a child. (3) I was read to as a child. (4) Mother exposed me to the library while I was young, leading to a lifetime addiction and commitment. (5) The love of books did not mark me as left-handed. (6) I had English teachers who saw a spark of talent in me and employers who utilized my creativity. (7) As a teacher I always loved 'story hour.' (8) From the time I was seven (fully determined by the time I was ten), I wanted to be a writer (whatever that was), a teacher, a nurse, and to run an orphanage. (The orphanage is the only unfinished dream.) When I showed my mom my first attempt at rhyming couplets, she did not laugh but gave me a sense of pride and destiny. When I was fifteen (and still not walking with the Lord), I got down on my knees in my bedroom . . . and specifically asked the Lord Jesus that I might one day write for His glory."

Fell states that she began writing Christian fiction because it chose her. " I was willing to go through whichever door opened first. I have published in both secular and inspirational magazines. Thirteen of my original English-speaking books were with inspirational houses. Franke (German translation) is also a Christian publisher." Recently, just as this book was going to press, Fell accomplished another of her career goals when she published the first of two books with a secular publisher. The large-print books are also with a secular publisher.

When asked about her research process, Fell stated that it is "detailed, thorough, creative, and challenging—providing some of my most memorable experiences." She went on to say that she might begin in the children's department, with books on tape, or with a novel by a favorite author, such as Helen MacInnes; then, as her creative spark is ignited, she moves on to books, videos, or brochures to gain a feeling for a group of people or an intriguing geographic location. "Something serves as the catalyst, and the research mushrooms." As stated previously, Fell's career and passion for travel have taken her to many of the settings that she uses in her books, adding credibility to her novels.

When asked to describe her target audience, Fell stated that most are women. However, Fell is assured that men also read her books, especially those works with plots of suspense and mystery. She characterizes her readers, male or female, as those who enjoy books that have multiple characters and multiple plots, such as found in real life, especially those who are "rebels with tender hearts." She says candidly, "I understand them."

Fell classifies her books as both character and action driven, as one would expect from her Seasons of Intrigue suspense series. However, the action does not override her well-developed characters. "My characters are often based on an emotional experience or past memory or something that intrigues me: the first glimpse of a snow-capped mountain; the majesty of the Alps; the *warmth* of a cold, frail hand of the elderly in mine; the fresh delight of a Bible verse; the times with my great-niece; the love of nursing; the cry of the newborn; the companionship of a good book; a chuckle remembered; the sound of quality music, time, and/or tea for two with another writer just talking about writing; the kindness of a gentle rebuke; flying above the clouds; knowing that eternity is mine and that God keeps His word; and Memorial Day breakfast with friends; etcetera, etcetera!" Fell's characters, with their conflicts and victories, step right off the page and speak to her readers precisely as a result of the moments and impressions just mentioned.

Although planned themes run throughout her work, Fell states that her books are "not sermons. . . . Forgiveness, family relationships, stubbornness in characters, a touch of humor and bridges between generations" are threads running through her novels. In her Seasons of Intrigue series, she deliberately included at least one elderly character in each book. Her purpose was to increase the reader's awareness of the older generation and to "react kindly to them." She demonstrates such response quite naturally through her plots and character responses.

When asked which people or books have influenced her writing, Fell reported that authors as varied as Agatha Christie, P. D. James, Rosamund Pilcher, and Max Lucado have provided grist for her writing mill. Books that have had special significance include *Heidi,* the Nancy Drew and Hardy Boys series, the poetic writings of Daphne DuMaurier, biographies of Margaret Thatcher, and the Psalms of David. However, the people to whom Fell gives credit for inspiration are her mother (now deceased), who read to her and set an example by writing; Dr. Elva McAllaster (now deceased) and Dr. Anna Belle Laughbam, both college professors; and two author friends, Carole Gift Page and Lee Roddy (both featured in this volume). She states that "all five were examples of self-discipline, self-motivation, commitment to Christ (and to writing), and inspiration to me as an individual. All five had/have a passion for living and a compassion toward others; and all five of them believed in me."

Fell sees her commitment to respond as a Christian as the vital first step in the act of writing, followed by the practical step of doing the work. She expresses the interrelationship this way: "First of all I am a Christian, then I am a Christian writer. First, I must walk with the Shepherd, then I must walk to the computer. What I do now will count in eternity whether I write and publish in the Christian market or in the secular one—or whether I write at all. What I do with my time now will count or pile up as hay, wood, and stubble when I arrive where the tick of a clock no longer matters.

"As a Christian writer, I have to come to those checkpoints in life, these stop-and-go signals, those wait times, those re-reflections on where I'm going and why I'm going there. Writing delights me and fills my hours. . . . I need the stop, go, and wait of life's journey to remind me that it is not enough just to entertain and delight readers (although this is important), but my characters and my plots must also touch their hearts in deeper ways. But I can't do that on my own. I must keep in tune with the Shepherd of Psalm 23."

In considering goals that she might have for her readers, Fell reflects on her own response to her favorite authors. "I think of the influence of other authors on my own life—the sense of a personal friend in Helen MacInnes, the sense of admiration for writers like Rosamund Pilcher, the sense of ministry that comes from writers like Max Lucado, the bond that I see in writers like Lee Roddy to his young readers, and the ability of writers to touch my every emotion—to make me laugh and cry, to trust, to be comforted, to go on toward the finish line.

"In the same way, I trust that out there somewhere a reader considers me as a friend. That a reader trusts me. That a reader is entertained or transported even for a short space of time to some setting that I've been privileged to visit. That someone out there is ministered to or is reminded that the scarlet thread of forgiveness is still available—that some broken relationship may be mended or some reader is touched for a moment in time, or for a season, or through the life of one of my characters touched and changed for all eternity."

Fell sees the future of Christian fiction as being a blend of dreams and corporate support. "Without vision, people perish, without vision, writers decay. Without a vision for fiction, the publishing industry cannot grow in that area. Without the vision of the publishing houses mushrooming, novelists will labor in vain, and dreams will fall by the wayside. But with real vision—and the recognition that fiction is ministry—and with corporate backing from the publishing houses, novelists and publishers can make a difference and can touch hearts and lives for the good in the process."

SUMMARY

The following are brief summaries of the first five books in the Seasons of Intrigue series written in the author's own words. These tidbits should whet any reader's appetite for the whole banquet.

ALWAYS IN SEPTEMBER (BOOK 1)

Andrea York went to Paris a fashion journalist—she left a fugitive. Terrorist threats. Airport bombings. A dying grandmother. Nothing could stop her race for the top—nothing short of an assassination.

BEFORE WINTER COMES (BOOK 2)

Robyn Gregory flew to Zurich to save her family business—now she's running for her life. Caught in the high stakes of the art world in Beverly Hills and Europe, she is propelled into a dangerous web of intrigue that brings her face to face with the father who deserted her sixteen years ago.

APRIL IS FOREVER (BOOK 3)

Luke Breckenridge gave up everything to defend his country—even Sauni. How could he be a traitor? Sauni can believe that her husband died in Vietnam twenty years ago, but she'll need a lot more than a military report to convince her that he betrayed his country.

THE TWELFTH ROSE OF SPRING (BOOK 4)

For years Drew Gregory and Nichlos Trotsky had chosen their governments over their loved ones, danger over safety, silence over exposure. With this choice, one man's secret hangs in the balance high in the mountains of Austria.

TO CATCH THE SUMMER WIND (BOOK 5)

At the height of her literary career, when Olivia Renway has achieved success and recognition, her past comes back to haunt her. When she dies mysteriously on Downing Street, she leaves behind dark, unanswered questions about her life in Prague, her loyalty to England, her unfinished novel, and a missing sapphire bracelet. But Chase Evans, a curious Columbia grad student, risks her own life to find the answers.

Robert Funderburk

Robert Funderburk shares that he was born "on July 10, 1942, in a tin-roofed farmhouse by coal-oil lantern light, six miles outside of Liberty, Mississippi," to Ezra B. Funderburk, carpenter (now deceased), and Norma Shaw Funderburk, housewife. His devoted readers might recognize that in reporting the event of his own birth, he creates setting and character descriptions and might wonder whether even at that tender age he was storing up picturesque material for later use.

On May 30, 1968, Funderburk married Helen Anderson. They have one daughter, Amy Elizabeth. Helen is currently a nurse at the Rehabilitation Hospital of Baton Rouge.

PROFESSIONAL

Education
B.A. in sociology, Louisiana State University

Career
Louisiana state probation and parole officer, retired, 1986; U.S. Air Force Reserve, staff sergeant, 1965–1971

Awards
Bookstore Journal's National Best Seller List, *These Golden Days,* March 1996; Angel Award, Excellence in Media, *Love and Glory,* 1995

PUBLICATIONS

Dylan St. John Novels
The Fires of Autumn, 1996
All the Days Were Summer, 1997
Winter of Grace, 1998
The Spring of Our Exile, 1999
The Innocent Years Series
Love and Glory, 1994
These Golden Days, 1995
Heart and Soul, 1995
Old Familiar Places, 1996
Tenderness and Fire, 1997
The Rainbow's End, 1997

Coauthored with Gilbert Morris

The Price of Liberty Series
A Call to Honor, 1993
The Color of the Star, 1993
All the Shining Young Men, 1993
The End of Glory, 1993
A Silence in Heaven, 1993
A Time to Heal, 1994
The Far Fields Series
Beyond the River, 1994
The Remnant, 1997

PERSONAL

After his first birth, which was noted previously, Robert Funderburk relates that he experienced a second birth, "in a revival in a little white frame Baptist church near Kentwood, Louisiana, and [was] baptized in the local 'swimmin' hole' in the Tangipahoa River." His grandfather was a Church of God preacher, and as a child, Bobby (as he was known) spent a lot of time in the Louisiana countryside.

However, Funderburk grew up in Baton Rouge, having resided there from about the age of four or five. After college he went to work for the Louisiana Welfare Department across the river, where there were "antebellum homes, slave cabins, sugarcane plantations, swamps, and bayous." For one year he worked across the river from New Orleans in the Barataria-Lafitte area, "the haunt of the pirate Jean Lafitte." He describes most of his twenty-plus years with the state in probation and parole work as "midnight arrest runs, scuffling with men who weren't particularly fond of going to jail, guns, investigations, prisons, courthouses, handcuffs—a smashing good time was had by all." Most of his caseload was comprised of juveniles who were on probation and parole.

However, not all of Funderburk's time was spent with those on the opposite side of the legal system. While attending high school, he taught Sunday school and worked in the church nursery. In later years, he has served in various ways—as an usher, in Light for the Lost, in men's ministry, in MAPS (an Assemblies of God construction program), and at Home of the Sons (a Christian-Arab orphanage) in Ramallah, Israel.

Funderburk responded conversationally to questions about his getting started as a writer and spoke candidly about his own experience as an aspiring writer. "If you have made reading a part of your life, you have the first requirement for being a writer. Then you need some talent. You also need to be teachable. No one likes their work sliced and spliced—take out the bad, graft in the good—but it's a necessary part of the learning process. Timing is important, getting your particular work to a publisher when they're looking for something of that particular type, but you have little control over that.

"The most important quality is *tenacity!* You have to keep walking to the mailbox week after week, month after month, and seeing that brown envelope that tells you your manuscript has been rejected—again! Imagine a young mother showing off her first child and someone says, 'Uggh—get that ugly baby away from me!' The publishers have said that about your manuscript, the child you have so carefully and lovingly birthed—but you have to keep showing the baby. My first novel was rejected forty times, and I was collecting more rejection slips on my second when I got my first contract."

Funderburk gives credit to well-known Christian novelist Gilbert Morris for helping him launch his writing career. "My first writing course was the Price of Liberty series we did for Word Publishing. In speaking to their staff, someone asked him [Morris] how we wrote the books. He said that it was a fifty-fifty effort. 'I sit down and write a plot in three hours, give it to Bobby, and three months later he comes back with the book.' Actually, we'd sit down together chapter by chapter for the editing process. Sometimes he used a penknife and sometimes he used a chainsaw."

When asked about the mechanics of his writing process, Funderburk responded much like his hardworking hero in the Dylan St. John novels. " I try to write seven days a week . . . and produce five pages a day. I write in a study that is cluttered with shelves and stacks of books; an old Royal typewriter that my grandfather used when he was the Church of God state overseer . . . [shades again of St. John]; Mac computer and printer; tennis racquets; an empty shell casing from a twenty-one-gun salute by a squad of Marines for an old veteran of Guadalcanal [both Dylan and Lane Temple in racquet and shell]; name plates from book signings; a print of an angel watching over two small children crossing a treacherous bridge in the night [see *The Fires of Autumn*]; pictures of my wife, daughter, family, and friends; and a round, metal picture ID badge of my father . . . from his work in a shipyard in Orange, Texas. Shortly afterward the Army trained him as an infantryman and sent him to Italy."

When asked which books or writers had influenced his life, Funderburk gave responses ranging from his boyhood through the present. "As a child, I loved Tarzan comics. Graduated to Hemingway, Faulkner, Steinbeck, William Styron, William Butler Yeats, James Dickey, and Dylan Thomas. Works I recommend are *The Winter of Our Discontent,* by Steinbeck; *The New Yorker Book of Poems; Root out of Dry Ground* (Biblical characterizations in verse by Gilbert Morris), and the letters of Paul the Apostle."

When asked which goals Funderburk has for himself as a writer and for his readers, he responded by reflecting on his earlier vocation in the correctional field. "In my years as a parole officer, I witnessed the dismal failure of social programs beginning with Lyndon Johnson's 'Great Society' in the sixties. I don't say this to condemn the intentions of the people behind them, but the results are all too clear. Only Jesus Christ can truly change lives and give a person lasting peace and joy. My books are written to reach people (those who may never go to church or read a Bible) with His gospel. I hope they'll be interesting, encouraging, and fun for all readers, like a visit from an old friend." Funderburk's desire for his fellow authors is that they "strive to give the world quality literature without the sordid and unnecessary trappings found in much of mainstream fiction."

SUMMARY: *LOVE AND GLORY* (THE INNOCENT YEARS SERIES)

Returning victoriously at the end of World War II, ex-Marine Lane Temple strives to leave behind the traumatic memories of Guadalcanal and the faces of both friends and enemies whom he met there. On the home front, Catherine, Lane's young wife, has struggled valiantly to stretch her meager finances to meet the needs of their four young children. Both Lane and Catherine feel that life will be glorious once they are reunited and can become established as a real family.

Sweetwater, Mississippi, his hometown, is the place that Lane has dreamed about through the danger and drudgery of war in the Pacific islands. Given time, establishing a law practice among people who remember him as a football star should be simple. Catherine is also a native of Sweetwater and looks forward to relinquishing the stress of trying to meet the material needs of her children and to enjoying the status acquired by being Lane's wife. Despite their dreams, both Lane and Catherine soon learn that there is not enough business in their beloved little town to support another lawyer, even a war hero.

Responding to an invitation from another soldier whom he met on the homebound train, Lane packs up his family and heads to the bright lights and city streets of Baton Rouge, Louisiana. Neither he nor Catherine is prepared for the demands exacted by their new life on their time, relationship, or morals. As the children settle into their new surroundings, Lane and Catherine seem to be drifting apart, until they reach a crisis that neither thought could ever happen.

The radio message by Billy Graham that helps Catherine find direction for life is just one of the many familiar sights, sounds, or smells that Funderburk incorporates as he takes the reader back to the late 1940s. For those who miss the popular songs with lyrics that do not embarrass the listener, this novel will bring a smile of remembrance and a feeling of "Yes, I've been there."

This work is significant not only because it paints a loving portrait of a time when life seemed simpler, at least to those who are now in middle age, but also because it meets issues head-on that inspirational writers often do not address. Materialism, graft, rebellion, and infidelity create conflict for his compelling plot. Friendship among those of various cultural groups and a hero in a wheelchair add color to Funderburk's character development. Faith, family, and warm, intimate expressions of love between marriage partners strengthen the theme. For the reader who fondly remembers the 1950s, reminiscent pleasure awaits in this introduction to The Innocent Years series.

THE FIRES OF AUTUMN **(DYLAN ST. JOHN NOVELS)**

Children are disappearing, and so is the marriage of parole officer Dylan St. John. In the first disappearance, innocence is lost; in the second disappearance, innocence has become jaded.

As a former juvenile probation officer, Dylan has reached out beyond the demands of duty to help young offenders who are slipping into the lifestyle of their already errant fathers. Mysteriously, these children are being taken from foster homes or straight from courtrooms to correctional institutions for minor offenses. Yet, when either the occasional social worker or a mother tries to reach the children, they seem to have vanished. Dylan risks life, limb, and an already shaky marriage in an effort to find the lost boys.

With a passion made possible only through experience, Funderburk escorts the reader to jail cells, judges' chambers, back alleys, and barrooms to meet thieves, murderers, scheming politicians, and hopeless children who are caught in "the system." From the cryptic dialogue hammered across steel desks to the hollow clang of barred prison gates, the reader experiences the precarious life of the overworked, stress-stretched parole officer who is never far from those who desperately need his help and those who would rather die than accept it.

Characters are so real that one can almost smell the aftershave, cigarette smoke, or stale sweat speak with dialogue in a dialect so honest that it could come only from someone who had been there and learned to listen. From ancient tenant shacks and tiny houseboats to the richly paneled halls of state offices, Cajun, black, and white step off the pages, each with his own intriguing story.

The reader comes to care deeply about Dylan and his estranged wife, Susan, as well as the fate of the boys, and Funderburk keeps the suspense alive and conversation lively with a spunky sense of humor right through the epilogue. Perhaps it would be wise to have *All the Days Were Summer,* the next title in the series, close at hand and ready to read when the last page is complete. It would save a trip to the bookstore.

***ALL THE DAYS WERE SUMMER* (DYLAN ST. JOHN NOVELS)**

Dylan has departed the city, moved to a new residence, and adopted a new role. Taking its tempo from the ebb and flow of the nearby bayou, the little town of Evangeline suggests a more leisurely pace, which the workaholic probation officer needs to reorder his life. Even the change of job to chief deputy seems to hold the delightful promise of becoming better acquainted with Cajun food, eaten at regular intervals, and perhaps the respect usually afforded an officer of the law in rural settings. Dylan is even employed by his good friend, Emile. Everything seems to be moving smoothly until the mayor is murdered.

Just as *The Fires of Autumn* careened along with the breakneck pace of a high-speed chase through city streets, this second in the series takes on the life of its setting. From the stillness of small-town streets at midnight to the clamor of New Orleans bars, the reader follows a shadowy suspect. As our hero attempts to solve the murder (and others that follow), he must draw on his knowledge of sociology, psychology, and literature in facing a new kind of danger, right out of the pages of the legendary Camelot.

Funderburk does not disappoint with his succinct, sincere, and often humorous observations on life, love, and the legal system. He leaves his readers eagerly awaiting the next title in the series, *Winter of Grace*.

Jean Grant

Jean Grant was born on January 1, 1934, to Robert and Lillias Grant in Traverse City, Michigan. Currently, she makes her home in Santa Rosa, California. Although she began writing as a second vocation, the spoken and written word has always held special charm for Grant. When she was only seven or eight years old, she recalls hearing a neighbor say, "That child was born with a Webster's Dictionary in her mouth."

Grant relates that "the little girl with the big vocabulary was also born with a cleft palate, which kept me from using those words effectively. . . . Writing was my communication with the world; yet I never seriously considered it a vocation. In my teens I recall singing the old hymn *Oh for a Thousand Tongues* and praying for 'Just one, Lord.' And yet I didn't dare dream that would be answered many years later, in God's time and in His abundant way."

After spending thirty years as a clinical laboratory technologist, Grant has now begun a career through which she can express her passion clearly as a writer of Christian fiction.

PROFESSIONAL

Education

A.B. in microbiology, University of California, Berkeley; creative writing classes; Christian writers' conference

Career
Clinical laboratory technologist

PUBLICATIONS

Adult Fiction

The Revelation, 1993
Salinas Valley Saga
The Promise of the Willows, 1994
The Promise of Peace, 1994
The Promise of Victory, 1995
The Promise of the Harvest, 1996

PERSONAL

In response to questions regarding Christian fiction as a genre, Jean Grant replied, "Christian fiction is my gift. It is the means God has given me to make Him real to others. Fiction must be larger than life, or it has no appeal, but must be true to life, or it has no purpose. So my goal in writing Christian fiction is, first, to tell a good story about real people, and second, to illustrate a growing, fulfilling relationship with Jesus Christ.

"I am uncomfortable, though, with the phrase 'Christian fiction' as it is used in the marketplace. Fiction from a Christian viewpoint has to compete with the world's fiction on its own terms if it is to reach the world for Christ. It must be just as well written, just as carefully plotted, with just as strong characterization. No, better! We have a wonderful God to present, and so we have an obligation to make our work the best possible. And to God be the glory."

SUMMARY: *THE PROMISE OF PEACE* (SALINAS VALLEY SAGA)

Set in both California and China in the post–World War I era, this book continues the story of the Hanlon family, who were introduced to readers in *The Promise of the Willows.* As the Hanlons have grown, married, and bore children, they have also spread out over more farming territory in the Salinas Valley. Close family ties, lasting wounds of war, and the effect of drugs, alcohol, and sexual assault are some of the issues addressed in this timely historical fiction novel.

Told in flashback format, this story reveals the psychological and physical pain inflicted by a war that leaves scars across two continents. It is also the story of an extended family reaching out with healing hands to its hurting children.

Contemporary in topic yet expressed in attitudes realistic to the early decades of the twentieth century, this work takes the reader inside the heart of an innocent victim of sexual assault. Grant confronts a sensitive issue with compassion and grace. Any reader who has experienced such violation will relate to the confusion and shame felt by the brave survivor. Her response to the pain, although not perfect, reflects her humanity. She provides an inspiring example to others who have been wounded in the same way. Complex in its resolution, this novel carries the reader along to a most satisfying conclusion.

Robin Jones Gunn

Born in Wisconsin in 1955, Robin was the second daughter of Travis and Barbara Jones. At age five, radical change occurred in Robin's life as her family moved to California, where her father began a teaching career. She has since lived in places as diverse as Hawaii, Nevada, and Oregon. Her husband, Ross, whom she married in 1978, has served as a full-time youth pastor for eighteen years. They are the parents of two children: Ross IV and Rachel. Gunn's love of writing is not limited to writing her own books, for she enjoys collecting antique books as well.

PROFESSIONAL

Education
Biola University, two years

Career
Clerical work at Christian Resource Management for clients such as Corrie ten Boom and Brother Andrew

Awards
First Place, Article Writing Contest, Biola Writer's Conference, 1988; Sherwood E. Wirt Award, 1989; Poetry Award, Mount Hermon Christian Writers

Conference, 1993; Evangelical Press Association, Article of the Year, 1994; Pacesetter Award, Mount Hermon Christian Writers Conference, 1996; Second Place, EPA Article of the Year, 1996

Memberships

Romance Writers of America

PUBLICATIONS

Adult Fiction

Palisades Pure Romance Series
- *Secrets,* 1995
- *Whispers,* 1995
- *Echoes,* 1996
- *Sunsets,* 1997
- *Clouds,* 1997
- *Waterfalls,* 1998

Juvenile Fiction

Mrs. Rosey-Posey Series
- *Mrs. Rosey-Posey and the Chocolate Cherry Treat,* 1991
- *Mrs. Rosey-Posey and the Treasure Hunt,* 1991
- *Mrs. Rosey-Posey and the Empty Nest,* 1993

Billy 'n' Bear Series
- *Billy 'n' Bear Go to the Grocery Store,* 1985
- *Billy 'n' Bear Visit Grandpa and Grandma,* 1985
- *Billy 'n' Bear Go to Sunday School,* 1985
- *Billy 'n' Bear Go to a Birthday Party,* 1985
- *Billy 'n' Bear Go to the Doctor's,* 1985

The Christy Miller Series
- *Summer Promise,* 1988
- *A Whisper and a Wish,* 1989
- *Yours Forever,* 1990
- *Surprise Endings,* 1991
- *Island Dreamer,* 1992
- *A Heart Full of Hope,* 1992
- *True Friends,* 1993
- *Seventeen Wishes,* 1993
- *Starry Night,* 1994

A Time to Cherish, 1994
Sweet Dreams, 1994
A Promise Is Forever, 1994
From the Secret Place in My Heart: The Diary of Christina Juliet Miller, 1999

The Sierra Jensen Series
Only You Sierra, 1995
In Your Dreams, 1996
Don't You Wish, 1996
Close Your Eyes, 1996
Without a Doubt, 1997
With This Ring, 1997
Open Your Heart, 1997
Time Will Tell, 1998
Now Picture This, 1998
Hold on Tight, 1998
Take My Hand, 1999
Closer Than Ever, 1999

Adult Nonfiction

Mothering by Heart, 1996

Juvenile Nonfiction

Jesus Is with Me Series
When I Help My Mommy, 1988
When I Celebrate His Birthday, 1988
When I Go to the Park, 1988
When I Have a Babysitter, 1988

PERSONAL

Robin Jones Gunn shares, "I was always a storyteller, so the desire to put those stories on paper came about naturally. I was not much of a reader when I was younger because I could often figure out the ending ahead of time and I lost interest. I wondered if I could ever do better if I wrote a story."

Specific motivation for Gunn to begin writing came when on a camping trip with their church youth group. "I was amazed to see girls tucked away in their tents reading when the beach was right out their door. I crawled into their tent and asked to read what they were reading. I read three of their library novels and was horrified at the content. I told them they shouldn't be reading such books, and they asked me to give them something else to read. A week later I went to the Bible bookstore and bought everything that I thought might interest them. They read them all in less than a week and asked for more. I told them there weren't any more Christian novels, and they told me to write one. Until that time, I'd only written articles and children's books. They told me it would be easy—they'd even tell me what to write!

"Each week, I took a chapter to my Sunday school class, and after I'd taught the lesson, those students listened to my story and ripped it to pieces." As she worked, Gunn sent the first few chapters to eleven publishers, who turned them down. Focus on the Family Publishers finally saw the promise of the books and asked her to do a whole series. "It took two years, but *Summer Promise,* the first book in the Christy Miller series, was finished after our group effort. That book was published in 1988 and now has sold over 120,000 copies. After seeing the profound impact fiction can have in establishing a role model for readers, I became committed to doing what Jesus did—telling stories that change lives."

Writing from a romantic viewpoint, Gunn sees her audience as "young hearts and women." In this respect, her plots are definitely character driven. Not content to write pure romance, she mixes into her stories elements of spiritual and emotional growth. "Sometimes, they even surprise me. The characters and situations are realistic, but I cover them with a thin veil of wishes and a dreamy mist of hope." For Gunn, romance is at the core of the redemptive process.

Answering the question whether her characters are frequently based on people she knows, Gunn replied, "Christy Miller and I both were born in Wisconsin. We both grew up in southern California during our high school years and spent our most memorable days and nights on the beach with good friends. In *Whispers,* Teri and Gordon hike through the Haleakala crater in Maui. Ross and I hiked the same trail with a group of college students. Lauren, in *Echoes,* is enamored with the writings and the love affair of Robert and Elizabeth Browning. I spent a summer reading everything they ever wrote."

As a basic research method, Gunn says, "I take an imaginary basket with me through each day and collect real life scenarios, senses, personalities, and dilemmas. When I sit down to write, my heart and mind draw from this basket and find the right pieces to fit a particular project.

"I cut pictures from magazines of characters and locations and prepare a notebook before I begin writing. Since these characters are all imaginary, I must create a history for them before I can let them walk onto the page. They need more than just a description. They need a birthday and a favorite food.

They need a traumatic experience and a secret wish. They need to be the kind of person I'd be intrigued by if I ever met them face to face.

"For locations, I've gone to the sites mentioned in my books. I've interviewed professionals in different fields to find out the particulars of their occupations as they related to the characters."

Responding to the question of who has most influenced her writing, Gunn replied, "I was and still am greatly influenced by Ethel Herr, who welcomed me into her critique group for six years and patiently taught me the basics of writing. Bill Myers has also influenced me greatly.

"With each book, I'm influenced by current relationships. I'm also affected by whatever recurring theme the Holy Spirit is breathing over my life at that time." If there is one theme that appears most often in her books, it is that "God is the relentless lover. He continually pursues us, because we are His first love. He will not give up until we are at last His and His alone."

As a goal for her readers, Gunn wants her readers to "soften up. I want them to open the gate to the garden of their heart and let the Savior in. If He's already there, I want the story to compel them to surrender more of their heart's garden to Him."

In regard to the future of Christian fiction, Gunn states, "We serve an infinite God. His creativity in communicating Himself to the world is limitless. I think of the little boy who gave Jesus all he had—some bread and some fish. Not a feast by the world's standards, but it was his best to offer, and it was all he had. Jesus was the one who blessed it and used it to satisfy the multitude. If Christian fiction is going to be used to feed the hungry masses, I don't think it will be so much a result of a feast of great talent but rather the work of God in a supernatural way. Should He choose, God can take that which honest storytellers offer in complete surrender to Him and bless it so He can use it widely.

"Stories are the common ground of all peoples of all nations. Stories written by Believers belong on the bookshelves of every bookstore in the world."

SUMMARY: *ECHOES* (PALISADES PURE ROMANCE SERIES)

Gunn mixes humor with heartbreak and suspense with romance in this romantic novel for the adult reader. Lauren Phillips is one of those persons for whom nothing goes smoothly. She flies to her roommate's wedding in Burbank and ends up in Fairbanks, dumps taco salad all over herself at a picnic, and sends e-mail messages to the wrong boyfriend. Beginning with a broken engagement and ending with a romance pursued over the Internet, *Echoes* is an encouraging novel of God's faithfulness in spite of our blunders.

IN YOUR DREAMS (SIERRA JENSEN SERIES)

Sierra Jensen is concerned with the same things that capture the attention of many teenagers: measuring up to a "perfect" older sibling, finding a job, and making friends. Her situation is complicated by the fact that her family has just moved to Seattle to live in her grandmother's house. Normally bright and outgoing, Sierra finds adjustments to a new school and new surroundings difficult to manage. She even considers taking out a personal ad: "Looking for a pal? I've been looking for you." Her grandmother's sudden surgery and Randy's applying to be her friend are events that restore Sierra's confidence and give her a new perspective on her future. Will that future also include the mysterious Paul?

In the Sierra Jensen series, Gunn has created stories that embody the joys and sorrows and the struggles and achievements of the teenage years. She skillfully mixes romance with elements of spiritual growth and personal discovery. Set in a Christian school, this series fills a gap for readers whose experiences are not touched by other authors.

ISLAND DREAMER (CHRISTY MILLER SERIES), REVIEWED BY LINDSAY HECKMAN, EIGHTH GRADE

Christy Miller and her best friend, Paula, get a vacation in Maui. Here she would celebrate her sixteenth birthday and spend time with her boyfriend, Todd. The problem starts when Paula lays her blue eyes on Todd. No teenager would want to miss this book. It is one of the best I have ever read. It resembles a teenager's life "today."

Dave Gustaveson

Born on October 4, 1946, to John and Thelma Gustaveson, Dave must have been well nourished both spiritually and physically by his father, a minister, and his mother, a dietician. He and his wife, Debbie, a kindergarten teacher and codirector (with Dave) of the Global Opportunity Network, are the parents of two daughters, Jamie and Katie. The Gustavesons live in Lakeview Terrace, California.

PROFESSIONAL

Education
California Graduate School of Theology

Career
Youth with a Mission (YWAM) Missionary, 1976 to present; associate pastor, 1970–1976

Awards
Various awards and honors in Youth with a Mission

PUBLICATIONS

Young-Adult Fiction

The Reel Kids Adventures Series
- *The Missing Video,* 1993
- *Mystery at Smokey Mountain,* 1994
- *The Stolen Necklace,* 1994
- *The Mysterious Case,* 1995
- *The Amazon Stranger,* 1995
- *The Dangerous Voyage,* 1995
- *The Lost Diary,* 1996
- *The Forbidden Road,* 1996
- *The Dangerous Zone,* 1997
- *The Secret Footage,* 1998

Adult Nonfiction

Personal Life Notebook, 1990

PERSONAL

Dave Gustaveson relates that his initial writing experience originally grew out of specific needs in his ministry and that his earliest works were nonfiction. He developed newsletters and training manuals to assist with his role as associate pastor, and in 1980 his first devotional book, *Personal Life Notebook,* was published by Bethany Fellowship.

Gustaveson's shift in focus to begin writing fiction came about in a most memorable way. His interest in writing for a younger audience was sparked at a seminar led by an author of fiction for children. "For three days I listened to her talk about the power of writing fiction to kids, and I cried the whole time. Then it became very clear that I was to write a series for kids."

Through Youth with a Mission, Gustaveson decided that the target audience for this series would be Christian children and young adults. It was his desire to challenge Christian kids to seek out those values and principles that would make a difference in their lives and to make them aware that they had a God-given destiny.

Gustaveson describes his research process as being about fifty percent of the total writing effort. Creating one book takes about six months, three of which involve research. Any reader of his books would verify that his thorough investigation of setting is evident in the wealth of factual information packed into each small novel.

Although boys and girls from the ages of nine to fourteen make up the typical audience for The Reel Kids Adventures series, adults also read the series to soak up the geographic and historic information cleverly camouflaged in the fast-paced action.

Gustaveson sees his plots as both action and character driven. He describes his style of writing as "purposeful, informative, and full of action." He keeps the pace moving and therefore holds the attention of his adventure-oriented readers. His dual themes of teens making an impact on the world for God and having the courage to find their individual destinies unfold as a natural part of the story and are presented forcefully. Settings vary from book to book as the Reel Kids travel to a different country in each episode. Such variety accounts for the time that Gustaveson spends in research. Yet even the locations he chooses are the result of a spiritual decision. Gustaveson states that his sense of place for each book is affected by God-given direction, following much prayer.

The characters in Gustaveson's books are based on his more than twenty years of service with Youth with a Mission. He relates that his experiences in travel often give him inspiration. For example, a scene in *The Stolen Necklace* describes the fear that grips a character who is trapped by angry elephants. The feelings that are expressed reflect those that the author experienced when he and others found themselves in a similar situation.

Loren Cunningham, the founder of Youth with a Mission, and fellow missionaries have greatly influenced Gustaveson's writing. Others who have made their mark on his life are Jan Rogers and another prolific writer of Christian fiction for children, Lois Johnson.

The audience on which Gustaveson focuses is the generation of young people born after 1982, known as Generation Y. These younger adults follow the now famous Generation X, who have been marked as those who are often prone to hopelessness and despair. His goal is that his readers will develop a new attitude toward a hurting world and will realize that, even as adolescents, they can be a powerful force for God.

His desire for the future of Christian fiction is that God will raise up many authors to communicate His great heart to children and young adults.

SUMMARY: *THE MYSTERIOUS CASE* (THE REEL KIDS ADVENTURES SERIES)

When Jeff, his sister Mindy, and their friend K. J. arrive in Bogota, Colombia, to create a film focusing on mission houses for homeless street kids, they are anticipating adventure. What they do not expect is a mix-up with suitcases, a kidnapping, a mysterious airplane engine fire, and threats from a drug cartel. Neither are they prepared to be personally drawn into the desperation characterizing the daily lives of children.

In previous books in the series, the young people have traveled to Cuba, the Philippines, Kenya, and Smokey Mountain as a part of the Reel Kids Club. Always there is intrigue, and someone's life is changed as these teens live out their mission.

Through the enthusiastic exploits of Jeff, Mindy, K. J., and others, Gustaveson exposes his readers to the excitement of evangelism. Plots are plausible, dialogue is realistic, and settings are convincingly portrayed. Reading one Reel Kids Adventure is certain to be the passport to discovering others in the series.

Ernest Herndon

When one considers the career experiences of Ernest Herndon, there is little wonder that he places his characters in a wide variety of settings, usually in wide-open spaces. Born to the late Bob Herndon and Maude Herndon Riales, whom he lists as management analyst/preacher and nurse/homemaker, respectively, Herndon reveals that he has been employed as a deckhand, bingo caller, housepainter, fur trapper, rural mail carrier, and pest control specialist. A native of Memphis, Tennessee, he currently lives in Mississippi with his wife, Angelyn, an elementary school teacher. They have one child, Andy Coy.

PROFESSIONAL

Education

M.S. in community health, University of Memphis; B.A. in English and anthropology, University of Memphis

Career

Reporter for the *Enterprise-Journal,* McComb, Mississippi, since 1979

Awards

More than thirty writing awards, including five first places in Louisiana–Mississippi Associated Press annual contests, six first places in Mississippi Press Association Better Newspaper Contests, two first places from the Mississippi Sportswriters Association, the 1995 Special Merit Award from the Mississippi Wildlife Federation, one first place in the eleven-state Southeastern Outdoor Press Association, and two honoraria from the Mississippi Humanities Council/Mississippi Press Association Newspaper Project

Memberships

World Tang Soo Do Association

PUBLICATIONS

Adult Fiction

Morning, Morning True, 1988
Island Quarry, 1990
Backwater Blues, 1991

Juvenile Fiction

Eric Sterling: Secret Agent Series
The Secret of Lizard Island, 1994
Double-Crossed in Gator Country, 1994
Night of the Jungle Cat, 1994
Smugglers on Grizzly Mountain, 1994
Sisters of the Wolf, 1996
Trouble at Bamboo Bay, 1996
Death Bird of Paradise, 1997
Little People of the Lost Coast, 1997

Adult Nonfiction

Self-Defense: A Body-Mind Approach, with Dr. Tom Seabourne (college textbook), 1987
In the Hearts of Wild Men, an account of an expedition in Papua New Guinea, 1987 (re-released, 1997)

Anthologies

"Rural Scenery" and "A Kayak Adventure," included in *The Magnolia Club: Fine Times with Nature's Finest,* 1990

"Meeting a Blues Master," included in *From Behind the Magnolia Curtain: Voices of Mississippi,* 1988

Articles

Feature and news articles published in a variety of newspapers, over the Associated Press wire service, and in such magazines as *Canoe and Kayak, Paddle, Sea Kayaker, Sports Afield, Bowhunter, Black Belt, Inside Kung Fu, American Karate, Frets, Interest, Fur-Fish-Game, Mississippi, Mississippi Wildlife, Mississippi Game and Fish, Mississippi Forestry,* and *Mississippi Health*

PERSONAL

Ernest Herndon states that his interest in writing arrived at birth and that his choice to write Christian fiction "just happened." He describes his research process as "nine-tenths" personal experience and the rest as a result of reading. No one who has read his novels for young adults would question the fact that his style is fast paced and, as he states, "with a strong sense of place." One of the strengths of the Eric Sterling series is that young readers can almost feel and taste the setting, and therefore they learn about nature and its precarious existence as they are drawn into the adventure of the plot.

For the target audience of his juvenile fiction books (ages eight to twelve), Herndon's goal is that they see his characters "tested by nature" and "redeemed by God." He accomplishes this through action-driven plots that are laced with an understated sense of humor and humility so appealing in protagonist Eric that he endears himself to the adult reader as well as to the teen. The all-too-normal "hero" is so average that any adolescent can relate to his feelings of inadequacy on the one hand and to his occasional pride on the other. He is so real that one knows that someone like him must exist somewhere and that he would be easy to get to know and would definitely be a loyal friend.

Herndon reports that he bases his characters on people whom he knows. He says that the karate expert in *Eric Sterling: Secret Agent* is his "lifelong friend Tom Seabourne." Others who have influenced his writing are authors of juvenile fiction Scott O'Dell and Jim Kjelgaard.

Herndon's personal goal, stated so succinctly, is "to keep writing." The goal he has for those who read his work is "to respect God and His creation" and to "learn to have confidence and faith." What he hopes to see in the future of Christian fiction are more "literary and experimental works."

Delighted readers hope to see more of Eric Sterling and his friend, Erik Stirling.

SUMMARY: *THE SECRET OF LIZARD ISLAND* (ERIC STERLING: SECRET AGENT SERIES)

In a case of mistaken identity, plain, average Eric Sterling (age twelve) is selected for the job of secret agent for WSI (Wildlife Special Investigations), a division of the CIA, instead of Erik Stirling, extraordinaire (age thirteen). Eric describes himself as a benchwarmer in sports, average in academics, and, in general, nothing special. Erik speaks several languages, earns straight A's in academics, and has a black belt in karate. Yet it is Eric who is dropped to an offshore island to attempt to infiltrate a compound where scientists are experimenting with the genetic engineering of lizards. In the course of events, both the right and the wrong Eric/k join forces to thwart the plans to breed giant lizards.

Herndon has created a memorable character in our insecure hero. The reader is cheering Eric not only because he is on the side of good but also because it will be a surprise to both reader and character if he succeeds. Adventure linked with a ready wit makes this little volume a winner and a good introduction to the series.

Ethel Herr

Perhaps it was being the child of a missionary and a building contractor that gave Ethel Funkhouser Herr the desire to build Christian writers. Perhaps it is the same nurturing spirit that causes her to be "always busy" with volunteer jobs and that has led her to mentor a number of contemporary Christian fiction authors. Whatever the reason, her leadership and contribution to the profession is widely felt today in the field of inspirational writing, as a number of the authors in this volume will attest.

Herr obviously finds interest in a wide range of activities. She lists her hobbies and other interests as playing with her six grandchildren, sewing, cooking, reading, traveling with her husband, and participating in the Women's Track of the AD2000 and Beyond Movement since its inception in 1991. She still serves as assistant editor of the international newsletter *Women of Vision 2000*. Ethel and her husband, Walt, to whom she has dedicated *The Dove and the Rose,* live in Sunnyvale, California, and are the parents of three children: Martha Doolittle, Timothy Herr, and Mary Jane Stajduhar.

PROFESSIONAL

Education

Multnomah Bible College; Modesto Junior College; Christian Writers Institute; Famous Writers School

Career

Full-time homemaker and mother; full-time freelance writer, speaker, historian, and teacher; teacher of writing workshops in the United States and India

Memberships

Institute for Historical Study, 1984 to present; Literature Ministry Prayer Fellowship, founder and director, 1982 to present

Awards

Pacesetter Award, Mount Hermon Christian Writers Conference, 1982; Encouragers Award, Sandy Cove Christian Writers Conference, 1995

PUBLICATIONS

Adult Fiction

The Seekers
- *The Dove and the Rose,* 1996
- *The Maiden's Sword,* 1997
- *The Citadel and the Lamb,* 1998

Adult Nonfiction

Chosen Women of the Bible (now in its twenty-seventh printing, having sold more than 107,000 copies worldwide), 1976
Growing Up Is a Family Affair (currently out of print), 1978
Chosen Families of the Bible (currently out of print), 1981
Schools: How Parents Can Make a Difference (currently out of print), 1981
Bible Study for Busy Women (currently out of print), 1982
An Introduction to Christian Writing (currently available only from the author), 1983

PERSONAL

Growing up as a missionary kid, I was convinced that the only occupations worthy of my time and energies were marriage, motherhood, and Christian ministry. My mother was a talented writer, but she was first of all a missionary, and most of her work never saw publication. She taught me to write as a way of life, but I could not think of it as a full-time ministry.

For years I followed her example, not realizing that in the process, God was at work making a novelist out of me. He was giving me a passionate heart for God, a probing mind, an insatiable curiosity about human nature, and an appreciation for the arts. Also, with each ministry came new opportunities to write. No one had ever written the materials I needed for my teaching, so I had to do them myself.

Then the U.S. Air Force sent my husband and family to the Netherlands for a three-year tour of duty. We all became fascinated with the country and its people. Later my curiosity led me to some Dutch history books. Here I discovered some significant people and events that begged me to write about them. After some preliminary research and a trip to a writers' conference in 1970, I decided I was not ready to write a historical novel. I put it in a thin notebook on my shelf and set myself to learn to write.

During the next twelve years, I discovered that my growing passion to write was a gift from God intended for ministry. I published dozens of articles, poems, and six books and finally had editors offering me assignments. I had decided the novel was a dream project that would never happen. That's when it came down off the shelf and demanded immediate attention.

Fiction was not marketable with Christian publishers in those days. Friends and editors wondered how I could get so excited about such an obscure time and place. Dutch Reformation history? They shook their heads and said no more. But I knew God was urging me, and I had to do it.

Thanks to a natural gift of stubbornness my mother had once dedicated to God back in my childhood, the first novel was finally ready fourteen years later. By now the market had learned to love fiction, and nobody else had saturated it with stories about my "obscure time and place."

The process was rich with discoveries, struggles, prayer, exhaustion, and ecstasy. I became a passionate browser of the stacks in the University of California at Berkeley library, which has one of the most extensive collections of Dutch language and history materials in the country. I buried myself in some incredibly helpful dusty volumes that carried me back to the sixteenth century. Later my husband and I spent three months digging around for all the remaining bits and pieces of "my other" century in Holland, Belgium, and parts of Germany and France.

After ten years of writing and rewriting, and collecting rejection letters, God connected me again with the man who had been my first editor twenty years earlier. He offered to be my agent. With his help, in 1996 Pieter-Lucas and Aletta, childhood sweethearts caught in the confusion and devastation of the Dutch Reformation, stepped out of the pages of a beautifully bound book and met the world.

My goal is to write character-driven novels with depth of purpose, richness and accuracy of historical setting, and challenging content. I refuse to write formula stories set in exotic surroundings. Each story must grow out of its specific historic place, time, and characters. It speaks to needs and values shared across the centuries but could only happen as it did in one time and one place.

My stories are designed to attract not only committed readers of substantial historical fiction. I also take aim at story lovers who think history is dry and boring as well as at the serious readers of "fact only" who believe fiction is spiritually shallow and a waste of time and intellect. Satisfied readers in all these categories tell me it has worked.

In the meantime, the series goes on growing out of my own special relationship with God. For as it chronicles the spiritual journey of Pieter-Lucas and Aletta and their friends and families living through some challenging times, it deepens my own spiritual journey as well. God only knows how many more novels from the same time and place in history He will guide me through. I face it with joy and freedom in remembering I am the manuscript God cares most about. All the lesser works He helps me write are some of the primary tools He uses to produce His work—both in my life and the lives of my readers.

SUMMARY: *THE DOVE AND THE ROSE* (THE SEEKERS SERIES)

Political upheaval and superstition provided fertile soil for the religious fanaticism that swept the Netherlands during the sixteenth century. The rout of William of Orange, coupled with raids and terrorism fueled by the Beggars, divided families and forced the persecuted to flee the country or to live as fugitives. Into this setting are born Pieter-Lucas and his young friend Aletta.

As time passes and the children grow into adulthood, conditions worsen. Both young people are forced to leave the village that has been so dear to them. The violence of religious fervor gone mad brings danger as both are caught between the beauty and tradition of their formal religion and the sincerity and grace of the Children of God who befriend them in time of extreme peril.

Herr gives credibility to both Catholic and Protestant believers and provides the reader with characters as memorable as a dear neighbor or a near relative. In addition to an atmosphere depicting political and religious unrest, the established use of holistic medicine and the peace gained from the release of demonic oppression round out this historically accurate story of the Dutch Reformation.

Marjorie Holmes

"You can write beautiful things for those who crave beautiful things." Those inspiring words from a junior high English teacher who later was also her college professor have been the banner under which Marjorie Holmes has expressed her talent for more than fifty years. The same teacher reminded Marjorie that when blessed with the talent for writing, one must assume the duty of developing that talent. Her now famous student has faithfully performed that duty with enthusiasm, to the joy of millions of readers. Holmes has also been motivated by the belief that she could write and that she must. For her it is "a gift from God, and that must be used. If not, it will be taken away! And it must be used for *good*."

PROFESSIONAL

Education

B.A., Cornell College; student, Buena Vista College

Career

Contributing editor, *Guideposts,* 1977; board of directors, *The Writer,* 1975; staff, Georgetown Writer's Conference, 1967–1968; teacher of writing, University of Maryland, 1967–1968; teacher of writing, Catholic University, 1964–1965

Awards

Alumni Achievement Award, Cornell College, 1963; Recipient Honor Iowans, 1966; Woman of Achievement, National Federation of Press Women, 1972; Celebrity of the Year Award, Women in Communications, 1975; Woman of the Year, McLean Business and Professional Women, 1976; D.Lit. (Honorary), 1976; Freedom Foundation at Valley Forge Award; Gold Medal, Marymount College, 1978; *Marquis Who's Who in the World,* 1995

PUBLICATIONS

Adult Fiction

Two from Galilee, 1972
Three from Galilee, 1985
The Messiah, 1987

Juvenile Fiction

World by the Tail, 1943
Ten O'Clock Scholar, 1946
Saturday Night, 1959
Cherry Blossom Princess, 1960
Follow Your Dream, 1961
Senior Trip, 1962
Love Is a Hopscotch Thing, 1963

Adult Nonfiction

Love and Laughter, 1967
I've Got to Talk to Somebody, God, 1969
Writing the Creative Article, 1969
Who Am I, God?, 1971
Nobody Else Will Listen, 1973
You and I and Yesterday, 1973
As Tall as My Heart, 1974
How Can I Find You, God, 1975
Beauty in Your Own Backyard, 1976
Hold Me Up a Little Longer, Lord, 1977
Lord, Let Me Love, 1978
God and Vitamins, 1980
To Help You through the Hurting, 1983
Writing the Creative Article Today, 1986

Marjorie Holmes' Secrets of Health, Energy and Staying Young, 1987
At Christmas the Heart Goes Home, 1991
Inspirational Writings of Marjorie Holmes, 1991
Gifts Freely Given, 1992
Writing Articles from the Heart, 1993
Second Wife, Second Life!, 1993
Cat Tales: Lessons in Life from Guideposts, 1995
Dog Tales: Lessons in Life from Guideposts, 1995
Still by Your Side: How I Know a Great Love Never Dies, 1997

Articles

Articles in magazines, including the following: *American Home, Better Homes and Gardens, Elks Magazine, Family Circle, Guideposts, House Beautiful, Ladies' Home Journal, The Man, Nation's Business, Reader's Digest, Redbook, McCall's, Today's Health, Woman's Home Companion,* and *Woman's Day*

PERSONAL

From the earliest years in Storm Lake, Iowa, Marjorie Holmes loved to read and write. While other children were playing, she often was busy creating poetry or prose. (She believes that all writers are poets at heart.) Encouraged by grandparents, parents, and teachers from first grade through college, the aspiring author never lacked material or motivation. From her first five-dollar manual typewriter to today's modern word processor, Holmes has created poetry, newspaper columns, magazine articles (for both sectarian and secular publishers), and books (both fiction and nonfiction). Sales of her hardcover books have reached more than six million, and she is also published in paperback, foreign, and book club editions.

What is Holmes's secret to success? When asked by Gene Shallit on the *Today* show why her books sold so well, she replied, "Identification and help." Readers identify with the situations that her characters face and receive help from the solutions they find. Certainly her warmth of words and sage advice through anecdotes have made her a resource for many readers traversing marriage, family, parenting, or relationship travails. Because most of her writing springs directly from her own experience and observation, and without her claiming any professional counseling credentials, many readers have come to think of her as a trusted friend, whether or not they have actually made her acquaintance. In one of her publications for *Writer's Digest,* "Writing Articles from the Heart," Holmes gives aspiring writers a book full of hints to assist them in becoming successful writers. Most of these suggestions hinge on the same classifications that she reported to Shallit years ago. It is that consistency of sparkle, caring for others, and seeing life as worthwhile that has continued to add new generations of fans to her readership. Her zest for life shines through in each article or full-length book.

After beginning school at Storm Lake's Buena Vista College, Holmes transferred to Cornell College in Mount Vernon, Iowa. She made this move mainly because of Toppy Tull, whom she refers to as "the patron saint of many writers." It was at Cornell that Holmes sold her first poem for the sum of seven dollars to a magazine called *Weird Tales*.

Following graduation, Holmes met Lynn Mighel, a just-graduating mechanical engineer, and within two months married him. To support themselves during the Depression, the newlyweds chose to raise cabbage in the Rio Grande Valley. Although floods, hurricanes, and aphids hampered their agricultural efforts, the young wife was successful in selling her first two stories just in time to pay hospital expenses for their first baby.

In the next few years, Lynn's career with Carrier Corporation created a rather mobile lifestyle for the family as he was attempting to start an air-conditioning business. During that time, Holmes worked at a radio station, including "a stint as a disc jockey." One day, realizing that she was missing the pleasure of rearing her own child, she decided to return to the typewriter so that she could also return to her family. She has continued to write while rearing four children and surviving the death of two husbands.

Holmes has chosen the Christian voice for her work because she wants to inspire as well as help her audience. Although she has drawn from family experience for many of her nonfiction articles and books, she has been scrupulous in maintaining privacy and anonymity for her family members. It is her desire to help others without bringing undue exposure to those closest to her. Holmes credits her ability to communicate with her readers to her commitment to write from the heart so that her readers will continue to say, "She understands."

SUMMARY: *TWO FROM GALILEE*

When Mary of Nazareth first comes of age, she is already considered a desirable bride for three young men in her village. Her ambitious mother, her protective father, and the rather determined young lady herself must reconcile their differences and settle on a suitor.

Intimate glimpses into the courtship and concerns of Mary as she approaches marriage flesh out the reader's knowledge of this significant biblical character. As the young couple bravely faces village gossip after Mary's pregnancy becomes evident, and later as they embark on the arduous journey to Bethlehem, the reader will likely grow in compassion for both the parents and the Holy Child.

One of Holmes's most beloved books, *Two from Galilee* made the *New York Times* Best-Seller List and became one of the ten best-selling books of 1972 and of the past fifty years.

James Byron Huggins

Born on August 14, 1959, in Alabama, Byron Huggins graduated from Morgan County High School. He later attended Troy State University, where he received a bachelor's degree in English and journalism. During the next three years, while working for the *Hartselle Enquirer,* he received numerous awards for his writing.

The year 1985 was one of change for the author when he went to work for members of the Christian Underground in Eastern Europe. From then on, his personal life reads like the pages from one of his suspense novels. Working to set up railing to smuggle people, Bibles, and information in and out of Iron Curtain countries, he was forced to become homeless, living in the woods and hiding in basements. Eventually, he was successful in making the contacts needed to achieve his goal.

After returning to the United States, he worked again in the field of journalism and then spent time as a bounty hunter. His last job before committing himself full time to a writing career was with the Huntsville (Alabama) Police Department. Today, Byron is married, the father of two children, and lives with his family in Alabama.

PROFESSIONAL

Education

B.A in English and journalism, Troy State University; Morgan County High School

Career

Journalist; agent for Christian Underground in Eastern Europe; bounty hunter; patrolman, Huntsville (Alabama) Police Department; full-time writer

PUBLICATIONS

Adult Fiction

Wolf Story, 1993

The Reckoning, 1994
Leviathan, 1995
Cain, 1997

PERSONAL

Byron Huggins always knew that he wanted to be a writer but says that he learned early that making a living as a novelist would not be easy. Therefore, although he knew that he had the talent to write, he spent a number of years smuggling Bibles, worked as a bounty hunter, and finally was employed as a uniformed patrolman. A life-changing experience finally tipped the scales for this writer, pushing him to pursue his desire to write as a career. One evening, when his son was ill, he found himself driving all over the city borrowing money from relatives and friends to pay for the medication that the doctor prescribed. At that point, he told himself and his son, "As God is my witness, I'll never let it happen again." For six months, while still employed by the Huntsville Police Department, Huggins worked from twelve midnight to six in the morning writing his first novel: *A Wolf Story*. The promise he made to himself fired his determination to succeed. "Anyone can start a novel, but finishing it and getting it accepted separates men from boys. There are long odds." When he began to market his first novel, Huggins did not know the difference between the CBA (Christian Booksellers Association) and the ABA (American Booksellers Association). He simply sent the manuscript to six or seven publishers, and three months later it sold. Bill Jensen of Harvest House saw his potential and agreed to publish the book.

Huggins does not target any particular audience with his novels, but rather writes for those who enjoy riveting action and gripping suspense. Although the backdrop of his stories is contemporary, he calls his story lines "classical," voicing the conviction that "there are only four or five great ideas. I have been rewriting them in a modern setting. *Leviathan* is a rewrite of *Beowulf*. *Cain* is a rewrite of *Dracula*." His character Hunter is a type of Dr. Jekyll and Mr. Hyde. Credit for conceptualizing *Leviathan* and *Cain* goes to Jan Dennis of Harvest House. "He kept building the idea with me, and after six weeks it was there," acknowledges Huggins.

Huggins conducts his research as the need arises. His advice is to "let the novel write itself. If you have a concept in your heart, let it come together. When you get to a point of need, look it up. Let the book happen. It has a life of its own. Characters have a life of their own. There are times when you want them to do a certain thing but you know they wouldn't do it. You have to give it to them. Characters write a novel themselves. They decide which way the novel will go. If you try to manufacture it, it will end up as an inferior novel."

If Huggins's characterization seems especially realistic, perhaps it is because he bases his characters on real people. He admits that *The Reckoning* is semi-autobiographical. His knowledge of espionage and combat techniques is real. The character of Kurtzman in *The Reckoning* is a real man. Other characters are patterned after policemen and bounty hunters whom he has known. When asked whether these people recognize themselves in the stories, Huggins indicated that they do. When asked whether they are ever offended, he answered, "No, they think it's great."

One classic writer who has influenced Huggins's writing is Edgar Allan Poe, whom he admires for his use of the language. Pulp fiction writer Robert E. Howard has proven to be a pattern for style, whereas James Dickey ranks as a favorite prose writer. Those who have personally encouraged Huggins to write include Ralph Adams, poet laureate of Alabama, who years ago inspired Huggins, telling him that he had talent "if he would only sit down and put it on the page." Larry Hanna, a writer for Marvel Comics, is also a friend and an encourager. Huggins credits Hanna with teaching him much about the discipline required to write.

Regarding a writer's spiritual beliefs, Huggins emphasizes that "a novel writes itself. When writing a novel, you use your own personal worldview. That dictates what you put on the page. It comes from the heart. You have to write what you believe. If you don't write what you truly believe, it won't have the power to come off the page and touch someone. . . . Go to the edge and take the chance someone won't like it. If you don't take that chance, it won't have the chance to be true writing. . . . Spirituality is your power. If you don't write from that, you are going to lose power."

When asked about his personal goals for writing, Huggins replied, "I write because I have to write. It's what I am. It's all I've ever wanted to do or to be. Maybe I write so that I know I'm not alone—so I can share. . . . I write to inspire, to encourage. I write to be what I am. I can't help it. I am compelled to create." For his readers, Huggins hopes that his writing "makes them stronger and inspires them."

Regarding the future of Christian fiction, Huggins sees increasing conflict between writers and Christian publishers. From his own experience, "publishers won't let writers write with true creativity. Too often they want writers to back up a certain platform or a particular denominational ideal. Publishers don't want great novels. They want novels that support their particular worldview."

If a common theme runs throughout Huggins's books, it is the age-old fight of good versus evil. As he has consistently portrayed in his stories, Huggins believes that "there is such a thing as evil. If you stand against it, you will have a fight, but I believe that evil can be taken on."

SUMMARY: *THE RECKONING*, REVIEWED BY DAVE BARNETT

The Reckoning, Huggins's second full-length novel, is a fast-paced adventure that keeps readers in suspense. Jonathan Gage, one of the most capable ex–Delta Force and CIA operatives ever trained, is betrayed and left for dead during an undercover operation in the Negev Desert. Nursed back to health by an aging priest who becomes his spiritual mentor, Gage spends three solitary years coming to grips with a new identity and a new faith. With the murder of his mentor, Gage is once again thrust into his former life of danger and intrigue as he seeks to recover a stolen ancient manuscript. Determined to rescue the ancient writing from the hands of those intent on its misuse and desiring to protect the one woman whom he loves, Gage pursues the assassins across two continents. No longer the "survival machine" that he had been trained to be, Gage now struggles to understand himself, his new faith, and the violent world in which he is again immersed.

A compelling novel, *The Reckoning* portrays a world that most readers have not experienced, a world in which violence, deception, and the physical struggle for life and death are ever present. Having lived through similar events in his own life, Huggins has the ability to write about such instances with passion, realism, and intensity. Yet even in the midst of the fast-paced action, we are able to journey with his characters through their pangs of self-discovery, leaving us with the hope and confidence that we too may emerge as victors from our own struggles with faith, emotions, and intellect intact. For those who enjoy edge-of-the-seat suspense, *The Reckoning* is an irresistible novel.

Angela Elwell Hunt

When one reviews the list and variety of her professional accomplishments, it seems impossible that Angela Elwell Hunt was born as recently as 1957. That she graduated from high school, community college, and a university with honors is no surprise for one so highly motivated to produce. Married and the mother of two children, Hunt continues to create quality literature in both fiction and nonfiction across all age and interest levels.

Along with her individual works, Hunt has worked with such well-known writers as Tim and Beverly LaHaye, John Donovan, and Joni Eareckson Tada as well as with evangelist Jay Strack. In the field of performing arts, she has been a member of The Re'Generation, with 500 concerts and three recorded albums to her credit. Since 1980 she has also served as a youth pastor's wife and is actively involved with both her family and her church.

PROFESSIONAL

Education

A.A., Brevard Community College (Florida); B.S., Liberty University (graduated magna cum laude)

Awards

Lorna Balian Award, 1987; Children's Choice Award, *If I Had Long, Long Hair,* 1988; Winner, Grand Prix de Treize (in France), *The Tale of Three Trees,* 1992; Gold Medal Finalist, Evangelical Christian Publishing Association, *A Gift for Grandpa,* 1991; Semifinalist, Campus Life Book of the Year, *If God Is Real, Where on Earth Is He?,* 1992; Honorable Mention for Book Design, Chicago Women in Publishing, *Calico Bear,* 1992; Gold Medallion Finalist, Evangelical Christian Publishing Association, *The True Princess,* 1993; Finalist, Romance Writers of America's RITA Awards, *Dreamers,* 1997; Silver Angel Award, Excellence in Media, *The Proposal,* 1997

Memberships

Novelists, Inc., 1997 to present; Romance Writers of America, 1994 to present; Author's Guild, 1990 to present

PUBLICATIONS

Adult Fiction

The Proposal, 1996
Gentle Touch, 1997
The Sleeping Rose, 1998
The Truth Teller, 1999
Legacies of the Ancient River
  Dreamers, 1996 (German rights sold, 1996)
  Brothers, 1997
  Journey, 1997
Keepers of the Ring
  Roanoke: The Lost Colony, 1996
  Jamestown, 1996
  Hartford, 1996
  Rehoboth, 1997
  Charles Towne, 1998
The Theyn Chronicles
  Afton of Margate Castle, 1993
  The Troubadour's Quest, 1994
  Ingram of the Irish, 1994
The Heirs of Cahira O'Conner
  The Silver Sword, 1998
  The Golden Cross, 1998

The Velvet Shadow, 1998
The Emerald Isle, 1999
Millennium Series (with Grant R. Jeffrey)
Flee the Darkness, 1998
By Dawn's Early Light, 1999

Juvenile Fiction

Where Dragons Dance, 1995
The Colonial Captives
Kimberly and the Captives, 1996
The Deadly Chase, 1996
Cassie Perkins Series
A Forever Friend, 1991
A Basket of Roses, 1991
No More Broken Promises, 1991
A Dream to Cherish, 1992
The Much-Adored Sandy Shore, 1992
Love Burning Bright, 1992
Star Light, Star Bright, 1993
The Chance of a Lifetime, 1993
The Glory of Love, 1993
The Nikki Holland Mysteries
The Case of the Mystery Mark, 1991
The Case of the Teenage Terminator, 1991
The Case of the Phantom Friend, 1991
The Case of the Terrified Track Star, 1992
The Case of the Haunting of Lowell Lanes, 1992
The Case of the Counterfeit Cash, 1992
The Case of the Birthday Bracelet, 1993
The Riddle of Baby Rosalind, 1993
The Secret of Cravenhill Castle, 1993

Adult Nonfiction

Just a Country Preacher (biography of B. R. Lakin), 1986
The Adoption Option, 1989
The Rise of Babylon (with Charles Dyer), 1991
Loving Someone Else's Child, 1992
Beauty from the Inside Out, Becoming the Best You Can Be (with Laura Krauss Calenberg), 1993
Listening with My Heart (with Heather Whitestone, Miss America, 1995), 1997

Juvenile Nonfiction

Too Old to Ride, Too Young to Drive, 1988
Now That He's Asked You Out, 1989
Now that You've Asked Her Out, 1989
Mom and Dad Don't Live Together Anymore, 1989
If God Is Real, Where on Earth Is He?, 1991
Keeping Your Life Together When Your Parents Pull Apart, 1995

Picture Books

If I Had Long, Long Hair, 1988
The Tale of Three Trees, 1989
Calico Bear, 1991
A Gift for Grandpa, 1991
The Singing Shepherd, 1992
The True Princess, 1992
Howie Hugemouth, 1993

Short Stories

Christmas by the Hearth, 1996

PERSONAL

Angela Hunt shares that she writes from what she sees God trying to teach her in her own life. She is not consciously trying to make a point or to teach a lesson, yet themes that emerge are those that will benefit the reader. Main characters are often self-disciplined and diligent—qualities depicted in the author herself.

Although she felt led by God to be a writer while still a child in summer camp, Hunt has been a cosmetics representative, a schoolteacher, a singer, a secretary, and a church worker. The desire to write was always strong, and she felt that she "had arrived" when her first book was published in 1988. Since that time, she has seen over sixty come into print.

Hunt states that although she finds writing across genre lines challenging, her favorite vehicle is fiction. She prefers to create her plots and characters because it allows space for working through issues. For example, in the Keepers of the Ring series, she deals with themes of grace, legalism, rejection, and the question of good people suffering. She feels that fiction has the power to communicate to different people on different levels and that the reader might identify with both problems and solutions.

Historical fiction has its own rewards. It offers rich resources of conflict and resolution as well as a painless way to gain knowledge of a time and place different from the reader's own. Although her main characters are fictional, the events are not, and Hunt believes that accuracy in research is essential. In writing *Roanoke: The Lost Colony,* Hunt and her family drove seventeen hours from Florida to the location of the action so that she could have an authentic feel for her setting. It is her desire in writing, whether depicting familiar biblical characters or those she creates from the pages of the past, to reveal God at work in human lives.

When one is such a prolific writer, there is always the question of whether quality is lost in quantity, but with Hunt there is no cause for concern. She sets out to tell a good story—and that she does, whether it is a traditional story retold (*The Tale of Three Trees*), a humorous picture book (*If I Had Long, Long Hair*), a teen dealing with the prospect of a new stepfather (*A Basket of Roses*), the struggle against abuse and poverty (*Afton of Margate Castle*), young-adult survival and adventure on the high seas (*Kimberly and the Captives*), or a contemporary adult thriller (*The Proposal*). Her characters are memorable, and the reader comes to care about the choices that they make. Her settings are well researched, and descriptions put the reader directly into the action.

Although Hunt strives to leave her audience with "hope and help," she also creates plots that unfold realistically, with no pretense that life's choices are easy but, rather, that God's grace is sufficient to meet one's needs. The following summaries are representative of Hunt's juvenile and adult works and demonstrate her talents in capturing a readership across age levels.

SUMMARY: *ROANOKE: THE LOST COLONY* (KEEPERS OF THE RING SERIES)

Thomas Colman, a young minister in England, desperately wants to book passage to the new colony in Virginia, but he has no money. John White, investor in the infant settlement, has promised his dying brother to find a husband for his daughter, Jocelyn. White sees his payment of Colman's fare as a solution to both their problems. Jocelyn, completely unaware of the arrangement made by her uncle, wants only to stay with her beloved father.

On board the ship, Colman is able to persuade Jocelyn to marry him, but it is not until the ship reaches its destination that the two can live as man and wife. The hardships of the primitive lifestyle and the psychological baggage that both bride and groom bring into the marriage create monumental challenges for the couple.

This is a story both of unresolved grief and guilt and of grace and patience. Hunt's ability to place the observer on the shores of the struggling colony gives readers a renewed appreciation for those who evidenced immeasurable courage in settling this nation. Both Thomas and Jocelyn will live on in the memory long after the last page is turned.

A BASKET OF ROSES (CASSIE PERKINS SERIES)

Cassie Perkins gives voice to the thousands of children and teens who are survivors of divorce in contemporary America. Her responses to her parents, her brother, and her new school are thoroughly realistic, as are those of the adults involved. As readers we live through the confusion, mistakes, misgivings, and deception with this young lady.

We, along with both Cassie and her brother Max, want life to be whole again with natural parents in the traditional family setting. We see the weakness on the part of both parents and children as they strive diligently to protect themselves against more pain while being not fully aware of the hurt that they inflict on the others they love.

The author has created a remarkable portrait of a family in the process of fracturing as seen from the perspective of the first-born child. Cassie's personality, winsome even under fire, will draw readers to each book in this series.

KIMBERLY AND THE CAPTIVES (THE COLONIAL CAPTIVES SERIES)

When fourteen-year-old Kimberly Hollis and her mother sell all their meager possessions to book passage for the New World, they anticipate meeting the father and husband whom they have not seen in seven years. Truthfully, Kimberly remembers little of her father and would rather remain in London. However, Mistress Hollis is eager to see the man whom she loves deeply and who has been laboring as an indentured servant so that he can provide a better life for his little family than they would ever have had in England.

However, the two ladies do not anticipate that they are the only paying passengers on the ship. The other 100 are children who have been kidnapped to be sold as indentured servants across the Atlantic. When Mistress Hollis is adopted as mother by all the children, her own daughter struggles with jealousy. However, as life-threatening illness, severe storms, and pirates press in around the hostages, Kim not only accepts the waifs into her heart but sincerely tries to demonstrate maternal strength herself.

Kimberly, who is Christian, and fellow passenger Ethan, who is Jewish, find common ground in prayer and unite to bring organization, a measure of cleanliness, and the spirit of survival to the sea-bound orphans.

The author has taken a fascinating excerpt from the *Encyclopedia of American Facts and Dates* (1627) regarding the ultimate success of one kidnapped child who was sold as an indentured servant, and built an enthralling adventure novel for young people. Kimberly, Ethan, Brooke, and the others step right off the page and beckon the reader to come on board—if the reader has the courage to try.

Dave and Neta Jackson

Dave and Neta Jackson are award-winning authors or coauthors of over seventy-five books, including the Trailblazer series of historical fiction for young people (over a half million copies sold) and novelizations of the Secret Adventures video series. They have two children: Julian, married and illustrator of the Trailblazer and the Secret Adventure series, and Rachel, married and mother of their granddaughter, Havah. They live in Evanston, Illinois, and have been members and lay leaders of Reba Place Church, a Christian church community, for twenty-five years.

When they are not writing in their basement office, the Jacksons enjoy singing in the "Racial Reconciliation" gospel choir, watching *Mystery!* and *Masterpiece Theatre* on public television, and gardening, camping, and biking. Dave enjoys fishing and bowhunting.

PROFESSIONAL

Education

Dave: Multnomah Bible College; Judson College; some graduate work, Wheaton College

Neta: Multnomah Bible College; Wheaton College

Shared Careers

Writing and editing

Awards

Silver Angel Award, *Listen for the Whippoorwill,* 1994; Gold Medallion Book Award, *Breaking Down Walls: A Model for Reconciliation in an Age of Racial Strife,* 1994; C. S. Lewis Award, Best Series, Trailblazer series, 1995; Best Children's Book of the Year, Christian Booksellers Association, New Zealand, Trailblazer series, 1995; Silver Angel Award, *Attack in the Rye Grass,* 1995

PUBLICATIONS

Juvenile Fiction, Shared Works

Trailblazer Series

Kidnapped by River Rats, 1991
The Queen's Smuggler, 1991
Spy for the Night Riders, 1992
The Hidden Jewel, 1992
Escape from the Slave Traders, 1992
The Chimney Sweep's Ransom, 1992
Imprisoned in the Golden City, 1993
The Bandit of Ashley Downs, 1993
Shanghaied to China, 1993
Listen for the Whippoorwill, 1993
Attack in the Rye Grass, 1994
Trial by Poison, 1994
Flight of the Fugitives, 1994
The Betrayer's Fortune, 1994
Danger on the Flying Trapeze, 1995
Abandoned on the Wild Frontier, 1995
The Thieves of Tyburn Square, 1995
The Runaway's Revenge, 1995
Quest for the Lost Prince, 1996
The Warrior's Challenge, 1996
Traitor in the Tower, 1997
The Drummer Boy's Battle, 1997
Defeat of the Ghost Riders, 1997
Fate of the Yellow Woodbee, 1997
The Gold Miners' Rescue, 1998

The Mayflower Secret, 1998
Assassins in the Cathedral, 1999
Mask of the Wolf Boy, 1999
Race for the Record, 1999
Ambushed in Jaguar Swamp, 1999
Secret Adventures Series
SPIN, Truth, Tubas, and George Washington, 1994
SNAP, How to Act Like a Responsible Almost-Adult, 1994
SMASH, How to Survive Junior High by Really Trying, 1994
SNAG, "I'm Dreaming of a White Christmas", 1994
SHRUG, The Self-Doubting Thomas, 1995

Adult Nonfiction, Shared Works

Living Together in a World Falling Apart, 1974
The Christian Family: A Woman's Perspective, 1983
What Makes a Christian Family Christian, 1983
STOREHOUSE: A Treasury of Family—Time Ideas (vol. 1), 1987
STOREHOUSE: A Treasury of Family—Time Ideas (vol. 2), 1987
Glimpses of Glory: Thirty Years of Community—the Story of Reba Place Fellowship, 1987
The Best Loved Stories from the Bible, 1989
On Fire for Christ: Stories from Martyrs Mirror, 1989
Growing Together with Your Teen: Studies for Parents of Teens, 1993
Starting Out Together: Studies for Newly Married Couples, 1993

Juvenile Nonfiction, Shared Works

Hero Tales: A Family Treasury of True Stories from the Lives of Christian Heroes (vol. 1), 1996
Hero Tales: A Family Treasury of True Stories from the Lives of Christian Heroes (vol. 2), 1997
Hero Tales: A Family Treasury of True Stories from the Lives of Christian Heroes (vol. 3), 1998

Adult Nonfiction Coauthored with Other Writers

Overcoming Homosexuality (with Ed Hurst), 1987
The Challenge to Take the Land (with Charles Simpson), 1987
A Time for Heroes (with Brother Andrew), 1988
Help! Crisis Ahead (with Joseph Bayly), 1988
WITNESS: Empowering the Church through Worship, Community, and Mission (with A. Grace Wenger), 1989

Between Life and Death—the Life Support Dilemma (with Kenneth Schemmer, M.D.), 1989
Cities of Lonesome Fear: God and the Gangs (with Gordon McLean), 1991
The Gift of Presence (with Beth Landis), 1992
Tinkering with People (with Kenneth Schemmer, M.D.), 1992
Heritage and Hope: The Legacy and Future of the Black Family in America (with Howard and Wanda Jones), 1992
Breaking Down Walls: A Model for Reconciliation in an Age of Racial Strife (with Raleigh Washington and Glen Kehrein), 1993
Becoming the Parent God Wants You to Be (with Kevin Leman), 1998
Too Young to Die: Bringing Hope to Gangs in the 'Hood' (with Gordon McLean), 1998
Recovering Hope in Your Marriage Series (with Dr. Stephen K. Wilke)
When It's Hard to Trust, 1992
When We Can't Talk Anymore, 1992
When We Fight All the Time, 1995
When Alcohol Abuses Our Marriage, 1995
When the Odds Are Against You, 1995

Juvenile Fiction, Neta Jackson

Pet Parables Series
The Parrot Who Talked Too Much, 1991
The Hamster Who Got Himself Stuck, 1991
The Cat Who Smelled Like Cabbage, 1991
The Dog Who Loved to Race, 1991
Loving One Another, 1993 (anthology of the Pet Parables series and the following stories: "The Ferret Who Slept in a Sleeve," "The Duck Who Quacked Bubbles," "The Rabbit Who Kicked the Door," and "The Pony Who Tipped the Cart")

Adult Nonfiction, Neta Jackson

A New Way to Live, 1983
Building Christian Relationships, 1984
Building Christian Relationships, Teacher's Guide, 1984
Who's Afraid of a Virgin, Wolf?, 1991
From Sod Shanty to State Senate, 1992

Coauthored by Neta Jackson with Other Writers

Called to Caregiving, 1987
Passport to Palestine (with Joyce Fifield Poley), 1989

Juvenile Nonfiction, Dave Jackson

Storybooks for Caring Parents
Tired, but Not Too Tired, 1985
Angry, but Not Too Angry, 1985
Bored, but Not Too Bored, 1985
Scared, but Not Too Scared, 1985
Disappointed, but Not Too Disappointed, 1986
Unfair, but Not Too Unfair, 1986
Shy, but Not Too Shy, 1987
Stubborn, but Not Too Stubborn, 1987

Adult Nonfiction, Dave Jackson

Coming Together, All Those Communities and What They're up To, 1978
DIAL 911, Peaceful Christians and Urban Violence, 1980
DIAL 911, A Study Guide, 1982
Keeping Your Teen in Touch with God, 1992
Lost River Conspiracy, 1995

Coauthored by Dave Jackson with Other Writers

The Christian as Victim (with Howard Zehr), 1981
Just Me and the Kids (with Patricia Brandt), 1985
The Freedom Years (with Larry Ferguson), 1985
Teen Pregnancy (with Matthew and Lea Dacy), 1989

PERSONAL

I [Dave] was born July 16, 1944, in Glendale, California. My parents became home missionaries to small logging and ranching towns in northern Idaho and California. We moved often because my dad's special ministry was starting new churches. So, when they got going well (after a couple of years), the mission board would send us to a new town. It was hard being the new kid in a small school where everyone knew each other. When I was in seventh grade, we moved to central California, where my father worked at an airport and learned to fly and repair planes. He hoped to become a missionary pilot, but that never happened. We lived there until I went away to college at Multnomah School of the Bible in Portland, Oregon. There I met Neta Thiessen.

Neta was born October 26, 1944, in Winchester, Kentucky. Her father was a Christian school principal. They lived in Boston and Texas and finally moved to Seattle, where Neta's father became the principal of King's Garden

Christian Schools and later Seattle Christian Schools. Neta's mom was a high school teacher at King's. Neta was very imaginative and liked to read and write, but she thought she was going to become an artist because she liked to draw (especially horses). However, in her senior year in high school, she wrote a story that won an award and got published in *Scholastic Magazine*. This caused her to consider writing more seriously. She had planned to go to Wheaton College back here in Illinois but decided to take her first year closer to home at Multnomah School of the Bible. (Lucky for me!)

I was a slow reader and a poor speller, but I loved good stories. I never imagined that I could become a writer. Writers seemed like people from another planet. I thought I might become a chemistry teacher because I was good at math and science. However, at Multnomah I tried working on the student newspaper and enjoyed it. Soon I became a journalism major. After Multnomah and a short stint in the Army, Neta and I got married. We then moved back to the Chicago area, where I went to work for David C. Cook Publishing Company as an editor. I continued my schooling at Judson College and did some graduate work at Wheaton College.

After Neta's first year at Multnomah, she decided to transfer back to Wheaton, which had been her plan all along. We were going together by then, so this decision was very hard for both of us. But we trusted that if we were meant for each other, God would help us maintain our relationship. Actually, it was good writing practice since we wrote two or three letters every week. After Neta graduated, she returned to Seattle, and we got married and lived for a while in Portland before we moved back here to the Chicago area. She went to work as an editor for Pioneer Girls (now called Pioneer Clubs).

We worked in Christian publishing for many years and wrote several books and articles on the side until 1986, when we went into business for ourselves as full-time writers.

Our Trailblazer books have been our most enjoyable work. They are historical fiction about great Christian heroes. There are twenty-six out currently. So far, the Trailblazers have sold over a half million copies and have won several awards.

We have also written many adult books. In fact, all together, we have written about seventy-five books.

SUMMARY: *THE CHIMNEY SWEEP'S RANSOM* (TRAILBLAZER SERIES)

Life in northern England seemed hopelessly hard for young Ned Carter. At the age of thirteen, he was already a veteran mine worker, helping to support his family. Now his mother was ill, his father was drinking away his despair, and his younger brother Pip was turning five—old enough to be sent underground to join the other miners. Sure that his little brother could never survive the rigors of this life, Ned desperately sought to prevent its happening. But an injury put him out of work, and Pip was sold as a chimney sweep to replace Ned's wages. When hope was low, Ned crossed paths with John Wesley, an itinerant Methodist preacher. Despite Ned's doubts and suspicions, Wesley worked to help Ned look for little Pip. It was through the practical compassion and instruction of this man that Pip learned of grace and the power of redemption.

THE QUEEN'S SMUGGLER (TRAILBLAZER SERIES), REVIEWED BY RACHEL HASSENPFLUG, FOURTH GRADE

Sarah Poyntz meets Anne Boleyn, the future queen of England, and saves her life. Later Sarah goes to be a maid-in-waiting for Anne while trying to save William Tyndale's life. I liked this book because it is adventure filled and takes place in another country.

DANGER ON THE FLYING TRAPEZE (TRAILBLAZER SERIES), REVIEWED BY SARAH MEYER, FOURTH GRADE

Fourteen-year-old Casey Watkins wants nothing more than to escape from school in Philadelphia. He wants to go back to his old farm, but one day he got a job at the circus. And I'll let you find out the rest. I really liked this story. I think it's the most interesting story I've ever read.

Jerry B. Jenkins

Born in Michigan to Harry and Bonita Jenkins (retired police chief and homemaker), Jerry Jenkins and his wife, Dianna, are the parents of three children.

Jenkins's interest in writing was initiated in high school by a sports injury. "I began sportswriting for the school paper to stay close to the athletic scene. I immediately realized I had found my niche." Although since that time editors, teachers, and others have been an influence in his writing career, he has "been most inspired, encouraged, and motivated by a supportive wife." So strongly does he feel about his writing today that he states, "I sincerely believe that writing is my one gift and that I am thus obligated to exercise it to the fullest. This is all I do. I don't sing or dance or preach. Any ministry, message, or legacy I might communicate will have to come through this medium." Currently, that legacy includes more than 125 titles.

Jenkins's current project, the Left Behind novels, which he has been cowriting with Timothy LaHaye, have become one of the fastest-selling series of books ever published. The first title was released in September 1995, and by the end of 1999 the first 6 of a projected 12 had generated over a million dollars in sales. All of the Left Behind novels have sold more than a million copies apiece.

PROFESSIONAL

Education

Moody Bible Institute; The Loop College; William Rainey Harper College

Career

Radio news writer; sportswriter and photographer; sports editor; editor, *Moody Monthly;* director, Moody Press; vice president for publishing, Moody Bible Institute; writer-in-residence, Moody Bible Institute; writer of nationally syndicated sports comic strip "Gil Thorp"

Memberships

National Scrabble Association (current); American Association of Professional Journalists (past); American Society of Magazine Editors (past); Writer's Guild (past); Evangelical Press Association (past); Evangelical Christian Publishers Association (past); National Table Tennis Association (past)

Awards

Gold Medallion Award (seven nominations); *New York Times* Best-Seller List (three times)

PUBLICATIONS

Juvenile Fiction

The Bradford Family Adventures Series
- *Daniel's Big Surprise,* 1984
- *Two Runaways,* 1984
- *The Clubhouse Mystery,* 1984
- *The Kidnapping,* 1984
- *Marty's Secret,* 1985
- *Blizzard,* 1985
- *Fourteen Days to Midnight,* 1985
- *Good Sport/Bad Sport,* 1985
- *In Deep Water,* 1986
- *Mystery at Raider Stadium,* 1986
- *Daniel's Big Decision,* 1986
- *Before the Judge,* 1986

Dallas O'Neil and the Baker Street Sports Club Series
- *The Secret Baseball Challenge,* 1985
- *The Scary Basketball Player,* 1985
- *The Mysterious Football Team,* 1985
- *The Weird Soccer Match,* 1985
- *The Strange Swimming Coach,* 1986
- *The Bizarre Hockey Tournament,* 1986
- *The Silent Track Star,* 1986
- *The Angry Gymnast,* 1986

The Dallas O'Neil Mysteries Series
Mystery of the Kidnapped Kid, 1988
Mystery of the Mixed-Up Teacher, 1988
Mystery of the Missing Sister, 1988
Mystery of the Scorpion Threat, 1988
Mystery on the Midway, 1989
Mystery of the Golden Palomino, 1989
Mystery of the Skinny Sophomore, 1989
Mystery of the Phony Murder, 1989
Tara Chadwick Books Series
Springtime Discovery, 1990
Time to Tell, 1990
Operation Cemetery, 1990
Scattered Flowers, 1990
Global Air Troubleshooters Series
Crash in Cannibal Valley, 1996
Nightmare in Branco Grande, 1996
Disaster in the Yukon, 1996
Toby Andrews and the Junior Deputies Series
The House of Tunnels, 1996
The Man with the Terrible Secret, 1996
The East Side Bullies, 1996
The Neighborhood's Scariest Woman, 1996
Left Behind: The Kids
The Vanishings, 1998
Second Chance, 1998
Through the Flames, 1998
Facing the Future, 1998
Nicolae, 1999
The Underground, 1999

Adult Fiction

The Operative, 1987
The Deacon's Woman, 1992
Rookie, 1997
'Twas the Night before Christmas: A Love Story, 1998
Left Behind Series (with Tim LaHaye)
Left Behind, 1995
Tribulation Force, 1996
Nicolae, 1997

Soul Harvest, 1998
Apollyon, 1999
Assassins, 1999

Margo Mysteries Series
Margo, 1978
Karlyn, 1980
Hilary, 1980
Paige, 1980
Allyson, 1981
Erin, 1981
Shannon, 1981
Lindsey, 1981
Meaghan, 1982
Janell, 1982
Courtney, 1982
Lyssa, 1982
Margo's Reunion, 1983
Margo Mysteries, Vol. I, 1985
Margo Mysteries, Vol. II, 1986

Jennifer Grey Mysteries Series
Heartbeat, 1983
Three Days in Winter, 1983
Too Late to Tell, 1984
Gateway, 1984
The Calling, 1984
Veiled Threat, 1985
The Jennifer Grey Mysteries, 1986

Adult Nonfiction

Biographies
Sammy Tippit: God's Love in Action, 1973
The Luis Palau Story, 1980
A Generous Impulse: The Story of George Sweeting, 1987
Nolan Ryan: Miracle Man, 1992
Karsten's Way: The Remarkable Story of Karsten Solheim—Golf Genius, 1999

Christian Education
VBS Unlimited, 1973
You CAN Get thru to Teens, 1973
You Me He, 1978

Light on the Heavy, 1979
Reproduced by Permission of the Author, 1980
Documentary
History of the Christian Booksellers Association, 1974
Three Behind the Curtain, 1976
The Night the Giant Rolled Over, 1981
Marriage and the Family
Loving Your Marriage Enough to Protect It, 1989
12 Things I Want My Kids to Remember Forever, 1991
As You Leave Home: Parting Thoughts from a Loving Parent, 1993
Still the One: Loving Thoughts from a Devoted Spouse, 1995
And Then Came You: The Hopes and Dreams of Loving Parents, 1996
General
Hymns for Personal Devotions, 1989
Lessons Learned Early, 1990
Winning at Losing, 1993
Life Flies When You're Having Fun, 1993
Coauthored
Bad Henry (with Hank Aaron), 1974
The Gingerbread Man (with Pat Williams), 1974
Stuff It (with Dick Motta), 1975
The World's Strongest Man (with Paul Anderson), 1976
Running for Jesus (with Madeline Manning), 1977
Sweetness (with Walter Payton), 1980
Home Where I Belong (with B. J. Thomas), 1980
The Power within You (with Pat Williams), 1984
Rekindled (with Pat and Jill Williams), 1985
Keep the Fire Glowing (with Pat and Jill Williams), 1986
Meadowlark (with Meadowlark Lemon), 1987
Kindling (with Pat and Jill Williams), 1987
Carry Me (with Christine Wyrtzen), 1988
Out of the Blue (with Orel Hershiser), 1989
Commitment to Love (with Deanna McClary), 1989
Baby Mayfield (with Larry and Diane Mayfield), 1989
Singletary on Singletary (with Mike Singletary), 1991
Fourth and One (with Joe Gibbs), 1991
Just between Us (with Pat and Jill Williams), 1991
I Almost Missed the Sunset (with Bill Gaither), 1992
No Matter What the Cost (with Sammy Tippit), 1993
Verbal Judo (with George Thompson), 1993
Addicted to Recovery (with Gary and Carol Almy), 1994

Field of Hope (with Brett Butler), 1997
Just As I Am (with Billy Graham), 1997
Homecoming (with Bill Gaither), 1997

PERSONAL

Jerry Jenkins began his writing career in the field of nonfiction, but, he states, "After having written seventeen or eighteen nonfiction books (biographies, Christian living, and so on), I was asked to try my hand at contributing one novel to a series that a friend of mine was editing. The novel was *Margo* and was intended to be a stand-alone book. It eventually became a thirteen-book series, and fiction became a major part of my writing."

When asked whom he sees as his audience, Jenkins replied, "I always write for myself. I don't do this out of a sense of ego but rather with the belief that if it interests me or inspires me, it will do the same to other normal people like me." When it comes to research, Jenkins says, "I research as necessary, striving not to let the research show in the final product. Fiction needs to be accurate, but the work of research needs to be blended in seamlessly." The author goes on to say, "I especially appreciate writers, such as the late Truman Capote, who understand the art of getting out of the way of their content. The ultimate goal of a writer, in my opinion, should be to be invisible. The reader should forget he or she is reading and be drawn totally into the story."

Influences for Jenkins's writing come from without and within. "I am a devotee of Strunk and White's *Elements of Style*. I'm also a big William Zinsser fan (*On Writing Well*). As for a love of reading, in my mind there are few writers who can match the lyricism of Pat Conroy. . . . [However], my writing is most influenced by my previous book. I want each book to be better than the last. Otherwise, I am stagnating or regressing. Despite the amount of writing I do, it seems I am writing more and more slowly all the time as my standard of satisfaction with my own work increases.

"My mother says she sees part of me in every character I include. There is some truth to that. Whether the characters are old or young, male or female, happy or sad, successful or unsuccessful, I try to put myself in their shoes and imagine how I would respond to various situations. Some characters look like friends and acquaintances of mine; others have similar names. . . . Even when writing action fiction, I try to keep it character driven.

"The theme, while overarching and undergirding, should be nearly invisible. If the reader doesn't get the point, then I have failed." When asked whether there is a single theme that appears in his work, Jenkins replied,

"I wouldn't call it a recurring theme, but my Christian worldview should come through. Stated simply, it is that there is a loving and just God and I am not Him. . . . Even when a novel of mine does not appear to be overtly evangelical, such as *Rookie,* my Christian worldview comes through, in that themes such as forgiveness, reconciliation, and restoration" are always there.

When it comes to actually putting thoughts on paper, Jenkins says, "I have graduated from a manual typewriter to portable typewriter to electric portable to correcting Selectric to memory typewriter and finally to word processing computer, which I have been using since 1980. I most often write on my desktop computer in my home office, though I sometimes enjoy the freedom of writing anywhere I wish on a laptop computer. I do a lot of writing on airplanes and in hotels."

As to the future of Christian fiction, Jenkins states, "I believe Christian fiction is here to stay; however, I am a bit troubled by how wide and shallow much of it seems. We must take comfort in the fact that cream rises. I sometimes worry that a glut of mediocre fiction might convince the market that the trend is past. I suppose this is a natural winnowing process, and we'll all be the better for it in the end."

SUMMARY: *TRIBULATION FORCE* (LEFT BEHIND SERIES)

Forty-year-old Rayford Steele paid no attention to the warnings of his wife about the coming end of the world. Thinking that her religious fervor was extreme, he was content to live for the present, ignoring spiritual things. However, the sudden disappearance of his wife, son, and millions of others all over the world shakes him from his skepticism, creating in him a desire to know the truth behind this catastrophic event.

Rayford, his daughter Chloe, Pastor Bruce Barnes, and Buck Williams, reporter of these strange phenomena, each seek for the truth in their own way. In *Tribulation Force* they become part of a group of new believers now living in grave danger. As Nicolae Carpathia, who they believe to be the Antichrist, consolidates his political power, all those who believe as Christians find themselves in a battle to defend their faith.

THE OPERATIVE

When NSA (National Security Agency) agent Jordan Kettering discovers plans of a nuclear threat to the United States, the knowledge places not only his life but also those of the people around him in danger. Determined to eliminate the risk of having their plot exposed and believing that they are killing him, his enemies murder both his wife and a stranger who resembles him. The stakes escalate as both his house and his uncle's house, where he has taken refuge, are destroyed. As it becomes apparent that the evil that he is battling resides within the NSA itself, Jordan must initiate clandestine operations to uncover and stop the danger before it is too late.

When it appears that everything of importance to Jordan has been taken from him in his pursuit of ambition and dedication to his career, a love long lost returns to bring him comfort, courage, and a renewed hope.

Michael Joens

Growing up in Virginia, Michael Joens was already creating stories, but instead of writing he drew his ideas as cartoon strips. In school his artistic talent gained him recognition from teachers and friends as his cartoons were being published in the school newspapers. After high school, Joens joined the Marine Corps and found his artistic ability being put to use as base cartoonist. In 1972, while still in the Marine Corps, Joens found a relationship with God and felt that he was called to ministry. To fulfill that call, he entered Bible school to train for the chaplaincy. During his last year there, it became apparent to him that God had a different direction for him. After graduating from college, Joens felt God calling him to the field of animation. With experience working in various levels of the animation business, he is now the owner of his own animation company, The Stillwater Production Company, which has produced the animation for the McGee & Me video series and the animated Adventures in Odyssey series. During the production of Adventures in Odyssey, the author attended a Christian booksellers' convention in Orlando, Florida, where his writing career was born. After talking with other Christian authors whom he met at the meeting, "something ignited. I came back home and decided to write." The resulting series was Twilight of the Gods.

PROFESSIONAL

Education
B.A. in literature/theology, Bethany Bible College

Career
All facets of the animation industry

Awards
Alumnus of the Year, Bethany Bible College, 1995; *Who's Who in American Colleges and Universities,* 1997; numerous Angel Awards

PUBLICATIONS

Adult Fiction

Triumph of the Soul, 1999
Twilight of the Gods Series
  The Crimson Tapestry, 1995
  The Shadow of Eden, 1995
Winds of Change Series
  The Dawn of Mercy, 1996

PERSONAL

With the responsibilities of owning an animation business demanding full attention, morning is the best time of day for Michael Joens to write. Although at some time he would like to have a career as a full-time writer, he presently spends about an hour and a half a day writing before going to work. Occasionally in the evening when he starts to read, his desire to write is stimulated, and he returns to his craft. Although Joens usually uses a computer to write, he finds that switching to longhand stimulates the thinking process when he is stumped by a difficult passage.

Joens's research methods vary, depending on the needs of the particular novel he is writing. Using fifth-century England as the backdrop for his Twilight of the Gods series demanded much research, but the lack of written historical reports made the writing more difficult than it would have been for other eras. *The Dawn of Mercy,* the first novel in his Winds of Change series, focuses more on human interest without demanding a great deal of technical information. With father/son relationships as the central theme, this story grew out of the wellspring of Joens's own experience. Being set in a location with which the author is very familiar, it demanded less research time. His manuscript in progress about the lives of two fighter pilots during World War II (*Triumph of the Soul*) has required extensive research so that it will be technically accurate.

On the whole, Joens sees his works as character driven, being filled with people whom he creates from his observations of humanity. These are woven into a plot that demonstrates God's sovereignty and His ability to redeem. For example, *The Dawn of Mercy* shows the mercy of God at work in relationships between people. In *The Crimson Tapestry,* the redemption of Aeryck's life from beggar and thief to noble defender of his countrymen and of his faith again displays the work of a God who removes the dross of people's lives and makes something significant of their lives.

Although all of Joens's books have at least one love interest, they also contain enough action and suspense to appeal to those who would choose adventure over romance. He does not see himself as a writer for men or women, Christian or non-Christian. His desire is not to sing to the choir, and he does not like the separation between secular and Christian literature. "What I write is not necessarily suited to the demographics of those who go into Christian bookstores." He simply wants to write what he sees as the truth and to write it for an adult audience.

Acceptance came fairly quickly for Joens's material, with his first manuscript being published by Moody Press. Ongoing support for his writing efforts comes from his partner Ken Johnson, who reads his work and encourages him in his efforts. His wife also contributes her objective opinions and suggestions. Other authors whom Joens admires and to whom he looks for patterns of style include Ernest Hemingway, John Steinbeck, and Harper Lee, although Hemingway is a special favorite. He loves the way Hemingway put his books together, unfolding the truth as he saw it while making the reader feel what his characters experienced.

Reconciling his desire to portray what he sees as the truth in situations without violating his own beliefs or the sensibilities of the Christian Booksellers Association's market is an ongoing struggle for Joens. With a strong desire to portray the reality of life while remaining true to who he is as a believer, he wants to help people recognize that there is more to life than what we see with our eyes. He wants to "communicate truth in such a way that men and women could accept it and move closer to an awareness of God."

With a personal goal of moving out of animation and into full-time writing, Joens hopes that the field of Christian fiction continues to remain strong.

However, he believes that its future is tied to a number of factors. As more people seek answers to life's questions, many of these people are becoming dissatisfied with the available reading fare. As indicated in the *Wall Street Journal,* the mainstream market has begun to tap into the field of Christian fiction, and the challenge for authors in this field, according to Joens, is to "move into truth and away from Christian fantasy. Truth will win out as Christian authors move into relating their real experiences. Not everything in life turns out rosy. There is not always a happy ending, but God is in the midst of it. The goal is to be conformed to His image."

SUMMARY: *THE CRIMSON TAPESTRY* AND *THE SHADOWS OF EDEN* (TWILIGHT OF THE GODS SERIES)

Life in fifth-century England was hard, crude, simple, and rough. There were few comforts and many dangers. The Saxon armies held the Britons under fear of attack from the south, and the Picts in the north were a cruel and fearsome enemy.

It was a time when brute strength was the sign of manhood, a time when frequent raids were made over Hadrian's Wall to destroy the towns of the Britons, with attackers taking both plunder and captives. It was a time when Druid priests claimed that human sacrifice was the way to appease the gods they served.

Orphaned at six, Worm seems to be an unlikely hero. Spending the first years of his life as a thief, living in alleys, and eating the scraps of others' tables, he seems to possess few qualities other than the ability to make himself scarce. Rescued from certain death at the hands of Saxon soldiers by Terryl, a young Briton, Worm is carried on the back of an enormous bear to the safety of Killwyn Eden. It is there that he discovers his true identity and begins the journey toward his destiny as Aeryck, son of Caelryck, a man known for his courage, his swordsmanship, and his deep faith in God.

Through fierce battles and narrow escapes, the war raging over the British Isles is played out in the lives of Joens's characters as political factions clash in their drive to gain control of the land. At the same time, spiritual forces are pursuing control of men's hearts and minds. Something unnatural is afoot. Wolves traveling in packs of 200 or more are attacking those whom they would not normally attack. As the battle of good and evil intensifies, Terryl and Aeryck take center stage in the conflict. Brave, strong, and sometimes foolhardy, these two young men make engaging heroes.

In volume 2, *The Shadows of Eden,* action intensifies as Norduk, the Wolf, an old enemy of Aeryck's father, seeks to destroy the boy. Aeryck finds himself running from the grasp of one who has sold his soul to the powers of evil. Although the physical battles rage, bringing on fear, Aeryck must face the fiercest enemy of all: the hatred for his merciless pursuer that would try to consume his soul.

These are high-adrenaline books and not necessarily ones to read before trying to fall asleep. Intensity of plot, coupled with the descriptive power of the author's words, makes this series difficult to put down. Joens presents his story with elegance of language without losing the powerful impact of the story line.

Lissa Halls Johnson

Born to Jim and Pat Halls on May 5, 1955, Lissa Halls Johnson shares that at age nine she read a book that "changed her life." Madeleine L'Engles's *A Wrinkle in Time* so impressed her as a child that, as she closed the book, she breathed a prayer asking God to allow her to "write like that someday." She goes on to say that the strong desire stayed with her into adulthood and that God continued to confirm His call through people and situations.

Johnson is a single mother of three children: Trevor, Stacie, and Misty. It seems that as an adult, she has achieved her childhood goal. Her many readers would attest that Johnson writes with power and that her books have the potential to change lives.

PROFESSIONAL

Education

Attended Biola University and various junior colleges

Career

Since 1982, Johnson has shared her interest in teen issues and her expertise in Christian creative writing by speaking at more than thirty conferences all across the United States, frequently serving as keynote speaker. Other speaking credits include English classes in high schools, in which she critiques stories written by elementary children and to give them encouragement. She has also appeared on radio and television interviews to discuss her books. Other writing includes scripts for teen shows.

Awards

Special Recognition Award, Mount Hermon Writers Conference, *Just Like Ice Cream,* 1983; Campus Life Fiction Book of the Year, *No Other Choice,* 1987; C. S. Lewis Silver Medal, *Just Like Ice Cream,* 1995

PUBLICATIONS

Juvenile Fiction

Just Like Ice Cream, 1983
Runaway Dreams, 1985
No Other Choice, 1986
Something to Live For, 1986
Lambs of the Lie, 1987 (Danish edition, 1989)
Homeward Heart (book 2 in the Pacific Cascade University series), 1996
China Tate Series
  Sliced Heather on Toast, 1994
  The Secret in the Kitchen, 1994
  Project Black Bear, 1994
  Wishing upon a Star, 1995
  A Comedy of Errors, 1996
  The Ice Queen, 1996
  The Never Ending Day, 1997

Nonfiction

Articles in the following publications: *Faith 'n' Stuff, Reader's Digest,* and *Family Life Today*

Short Stories

Numerous short stories, which can be found in the following magazines: *Brio, Breakaway, Clubhouse,* and *TQ*

Other Writing Credits

Contributor, *Christmas by the Hearth,* 1996
A Reason to Live, edited by Melodie Beattie, 1991
Affirmation for the Inner Child, by Rokelle Learner

Ghostwriter, *Dying to Live,* by Georgia Comfort, 1992
Prisoner of Another War, by psychologist Marilyn Murray, 1991
Editor, *Helping Women Recover from Abortion,* 1988
Rewrote, edited, and condensed *Defender of the Faith, Charles Ludwig,* 1988

PERSONAL

Lissa Halls Johnson states that she did not choose to write Christian fiction; rather, it chose her. She credits an overactive imagination, a love of books that began even before she could read, her acceptance of Christ at age four, and a voracious appetite for the printed word as the factors that led to a career writing inspirational novels. She says that it was not planned—it just unfolded as a natural result of her love for the printed word and her desire to share her faith.

Describing her style of writing as realistic, Johnson frequently bases her investigative process on primary sources. She interviews or simply talks with whomever might be an expert on the topic that she is currently researching, stating that the process varies from book to book. Being an avid reader, she naturally explores whatever material she can discover that is valid or insightful. She states that she tries to write stories that her readers will find relevant to their own needs, and therefore she incorporates "more about the emotions of people, rather than the surface things, such as what they look like or what they wear." She feels that what goes on inside a person is "far more interesting" than physical appearance.

In analyzing the literary elements in her novels, Johnson describes her plots as character driven and feels that caring about what is going to happen to the main character is what keeps the reader involved. The themes that recur are God's willingness to accept man where he is with his failures and to forgive him as well as remain faithful for the next trial. Her characters are often composites of people she has known. Rarely does she take the whole personality and description of only one person to create a character.

When asked what has most influenced her writing, Johnson stated that personal experiences and her own spiritual growth provide the realistic combination that have come to characterize her novels. Books that she has read, as well as her friends, play a significant role in her production. "I think many people think of writing as a magical process. In some ways, I suppose it is. Mostly, it is hard work. And when writers are alone, working hard, they need encouragement from outside sources. That's when friends and fan letters come in handy. They remind the lonely writers that, yes, their books are being read and it is worthwhile to pursue churning out more."

In discussing her personal goals, Johnson states that "writing is as important to me as breathing," yet she wants all that she writes to be pleasing to God. Her desire is "to glorify God, reveal Him, or beckon others to check out the promise of Salvation for those who believe." She feels that if these are the results of her writing, her work has exceeded what she could have imagined.

The foremost goal Johnson has for her readers is to create empathy. "So often humans condemn what they don't understand. If I can help readers understand why a person would commit suicide, get pregnant, or be rude to others, perhaps those readers will then offer kindness and compassion to those around them."

SUMMARY: *JUST LIKE ICE CREAM*

When sixteen-year-old Julie first meets Kyle, she is overwhelmed by his charming manner, his handsome face, and the sheer excitement of being near him. As the relationship moves toward intimacy, Julie resists and Kyle entices her by saying that sex is "just like ice cream." It is delicious and something that her parents or her outdated standards are keeping her from enjoying. Following the whirlwind summer romance, Julie discovers that she is pregnant. When she informs Kyle, he leaves no question that it is her problem and that she will have to resolve it. He does not care how she does that, as long as it does not interfere with his life. Embarrassed to tell her parents and with no one else she can trust, Julie's first resource is an abortion clinic.

This landmark book (which has sold more than 100,000 copies) faces honestly the how's and often the why's of teen pregnancy. Its frank treatment of medical procedures might leave some readers abashed, but the significance of the message is one that both parents and teens should confront, whether it applies to the reader or to a friend.

LAMBS OF THE LIE

Feeling overlooked or isolated has created fertile ground for manipulation in the lives of sixteen-year-olds Deanna and Jeff. Jeff's desire to serve God is apparently being fulfilled through his association with an enthusiastic and supportive group known as The Flock. Deanna is new in town and has yet to make any real friends. Jeff has learned through his training with The Flock that lonely people are often the easiest converts, and, besides, he finds Deanna attractive and intriguing. When Jeff invites Deanna to attend a concert and later a Flock meeting, she is delighted because it gives her a place to belong, and she also is drawn to the gregarious and handsome Jeff.

In the ensuing months, both young people, virtually ignored by their parents, find a family substitute in the group. Gradually, the sinister nature of The Flock, and especially of Shep, the leader, is revealed to Jeff, but Deanna has become brainwashed and rejects his warnings.

Johnson has created a believable story with a plausible plot that is chillingly possible. Parents, teachers, youth leaders, and teens should read this little novel and discuss, discuss, discuss.

THE ICE QUEEN (CHINA TATE SERIES)

China Tate and her friend Deedee are experiencing the joy of being camp counselors for ten-year-old girls. China agrees to this grueling experience only so that she and Deedee can be together. On receiving their assignments, the girls discover that they are at opposite ends of the campground and that China will be working in partnership with a former camping acquaintance who hates her. Heather the snob does not attempt to hide her disdain for her partner, nor does she intend to cooperate with her in any way.

China comforts herself with the thought that among her five little ten-year-old charges, she will make a difference. She prays for God's direction to reach the one camper in whose life she may become a pivotal force. It must be Irene, the misfit. Yet China struggles tremendously simply trying to like the rejected child, much less breaking through her wall to improve her life.

Adventure, humor, and a surprise ending make this a delightful addition to the China Tate series.

Lois Walfrid Johnson

Lois Walfrid Johnson was born in a parsonage on November 23, 1936. Her father, Alvar Bernhard Walfrid, was a pastor, and her mother, Lydia Christiansen Walfrid, worked as a business manager and bookkeeper.

From the age of nine and a half, Johnson has known that she wanted to write, a dream that has been encouraged by her husband, Roy. "During my college years, I kept a journal. Years later, after a number of Northwoods novels had been published, I went back to that journal and found these words: 'I want to write about people who have that insurmountable something in their lives. How the answer is God—not God in a wishy-washy way, but God with strength and purpose and power.' I had forgotten about those words, but God hadn't. Instead, He led me to do exactly what I said I wanted to do!"

PROFESSIONAL

Education

B.A., Gustavus Adolphus College (graduated magna cum laude); Northwestern Seminary, graduate classes; University of Oklahoma, courses in professional writing

Career

Author and speaker, 1969 to present; editorial associate, 1974–1977; English teacher, 1958–1959

Memberships

Society of Children's Book Writers and Illustrators; Children's Reading Round Table of Chicago; Council for Wisconsin Writers; Minnesota Christian Writer's Guild (former president and vice president)

Awards

Dwight L. Moody Award for Excellence in Christian Literature, 1969; Distinguished Alumni Citation for Distinguished Service and Significant Attainment in the Field of Christian Literature, 1983; C. S. Lewis Medal for Best Series Published in 1988; Gold Medallion Book Award, *You're Worth More Than You Think!, Secrets of the Best Choice, Thanks for Being My Friend,* and *You Are Wonderfully Made!,* 1989; Book Award of Merit for Distinguished Service to History for Adventures of the Northwoods series, 1991; Arthur Tofte Juvenile Book, 1992; Silver Medal, C. S. Lewis Honor Book, *Escape into the Night,* 1996; Silver Angel Award: *The Disappearing Stranger,* 1991; *Trouble at Wild River,* 1992; *The Runaway Clown,* 1994; *Disaster on Windy Hill,* 1995; and *Escape into the Night,* 1996

PUBLICATIONS

Juvenile Fiction

Aaron's Christmas Donkey, 1974
Hello, God!, 1975
Come As You Are, 1976
Young Readers Series
  Just a Minute, Lord, 1973
  You're My Best Friend, Lord, 1975
Adventures of the Northwoods Series
  The Disappearing Stranger, 1990
  The Hidden Message, 1990
  The Creeping Shadows, 1990
  The Vanishing Footprints, 1991
  Trouble at Wild River, 1991
  The Mysterious Hideaway, 1992
  Grandpa's Stolen Treasure, 1992

The Runaway Clown, 1993
Mystery of the Missing Map, 1994
Disaster at Windy Hill, 1994
The Riverboat Adventure Series
Escape into the Night, 1995
Race for Freedom, 1996
Midnight Rescue, 1996
The Swindler's Treasure, 1997
Mysterious Signal, 1998
The Fiddler's Secret, 1998

Juvenile Nonfiction

Let's-Talk-About-It Stories for Kids Series
Secrets of the Best Choice, 1988
You're Worth More Than You Think!, 1988
Thanks for Being My Friend, 1988
You Are Wonderfully Made!, 1988

Adult Nonfiction

Gift in My Arms: Thoughts for New Mothers, 1977
Either Way, I Win: A Guide to Growth in the Power of Prayer, 1979
Songs for Silent Moments: Prayers for Daily Living, 1980
Falling Apart or Coming Together: How You Can Experience the Faithfulness of God, 1984

PERSONAL

From my earliest memory, I loved having someone read to me, then being able to read myself. I devoured good books and especially enjoyed the kind of high adventure/mystery books that I now write. My love for stories soon contributed to what happened to me spiritually.

On a warm spring day when I was nine and a half years old, I did something—neither my mother nor I remember what—that needed discipline. I had an older sister who would say, "Spank me quick so I can run outside and play." With me that was not an option. My mother knew that I was too tender emotionally for a spanking and that sending me to my room was not a punishment. I would simply read a book. My mother decided that I should clean the leaves out of the barberry bushes in front of our home. The thorns pricked and scratched my fingers, and I poked along, moving more and more slowly. Finally I sat down on the sidewalk warmed by the spring sunlight.

At the time, we lived in the strongly Swedish town of Scandia, Minnesota. Across the lawn from our home was the red brick church where my father was pastor. While I sat on the sidewalk, the church bell began to ring, and I knew that someone had died. As the long tolls rang across the countryside, I counted: 89, 90, 91. Then the bell stopped. "Ninety-one years old," I thought. "What a long time for someone to live. I wonder what that person left behind?"

In that moment, I didn't remember all the gifts of love and encouragement every one of us can give to others. Instead, I felt if I could ever write a book, that was what I wanted to leave behind. I wanted that book to tell others what I believed about Jesus Christ. At nine and a half, I didn't realize that God had already called me to a specific kind of work. As it turned out, I could never shake off nor forget that experience. Even now it influences me when I write for children because I know what they are capable of thinking.

Though I didn't tell anyone about that experience until after my first book was published, I immediately started to do what I could to become a writer. Each night after supper, I went to my room and worked on what I hoped would be a novel. I finally finished that manuscript as *The Runaway Clown* (1993). When I was old enough to work outside the home, I tried to get a different kind of part-time job each time I needed work. I believed that if I knew how people acted in a variety of work situations, it would help me understand the rest of their lives.

When our youngest child was four years old, I began setting goals and wrote when my husband and children were at work and school. At first my goal was to write four pages a day. Then, when our children attended school for longer periods of time, I expanded my writing time. During those early years, I wrote on the kitchen table, then in a three-by-six-foot alcove in our kitchen. Next in a basement office, then an upstairs room, an office outside our home, and now in our home once more. I have written with whatever I had at hand: a pencil, a pen, a scrap of paper, a notebook, a manual portable, an electric typewriter. Currently I enjoy using a notebook computer because it gives me more freedom for researching and writing the Riverboat Adventures. In short, I work wherever I am and often use routine tasks such as doing dishes or cleaning as think time. To me, it's important that I work within the needs of my family. When our children were young, I set aside my writing if they were sick. Yet, whenever possible, I kept up a regular schedule of starting to write after they left for school.

Though I had been interested in writing fiction for many years, I didn't know how to begin until we moved to northwest Wisconsin. There I met people whose families had been friends and neighbors for three and four generations. I listened to their stories, thought about the way of life they had known, and decided it was too good to be lost. Then on a warm spring evening, sweet with the scent of lilacs and plum blossoms, I walked along a country road. I came to a cluster of trees and found within it the foundation for an old farmhouse. I thought, "What if a farm family lived here? What if there was a girl named Kate who moved from Minneapolis to northwest Wisconsin? What if she had a stepbrother named Anders who teased her all the time? And someone named Erik who could become a special friend?" That was the beginning. I kept asking questions and talking to a wide variety of people. I continued thinking about Kate, Anders, Erik, and the Windy Hill family until I felt as though that family were mine. I'm glad for each time someone tells me they feel that family is also theirs.

For one summer my husband and I lived without electricity, indoor plumbing, or our own well. At the end of that time, I felt as if I had lived in 1907. Later on, in addition to my electric stove, I had a wood cook-stove in my kitchen. While living on a country road, I was a beekeeper and kept a garden. My husband and I heated with wood and were visited by bears. Those experiences helped me to write about the transition years between the old and the new in northwest Wisconsin.

The audience I have in mind for my writing . . . depends on which book, article, or story you read. I have written for four age levels, using a variety of literary forms. With my most recent books, the Northwoods and Riverboat novels, my target audience is boys and girls, ages eight and up. Average, strong, and reluctant readers read the novels. One of these reluctant readers, a seventh-grade boy, found *The Disappearing Stranger* and talked his entire class of reluctant readers into reading the series.

I have received mail from nearly every state, Canada, and such foreign countries as Australia, Korea, Norway, Mexico, Japan, Saudi Arabia, Germany, South Africa, Spain, the Ukraine, and Northern Ireland. I enjoy the great variety of things children tell me about the novels. "If a video is made, I want to be Kate," girls often write. Many children read the books again, sometimes five or six times.

It surprises me that the novels are also read by men and women of all ages. I receive letters from fifteen-, eighteen-, and twenty-two-year-olds who ask, "Is it okay if I read your books?" I've also heard from men and women in the thirty-to-seventy age range. Frequently the books are read aloud in family, school, camp, nursing home, or other kinds of groups. One thirty-six-year-old woman told me she had never read a book completely through and found reading so hard that she did not want to begin trying. The people in the factory where she worked talked so often about the Northwoods novels that she felt she had to read them in order to take part in the conversation. That first book was difficult for her, but it came easier with the novels that followed. "I learned to read with your series," she said. "By the time I got to number six, I was reading lickety-split."

Often children write to tell me, "I'm glad you include God in every book." I especially appreciate hearing that the Lord has used a book to help someone spiritually. One young woman said, "Your books changed my life." When she started reading the series, she had stopped going to church. With *The Disappearing Stranger* she went back. In the second or third novel, she started thinking Kate's thoughts. With the fourth book, she had put her relationship with the Lord in order.

With the Riverboat novels, boys and girls tell me they had never before thought about slavery and the courage that it took for fugitives to reach freedom. God has used the books to give these readers new understandings about their most treasured possessions, what it means to stand for what they believe, and how free blacks and whites worked together in the Underground Railroad to help fugitives reach safety and freedom.

In each novel I combine action, character, and theme rather than allowing one or another to drive the work. I create double-line plots with two separate threads. One of these story lines develops the mystery—the compelling action that sends a plot forward. In the Riverboat Adventures that means something suspenseful connected with the Underground Railroad. The other thread shows the personal and spiritual growth in my viewpoint character and often other characters as well. Throughout a novel, I alternate character and action-driven scenes and weave the theme into both. All of these elements intersect at the resolution, close to the end of the book.

After writing my first thirteen books, I realized that in picture books for children, as well as in devotional books for three other age levels, I had used the same theme in thirteen different ways: If we depend on the Lord, He will give the help we need in every circumstance we face. In the novels I write now, the theme needs to be true to whatever the viewpoint character is learning at that point. Fiction demands that the hero or heroine be an overcoming person. Christian fiction, therefore, becomes a natural opportunity to show how a character overcomes with the help of the Lord.

I don't create characters exactly like someone I know. I'm afraid that if I did, I would have trouble making that character act in the way that is needed for the story. However, all I know in a general way about people *does* influence my character development. That knowledge helps me describe a character reacting to fear, or danger, or being loved. It helps me give an important character strong motivation and, out of that, a strong plot.

Though I don't lift a character from real life into my work, the experiences of my characters sometimes reflect what has happened to me. Before our marriage, my husband, Roy, was a widower, just like Papa Nordstrom. When Roy and I were married, Roy's daughter, Gail, became our flower girl. In time, two additional children, Jeffrey and Kevin, were born and grew tall like

Anders and Erik. While Kate is my viewpoint character, I also wanted strong male characters because of my experience in having sons.

Something subtle often happens in my development of characters. Kate (Northwoods) is a person I'd like to be. She's small and petite and has dark hair and blue eyes. She and Libby (Riverboat) are both curious and love to solve mysteries, two of my deeply embedded characteristics. Yet I had written several Northwoods novels before I realized that Anders and Erik remind me of two young men I know well: our sons, Jeff and Kevin. Mama is like all the old-time Scandinavian mothers I know rolled into one. Now and then, Pa, captain of the steamboat *Christina,* gives tiny glimpses of the wisdom, stability, and prayer life of my own father. Pa also reflects the Christian beliefs and parenting skills of my husband, Roy.

I set the Northwoods Series in 1906–1907 for two reasons. Those were transition years in northwest Wisconsin. It was still possible to see the old way of doing things— horsepower, hand pumps, clearing of the land. Yet the new was coming in—electricity, rural telephones, even automobiles. Also, Big Gust, a much-loved 360-pound, seven-foot, six-inch Swedish immigrant, was village marshal in Grantsburg, Wisconsin, during those years.

Whenever I could, I used historic characters—people who actually lived in the time and place about which I wrote. A note at the front of each novel tells which characters really lived. Kate had Irish and Swedish parents and soon discovered that she, Harry Blue, and Reverend Pickle were the only non-Swedes in the Trade Lake area. Being Swedish was true to the settlement of that part of northwest Wisconsin, but I also wrote out of what I knew from my own background.

Within the novels are "secrets" that reflect both my family and that of my husband, Roy. We are still close to the immigrant heritage that made America strong. As a young woman, Roy's mother came from Norway. In a wave of homesickness, she had her picture taken and sent back to her family. The result was the family picture described in *The Disappearing Stranger* and other novels.

Carl Nordstrom is named after two more immigrants: my Swedish grandfather, Carl Johnson, and my Swedish grandmother, Mathilda Nordstrom. While a young woman, Grandma worked on a farm outside Walnut Grove, Minnesota, and often watched wagon trains pass through to settle in the West. When Grandpa and Grandma Johnson were married, they bought a farm on the banks of Plum Creek. My father grew up there, and many of my stories about runaway horses come out of his experience in riding and breaking broncos. Years later, during summer vacations, my sisters and I played in Plum Creek. From where we waded, the water flowed under a bridge into the land once owned by the family of Laura Ingalls Wilder.

The Danish side of my family is also represented in the Northwoods novels. When my Grandpa Christiansen came to America, he worked for about a year to save enough money to bring my grandmother and their three-year-old daughter, Lydia, across the Atlantic. While passing through Ellis Island, Grandma and Lydia had pieces of paper pinned on their coats, as described in *Grandpa's Stolen Treasure*.

Some of the country school experiences in the Northwoods novels also came out of my own childhood. I attended my first four grades in a two-room country school on the shores of Goose Lake, near Scandia, Minnesota. Miss Sundquist gives spelling words exactly as my teacher, Miss Guslander, did. There were drafts through the knotholes in the floor at Goose Lake, too, as well as box socials, a woodshed, and a large wood stove. Even as a child, I knew it was special to attend a school with woods and water for a playground.

The Lord has been the greatest influence on my writing. In addition to the direct help he gives, He has used a wide variety of people who offered encouragement at just the right moment. These include friends, teachers, other writers, and readers of all ages. Often I feel amazed by children who know only my books yet write to give me a thought or verse. Countless times they have spoken so specifically to my need that I know they have heard from God about what to say.

In the acknowledgment section of each novel, I give information about the writing process and the people who help. Walter Johnson, a ninety-year-old man who still climbs trees, was a resource with most of the Northwoods novels. Students and faculty members at the Illinois School for the Deaf helped me develop Peter, a Riverboat character. Two persons have provided long-term and consistent encouragement. One of these is my husband, Roy, a former public school elementary teacher and a counselor for children at risk. While working on my first book, *Just a Minute, Lord,* I asked him, "Tell me everything you know about a fifth-grade girl." Roy talked for two hours. I wrote it all down and used those insights to make my writing real. When girls tell me, "Your book knows me," the credit should go to Roy, not to me. In addition to understanding the average child, he is uniquely gifted in helping troubled youth. Often people comment about the way I developed Stretch (early Northwoods novels). I gained those insights from Roy's ability to understand a young person in trouble.

In everything I write for children, he tells me whether the topic and concepts are appropriate and whether readers will understand what I'm saying. Roy also helps me with vocabulary and writing to grade level. When we travel to research novels, he often discovers something I might have missed. As I write a first draft, we frequently talk about how to develop a scene. I'll say, "This is what I need to do. How can I make it work?" Almost without exception, Roy is able to give me the idea that helps me move on. With every novel there's some variation of that thinking-things-through process.

One day, after I had written a number of Northwoods novels, I said to Roy, "I'm having so much fun doing this. I'll miss my characters when it's time to stop. What could we do next?" That morning he went out for coffee. Taking a napkin, he wrote down his concept for the Riverboat Adventure series. When he told me his ideas, I said, "That's it!"

We felt that by having my main characters live on the steamboat *Christina,* they could travel as needed to make a story work. For three years, while I was still writing Northwoods novels, Roy and I traveled up and down the Mississippi River, researching for ideas and historical accuracy. Soon the year 1857 became especially interesting to me. I could reflect the golden era of steamboats, for rivers were the highways of that time. I could show the pioneers using those steamboats to reach their new homes along the waterways of the Midwest. But I could also reflect the social and political upheaval of the times and give a Christian perspective on the exciting story of the Underground Railroad.

Again I use a girl as my viewpoint character—Libby, who comes from Chicago to join her father, a steamboat captain. Again I use strong boy characters—Caleb, who has worked with the Underground Railroad since the age of nine, and Jordan, a fugitive slave who escapes from his cruel master. With every novel I try to create strong reader interest by having fast-moving plots and cliffhangers at the end of each chapter. I also seek to reflect important truths of our American heritage.

To research these books, my husband and I visited the Underground Railroad sites in a number of states. We grew to love and value the runaway slaves about whom we learned. We grieved about their hardship and suffering. But we also respected their courage and daring as well as the integrity and honor of the people who helped them.

When readers write to say, "I want to know what happens to Jordan's family," I feel deeply moved. I, too, want to discover what happens to his family! By now Libby, Caleb, and Jordan have become part of our lives. When Roy and I talk, we sometimes say, "Could Libby do that?" Often we think of something that would be perfect for such a leap-before-she-looks person. Other times we decide, "No, that would fit Caleb or Jordan better." Like my readers, we often wonder, "What will these characters do next?"

Perhaps the way in which a character might be created is best explained through Annika, a teacher in the fifth Riverboat novel, *Mysterious Signal*. Annika came to me full-blown. I knew her the moment she entered my mind. I knew what she would say, how she would act, and what she would think. . . . But Annika still had to pass muster with Roy and Ron [Klug]. With both of them, it's as though we're talking about real people instead of characters. When Ron read *Mysterious Signal,* he said, "I liked Annika."

My content editor, Ron Klug, has also been a strong influence in my writing. Ron is especially good with plot lines, developing details needed, tying up loose ends, and the long-term direction of a series. At this point, he has edited nineteen of my books, and story lines become an important part of our discussion.

I cannot overstate how profoundly a good editor influences the development of a book, whether fiction or nonfiction. In *Midnight Rescue,* my runaway slave, Jordan Parker, wants to make a dangerous trip back into the area from which he came in order to help his mother, two sisters, and brother escape from slavery. This is the third novel in which Jordan has expressed his desire to lead his family to the Promised Land of freedom. After much pain, danger, and a long separation from his family, Jordan finally is reunited with his mother. When Ron read the first version of that scene, he said, "You've been building up this family's reunion for three books. Yet when Jordan see his mother, nothing happens. Don't you think you need to develop that scene more?" If Ron hadn't pointed out my need to rewrite that scene, I never would have received a truly great gift. I knew that Ron was right and started thinking about how I would feel if I saw my mother after believing I would never see her again. Next, I wondered how I would feel if I were a mother who thought I'd never see one of my children again. Then I wrote the scene.

In all that I do, I want to depend on the Lord. I seek Him about what projects to accept and desire to follow that leading. I specifically invite Him to be with me in my work. Often I stop in the midst of writing and ask what He wants me to say.

I believe that I will help my readers only to the level at which I have a relationship with the Lord. That means I need to grow not only in my craft but also in the Lord. At key points in my life I have often been reminded of Ephesians 4:15 (Revised Standard Version): "Grow up in every way into Him who is the head, into Christ." I want to continue growing in the Lord, to know and worship Him. Out of that relationship I want to make him known—to bring the hope of His love, forgiveness, power, and healing.

As a writer, I am called to build on the foundation of Jesus Christ, using gold, silver, and costly stones (1 Cor. 3:10b–14). I want to let the Lord use both my happy experiences and my times of suffering. In *Either Way, I Win,* I talk about my life-threatening experience with cancer. In the twenty years since diagnosis, the words of Romans 14:7–8 have continued to shape my thinking.

My first goal is to make whatever I write as compelling as I possibly can. I want readers to have fun with my books, to look forward to reading them, to find it hard to put them down. . . . I include a mystery in every Northwoods story and the compelling suspense of the Underground Railroad in every Riverboat Adventure. I put a cliffhanger at the end of every chapter.

I set this goal first because if I do not keep my readers interested, they will not continue reading. Yet in everything I do, I sense a responsibility because children take my writing seriously. They use my characters as their own role models. Therefore, I want to show a way of life that will be valuable to them. I want to give them role models that help them grow strong. I want readers to catch the vision of being part of a never-give-up family—a family that works together, believing in one another, even in very difficult times.

I also want readers to know and appreciate the past, becoming better equipped for the present and future. Often children tell me, "I never read a historical novel before yours. I didn't know it could be so exciting." I want them to have that excitement about other times and ways of living. I want them to think about what it means to cope in a world with less money and fewer conveniences. With the Northwoods books, I want them to see a way of life that was not easier but was in many ways simpler.

With the Riverboat books, I want my readers to understand some of the crucial issues sought by our founding fathers in the Declaration of Independence. I use the Declaration to help readers see a Christian perspective of the Underground Railroad. In story form, I blend my fictional characters with people who lived or still impacted life in the 1857 time period. By using my Riverboat family and a runaway slave, I show how people from a variety of church and work backgrounds, rich and poor alike, African-American and white, worked together for a common purpose: the dignity, worth, and freedom of those who had been enslaved.

Most of all, I want my readers to know and love the Lord and grow in Him in whatever way is needed. I want them to understand and accept his call on their life and receive his love, comfort, and empowerment.

Historically, the Christian perspective was a vital part of American thought in government, education, and daily life. Where once a biblical viewpoint was a normal and even expected part of literature, Christian literature has become "Christian" instead of "mainstream." The future in Christian fiction lies in our willingness to understand what the average person needs to face each day. Armed with that wisdom, we as authors need to seek God about how to bring light into those places. Our hope for relevance lies in knowing him and hearing his voice, then saying what He wants said under His anointing. This means working within the specific niche he has given us in order to honor Him. We also need to use universal themes and story problems that are true to the time about which we write yet speak to present-day readers. Well-crafted fiction offers a natural way to show what it means to live an overcoming life.

I believe it was Mother Teresa who said, "We are not called to be rich or successful. We are called to be faithful." I want to be faithful to my Lord.

SUMMARY: *TROUBLE AT WILD RIVER* (ADVENTURES OF THE NORTHWOODS SERIES)

Danger and suspense fill the pages of this novel set in the woods of northwestern Wisconsin in the early 1900s. With timber a major source of income for the area, the discovery of a timber thief is serious business. On a nighttime visit to their friend Joe, a Chippewa Indian, Kate O'Connell, her brother Anders, and friend Erik spy a man dressed all in black changing the ownership markings on logs that the farmers plan to send downriver to market.

Further mystery is added when a letter comes from Mama's younger brother Ben, who wants to visit. Ben had stolen money in Sweden before coming to the United States and wants to know whether he is forgiven. With her baby due any day, Mama cannot make the trip to meet Ben. Kate and Anders must go in her stead. With only two days to make the trip and a timber swindler working in the woods between their home and their destination, the young people must use all the courage and ingenuity they possess to meet their deadline.

Along with mystery and intrigue, Johnson weaves into her stories such timeless topics as blended families, sibling rivalry, and appreciation of other cultures. Without preaching, she portrays to young people the importance of such virtues as cooperation, trust, and forgiveness.

ESCAPE INTO THE NIGHT (THE RIVERBOAT ADVENTURE SERIES), REVIEWED BY SARAH BARNETT, AGE THIRTEEN

Escape into the Night is the first book in a series called the Riverboat Adventures. Authored by Lois Walfrid Johnson, this book is set in the year of 1857. Twelve-year-old Libby Norstad moves from her aunt and uncle's home in Chicago to her widowed father's steamboat on the Mississippi River. When a runaway slave comes aboard the *Christina,* Libby finds herself caught up in the adventure and danger of the Underground Railroad. Through it all, Libby learns what it is like to have a "never-give-up" family.

Johnson does a wonderful job of keeping *Escape into the Night* exciting while teaching valuable lessons. She emphasizes the importance of family, friends, and, most of all, an unwavering faith in God. This is a great book for anyone who enjoys adventure and suspense.

Jan Karon

To follow the life of Jan Karon from her birth in Lenoir, North Carolina, through her educational background and career experiences to the present, is to read a modern version of a female Horatio Alger. Karon has, with an eighth-grade education and high motivation, educated herself, become the vice president of an advertising agency, and joined the select ranks of inspirational fiction writers to make secular best-seller lists.

Karon still has time for hobbies, such as cooking, drawing, reading, singing, and music. Each of these recreational activities has found its way into her novels in some way. Her leisure activities also reflect the talents of her mother, Wanda Setzer, who is a china painter, and her daughter, Candace Freeland, who is a photojournalist and musician. What a creative delight their times together must be.

PROFESSIONAL

Career

Advertising executive

Awards

Stephen Kelly Award for Best Magazine Ad Campaign in America, 1987; Logos Bookstores Award for Best Fiction of the Year, 1995, 1996, 1997; Abby Honor Book, *At Home in Mitford,* 1997

PUBLICATIONS

Adult Fiction

New Song, 1999
The Mitford Years
At Home in Mitford, 1994
A Light in the Window, 1995
These High Green Hills, 1996
Out to Canaan, 1997

Juvenile Fiction

Miss Fannie's Hat, 1998

PERSONAL

I became interested in writing at a very early age because I was an omnivorous reader. At the age of six, I had an experience in which I began to preach with great feeling. At the age of ten, I knew without any doubt that I wanted to be an author. Half a century later, I'm an author writing about a preacher—an Episcopal clergyman, to be precise. I do not, however, consider myself a writer of Christian fiction.

I write fiction that happens to have a Christian setting and theme, but it is written primarily for a secular audience. That many Christians read and appreciate the Mitford series is a great bonus and consolation to me.

My research process is very hands-on. I do not rely on the Web. I typically go to people and experiences for research. For example, I sat down with my doctor when I had to choose an illness for my main character. After giving my doctor the character's symptoms, he said, "Hmmm. Could be one of two things. What would you prefer, diabetes or lupus?" In researching the experience of being lost in a cave, I went deep into a wild limestone cave in Virginia and found that one can, indeed, be hopelessly lost in less than five minutes. I did not want to do this research, but I'm glad I did and believe that it added immeasurably to the authenticity of my writing.

I write on a word processor in my studio, which is filled with natural light and overlooks a sloping lawn and copse of trees. In winter, I can see the blue ridges of our mountains wrapped in mist.

My audience is comprised of people of every age and various religious persuasions and reading interests. The male audience is growing rapidly. The age of my readers begins at ten and ends in the late nineties. Whole families share my books, and I have received more than 6,000 letters from men and women around America, Canada, and England.

I have been motivated and inspired by legions of writers, including Wordsworth, the Brontes, Goethe, Churchill, Charles Wesley, Charles Dickens, Miss Read, James Herriot, and others too numerous to mention. People inspire me daily, and I am always looking for the way people turn their phrases, speak in dialect, walk, stand, or even hold their mouths!

My books are character driven, and for that reason the observation and genuine love of people is critical to me and to my work. If there is a recurring theme in my work, it is that of forgiveness. My characters are almost never based on any one individual but are compilations of certain individuals I've known over the years. Often my characters are drawn from all those who peopled my childhood and influenced my early life. On rare occasion, a character will be drawn from an actual person, as Harley Welch, in my third and fourth novels, is loosely drawn from a native mountain man who painted my house several years ago. I thought very highly of this person, who was colorful, funny, and had the Irish gift for storytelling and good humor.

God influences my writing more than any particular person or book or writing style. I do what I do because He called me to it; it is definitely a calling, and it is definitely a ministry. It is also the great joy of my life. I love my craft beyond all telling.

My personal reading always shapes my writing. If one writes, one must read—period. Favorite books of my childhood included *Rackety Packety House, The Tale of Peter Rabbit, The Adventures of Tom Sawyer, The Adventures of Huckleberry Finn, Heidi* (a great favorite), *The Girl of the Limberlost,* and *Lorna Doone*. The most prominent shaper of my work is my spiritual belief. I have no interest in writing without these beliefs undergirding the work.

I would like to know that my work is a consolation to readers, that it makes them laugh and causes them to be free, for a time, of anxiety and care. Though the world tells us otherwise, I have learned that it's all right to be good and to love good things. I hope to expose a certain goodness of the human spirit in my work that causes a reader to say, "Yes! That's how I feel! That's who I am!"

The value systems we see/read/hear in today's media do not reflect my values—at all. Many of us feel isolated, disconnected because we seldom see ourselves reflected in television, magazines, and so on. My work reflects my readers—they look into the Mitford books and find themselves, and I believe they like whom they find.

My view regarding Christian fiction is that its potential is great, but the general writing skills must improve, as readers demand more and more "religious" reading material. I believe Christian fiction needs to deal aggressively with the world as we know it. We need to move authentically away from the realm of the historical novel and into the reality of today. We need to deal with some of the deep issues that divide and challenge us as believers. I am not saying that the historical setting isn't viable; I am saying that we must build on this narrow category and offer more contemporary settings in which we see faith at work in a way that speaks to our lives directly.

My clergyman in the Mitford books is not perfect. He doesn't even attempt to be. He's human and frail and sometimes fragile. He bumbles along, he makes mistakes, he can be peevish and short-tempered. Voila! A human being who happens to be a man of God. He can also be sacrificially loving, patient, tender of heart, thoughtful, generous to a fault, spiritually deep, and funny. As far as I can determine, he's the first decent, ordinary preacher since "Elmer Gantry" seriously contaminated fictional clergy more than four decades ago.

I am pleased that God appointed me to write and specifically to write fiction.

Author's note: Karon's The Mitford Years series, with the first novel published in 1994 and the fourth in 1997, has sold more than one million copies. To deal with her ever-increasing fan mail, Karon publishes a newsletter that is free to her readers and can be received by writing to More From Mitford, Penguin Marketing Department, 375 Hudson Street, New York, N.Y. 10014.

SUMMARY: *A LIGHT IN THE WINDOW* (THE MITFORD YEARS SERIES)

Readers were introduced to the cast of characters and their sometimes friendly, sometimes fiery intrusions into the lives of each other as they experience their own personal dramas in the first volume of the series, *At Home in Mitford*. In *A Light in the Window,* Karon serves as guide for her readers as she escorts them through the patches of sunlight and shadow in the small southern town of Mitford, North Carolina. Through episodes of sorrow and joy, Father Tim, the confirmed bachelor, meets the needs of his flock while also reaching out to the resentful, angry, downtrodden, and homeless not of his fold. Cast as a flesh-and-blood hero, with both faith and foibles, Father Tim quickly wins over the reader and most of those to whom he ministers.

Cynthia Coppersmith, owner of the Light addressed in the title, is Father Tim's petite neighbor. Her spirit, bright humor, and loveliness have long ago stolen the heart of the priest. However, a fear of being vulnerable to anyone prevents the middle-aged bachelor from declaring his feelings or making a commitment.

This is a warm, humorous story, even earthy at times, that will invite the reader in from the first page and whet the appetite for both the prequel and the sequels.

Harry Kraus

Husband, father of three boys, surgeon, and best-selling author are all descriptors appropriate for Harry Kraus. Son of a family physician, Kraus has continued the family trend of practicing medicine and has used his work as inspiration to create a series of modern medical thrillers. Kris, his wife, encourages and reviews his writing while maintaining their home, raising their three sons, and running marathons. Despite his busy schedule, Kraus fills the position of worship leader in their local church.

PROFESSIONAL

Education

B.S., Eastern Mennonite University; M.D., Medical College of Virginia; surgical residency, University of Kentucky

Career

Short-term medical missions in Kenya, Swaziland, and Albania; surgical practice

Memberships

American College of Surgeons, fellow; Christian Medical Society

Awards

A Closer Look Book Club Selection, *Lethal Mercy*; Christian Booksellers Association Best Seller List, *Lethal Mercy* and *The Stain*

PUBLICATIONS

Adult Fiction

Stainless Steal Hearts, 1994
Fated Genes, 1996
Lethal Mercy, 1997
The Stain, 1997
The Chairman, 1999

PERSONAL

My interest in writing fiction grew directly from my love of reading it. In spite of my busy schedule as a resident in surgery and the phenomenal amount of nonfiction that I was required to read, I found a relaxing escape in the wide world of novels, particularly suspense and mystery. I first enjoyed contemporary secular authors like Tom Clancy before finding an exciting Christian alternative in Frank Peretti.

I actually began writing my first novel manuscript (which was published by Crossway Books as *Stainless Steal Hearts*) as a surgery resident . . . not something that I would encourage others to try! I had little time for my family and even less for an extra pursuit of that magnitude. After twelve chapters, my wife prodded me to my senses and recommended postponing my passion until after I had settled into a relatively sane lifestyle in a private surgical practice. I complied, and later, after taking my American Board of surgery exams, I turned my attention back to the business of writing. I had no formal instruction in literature beyond freshman English. All my studies were in biology and chemistry. All I knew was that I had a strong idea about a story and the courage (naivete, maybe?) to try to write it down.

My schedule was, and is, surgery during the day (and an occasional night) with writing fitting in wherever I can manage . . . including between cases, late at night, and while on vacation. Did I mention that I am a father of three young sons, a husband to my wife, and that I'm active in my local church as a worship leader? I know it sounds stressful, but writing is very enjoyable to me, and my work schedule is a bit more relaxed than many physicians because I am working with a group of surgeons who value time over money!

A laptop computer helps with my weird writing schedule, and I take it with me to the hospital when I'm in the middle of a project. At home, I position myself in an easy chair, with my Powerbook on my lap and with the phone and a diet Pepsi within easy grasp. There I sit, hour upon hour, writing, smiling, frowning, squinting, laughing, thinking, and even crying, as my characters are tested, proven, and experiencing the elated ups and suspenseful downs of life.

Why do I write fiction? Simply because I think it is a powerful messenger tool that will challenge many who could never be reached with another (nonfiction) format. Sure, I entertain, but my goal is to stimulate thinking about current issues, including difficult and often distasteful topics such as fetal tissue research and physician-assisted suicide. These topics can be tastefully addressed in fiction in a way that will make readers stop and consider biblical truth. Ultimately, I want my readers to be challenged with the truth of the gospel of Jesus Christ. I don't want them to feel preached to, but I do desire to stimulate spiritual thirst.

There have been recurring themes in my novels. I have written over and over again about the value of human life . . . life which is a beautiful gift from God whether preborn, associated with disabilities, or in old age. Certainly, my studies as a medical student and as a physician have helped me to realize the wonderful miracle of our physical life.

All of my books are considered medical thrillers but are arguably more about people struggling with the truth rather than medicine. I write from a medical orientation simply because that is the life that I know best. The authentic medical flavor of a Kraus novel is my signature. Never forget the dictum "Write what you know!"

Many other authors have influenced my writing. My personal favorites are Hannah Whitall Smith, Neil T. Anderson, and Brennan Manning. Their precious words have helped my understanding of forgiveness, grace, and self-image based solely on God's acceptance.

My hope for the future of Christian fiction is that the market would open wider for fiction with a broad appeal for men. For too long there have been few wholesome, challenging alternatives for the Robin Cook, Tom Clancy, and John Grisham lovers out there. Hopefully, I can be a part of that alternative.

SUMMARY: *LETHAL MERCY*

Sarah Hampton is radiant with joy at the news that she is pregnant with her second child, until cancer is found in her breast. Determined to protect her unborn child from dangerous chemicals and radiation, Sarah seeks help at an alternative cancer treatment facility. Her sudden death brings suspicion on her husband, Jake, whose displeasure with her choice of treatment was well known. Had he abandoned his stand against assisted sucide to bring relief from her terrible pain, or were more sinister forces at work?

Suffering from traumatic amnesia following Sarah's death, Jake seeks peace for his life by joining in medical practice with Dr. William Dansford in his old hometown. To be successful there, Jake must overcome the suspicions of the community as well as his own grief. Pressure builds as Jake finds subtle hints that a stalker is threatening his life and the lives of those close to him. He must find the answers to these matters before they destroy his practice and the life of his young son.

NOTES FROM THE AUTHOR

Lethal Mercy is the third in a series of suspense novels from Crossway Books. The trio of books began with *Stainless Steal Hearts* (1994) and includes *Fated Genes* (1996) as well as *Lethal Mercy*. The books are readable as "solos" but are linked by a common character, Matt Stone, who is the protagonist in the first novel and a supporting cast member in the second and third.

In each novel, I desired that the theme of the sanctity and value of human life (whether preborn, infant, or disabled) be an integral part, not an afterthought or a tacked-on message. My commitment is not just to entertain but to challenge my readers with the tough ethical issues that we face today. It is my prayer that the books be high in "pass-along value"—that is, acceptable to pass on to your unbelieving friends as a challenge to them. The novels are considered "medical thrillers" but are arguably more about struggling people encountering biblical truth than about medicine.

The book reviews have been outstanding and, I assure you, are only evidence of the grace of our wonderfully creative Heavenly Father. He is the source of everything good. Happy reading!

William W. Kritlow

Writing has been an essential part of life for William Kritlow from a very young age. "I started writing when I was about seven and had a manuscript that I wrote when I was ten or so. It's always been the way I express myself. I can remember making up stories to talk myself to sleep as a kid. I came out of an alcoholic home, and it was a way to escape."

Kritlow's father is now retired from the construction industry, and his mother works for a newspaper. He and his wife, Patricia, have reared three children of their own. His present goal for his writing is that it will become his sole means of support.

PROFESSIONAL

Education

M.S. in cybernetics, San Jose State University; B.S. in math, Santa Clara University

Career

Life insurance sales, 1990 to present; computer sales, 1978–1990; systems engineer, 1971–1978

PUBLICATIONS

Adult Fiction

Driving Lessons, 1994

Lake Champlain Mysteries Series

Crimson Snow, 1995

Fire on the Lake, 1996

Blood Money, 1997

Juvenile Fiction

A Race against Time, 1995
The Deadly Maze, 1995
Backfire, 1995

PERSONAL

Unlike many authors who credit their writing to a voracious appetite for reading, William Kritlow states, "I don't read much. If I do, I find I end up stealing something. Plus I read slowly. I'm not a reader. I'm an imaginer. I put what I see down and try to shape it with words. I feel, and I like to put what I feel down in such a way that the reader feels it too."

The greatest influence on his writing has been from his critique group: Terry Whalen and Larry Clark. "It took three or four years of them tearing my stuff apart before I was ready to be published."

The writing process is continual for Kritlow. "Anywhere, anytime—all places—all times. Even when I'm not writing, I'm writing in my head." Actually putting words onto paper is done with a word processor.

Kritlow does not have the luxury of many hours to devote to research. Such work must be planned around the need to support his family. "I know where my story is going so I research enough to get it there. I know I'd do better if I could immerse myself in things, but I can't. I have to earn a living from something other than writing because I'm not as well read as some others. That's fine. No complaints. It's just that I have a limited amount of time."

Kritlow sees his works as theme driven "with action and strong characters." If there is a recurring theme, it is that "God is a planning God, and He works things out according to His plan. God is an active character in all my work. He's working out his plan, and my characters are a part of that drama."

The ideas for Kritlow's works come from "everywhere. Jesus influences my work, and that sounds trite, but it's true. He's in my work—or as I see Him. I see Him working in my own life and I translate that to my stories. Are my stories divinely inspired? Who knows? They're certainly not Scripture, and they're certainly not perfect. But if there's truth in them, it's not because I'm particularly bright."

Seeing his audience as "mostly other Christians" or those who "want to think about something Christian—want to face a Christian issue," Kritlow's goal is that "they are edified—enlightened—that they feel, that they come back for the next one."

When asked why he chose to write Christian fiction, Kritlow replied, "I committed my talent to Christ. He gave it to me. He should benefit from it.

I'm not a good witness verbally. I get tongue-tied, come across a little holier-than-thou. But my writing is based on a lot of thought. It's what God's given me to do. How could I possibly use it any other way? I only write what I believe. How could anyone with conscience write anything else?"

In regard to the future of Christian fiction, Kritlow states, "I think that fiction is a medium of truth. Not just facts. People don't mind being told how to do something—but they seem to mind seeing themselves in a less than flattering light. Fictional Christian characters can expose the reader that way. I have no clue to fiction's future, but since I enjoy writing it, I hope it's bright."

SUMMARY: *DRIVING LESSONS*

Unique in Christian fiction, this novel is a wild, wacky, wise, witty, and wonderful tale. With circumstances totally out of control, Nancy Bernard and her Great Dane are forced to ride out West with Mark Brewster and his salt-and-pepper fur-ball dog in a 1973 Pacer. Nancy is a klutzy, somewhat paranoid "neat freak," and Mark might be known as the king of the messies. Mark is determined to sell his movie script in Hollywood and strike it rich. Nancy, a new Christian, is seeking reconciliation with an alcoholic father. Hardly able to stand each other, the travelers find bizarre, funny, frightening, and enlightening experiences overtaking them as they discover unexpected things about themselves and about God.

A RACE AGAINST TIME

When their Uncle Marty is called in by the FBI to try to stop a deadly virus developed by his former rival Matthew Helbert, Kelly and Tim, his niece and nephew, are invited along. After Uncle Marty catches the virus himself and is sidelined from the hunt, the young people enter the virtual reality world of Helbertland themselves, desperate to track down the cure that is hidden there before their uncle dies. With the lives of their uncle and many others in jeopardy, they must meet the many dangers embedded in a make-believe world that has been created by a twisted, evil mind. Not alone in their search, the young people must defend themselves against attacks by Matthew's evil brother Hammond, who is bent on using the virus for his own wicked ends.

Nancy Simpson Levene

As a young girl, Nancy Simpson Levene wrote short stories to read to her younger sister. She wrote poems for her parents and teachers and plays for her friends to perform at summer camp. Today, Levene is still writing, but this time for publication. The popularity of her Alex series for girls and T. J. series for boys attests to her skill.

Pleased with her success, Levene now desires to expand her writing. "For over ten years, I have written books for children with spiritual messages but now wish to switch to adult audiences. I am pursuing a master of divinity degree to enhance my qualifications as a minister and Christian writer."

Although extremely busy studying at George W. Truett Seminary at Baylor University, Levene makes time for speaking to children and other groups about the craft of writing. For her own relaxation, she plays tennis, swims almost every day, and plays the piano.

PROFESSIONAL

Education

B.A in legal studies, Avila College; A.A. in business, Johnson County Community College

Career

Paralegal; freelance author; public speaker

PUBLICATIONS

Juvenile Fiction

The Alex Series (for Girls)

Shoelaces and Brussels Sprouts, 1989
French Fry Forgiveness, 1989
Hot Chocolate Friendship, 1989
Peanut Butter and Jelly Secrets, 1989

Cherry Cola Champions, 1989
Mint Cookie Miracles, 1989
Salty Scarecrow Solution, 1989
Peach Pit Popularity, 1989
T-Bone Trouble, 1990
Grapefruit Basket Upset, 1991
Apple-Turnover Treasure, 1995
Crocodile Meatloaf, 1995
Alex's Triple Threat, 1996

T. J. Series (for Boys)
The Pet That Never Was, 1992
The Fastest Car in the County, 1992
Trouble in the Deep End, 1993
Hero for a Season, 1995
Master of Disaster, 1995

Juvenile Nonfiction

Chocolate Chips and Trumpet Tricks: A Devotional, 1995
Face to Face with Women of the Bible (published under the name Nancy Simpson), 1996

Articles

"Babysitting and Baseball," *Clubhouse* magazine, Focus on the Family

PERSONAL

Writing has always been a part of the life of Nancy Simpson Levene. "I had a good friend, an older lady, who encouraged me to write when I was quite young. She always believed in me and in my writing abilities. Everyone needs someone like that for encouragement."

Despite her early encouragement, Levene has known great difficulty. Abandoned by her first husband when her daughter was three months old, she raised and supported her child by herself. Later a second marriage was devastated by alcohol abuse. Refusing to be destroyed by these problems, Levene worked as a secretary during the day and attended junior college at night until she was able to graduate with an A.A. degree in legal studies. After working for two years in a paralegal position, she returned to college for her four-year degree. "No matter what happened, my faith just kept getting stronger." After my first divorce, I began to learn about Jesus, and I have been close to the Lord ever since. He has helped me through every situation and has even made the difficult times turn out well."

Returning to college presented Levene with a number of challenges. "This was quite a strenuous but exciting time for me. I was not able to make ends meet. I knew I needed further education to get a higher-paying job, but I had no money. I did what always worked when I hit an impossible situation: I prayed. The Lord came through for me in a big way. Because of my good grades at the junior college, I was given a full scholarship for tuition and books at a four-year college. They even paid for gasoline and child care expenses."

After earning her four-year degree, Levene worked for ten years at a law firm as a paralegal. This did not bring her the satisfaction she sought. "I found that I wasn't happy merely being a regular part of the workforce. I wanted to do something special—something neat and out of the ordinary for God. I wanted my life to count for Him. So while lying in bed one night, I asked God what else I could do with my life. To my joy, He answered with one word: 'Write!'"

Levene began writing while working as a paralegal. After researching the book market, she chose to fill a gap by creating Christian stories for children. Her first story was *Shoelaces and Brussels Sprouts*. "I wrote and rewrote the manuscript. I asked everyone I knew to read it and give me their comments. Finally, I began submitting it to publishing houses. It took a year before it was accepted for publication by David C. Cook. During that year of waiting, I wrote my second novel, *French Fry Forgiveness,* to evidence my belief that the Lord would find a publisher."

Both books were accepted for publication, and two additional books were requested at the same time. "My first contract was for four books! It was amazing." Most of the story lines for what became Levene's Alex series for girls and T. J. series for boys came from incidents that occurred in her or her daughter's life.

In the future, Levene plans to keep writing but to expand her focus. "I want to write everything, from novels to devotionals to biographies for children and adults. But whatever I write, it has to be for God. He gave me the spark, and with it I plan to set the world on fire."

SUMMARY: *THE FASTEST CAR IN THE COUNTY* (THE T. J. SERIES)

Anthony Biggins is a boaster who loves to tease other children. Timothy John Fairbanks Jr. is one of his favorite targets. Even though his parents tell him not to seek revenge, T. J. longs to get even. When both boys enter cars in the Pinewood Derby, T. J. is determined to win, but how can he produce a winning car when his little sisters put Sesame Street stickers and pink crayon all over the body? How can he beat someone who cheats on the weight of his car?

With her T. J. stories, Levene has created a series to which many young boys can relate. As T. J. experiences the joys and sorrows of daily life, his family helps him discover that God really can help with everyday problems.

THE FASTEST CAR IN THE COUNTY (THE T. J. SERIES), REVIEWED BY MARK JONES, AGE SIX

This story is about a boy named T. J. who makes a Pinewood Derby car. He thought he would be the first-place winner because his car was so fast. When Anthony, who always cheated and was mean to T. J. and his friends, made his car two ounces heavier than the weight limit and won the race, T. J. wanted to get revenge. His father told him not to because God would take care of it. At the county championships, Anthony's car was disqualified because of its weight, and T. J. won first place.

I liked the part when T. J. let God handle the situation after Anthony cheated. He got a chance to race again in the county meet, and this time he won the trophy.

PEANUT BUTTER AND JELLY SECRETS (THE ALEX SERIES), REVIEWED BY STACIE ROY, AGE TEN

Peanut Butter and Jelly Secrets is a story about a girl named Alex who spends her lunch money at a carnival. Now she does not have any money for lunch. What will she eat, and how will she tell her Mom? Well—what would you do? I thought *Peanut Butter and Jelly Secrets* was a good book. It taught about telling the truth and obeying your parents.

T-BONE TROUBLE (THE ALEX SERIES), REVIEWED BY JAIME LIMPSCOMB, FOURTH GRADE

Alex finds out that people are gossiping about her. She know it's not true. She tries to get back, but she finds out that revenge is not the best way. I like this book. I would recommend it to anyone. It teaches a lesson in a good, kind way. It is a very good book.

Max Lucado

Perhaps it was being born in the creative 1950s or on a month and day of all 1's, but more than likely it was the finger of God touching the child born on January 11, 1955, that gave Max Lucado the potential to achieve such incredible success as an award-winning author of fiction and nonfiction, with a voice understood and loved by adults and children alike. In every book, using each genre, he speaks to the reader's heart.

Lucado and the former Denalyn Preston were married on August 8, 1981. They are the parents of three daughters—Jenna, Andrea, and Sara—all of whom were born within five years of one another and who served as coauthors for *The Crippled Lamb*. Each of these ladies has become known to readers, to some degree, in anecdotes scattered throughout Lucado's very personal books. Perhaps it is the inclusion of his wife and daughters that makes him seem like a member of each reader's family.

PROFESSIONAL

Education

M.A. in biblical and related studies, Abilene Christian University; B.A. in mass communications, Abilene Christian University; Andrews (Texas) High School

Career

Senior minister, Oak Hills Church of Christ, San Antonio, Texas, 1988 to present; church planting missionary, Rio de Janeiro, Brazil, 1983–1987; associate minister, Miami, Florida, 1980–1983

Awards

Teenage Christian Magazine Writer of the Year, 1983; Outstanding Young Man in America, 1983; Churchman of the Year, San Antonio Community of Churches, 1991; *Christian Reader* Reader's Choice Award, *The Applause of Heaven,* 1991; Gold Medallion Finalist, *The Applause of Heaven,* 1991; Choice Award and Gold Medallion Award, *Six Hours One Friday,* 1991; Young Alumnus Award, Abilene Christian University, 1991; Campus Life Award, *In the Eye of the Storm,* 1992; Gold Medallion Award, *In the Eye of the Storm,* 1992; named one of seven Most Admired Christian Authors, *Christianity Today,* 1993; Gold Medallion Finalist, *And the Angels Were Silent,* 1993; Gold Medallion Award, *Tell Me the Story* and *Just in Case You Ever Wonder,* 1993; Campus Life Award, *And the Angels Were Silent,* 1993; Campus Life Award, *He Still Moves Stones,* 1994; Gold Medallion Finalist, *He Still Move Stones,* 1994; Gold Medallion Award, *Tell Me the Secrets,* 1994; Evangelical Christian Publishers Association/Christian Booksellers Association (ECPA/CBA) Christian Book of the Year, *When God Whispers Your Name,* 1995; Gold Medallion Award, *The Crippled Lamb,* 1995; Gold Medallion Finalist, *The Final Week of Jesus,* 1995; ECPA/CBA Christian Book of the Year, *In the Grip of Grace,* 1996

PUBLICATIONS

Adult Fiction

Cosmic Christmas, 1997

Juvenile Fiction

Tell Me the Story, 1992
Just in Case You Ever Wonder, 1992
Tell Me the Secrets, 1993
The Crippled Lamb, 1994
The Children of the King, 1994
The Song of the King, 1995
Alabaster's Song, 1997
You Are Special, 1997

Jacob's Gift, 1998
Because I Love You, 1999

Adult Nonfiction

On the Anvil, 1985
No Wonder They Call Him the Savior, 1986
God Came Near, 1987
Six Hours One Friday, 1989
The Applause of Heaven, 1990
In the Eye of the Storm, 1991
And the Angels Were Silent, 1992
He Still Moves Stones, 1993
When God Whispers Your Name, 1994
The Inspirational Study Bible (general editor), 1995
A Gentle Thunder, 1995
In the Grip of Grace, 1996
The Great House of God, 1997
Just Like Jesus, 1998
Let the Journey Begin, 1998
The Christmas Cross, 1998
God's Open Arms, 1999
Touch of the Master: Studies on Jesus, 1999
Gift for All People, 1999

Articles

Articles in magazines such as *Image, His, Chinese Churches Today, Up-Reach, Teenage Christian, 20th Century Christian, Discipleship, Christian Reader*, and *Wineskins* and in numerous other publications

PERSONAL

From his first job as a gas station attendant, to becoming a best-selling author and pastor of a church that averages more than 1,800 worshipers at Sunday morning service, Max Lucado still maintains that "success is relative." Describing himself as "happy and content," Lucado admits that although his life sounds like a golden existence, it has not been without its challenges. Perhaps the key to his joy comes from his philosophy of goal setting. Instead of gauging achievement by membership, money, or any other measurable degree, Lucado believes that any Christian should determine his success by whether he has been obedient and tenacious in whatever he understands that God is leading him to do.

In describing his church planting in Brazil, Lucado candidly relates that he experienced frustration and disappointment when the work did not advance as rapidly as he had expected and when new converts did not display the strength of conviction that he felt they should have. It was in South America that he learned real obedience and endurance. Consistency in the day-to-day requirements of his ministry, regardless of the results (or lack thereof), taught him the value of being a foundation builder. He came to understand that success lies not in the visible but in the vision.

Professional recognition of Lucado's talent as a writer came in 1980, when, at the prompting of other staff ministers, he submitted a compilation of columns that he had written for his church newsletter to *His* magazine. To his surprise, it was published. When the Lucados went to Brazil, writing (in English at least) was put on hold while Portuguese became the language of daily life. Yet he continued to put his thoughts on paper and to pull together the assortment of thoughts he had written for the church newsletter. Thus began the long process of submission. After persevering through fourteen rejections, Lucado was rewarded when Tyndale House accepted his work, and *On the Anvil* was forged in book form.

When asked about the possible conflict of being involved in two full-time jobs, Lucado shared his method of dividing his time and multiplying himself. In their initial interview, he and the elders of his church understood the significance of setting priorities and limiting speaking engagements and thus established a system of regulation to keep one calling from swallowing up the other. The underlying principle in the success of their program is that pastor/author Lucado acknowledges his strengths (getting the message out by preaching and writing) and his weaknesses (administration, counseling, and saying "no"). To utilize his talents most effectively, Lucado concentrates on what he does well and delegates the other responsibilities.

One of the survival techniques that allows Lucado to balance such demanding roles is his philosophy of what constitutes success and failure. To him, success is measured in what he can do well and what he can control. Recognizing that he cannot control the opinions of others, he simply attempts to be obedient to God—to do his best at what he knows he can do well, leaving the responses and the results to God. His positive, realistic approach to life might spring from his healthy view of failure as well. He states that he has learned as much from failure as from success and that success is more dangerous than failure. He reveals that at times he has felt that his only success lay in his relationship with his family. He continues to take joy in his favorite roles of husband and father and says that Denalyn is his best friend.

When asked to respond to the phenomenal success of his books, with sales numbering in the millions, Lucado seems amazed that his gift has reached so deeply into so many hearts. He states that it "has to be God working." Recognizing the mobility of books as compared to sermons, he acknowledges, "Books go where I could never go." He notes that even when he is having a bad day and does not feel like ministering to anyone, "somewhere, one of those books is helping someone."

Although Lucado states that he is not a counselor, an avid fan of his many works might dispute that admission. Themes of God's free-flowing and unmerited grace, forgiveness, and unconditional love abound in both his fiction and his nonfiction. Readers of his books, both adults and children, sense that he has been right where they are—spiritually and emotionally—and that together they have discovered a new and intimate glimpse of their Creator.

When descriptors such as "brother," "neighbor," or "old friend" have been used to characterize the relationship established between the author and his readers, one can begin to grasp why Lucado's books are award winners. In addition, readers might not be surprised that he chose to refuse a pastor's salary and draws complete support from his pen. This is indeed encouraging, as it would seem that readers will continue to have available more of those books that speak to their spirits in Lucado's distinctive style.

SUMMARY: *JUST IN CASE YOU EVER WONDER*

Childhood is often a very scary time. Friends act unfriendly, monsters seem to hide in the shadows, and sometimes grades are bad and teachers get mad. Is there someone who will always be there for the young one? Is there anyone who loves her no matter what else happens?

In first-person style, Lucado writes simply with expressions that could have come straight from the hearts of his daughters. In language both childlike and profound, he reassures the little listener or young reader that both the loving parent and God will always be there, even into eternity, and will always love them—just in case they ever wonder.

COSMIC CHRISTMAS

Almighty God has entrusted the archangel Gabriel with the task of bestowing His Glory in a small vial on a virgin girl named Mary. It seems like a strange plan, but Gabriel is obedient. Each step of this cosmic event is shadowed by the forces of Darkness. Satan employs violence, deception, feigned repentance, and even the embodiment of an innocent-appearing human in an attempt to destroy his Creator's Design, and Gabriel must be alert to every strike.

In fewer than 100 pages, Lucado transports the reader from Matthew to Revelation, shedding light on those passages that are significant to that holy night when the birth of a tiny boy tolled the death knell for Satan. Never again will the familiar story of Christmas, with its silent, holy, peaceful night, be read without remembering that likely surrounding that simple stable were two armies: one good and one evil.

Paul L. Maier

Son of Dr. Walter A. Maier, founding speaker of *The Lutheran Hour* radio broadcast, Paul Maier has gone on to distinguish himself as a professor of ancient history at Western Michigan University and campus chaplain to the Lutheran students who are in attendance. Graduating from Harvard University in 1954 and Concordia Seminary in 1955, he received a Fulbright scholarship for postgraduate studies at the University of Heidelberg (Germany) and the University of Basel (Switzerland). While at the Swiss university, he was privileged to study under Karl Barth and Oscar Cullman.

The publication of the documentary novel *Pontius Pilate* in 1968 added another area of accomplishment for Maier. It was well received and has been reprinted in numerous editions and translations. His third novel, *A Skeleton in God's Closet,* became a number-one national best-seller in the religious fiction category. With his history of successful undertakings, the literary world can look forward to future contributions from Maier.

PROFESSIONAL

Education

Ph.D., University of Basel; B.D., Concordia Seminary; M.A., Harvard University

Career

Professor of history, Western Michigan University, 1960; Campus chaplain to Lutheran students, Western Michigan University, 1958

Memberships

American Historical Association

Awards

Alumni Award for Teaching Excellence, Western Michigan University, 1974; Outstanding Educator of America, 1974–1975; Distinguished Faculty Scholar Award, Western Michigan University, 1981; Professor of the Year Award, Committee for the Advancement and Support of Education, Washington, D.C., 1984; Academy Award, Michigan Academy of Science, Arts and Letters, 1985; Gold Medallion Award, *Josephus: The Essential Writings,* 1989; doctor of letters degree (*honoris causa*), Concordia Seminary, 1995; Russell H. Seibert Distinguished Named Professorship, Western Michigan University, 1998

PUBLICATIONS

Adult Fiction

Pontius Pilate, 1968
The Flames of Rome, 1981
A Skeleton in God's Closet, 1994

Juvenile Fiction

The Very First Christmas, 1998

Adult Nonfiction

A Man Spoke, a World Listened, 1963
First Christmas: The True and Unfamiliar Story, 1971
First Easter: The True and Unfamiliar Story, 1973
First Christians, Pentecost and the Spread of Christianity, 1976
The Best of Walter A. Maier, 1980
Josephus: The Essential Writings, 1988
In the Fullness of Time: A Historian Looks at Christmas, Easter, and the Early Church (compilation, revision, and expansion of the first three titles in this section), 1991

Josephus: The Essential Works (update and enhancement of *Josephus: The Essential Writings*), 1995
Usebius: The Church History, 1999

PERSONAL

As a professor and preacher, Paul Maier enjoys communication. That enjoyment is what motivated him to begin putting his thoughts into print, "as another important avenue for communication." Convinced that much important material relating to the New Testament accounts has been "largely unknown, for example, the politics behind Pontius Pilate's decisions on Good Friday," he wanted to share "such information with a wide audience in both popular and scholarly form; hence I write both fiction and nonfiction, novels, and also professional articles and books."

The author's research techniques involve "identifying an important problem or gap in our knowledge—about Jesus and the origins of Christianity, for example—and then trying to fill that gap by 'beating the bushes' of the ancient world for additional data. This usually involves archaeological, historical, and even geographical sources." Relating to experiences in his youth, he has pulled some of his inspiration from "the questions I asked my Sunday school teachers—many of which they could not answer at the time. I've tried to answer them since then in my research."

Putting these materials together for a varied audience of professors, scholars, and the general public is done on a word processor or a laptop "in the early morning, in the evening, or in airports between planes." Emerging from these efforts are books that present the "basic historicity of Christianity" in a highly readable form.

When asked which books influenced his writing career or inspired his love of reading, Maier replied, "There is no question that the Old and New Testaments have most influenced me, bookwise. They were also my childhood favorites." In addition to Scripture, C. S. Lewis has been a shaping force in the development of Maier's theology, and Henryk Sienkiewicz has provided inspiration for his fiction.

Stimulus for characters in Maier's novels comes from various sources. The main characters in *Pontius Pilate* and *The Flames of Rome* obviously are based on historical figures. "But with *A Skeleton in God's Closet,* which is contemporary fiction, the 'heavy' in the novel was based on my high school English literature teacher, the hero has *some* autobiographical aspects, and some of the characters are genuine personalities alive today, such as Billy Graham, Dan Rather, Tom Brokaw, Martin Marty, Walter Rast, Frank Moore Cross, and others."

As a result of his writing, Maier hopes to "impart important knowledge in a painless and interest-sustaining manner to the general reader and to advance the general fund of knowledge in the case of the professional. In the process, I also hope to demonstrate the historical reliability and credibility of the Christian faith." He desires that his readers "will be informed—maybe even engrossed and inspired—but, above all, that they will find my prose worth the price!"

For the future of Christian fiction, Maier hopes "that Christian fiction can break out into the literary mainstream to a greater extent than it has and that Christian authors will go beyond the almost 'obligatory' categories of rural romance, end-time fixations, prophecy projections, or the satanic supernatural."

SUMMARY: *A SKELETON IN GOD'S CLOSET*

Taking a sabbatical from his teaching duties at Harvard University, Dr. Jonathan Weber is invited by renowned archaeologist Professor Austin Balfour Jennings to be part of a dig at the ancient site of Rama. His excitement at this excavation is increased by the presence of Jennings's beautiful daughter, Shannon, a member of the archaeological staff.

Weber soon makes a stunning discovery, but his delight quickly turns to dismay as it appears that the bones he has uncovered might be those of Jesus. Much of the world reacts to this discovery with fear and anger as believers see the basis of their faith being shaken at its very foundation.

Resisting temptation to destroy the evidence he has found, Jonathan relentlessly pursues the truth of its origin. As pressures and dangers increase, this tenacity nearly costs him his career, his life, and his newfound love.

Addressing foundational beliefs of the Christian faith, Maier packages his message in an extensively researched thriller format.

Robert D. Massie

Through his firm, Massie & Associates, Robert Massie serves a wide variety of clients, from health-related industries to political groups and cultural organizations. Massie & Associates specializes in market research and business planning for emerging businesses and for nonprofit organizations and has "served as a partner in success for scores of organizations."

However, not content only to operate his own business, Massie shares his marketing experience through speaking and training engagements. His goal—to "demystify the concept of marketing so that the process can be better integrated into the life of a business"—is pursued through lecturing in the Midwest Entrepreneurial Educational Association's Fast Trac program and acting as a trainer for the Indianapolis Chamber of Commerce.

Education takes precedence in this family, with both husband and wife involved in teaching experiences. Massie's wife, Dianna, is a public school teacher, and Massie himself is founder and president of Dynamics of the Biblical World (DBW), a nonprofit educational organization that provides seminars on the culture and history of the Bible. These seminars are conducted in churches and colleges across the United States. Tens of thousands of people from more than twenty-five denominations have been the recipients of this volunteer effort. Massie's three children are currently pursuing their own education: Mary Katherine at Indiana University, Matthew at Purdue University, and Emily at Southport High School.

PROFESSIONAL

Education

M.Div., Southern Seminary, Louisville, Kentucky

Career

President, Massie & Associates, Inc. (a firm serving clients in marketing research and planning, direct marketing services, and direct-response advertising), 1987 to present; seminar leader, International Center for Learning, Ventura, California; member, City County Council of Indianapolis; bivocational pastor, Brethren Church; founder, Dynamics of the Biblical World, 1985; minister of three churches, 1975–1986

PUBLICATIONS

Adult Fiction

Mortal Intent, 1993

Adult Nonfiction

Marketing Is a Relationship, 1998
Wisdom for Men, 1994
The Search for Noah's Ark, 1989
Contributor to *Encyclopedia of Indianapolis*

Curricula

Ezra-Nehemiah, 1995
Author and editor of adult curriculum for G/L Publications 1980–1986 (included four book-length curricula yearly)

Coauthor

Teachers Are Made, Not Born (for Eddie Fine), 1990
Overture to Armageddon (with Moishe Rosen), 1991

Newspaper Columns

"Morning Coffee and the Bible" (syndicated in Illinois and Iowa), 1988–1989
"The Hoosier Poll" (syndicated in twenty-three newspapers), 1996 to present

PERSONAL

Robert Massie has drawn from his understanding of human nature that he has developed during his years in ministry and marketing to create fiction that accurately portrays the effects of ambition and success on people's lives.

SUMMARY: *MORTAL INTENT*

Just as Franklin Justice seems to have all the political power and success to guarantee a bright future, his life begins to fall apart. His selfish ambitions and his total disregard of his wife's needs have driven her to the edge of mental illness. His mistress is implicated in drug use and the mismanagement of political funds. However, determined to pursue his ambitions of running for higher office, Justice attempts to hold the wolves at bay with manipulation and deceit. Just how far will he go to protect his dreams of power?

In the midst of her depression and despair, Evelyn Justice seeks for new hope and wholeness. Her pursuit of a truth on which to rebuild her life and the determined efforts of a relentless team of reporters begin to apply the pressure that threatens to pull down the house that Franklin Justice has built.

Massie has created an intense and suspenseful novel that could easily be taken from today's front page. With a good mix of danger, romance, and character development, Massie portrays the reality of today's political maneuverings.

Paul McCusker

Paul McCusker was born on October 3, 1958, in Uniontown, Pennsylvania, to Thomas and Nancy McCusker. His father worked for United Airlines until his death in 1985. His mother has worked in a number of different capacities (e.g., in banking and real estate) and is now remarried and retired. Paul has three brothers: Jeff, Dale, and Dan.

McCusker's wife, Elizabeth, is English and has a degree in history from the University of Colorado.

PROFESSIONAL

Education

B.A. in journalism, Bowie State College (now Bowie University); two-year degree, Prince Georges Community College

Career

Advertising copywriter, Brady Publishing (division of Prentice-Hall, now Simon & Schuster); communications coordinator, Continental Ministries; freelance playwright, Jeremiah People and Custer and Hoose dramatic touring groups; writer/director, Adventures in Odyssey, Focus on the Family; writer of scripts for two Adventures in Odyssey videos and many novels based on the series; consulting producer writer and director, Focus on the Family

Memberships
American Society of Composers, Authors and Publishers (ASCAP); Dramatist's Guild

PUBLICATIONS

Juvenile Fiction

Adventures in Odyssey Series
Strange Journey Back, 1992
High Flyer with a Flat Tire, 1992
Secret Cave of Robin Wood, 1992
Behind the Locked Door, 1993
Lights Out at Camp What-a-Nut, 1993
The King's Quest, 1994
Danger Lies Ahead, 1995
Point of No Return, 1995
Dark Passage, 1996
Freedom Run, 1996
Stranger's Message, 1997
Carnival of Secrets, 1997
Time Twist Series
You Say Tomato (with Adrian Plass), 1995
Sudden Switch, 1996
Stranger in the Mist, 1996
Memory's Gate, 1996

Adult Fiction

Catacombs, 1997

One-Act Plays

Home for Christmas, 1982
The First Church of Pete's Garage, 1983
The Waiting Room, 1984
The Case of the Frozen Saints, 1985
The Revised Standard Version of Jack Hill, 1988

The Performance of a Lifetime, 1989
Season Tickets: The Christmas Collection, 1997
Season Tickets: The Easter Collection, 1997
Dear Diary, 1998

Full-Length Plays

Catacombs, 1985, 1995
Death by Chocolate, 1985
Family Outings, 1988
Camp W, 1989
Snapshots and Portraits, 1989
A Work in Progress, 1991
Pap's Place, 1993
Father's Anonymous, 1995

Musicals

The Meaning of Life and Other Vanities (with Tim Albritton), 1986
A Time for Christmas (with David Clydesdale, Steve Amerson, and Lowell Alexander), 1988
Dyno-Song Sing-a-Long, 1990
Shine the Light of Christmas (with Dave and Jan Williamson), 1991

Videos

Family Portrait, 1988
Dear Diary, 1989
Best of Friends, 1990
Stop the Presses, 1992
Father's Anonymous, 1992
Adventures in Odyssey series, 1992 to present

Lyrics

"Billy on the Boulevard" (with music by David Maddux, as recorded by First Call), 1986
"Hymns" (with music by David Maddux, as recorded by Cynthia Clawson), 1987
"Carols" (with music by David Maddux, as recorded by Cynthia Clawson), 1988
"Without You" (with music by Michael W. Smith, as recorded by First Call), 1990

General Resources

Youth Ministry Comedy and Drama: Better Than Bathrobes but Not Quite Broadway (with Chuck Bolte), 1987
Playwriting: A Study in Choices and Changes, 1995

Sketch Compilations

Sketches of Harvest, 1981
Souvenirs, 1982
Batteries Not Included, 1984
Void Where Prohibited, 1989
Quick Skits and Discussion Starters, 1989
Sixty-Second Skits, 1991
Fast Foods, 1991
Drama for Worship, Volumes 1–4, 1992
Short Skits for Youth Ministry, 1993
Vantage Points, 1986

Radio Dramatizations for Focus on the Family

Adventures in Odyssey series
A Christmas Carol (adaptation)
Dietrich Bonhoeffer: The Cost of Freedom
The Legend of Squanto
Radio dramatization of the *Chronicles of Narnia,* 1998
The Father Gilbert Mysteries: A Soul in Torment, 1999

PERSONAL

I'm not sure where my interest in writing began. From an early age, I was interested in creating new things through drawing, writing, and recording. Narrowing that down to writing plays, scripts, and novels as a possible career seemed to come as a matter of course. Since writing is an extension of who I am and what I believe, it was inevitable that I would write in the context of my faith as a Christian.

The kind of research I have to do depends entirely on the kind of thing I'm writing. I've just finished work on a radio drama about Dietrich Bonhoeffer, so I have to read through at least two dozen books about Bonhoeffer, his works, and Nazi Germany to try and get it right. I did a novel for Lion called *Stranger in the Mist* (about King Arthur) and had to read a lot of material. I prefer to buy new or used books and keep them with me at home.

I suspect that my audience (if I actually have one out there) is as varied as the books I write. Some of my sketches and plays are written for teens and adults. The Adventures in Odyssey series is geared for eight- to twelve-year olds (though we know we have a lot of adults listening). The Time Twists series is directed to twelve- to sixteen-year olds. *Catacombs* (the novel) is written for adults.

I've never been sure what my style of writing is. I'm inclined to work towards a balance of drama and humor in whatever I'm working on—laughter in the midst of tears, tears in the midst of laughter. A lot of that is determined by the genre I'm working in. Some stories are definitely action driven, while others require more of a character-based approach. I think the best writing integrates both action and character. I've been told, though, that I seem to lean more heavily to stories of relationships: what's happening to the people in the context of the action.

I'm not aware of a recurring theme in my writing. I guess if I'm as rational as some friends have said I am, then I'm constantly exploring what's happening between us and God, or between parents and their kids (and vice versa), or between friends or co-workers or enemies or whomever. Mostly I'm fascinated by ordinary people in extraordinary circumstances and how they react to them.

Where my stories are set often depends on the story itself and the constraints of the genre. If I'm writing a play, then I have to limit where the story takes place. If it's a novel, then it's determined by the characters and plot development. I don't have any typical places I return to. . . . I'm terribly suburban in my upbringing and find that writing for large cities or small towns can be difficult. If there's any particular situation I enjoy, it's people in isolation: shut up in a mountain cabin or an abandoned church and so on.

I think any honest writer will tell you that characters are a fusion of real people filtered through an individual imagination. Those "real people" may be people we know, have seen somewhere, or watched in other fictional settings (like books, TV, or movies). They may be characteristics of ourselves. But I have rarely ever written in a character who was undiluted—in other words, it's never an exact representation of someone I know. Even when I've tried to write an exact representation, the character (in the context of the story) has taken on a life of his or her own and changed into someone else. Examples would be difficult to give at this point since, even if I gave one, the people involved would be shocked to think that they were somehow the inspiration for my characters.

Influences for my writing depend on the project. If I'm writing a mystery, then I want to read the best-written mysteries I can find (in the hope that they'll rub off on me). The same with other genres. When I wrote the play *Catacombs,* I remember listening to side 2 of Daniel Amos's *Shotgun Angel* over and over just to get the right mood. When I wrote the novel based on the play, I immersed myself in the writings of Graham Greene because he seemed to capture the right combination of humanity in difficult circumstances.

Someone I know once said that movies need to either give you insight into your life or make you forget about your life altogether. I consider that a wise perspective. Personally, I hope that my writing tells a good story with insight into our human condition. And if it can't give meaning or insight, then I have to hope it'll at least be entertaining enough to serve as a brief escape.

I'd like to get rid of the tag "Christian" fiction. That's a marketing tag, not an artistic one. So please allow me to rephrase: I think "fiction from writers with a Christian viewpoint" has a lot of potential to impact not only the Christian community but the secular as well. But we have to get out of our evangelical subculture public-relations-commercials-for-Christ mentality, dispense with the utilitarian view that says "all art must be evangelical and lead to an altar call," and start communicating on a level that will reach outwards to our world. It's okay to keep preaching to the choir in some ways, but what about those who are out in the congregation and beyond the church doors? Art can be a tool, yes. But it isn't an evangelical hammer. It's a paintbrush, creating images and color and perspectives that may not be easily defined but still touch the heart and soul. Much like the Bible. The Bible isn't a textbook or a crossword puzzle; it's a work of art that expresses the mind, heart, and soul of the ultimate Creator as He reaches out to our minds, hearts, and souls. Besides, I believe that if we truly treat art as art, it will draw people to Christ.

If anything will kill the future of the arts (novels etc.) from a Christian perspective, it will be that we've reduced that art to mere paint-by-numbers.

SUMMARY: CATACOMBS

Captain Robert Slater, director of the government's Special Forces Division, pursues one single goal with relentless determination. His desire is to crush the "roaches" of society who call themselves Christian. Imprisonment, torture, and constant harassment are all part of his toolbox of terror to keep citizens faithful to the official government creed.

Joined together in their flight from these repressive forces, a handful of believers desperately work to survive.

THE SECRET OF ROBINWOOD (ADVENTURES IN ODYSSEY SERIES)

Mark Prescott has a conflict. Despite his close friendship with Patti, he very much desires to be part of a local gang of boys who call themselves the "Israelites" and actively seeks their acceptance. When both he and Patti receive the coveted invitation to join the group, Patti refuses, leaving Mark in a quandary. Patti has been as good a friend to Mark as any boy could have been. How can he reconcile both loyalties? Mark's intense desire to join the group, coupled with his frustration with Patti's stubbornness, tempts Mark to betray his friend and give away her most important secret just to impress the other boys. How will he ever make it up to her and regain her trust?

STRANGE JOURNEY BACK (ADVENTURES IN ODYSSEY SERIES), REVIEWED BY TIMOTHY LAI, FOURTH GRADE

Mark Prescott moved to Odyssey with his mother because his parents had a divorce. Mark thinks they divorced because of him. When he learns about a time machine, the Imagination Station, he sneaks into it at night and goes back to the time of his parents' divorce. There he learns the true reason for their separation.

Karen Mezek (Leimert)

Although presently living in Los Angeles, California, with her husband and three children, Karen Mezek Leimert most truly qualifies as "a citizen of the world." Calling a seventeenth-century castle home at the age of ten, she has subsequently lived in or visited over thirty countries in Europe and Africa. Mezek is now using her artistic ability and her gift for writing to share her love of the world's cultures with young children.

PROFESSIONAL

Education
B.A. in two-dimensional art

Career
Illustrator; creator and conductor of Inside Out, a creative writing group for young girls incarcerated at Central Juvenile Hall, Los Angeles, California

Memberships
Society of Children's Book Writers and Illustrators; Author's Guild

PUBLICATIONS

Juvenile Fiction

The Lost Princess, 1990
Goodnight Blessings, 1994
All the Children of the World, 1996

The Rumpole Series
The Rumpoles and the Barleys, 1988
A Picnic with the Barleys, 1989
Christmas at Rumpole Mansion, 1989
The Katie Series
Katie's Swiss Adventure, 1990
Katie Sails the Nile, 1990
Katie Goes to New York, 1991
Katie's Russian Holiday, 1991
Katie and the Amazon Mystery, 1991
Katie Lost in the South Seas, 1991

Juvenile Nonfiction

The Great Bible Adventure, 1990
In Search of Righteous Radicals, 1992

Books Illustrated

The Money Tree, 1989
Sunita Series
Sunita Makes Friends, 1985
Sunita's Special Day, 1985
Sunita at the Zoo, 1985
The Marble Tree, 1986

PERSONAL

Karen Mezek Leimert's whole life has been research for the books that she writes today. Riding a camel in Egypt, exploring the moors of England, sleeping in tent cabins in Russia, and swimming in the Black Sea are just a few of the adventures she had as a child. Drinking mint tea with a rug merchant in Morocco and celebrating her eleventh birthday under the stars in Turkey are memorable for her, but, she says, "the best adventure of all was living in a real seventeenth-century castle in Switzerland, complete with turrets and towers and winding staircases. There were scary dungeons down below and a mysterious attic up above. I attended the village school and lived in fear of my teacher, Madame Petriquin, a ferocious old lady who rode a bike to school and wore big black boots every day."

An event that caused Mezek to turn to writing as a career occurred when she was ten years old. "My family was traveling through Europe and staying in an old thatched house in the English countryside. It was a rainy, blustery day, and my sister and I wandered into the library where a fire was burning cozily in the fireplace. I pulled a book off the bookshelf, settled in a chair, and began to read *The Lion, the Witch and the Wardrobe.* It was pure magic to me. Although I already loved to read, it was then that I truly fell in love with books and the power of words."

As an adult, Mezek continued her world travel, attending college in the English town of York. "Afterwards, I lived part time in London and part time in a small village in the tiny country of Slovenia. If you look very hard, you might find Slovenia on a map." While living in England, she illustrated four books "that were among the first multicultural books published there."

However, it was when Mezek returned to Los Angeles that she began to write in earnest. The publication of her nineteenth book, *All the Children of the World,* is an effort to explain the various cultures of the world to children. "It was only natural that after my experiences living abroad, I would get the idea to write and illustrate this book. . . . I have a great appreciation for faraway places and especially for the diverse peoples who inhabit our world."

Besides publishing her own books, Mezek volunteers her time at Central Juvenile Hall in Los Angeles, conducting a creative writing workshop that she developed called Inside Out. Involved in the program are girls, ages fourteen to eighteen, who have lived through years of brutal tragedy. Mezek believes that these young girls have important things to say and that we need to listen to them.

Mezek has also developed a creative thinking and writing program called Word Power!, which she uses in elementary and middle schools. Through the program, she shows students the effect that words have on people to inspire, whether for good or for evil. Using writing exercises to guide the students from idea to finished product, she hopes to help them improve their communication skills, their ability to share ideas, and their ability to learn from others.

For all children, Mezek has this message: "Every one of us is an adventurer. Hey, sometimes just getting out of bed in the morning can be an adventure! And making it through a day at school can be an even bigger one. Enjoy the adventures in your life because, who knows, someday you might write a book about them!"

SUMMARY: *ALL THE CHILDREN OF THE WORLD*

Beginning on the inside cover of the book, Mezek, who also illustrated this book, works to inspire readers to seek more information about the cultures of the world. Featuring thirteen different groups of people, including Kashmiris of India; Samoans of Upolu, Western Samoa; and Iowans of the United

States, beautiful illustrations of parents and children are drawn in detailed settings. Mezek has stated that she wanted to show that everyone is the same and that everyone loves their children and has great hopes for them.

A PICNIC WITH THE BARLEYS (THE RUMPOLE SERIES)

A picnic in the country with their friends the Barleys sounds like great fun to the Rumpole family of mice who live in the attic atop the old Rumpole mansion. A glorious day of sunshine, good food to eat, and outdoor games of hide-and-seek, tug-of-war, and follow-the-leader fill the hours until Cordelia's jealousy over Prunella's pink parasol puts her life in danger. Then there is ample opportunity for the mice to practice the attributes of courage and forgiveness.

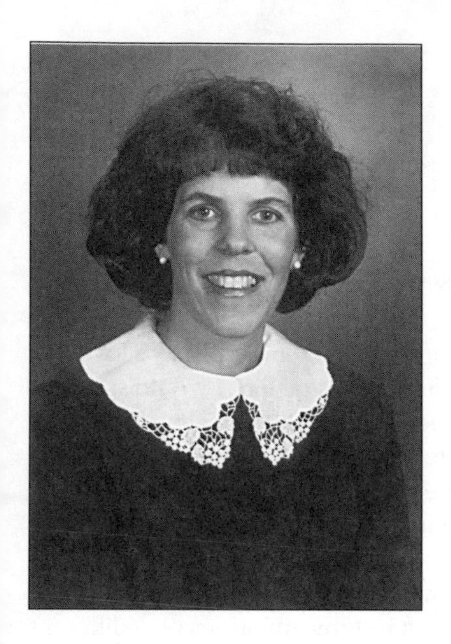

Mary Ann Minatra

Born to Ike and Nilla Avenger in Mascoutal, Illinois, Mary Ann Minatra now makes her home in Arizona with her husband and five children. "I married young and have been a mom and homemaker until I started writing about ten years ago. Between home schooling my five and writing, I don't have a 'hobby time.' But when I do take a break from the above, I enjoy playing tennis, roller blading, and basketball. I love to travel. I enjoy going through antique stores. I have very little time for reading besides for research, but I do enjoy settling in with a good book. I enjoy the old classic movies. And in the summer, after the monsoon rains, I enjoy canoeing with my hubby."

PROFESSIONAL

Education

Attended junior college

PUBLICATIONS

Adult Fiction

The Alcott Legacy Series
The Tapestry, 1993

The Masterpiece, 1994
The Heirloom, 1995
Legacy of Honor Series
Before Night Falls, 1996
A Darkness before Dawn, 1997

PERSONAL

Mary Ann Minatra shares, "As far back as I can remember, I have loved to read, especially fiction. When I was an elementary age girl, I would spin stories as I walked alone to school. I acted them out. I read voraciously. In high school, I feasted on Dickens, Hardy, Dostoyevsky. I went through a 'Russian' period, a 'mystery' period, a 'western' period. Zane Grey is one of my favorite authors. My all-time favorite fiction is *To Kill a Mockingbird.* So, by the time I was seventeen, I knew I wanted some career in writing. In college, I went for a journalism degree, thinking I would someday work on a big-city newspaper. But love, marriage, and children put my ambitions on a different track for a few years. I'm very thankful now that I've changed tracks."

Writing fiction seems a natural venue for Minatra because that is what she loves to read. Writing from a Christian perspective flows from the faith that she chose at the age of eighteen. Although her books are sold largely through Christian bookstores, they can also be found in public library collections. Minatra hopes "that my books are not confined to a strictly Christian audience. If a book is well written and interesting, then it could be read by anyone who loves to read."

Research is very frustrating at times, but Minatra enjoys the process because "I get to learn so much history I didn't get in school. I get a thrill over finding some 'tidbit' like the fact that a black regiment in World War I wore Civil War uniforms because there were no others available. Someone came across them stored away in a Washington, D.C., warehouse. I came across that when I was researching for *The Tapestry* but didn't use it until *The Heirloom.* I research mostly from libraries. I'd like to do more through the Internet but haven't had time to learn it so far."

Minatra's stories usually begin with her personal interest in a time period. As a plot unfolds, she sets her characters into that chosen period. "Then characters and conversations just start filling my head. So I sit down at the computer. I used to have to write it on paper, then transfer it to computer. That was difficult at first because a pen seemed more stimulating than a keyboard. But since I write under a deadline, I had to save time and go directly to the computer. With the first four books, I've written the endings first. That was a great encouragement to me as I wrote, knowing that there was an end in sight. . . . In *The Tapestry,* I actually wrote the beginning, ending, and then the middle. Now, again for the sake of time, I try to write sequentially. Often I end up writing a scene out of order, however, because it comes to mind and I don't want to forget it. I write in terms of 'scenes' in a chapter. A chapter can have at least six scenes."

Minatra's plots are a blending of action, character, and theme. "In *The Heirloom,* I wanted to include the drama of the sinking of the *Lusitania.* That was a big part of the book. But the theme was forgiveness. *The Tapestry* was definitely theme driven. That book is about being persistent in prayer. The *Masterpiece* is also theme oriented. It's about setting expectations and forgiveness. When it comes to theme, the settings may change, the events, and the times, but hopefully the characters come across as real flesh and blood, with struggles, small triumphs, wanting to hear from God, and hanging on to Him."

Before Night Falls, part of the Legacy of Honor series, is more action than theme driven. This series developed as a result of Minatra's fascination with the World War II era. Of special interest was "how a civilized nation could regress to such savagery and barbarism. Could it happen again? Are there parallels to our own times? The story of the Nazi regime is so much more than Adolf Hitler. There are the inspiring stories of the men and women who resisted the Nazi evil, often to the point of death. The current book I'm working on explores the seduction and persecution of the Christian Church in the Third Reich."

The settings and time periods that Minatra chooses are based on "personal bias! *The Tapestry* is set in Illinois as a tribute to the good memories I have of my growing-up days in a small, German, southern Illinois town. A book that is in the developing stage is set in a small Texas town because that is where I spent wonderful summers with my maternal grandparents."

Replying to whether her characters are frequently based on people she knows, Minatra states, "The main character in *The Tapestry* is very much like my husband. The sister and brother in *The Masterpiece* are reflections of my relationship with my older brother. But generally, no, the characters are just fictional creations."

After pondering the question of who or what was most influential in her writing, Minatra answered this way: "Reading has influenced me more than any person. I write books like those that I would like to pick off the shelf and read. The encouragement and support of my family and friends also influences me to keep writing. Knowing that the Lord gave me the gift to write and opened the door to the publishing world, I trust He is still working in me as I write. I could not sit down each day to work if I thought I worked alone. Last year, *The Tapestry* made the Bookstore Journal Best-Seller List in fiction at place number eighteen. That was a real thrill. Honestly, I'd like see more of my books make that list. But that's not in my hands. I just want to be faithful with the gift. As a big, big dream, I think my books would translate into good movies!"

Concerning her reading audience, Minatra states, "I know Christian women are the strength of my reading audience. That's who I get letters from most often. But I have heard from men as well. I know from comments I receive personally, or through letters, that my readers love historical fiction as much as I do."

One of Minatra's goals in her writing "is to make sure that when a reader gets to the end of my book they are left with a good, positive feeling. . . . I like to hear when they have identified with a character. I heard from a reader just this week who named her first child after a character from *The Tapestry*."

In addition to loving it when readers tell her that they could not put down her book until they were finished, Minatra wants them to receive "an education regarding a specific time in history." Most important is that something in her books "turns their thoughts to the Author of all things."

Pondering the future of Christian fiction, Minatra writes, "Well, I'm just a housewife out in a little Arizona town, so the world of Christian fiction is a little removed from my expertise. I do know the market has exploded in the last few years and is therefore very competitive. Any time period you're interested in is represented: science fiction, fantasy, contemporary. I just hope I can make a worthwhile contribution to the field."

SUMMARY: *THE MASTERPIECE* (THE ALCOTT LEGACY SERIES)

Set in Mississippi, *The Masterpiece* introduces readers to the Alcott family as Meg and her brother Andy are facing issues left in the aftermath of the Civil War. Meg Alcott, whose life in Illinois has been filled with many disappointments, accepts an invitation to visit her Mississippi relatives. It is there that she finds some fulfillment in establishing a school for the children of former slaves. Is it enough to fill the void of love that she feels?

Invited to recover from serious injuries at the elegant southern mansion of his friend Patrick Cash, Andy Alcott struggles against the growing love that he feels for his friend's wife. Hoping to escape the pressure of his growing love, he returns to a life at sea. Will he be able to forget?

Minatra has the gift of creating characters that are real. Her descriptive ability draws readers into the lives of this brother and sister from the first sentence, involving them in the young people's struggles to find their destinies and their loves. She manages in this, as in her other works, to weave numerous subplots into an intelligible and compelling whole.

Alan Morris

Joining his famous father, Gilbert, and creative sister, Lynn, Alan Morris completes the unique triangle of a family united not only by faith but also by fiction. Although Gilbert might have been the original inspiration for his initiation into the field of writing Christian novels and Lynn his encourager, Morris adds his own personal blend of adventure, one-of-a-kind characters, and compelling settings to each of his works. Simultaneously publishing as coauthor with his prolific father while establishing his reputation as an author alone, Morris is well on his way to continuing the family tradition of excellence in inspirational storytelling.

PROFESSIONAL

Education

Ouachita Baptist University, two years, in accounting (major) and English literature (minor)

Career

U.S. Army; U.S. Postal Service

Awards

Best Book Young Adult Library Services Award Nomination, *By Honor Bound,* 1996; Gold Medallion Book Award Nomination, *By Honor Bound,* 1997

PUBLICATIONS

Adult Fiction

Katy Steele Adventures Series (with Gilbert Morris)
Tracks of Deceit, 1995
Imperial Intrigue, 1996
The Depths of Malice, 1998
Guardians of the North Series
By Honor Bound, 1995
Heart of Valor, 1996
Bright Sword of Justice, 1997
Between Earth and Sky, 1998
Wings of Healing, 1999
Omega Trilogy (with Gilbert and Lynn Morris)
The Beginning of Sorrows, 1999

PERSONAL

As the father of one son, Zachary, and an obviously active man who enjoys tennis, baseball, and swimming, Alan Morris has the uncanny ability to write about women convincingly, without condescension, and often with tender amusement. Describing his books as action oriented, he still manages to create leading ladies with individual personalities and temperaments, ones to whom his primarily female audience can easily relate, something validated by the fact that most of his fan letters are from housewives and home-schooled girls. However, Morris observes that men would like his books, but, as he observes, "that branch of the market is very hard to penetrate." Perhaps men are reading his books but simply are not writing to him.

Morris's first attempt at writing inspirational fiction came after he had taken a test recommended by his father in his book *How to Write a Christian Novel.* After examining the test results, Gilbert related to his son that he had talent and that, if he would polish his skills, he showed the potential for success. Alan's response to his joy in writing can best be recounted in his own words: "I've always been fascinated with the printed word, and the happiest moment of my life, besides accepting Jesus and the birth of my son, was when I finally received the first copy of my first book." He shares that he has no interest in publishing for the secular market. "I will not compromise my God-given talent by throwing in gratuitous sex and violence. Because of that, there is no other market except the Christian one, and I'm very satisfied with that."

Describing his research process as "meticulous," Morris shares that it was a sobering experience to receive a letter from a person who truly loved his book yet pointed out that he had attributed a poem to the wrong poet. "I've since thrown away the reference book that caused that. Readers are important and are not stupid. They should be able to depend on the author when he says that something happened at a certain time in history."

When asked about his schedule for writing, Morris reports that his goal is to compose about five pages in the morning, punctuated by lunch and a nap, followed by five pages in the evening, "preferably before 5 P.M." This is, of course, rearranged by necessary research and new ideas that arise along the way. "There are times while writing that I am forced to stop and look up something pertaining to history, fashion, and so on that ultimately leads to distractions. I estimate five pages a day to be a good, steady workday—anything more is icing on the cake."

Sharing that in recent works he is building more on character development than he has in the past, Morris relates that he often does base his creations on people whom he knows or has observed. For example, Reena O'Donnell, "the missionary heroine in the Guardians of the North series, is physically based on the actress Courtney Cox. I chose her because she can appear both vulnerable and strong at the same time and has that innocent look."

Some authors have influenced Morris's writing because of his longstanding admiration for their work, such as John D. Macdonald, Pat Conroy (for his descriptive ability), and Larry McMurtry (for his "skill in creating quirky characters"). Others have affected him simply because they have written what he is currently reading; he notes Lawana Blackwell as an example. His all-time favorite novel is *Lonesome Dove*.

When asked how his beliefs have shaped his writing, Morris replied, "I like to spread the Message, and when I'm writing, I'm enthusiastic about it. I hope that shows in my work—I'm of the belief that it does. Obviously, writing is also work, and on those days that it seems like drudgery, I pray and ask the Lord to make me excited about it again, to put it back in perspective."

Like all writers, Morris would like to "be on the best-seller list someday." He sees such popularity as a means of reaching more people. His special desire is to see his work in "foreign printings and schools." With his careful research, as reflected in attention to historical and geographical detail, his books would be great candidates for the secondary Christian school classroom. Other goals for his readers include that they will "appreciate good, clean writing and take the message to heart—that they will believe in the characters and care about what happens to them."

In observing the present condition and future possibilities of Christian fiction, Morris observes, "It's apparent that the secular market is standing up and taking notice of our sales from [Frank] Peretti and Janette Oke. They want a piece of the pie, and that is good for spreading the word of God if they don't limit Christian content. Also, I believe that historical series fiction is going the way of the dinosaur—stand-alone contemporary books are the future."

SUMMARY: *TRACKS OF DECEIT* (THE KATY STEELE ADVENTURES SERIES)

When John Steele bids his daughter, Katy, farewell and returns to his job as a railroad detective, they have just enjoyed a special time of sharing together. As they part, he reflects on a familiar biblical passage and reminds his daughter, "Two are better than one." Little does Katy realize the significance that these words will hold in the days to come.

Within twenty-four hours, her secure, if stifling, world is shattered by the news of her father's death from an apparent heart attack. Katy finds herself feeling more alone than ever in her young life, and the person who seems least understanding is her Aunt Agnes, with whom she lives. Having been educated to be a teacher but never having been really comfortable with the role, Katy knows that this change in fortune may be her last chance at breaking out of the mold cast carefully by Aunt Agnes. When her knowledge of chemistry leads her to discover that her father's death was not of natural causes but rather that he was murdered, Katy applies to the railroad officials as a replacement for her beloved parent.

Because the jobs available to women in the 1860s do not include that of detective, she finds the gender barrier almost impossible to breach. The only option available to her to secure the position that she so strongly desires is to be accompanied by a man. The greatest difficulty with that requirement is that Katy knows no men. Her life has been sheltered and restricted by Aunt Agnes, who was for years locked in the bonds of matrimony with an unfaithful spouse and thus sees all men as suspect. Her overprotection of her niece has been thorough and successful.

Quite by accident, Katy stumbles on Sam Bronte, an unemployed actor who answers an ad she had placed in the paper. Through a series of fast-moving adventures, the unlikely pair is brought face to face with John Steele's killers, and it is then that Katy comes to understand how true is the proverb "Two are better than one."

In Katy Steele, Gilbert and Alan Morris have created a heroine who is determined and strong yet vulnerable and feminine. She does not retreat from difficulty or danger, and she reflects characteristics that are warm and compassionate. With single-mindedness, she pursues those who are responsible for her father's death while battling with a range of emotions that have the potential to draw her off her set course.

This novel clearly depicts the dangers involved in laying the transcontinental railroad and shines light on the difficulty created by prejudice against immigrant workers. Through this story, one develops a new respect for the Chinese and Irish pioneers who were responsible for putting down the tracks taken for granted so readily by those in the twentieth century.

BRIGHT SWORD OF JUSTICE (GUARDIANS OF THE NORTH SERIES)

Liam O'Donnell had planned to surprise his sisters, Megan and Reena, by simply riding into their settlement. However, he had not anticipated snow blindness; the dubious aid of a band of outlaws who sometimes kill just for the sport, or being arrested by the love of Reena's life, Hunter Stone of the Northwest Mounted Police.

Reena O'Donnell had planned to continue being the only missionary to the Blackfoot Indians after gaining the confidence of most of them and sharing her faith in Christ with some. That was before the handsome, young, idealistic Jack Sheffield arrived at their camp bearing his Bible, his zeal for evangelizing the lost, and his agricultural knowledge, which has the potential of wresting food from the land and being financially beneficial to the tribe.

Hunter Stone had planned one day to look more closely into what being committed to Christ really involved and to decide whether he was ready to lay aside bitterness and anger over past injuries and take that eternal step toward a new life.

In the winter of 1874, on the central Canadian prairies, the schemes, dreams, fears, and joys of all four were woven together for a time and brought to reckoning by both a physical and a spiritual Sword of Justice.

Gilbert Morris

It comes as no surprise when Gilbert Morris, a prolific writer, reports that he has always been a reader. Indeed, he shares that he "came into the world asking for a book." It was such a love of reading that led the former English professor to choose to write fiction from a Christian perspective. Evidently, Morris had just the approach that American readers were awaiting, and his creativity found a channel. In the past twelve years he has written over 100 novels, of which hundreds of thousands of copies have been sold.

Yet to say that Morris is productive or to designate him as simply being a prolific writer understates his significant contribution to inspirational fiction. A quick glance at the education, career, or professional accomplishments of this pacesetting author verifies that he has wasted little time in his soon-to-be seventy years. As teacher, pastor, and professor, he has touched many lives on a personal level. However, when one considers those who have been enlightened, enriched, or simply entertained through his role as a full-time writer, the number multiplies by the thousands.

Statistics serve as concrete evidence of book sales, and sales would seem to be representative of reader response. The House of Winslow series, following the history of America through the form of a family tree, has sold well over 1.25 million copies. The Appomattox Saga series, focusing on the Civil War and its effects on an extended family, lists sales of more than 250,000. The American Odyssey series, another historical fiction set, numbers over 100,000 books sold. The Wakefield Dynasty series, reaching deep into European heritage, has sales totaling more than 90,000. Finally, the Reno Western Saga series, focusing on the American West, notes more than 80,000 copies sold. These titles include only adult series written by Morris alone.

Morris also has the distinction of being an encourager of other writers. He is one of a select few to write in tandem as well as alone. His partnership has blessed fans of Christian fiction with the creative gifts of his friends Robert Funderburk and Aaron McCarver, as well as those of two of his children, Alan and Lynn Morris.

Readers and would-be writers might stand in awe of Morris's phenomenal success. Yet when asked about his consistent motivation to write, he responds with shades of the past influencing the present. He shares that he is compelled to write from surviving the Great Depression with its "if you want to eat, then you work" philosophy. If he wants to publish, then he must write.

Accompanying Morris through education, career, and life is Johnnie, his wife of nearly fifty years. He readily acknowledges the contribution that his partner has made to his knowledge of feminine psychology. He reports that many of his female characters reflect aspects of Johnnie, especially her strength and grace. The Morrises have been blessed with three children: Alan, Stacy, and Valerie Lynn.

PROFESSIONAL

Education

Ph.D., concentrating in eighteenth-century English literature, University of Arkansas, Fayetteville; M.S.E., in secondary education, Arkansas State University; B.A. in English (major) and history (minor), Arkansas State University

Career

Full-time novelist, 1990 to present; speaker at numerous conferences and workshops for writers; professor of English, World Evangelization College, Baton Rouge, Louisiana, 1986–1990; professor of English, Ouachita Baptist University, Arkadelphia, Arkansas, 1962–1986; high school English teacher, 1956–1961; pastor of Southern Baptist churches in Arkansas, 1950–1962

Awards

First Place for Dramatic Poetry, Mississippi Poetry Contest, 1963; Second Place for Short Fiction, Arkansas Round Table, 1970; Finalist for Poetry of the Year, "Last Chance," 1973; First Place, Jesse Stuart Poetry Contest, "Tennessee Burial," 1974; First Place, International Literary Contest, "No Escape for Ernie," 1978; Second Place, Light and Life Writing Contest, "Milton's Curse,"

1980; Amy Manning Award for Christian Fiction for short story, "The End of Daisy Potter," 1982; Golden Quill Award for Christian Fiction, *The Indentured Heart,* 1985; Angel Award, *The Wounded Yankee,* 1991; Angel Award, *The Union Belle* (ten other Angel Awards received), 1992; Gold Medallion Finalist several times; Angel Awards three times for the House of Winslow series and twice for the Appomattox Saga series

Memberships

College Teachers of English, 1989; Popular Culture Association, Texas, 1983; Arkansas Teachers of College English, 1970; Modern Language Association, 1965, 1972, 1975, 1985; National Council of Teachers of English, 1963, 1979; Arkansas Teachers of English, 1961

PUBLICATIONS

Adult Fiction

All That Glitters, 1999
The House of Winslow Series
The Honorable Impostor, 1986
The Captive Bride, 1987
The Indentured Heart, 1988
The Gentle Rebel, 1988
The Saintly Buccaneer, 1989
The Holy Warrior, 1989
The Reluctant Bridegroom, 1990
The Last Confederate, 1990
The Dixie Widow, 1991
The Wounded Yankee, 1991
The Union Belle, 1992
The Final Adversary, 1992
The Crossed Sabres, 1993
The Valiant Gunman, 1993
The Gallant Outlaw, 1994
The Jeweled Spur, 1994
The Yukon Queen, 1995
The Rough Rider, 1995
Iron Lady, 1996
The Silver Star, 1997
The Shadow Portrait, 1998
The Flying Cavalier, 1999

The Liberty Bell Series
- *Sound the Trumpet,* 1995
- *Song in a Strange Land,* 1996
- *Tread upon the Lion,* 1996
- *Arrow of the Almighty,* 1997
- *Wind from the Wilderness,* 1998
- *The Right Hand of God,* 1999

Cheney Duvall, M.D., Series (with Lynn Morris)
- *The Stars for a Light,* 1994
- *Shadow of the Mountains,* 1994
- *A City Not Forsaken,* 1995
- *Toward the Sunrising,* 1996
- *Secret Place of Thunder,* 1996
- *In the Twilight, in the Evening,* 1997
- *Island of the Innocent,* 1999

The Spirit of Appalachia Series (with Aaron McCarver)
- *Over the Misty Mountains,* 1997
- *Beyond the Quiet Hills,* 1997
- *The Spirit of Appalachia,* 1998
- *Among the King's Soldiers,* 1999

Price of Liberty Series (with Robert Funderburk)
- *A Call to Honor,* 1993
- *The Color of the Star,* 1993
- *All the Shining Young Men,* 1993
- *The End of Glory,* 1993
- *A Silence in Heaven,* 1994
- *A Time to Heal,* 1994

The Far Fields Series (with Robert Funderburk)
- *Beyond the River,* 1994
- *The Remnant,* 1997

The Appomattox Saga Series
- *A Covenant of Love,* 1992
- *Gate of His Enemies,* 1992
- *Where Honor Dwells,* 1993
- *Land of the Shadow,* 1993
- *Out of the Whirlwind,* 1994
- *The Shadow of His Wings,* 1994
- *Wall of Fire,* 1995
- *Stars in Their Courses,* 1995
- *Chariots in the Smoke,* 1997
- *Witness in Heaven,* 1998

The Wakefield Dynasty Series
The Sword of Truth, 1994
The Winds of God, 1994
The Shield of Honor, 1995
The Fields of Glory, 1995
The Ramparts of Heaven, 1997
The Song of Princes, 1997
A Gathering of Eagles, 1998
Reno Western Saga Series
Reno, 1992
Rimrock, 1992
Ride the Wild River, 1992
Boomtown, 1992
Valley Justice, 1995
Lone Wolf, 1995
The Katy Steele Adventures Series (with Alan Morris)
Tracks of Deceit, 1995
Imperial Intrigue, 1996
The Depths of Malice, 1998
American Odyssey Series
A Time to Be Born, 1994
A Time to Die, 1994
A Time to Laugh, 1995
A Time to Weep, 1996
A Time of War, 1997
A Time to Build, 1998
Danielle Ross Mysteries Series
Guilt by Association, 1991
The Final Curtain, 1991
Deadly Deception, 1992
Revenge at the Rodeo, 1993
The Quality of Mercy, 1993
Race with Death, 1994
Chronicles of the Golden Frontier Series
Unseen Riches, 1999

Juvenile Fiction

The Seven Sleepers Series
Flight of the Eagles, 1994
The Gates of Neptune, 1994

The Sword of Camelot, 1995
The Caves That Time Forgot, 1995
Winged Raiders of the Desert, 1995
Empress of the Underworld, 1996
Voyage of the Dolphin, 1996
Attack of the Amazons, 1996
Escape with the Dream Maker, 1997
The Final Kingdom, 1997

Bonnets and Bugles Series
Drummer Boy at Bull Run, 1995
Yankee Belles in Dixie, 1995
The Secret of Richmond Manor, 1995
The Soldier Boy's Discovery, 1996
Blockade Runner, 1996
The Gallant Boys of Gettysburg, 1996
The Battle of Lookout Mountain, 1996
Encounter at Cold Harbor, 1997
Fire over Atlanta, 1997
Bring the Boys Home, 1997

Time Navigators Series
The Dangerous Voyage, 1993
Vanishing Clues, 1996
Race against Time, 1997

Ozark Adventures Series
The Bucks of Goober Holler, 1994
The Rustlers of Panther Gap, 1994
The Phantom of the Circus, 1994

Dixie Morris Animal Adventure Series
Dixie and Iran, 1998
Dixie and Jumbo, 1998
Dixie and Stripes, 1998
Dixie and Perry, 1998
Dixie and Champ, 1998
Dixie and Bandit, 1998
Dixie and Dolly, 1998
Dixie and Sandy, 1998

Daystar Voyages Series
Revenge of the Space Pirate, 1998
Escape from the Red Comet, 1998
Dark Spell over Morlandria, 1998
Secret of the Planet Makon, 1998

Wizards of the Galaxy, 1998
Dangers of the Rainbow Nebula, 1999

Adult Nonfiction

Those Who Knew Him, 1997
How to Write (and Sell) a Christian Novel, 1994

Articles

Articles in numerous periodicals, including *Christianity and Literature, Southwest Review, Arkansas Quarterly Review, Collected Studies: Council of Teachers of English, Theology and Literature,* and *Learning Today*

Poems

More than 200 poems in periodicals, including *Hyacinths, Southwest Quarterly, Anthology of Southern Poetry, Arkansas Baptist, Arkansas Poetry Review, Arkansas Gazette, Missouri Quarterly, Wisconsin Poetry Magazine, Notable American Poets, Midwest Poetry Review, Southern Verse,* and *Christian Review*

PERSONAL

Labeling himself a "late bloomer," Gilbert Morris has nonetheless become one of the most popular authors of Christian fiction today. Since publishing his first novel in 1986, he has worked at the pace of producing twelve to twenty books a year, spanning genres from historical eras to futuristic times. Because Morris is such a versatile writer, one might wonder about his investigative process and how he makes the past, present, and future come to life so vividly. Describing his research process, Morris uses terms that seem paradoxical. He reports himself to be both "haphazard" and "intense." The "haphazard" classification springs from the fact that when he is examining a specific period, event, or place, he simply goes to the library, takes home lots of books describing the topic, and "reads, reads, reads." It is his immersion in the subjects that lend the intensity and realism that have led many readers to remark that they have learned much more from his novels about a specific event in history than they ever did from a history book.

The next obvious question would be, "How do you accomplish so much?" Morris relates that his method of writing has been modified since he had open-heart surgery. When this literally put him on his back, he was forced to use dictation, a method that he continues to use today. Although he puts his plots and characters on the computer, the narration will often be done with the use of a tape recorder, which his secretary later transcribes to disk. Morris claims that consistency is not one of his artistic strengths and admits that he works best when the pressure is on—sometimes staying up half the night to meet a deadline. However, he tells would-be authors that if they plan to be successful, they must discipline themselves to write whether they feel like writing or not. "I don't let the blank screen intimidate me. . . . I never wait for inspiration, I just keep on writing. If I have two chapters to write this morning, I'll write two chapters. . . . There's no mystique to writing, I just do it . . . it's just a lot of hard work and determination and putting in the hours actually writing. There's no secret to that."

When asked whom he sees as his audience, Morris responded that eighty percent of his readers are women and children, although he also receives some mail from men. He credits his ability to write about women and his knowledge of feminine responses to his wife, Johnnie, stating that he has learned much from her.

Morris's own reading has taken him through a wide variety of books. As a young person, his appetite for reading was satisfied with dog books, horse books, and detective stories. He reports having read all the Tarzan books at one time or another, and he was a Nancy Drew fan as well. The exposure to both the classic and the popular writing of others has given him "rich ground for invention." When one examines the styles of writers whose works have been influential in Morris's adult life, one begins to understand how he has had the courage and creativity to attempt genres as varied as futuristic and historical fiction, romance, mysteries, and westerns. He admires John D. MacDonald, a writer of detective stories, and the classic writer Jack London for their ability to move the reader. He sees Hemingway as an example of a writer who was successful in presenting his view of life clearly to his readers. In the field of Christian novelists, the masterful C. S. Lewis and contemporary Max Lucado have gained Morris's approval. With such varied interests, is it any wonder that he attracts readers across age and gender lines?

Morris views theme as the most significant literary element of his works. Characters are created specifically to illustrate a chosen theme, and action is governed by how a character then responds. For example, if he chooses jealousy as a theme, the work will focus on what jealousy will do to a person if that jealousy is not overcome. Therefore, when planning a novel, he works from theme to character to action. One theme pervasive in all of Morris's works is a person's relationship to God. In each book, "someone goes through the conversion process." Also important to him is the realistic unfolding of the Christian life. Combating the philosophy that everyone lives "happily ever after," his characters are styled to illustrate that a lifetime of learning, study, and openness are necessary to this effort. It is just such honest conflict that he portrays in his novels, whatever the genre.

Although elements of himself can be found in some of his books and some qualities for his feminine roles are drawn from his relationship with his wife, Morris does not try to pattern his characters after people he knows. As a writer of so many books, "I haven't known enough people to populate them all." Aspects of some of his male characters are remembered from an elderly gentleman named Robert Mitchell, obviously much admired by Morris.

Morris has a number of goals for his writing. First, he wants to survive as a full-time author. Second, he makes no apologies for wanting to simply entertain. Perhaps that is why his works are so popular. Third, he desires to convey his spiritual belief that God is the answer for man. He demonstrates the Creator's power by giving his character a weakness that becomes the balm for healing when the character surrenders to God.

In regard to the future of Christian fiction, Morris speculates that it will grow larger, although it is difficult to predict which books will be the big sellers. He does see a trend in interest toward contemporary fiction instead of historical themes. He also suggests that an adjustment in the size of the books would make them easier to shelve in secular bookstores and therefore increase sales to the mass market. With both his son and his daughter now writing, he is hoping that the field will continue to prosper.

SUMMARY: *THE DIXIE WIDOW* (THE HOUSE OF WINSLOW SERIES)

Capturing the raw emotions aroused by the conflict and pain of the Civil War, Morris continues his saga of the Winslow family in volume 9 of the House of Winslow series. Like so many families, the Winslows find themselves split on both sides by the issues of the war. Filled with anger by the death of her husband at Yankee hands, Belle, the daughter of Sky and Rebekah Winslow, determines to use her northern family connections to spy for the Confederate cause. Her actions bring more sorrow to the family by bringing about the death of her distant cousin Lowell, a soldier in the Union army. Consumed with hatred for Belle, Lowell's normally placid brother Davis joins the Union forces to seek revenge on those who took the life of the one he loved.

In the twists and turns of their lives, Belle and Davis are brought face to face with each other and with the results of their bitterness and hate. Only grace can intervene and heal their torn and broken lives.

THE SWORD OF TRUTH (THE WAKEFIELD DYNASTY SERIES)

Born into the meanest of circumstances in the year 1507, Myles Morgan has little hope of ever being more than a serf, living in a hovel on the estate of the Bourneville family. The rigid rules of English society in the sixteenth century leave little room for improving one's status. However, at the death of his mother, the identity of his father is revealed, and he finds himself the acknowledged heir of Sir Robert Wakefield, lord of a great manor. Sir Robert and his wife, Jane, take Myles into their home and their hearts, teaching him the skills and the manners appropriate to his new station.

As Myles is introduced to the privileges of nobility, he finds himself surrounded by the political intrigue and moral decay of the court of Henry VIII. Having become the friend of William Tyndale, who has given his life to making the Scriptures available to even the simple plowmen of England, Myles finds himself at odds with many powerful people, including the king. Crisis comes when he must choose between the faith exhibited by his mother and the enticement of the life represented by the beautiful but spoiled Isabella Bourneville.

The Wakefield Dynasty stands apart as a series rich in historical detail. In it Morris successfully portrays the feel and the fact of English life in the 1500s, the reality of the struggle for religious freedom, and an understanding of how events surrounding the lives of his characters fit into the larger sweep of world history.

WHERE HONOR DWELLS (THE APPOMATTOX SAGA SERIES)

Living as a riverboat gambler since he was a teenager has prepared Jake Hardin for almost all dangerous situations. He has learned how to read the eyes of other card players, how to predict a bluff, and how to draw and fire a gun quickly enough to save his life on the shortest of notice. Therefore, when life deals him a hand that seems a bit less than fair and he is offered a way out that involves deception and a cash reward large enough to live well for the rest of his life, he thinks that the stakes are about reasonable. All he has to do is play the role of a spoiled, self-centered, rich rebel for a time while the near stranger plays out his insidious scheme.

What Jake does not count on is the way in which his spirit is warmed as he is welcomed home by a whole house full of relatives. Nor is he prepared for the way in which his heart responds to a beautiful, spirited lady who makes all the other risks he has taken seem small by comparison. The only problem is that he has betrayed the trust of the family that nurtures him by pretending to be someone he is not, and the woman who has stolen his heart believes him to be her prodigal brother.

For readers who have enjoyed the first two volumes of the Appomattox Saga series, this third in the series will be a real treat, as it continues with the next generation of the Rocklin family, focusing on Amy's children. For those who are new to the series, this novel easily stands alone but likely will spark a desire to read those stories leading up to and following after it. Strength of family, pride in community and country, and the love of God are themes that run throughout this series of Civil War novels.

THE COLOR OF THE STAR (PRICE OF LIBERTY SERIES)

In the first volume of this series, *A Call to Honor*, readers meet the mainstream residents of Liberty, Georgia, and suffer with them as the advent of World War II explodes into their lives, bringing about permanent change. This book, the second of the series, introduces the elite and the outcast of the town and explores the war's effect on those on the periphery of society.

The survival of small, unwanted, neglected Jordan Simms, left in the care of her eccentric and poverty-stricken aunt Annie, forms the core of this novel. Through Annie's hard work, thrift, and scavenging, these two rejects from society eke a living from the ground and the scrap heap of Liberty. Their near destitute circumstances arouse the best in some of the townsfolk and the worst in others. Yet through Annie's determination and sacrifice, Jordan finds love and acceptance while developing a faithful servant's heart.

Annie's two best friends in Liberty—a black minister and J. T., the formerly prosperous lawyer-turned-alcoholic—symbolize the two warring sides of her temperament. On the one hand she is unselfish to a fault, but on the other she is bound by a dark secret that drives her to drink. Although successful at providing a secure place for Jordan to survive, Annie is herself teetering on the brink of self-destruction.

When Jordan grows old enough to get a job, she finds after-school employment in the office of Dr. Simmons, the small town's respected physician. As the doctor comes to recognize qualities in the dedicated teen that he believes would enable her to develop into a fine nurse, he sets about to secure a scholarship for her. However, because of her dedication to Annie and her aunt's failing health, Jordan is unable to complete the training offered. Instead she later chooses to enlist in the Navy, using her knowledge to serve her country and to give her ailing aunt much-needed financial support.

As Jordan is finding her place in the world outside of Liberty, across town another battle is raging. Billy Christmas, who has always been given everything he wants (except the freedom to choose his own friends), seeks to become his own person, apart from his wealthy, status-bound parents. With the escalation of the war, Billy begs his father to allow him to quit college and enlist in the armed forces. Denying support of his son's decision, the former general states emphatically that Billy can do no less than stay in college and become an officer. Anything less is beneath the family tradition. Billy eventually chooses this issue to become his defining moment, defying his father's wishes and enlisting in the Marines.

Jordan and Billy, former schoolmates, are reunited on the island of Guadalcanal, and Billy is able to pursue the relationship with her that had been denied by his parents. It is in this combat zone that heroism, death, and eternity meet with satisfying, if harrowing, results. The reader is catapulted into the carnage for which the island became famous, experiencing the sights, sounds, and tastes that demonstrate the horrors of war.

In the Price of Liberty, Morris and coauthor Funderburk have created a nostalgic series that transports readers back to the time when patriotism was an established national value, popular tunes were shared without embarrassment, and the traditional family was the norm. The strength of these novels lies not only in memorable character development but also in reminding the reader that fighting for one's country is a noble act. The prologue to *The Color of the Star* contains one of the most vivid characterizations in current Christian fiction and might well serve as a model for the novice writer.

WINGED RAIDERS OF THE DESERT (THE SEVEN SLEEPERS SERIES)

In this book, Morris takes his young readers into the surrealistic world of the People of the Desert. Resisting the efforts of the evil Lord Necros to force them into slavery, these bold tribes must constantly defend their camps from the attacks of the Winged Ones. Enlisted to service by Lord Necros, the Winged Ones raid the camps to capture all they can and kill those who resist.

Answering the pleas of the People of the Desert for help in their fight, the Seven Sleepers find themselves captured and forced into slavery. Slowly finding favor with their captors, the young Sleepers are also taught to fly and to use this newfound skill to defeat the evil Lord and bring peace between the tribes.

Lynn Morris

The fact that she considers her rather special childhood as fairly "typical," with two parents, a brother, and a sister, bears witness to the fact that the values of faith and family are a natural part of the life fabric of Lynn Morris. The academic environment that the child of a college professor assimilated and the spiritual climate surrounding the home of a minister perhaps influenced Morris's choice to take her B.A. degree at a Christian university and later gave her the impetus to start her own accounting business. Currently, Morris lives in Runaway Bay, Texas, with her daughter, Dixie Lynn.

Perhaps readers would question Morris's definition of the word "typical," considering that her father, Gilbert Morris, is one of the most popular authors of Christian novels on the contemporary market and that her brother, Alan, is a fast-rising star in the same field. Morris herself stands quite tall beside the two males as co-creator of the Cheney Duvall, M.D., series and winner of two awards from her first seven published volumes.

PROFESSIONAL

Education

B.A. in accounting, Ouachita Baptist University

Career
Accountant; writer

Awards
Angel Award, *Shadow of the Mountains,* 1995; Award of Merit, Angel Awards, *Toward the Sunrising,* 1997

PUBLICATIONS

Adult Fiction

The Balcony, 1997

Coauthored with Gilbert Morris

Cheney Duvall, M.D., Series
The Stars for a Light, 1994
Shadow of the Mountains, 1994
A City Not Forsaken, 1995
Toward the Sunrising, 1996
A Secret Place of Thunder, 1996
In the Twilight, in the Evening, 1997
Island of the Innocent, 1999

PERSONAL

It comes as no surprise that Lynn Morris names her father as the one who first encouraged her to write. However, the fact that she read his essay "How to Write a Christian Novel" and then attempted to write, just as any other novice might, may give hope to other aspiring writers. (Gilbert has since expanded that piece into a book that is available to others who would like to try their hand at the market.) When she tried his suggestions and shared her efforts with the seasoned writer, he saw promise, and a delightful new writing team of father and daughter was born.

Part of the charm of Morris's writing is that she successfully carries out her desire to "depict in a natural and unforced way the day-to-day life of a Christian." This is accomplished by including Christian themes, such as denying temptation, facing spiritual pride, and hearing the voice of God. Always she incorporates a salvation experience, seamlessly weaving it in as an integral part of the plot.

Morris describes her research process as "obsessive," and her many readers would attest to the fact that they feel as if they were living out the experiences of her characters through the sights, sounds, smells, and tastes of her settings. "No matter what I'm researching, I develop the most insatiable hunger to learn everything about it, whether it's the location of the theaters in Manhattan in 1867, or what kind of crinolines the women were wearing in 1865 to 1870, or exactly how a craniotomy was performed in the nineteenth century. Generally, I allow two months for research, though it never seems to be time enough.

"For the process itself, I naturally go first to bookstores and then to libraries. In general, there are always certain items that must be researched for any book: (1) The location. I always have a city map practically memorized by the time I finish a book, or in the case of a fictional geographic location, I create my own map. If travel is involved, I always have maps depicting the progress of the travel: mode of transportation, time allotted, interim cities, or stops. (2) The dwellings and other sites. I generally draw floor plans of all homes and other major sites, such as workplaces. Then I furnish them. (3) The physical conflict. Is it something, such as a war or a disease, such as the cholera plague depicted in one of my books? For another of my books, I learned all about boxing . . . in another it was voodoo curses; in another it was gunfights. (4) The spiritual theme. I try always to study the Christian theme (forgiveness, freedom from fear, temptation, and so on) that the Lord would have me illustrate in each book. (5) Characters. Before I begin each book, I try to have a complete list of characters (major and minor) completed, including birth dates, physical characteristics, history, and personality traits."

Morris describes her plots as action driven, with conflict coming first, followed by theme. Characters then mold themselves into what is required to carry off the idea. However, the avid reader of the Cheney Duvall, M.D., series would be reluctant to admit to themselves that the unique pair of Cheney and her Iron Man, Shiloh, did not really exist in the mid-1800s, so realistically are they portrayed. Perhaps the secret of Morris's successful characterization is that she peoples her novels with relatives, acquaintances, or even celebrities who have impressed her in some way. In one novel, two elderly ladies are based on her own great-aunts; in another, the physical description of a hero is that of a famous baseball player.

Influences on her writing career are varied, but Morris gives most of the credit for her initial interest in attempting the art to her father, Gilbert. She describes him as "a wonderful writer, a dedicated Christian," and she trusts his professional opinion because "he has a Ph.D. in English. He's read just about everything, he knows just about everything about writing, and he's a talented and experienced teacher. My first rule: If my dad says to do it *this* way, then do it this way. If he says *not* to do it, better not do it." She classifies him as "an infallible authority on the craft of writing."

Other influences that Morris sees on all writers are their past experiences and environments, personal opinions, how they spend leisure time, and their daydreams and hopes. She observes that the list is "endless." She states that all these are a part of her writing also, yet she finds herself becoming more dependent on the Lord to use the gift that He has given her. "I ask for His help for physical strength and stamina, for strength of mind and will, for a perfect comprehension of what He wants me to write about, and most especially for the skillful use of words to convey to my readers exactly what He wants them to absorb."

Morris shares that her own personal reading choices are "wide and varied and always have been." She emphasizes that "what a person reads is always reflected in the personality, opinions, and state of mind." Authors, both contemporary and classic, who have been reflected in her writing include William F. Buckley Jr., "with his love of big words," whom she emulates when appropriate, and Charles Dickens, "who gave even one-time walk-on characters a personality, an identity, and [did] not just present them as a device."

One book that has greatly influenced Morris is her father's *How to Write (and Sell) a Christian Novel*. She actually came across the text of this work when her father gave her a computer, and she "accidentally" discovered it on the hard drive. She printed it out, "out of curiosity," and read it. "I was so impressed—the principles and rules were right there, clear and simple—I thought, 'I can do this!' As it turned out, I could."

Other works, quite different from the adult fiction and nonfiction that have inspired Morris, are J. R. R Tolkien's Lord of the Rings series. "I stayed up for an entire weekend reading this trilogy, and that's when I learned that I'd rather read than sleep!" The mysteries of Nancy Drew; the Cherry Ames, R.N., books; Madeleine L'Engle's *A Wrinkle in Time;* and *The Scarlet Pimpernel* by Baroness Orczy complete her childhood favorites.

Beyond all human influence, Morris states that her spiritual beliefs supply motivation and inspiration. She views her writing as a ministry rather than as a career choice. She classifies writing as a spiritual gift, "though it is not listed in 1 Corinthians 12" as such. "I like to receive gifts, and a ministry is the end result of a gift the Lord has given me. My goal in writing is to cherish and perfect the gift and then to pour it out into a ministry. That in turn will mean that my gift and my relationship with my Lord will be always refreshed, renewed, and strengthened."

Recipients of that gift are those in Morris's audience, whom she believes are mainly Christian women and girls. For these readers, Morris hopes to accomplish two goals. First, each novel will reveal some spiritual insight. Second, through her literary skill, she hopes to uplift the spirit. She intends for her books to be "lighthearted," and she chooses to depict few heart-rending tragedies. She sees the value in great tragedy and enjoys the art involved in writing such, but in her own writing she aims for "a strong element of laughter, of merriment, of happiness." She believes that keeping alive a sense of humor is one root of hope and that hope can lead to faith.

When asked about her predictions for the future of Christian fiction, Morris stated, "God uses Christian fiction to uphold and strengthen the saints. . . . He will always bless this ministry. Christian fiction must stay exactly that—a work of literature whose main purpose is fiction, and those people will always be there, anxious to buy books that they know will be based on Godly principles with a strong moral base and purpose. As long as that kind of Christian fiction exists, there will always be a demand for it."

SUMMARY: *TOWARD THE SUNRISING* (CHENEY DUVALL, M.D., SERIES)

Readers may have already met Dr. Cheney Duvall and her prize-fighter-turned-nurse, Shiloh Irons, in one of the previous volumes in this series. If so, the renewal of acquaintance will no doubt be one of amused anticipation. If not, then a rare treat is in store. As a word of brief introduction to the series, the affluent and proper Cheney Duvall has graduated from medical school and is meeting with the expected degree of skepticism experienced by the small smattering of female doctors in the mid-1800s. Shiloh Irons, a foundling, credits his knowledge of medicine to battlefield practice as a medic in the Civil War. In the first book of this series, Cheney hires Shiloh to assist her as she attempts to establish a credible professional reputation against the formidable odds of being a woman doctor.

Toward the Sunrising reassures the reader that Morris and her father continue as a delightful writing duo and have created an evenly matched pair in Cheney and Shiloh. The consistency of character from book to book, the complex relationship between the two, and the sheer entertainment of their verbal sparring make this unlikely twosome contenders for the most memorable pair in Christian fiction. Through all their quipping, Cheney and Shiloh demonstrate a mutual respect while constantly accepting the challenge to maintain the virtue of humility in each other. The Morrises exhibit great skill in keeping male and female roles in perspective while developing two equally well-rounded, equally significant characters.

In this fourth volume, Cheney and Shiloh have arrived in Charleston, South Carolina, at the time when Reconstruction is at its worst. There they become intimately acquainted with the injustices imposed by the Freedman's Bureau, affecting the very life's blood of both blacks and whites. Midnight riders, masked men, wealthy southern ladies, a former Confederate general, and primitive medical care all await the unsuspecting doctor and nurse.

God's protection and grace are themes skillfully woven through this fast-moving novel. The reader feels not only a sense of post–Civil War empathy for those oppressed by the greedy power wielders but also a sense of security as God's hand is clearly seen in His care for His own.

IN THE TWILIGHT, IN THE EVENING (CHENEY DUVALL, M.D., SERIES)

Cheney and Shiloh find new adventure, intrigue, causes to champion, and lessons to learn as they become staff members at the St. Francis de Yerba Buena Hospital in San Francisco. Cheney accepts the hospitality of her wealthy friend Victoria de Lancie and shares her exquisitely furnished mansion. Shiloh chooses surroundings that are more masculine and less elegant in a less than affluent part of town.

Having worked independently for most of her medical career, Cheney has much to learn about being a staff physician, and with her usual impetuous courage, she marches into the fray to give her opinions about needed improvements. With time, she earns the respect due her knowledge and skill although not necessarily her tact.

Shiloh continues to use his unique talents in the paradoxical combination of being an ex-prize fighter and a gentle, competent nurse. He seems to makes progress in his search for identity, and readers are given a glimpse into the underlying complexities of his feelings for Cheney and the profound significance of his being an orphan.

Using Proverbs 9 as a framework for each chapter heading, the Morris team weaves a tapestry of mistakes made by a headstrong, young woman and lessons learned the hard way. Being both angelic and totally human, Cheney is a believable and memorable character. Issues of prejudice, social stigma, and the love of God are all included in this story as both Cheney and Shiloh struggle to discover who they really are and what they expect from each other.

Bill Myers

Born in Seattle, Washington, in 1953, Bill Myers has become a highly successful author, director, and screenwriter. His varied career began with acting in stage and film productions but has broadened into one as a full-time writer and director. When not writing and directing, Myers hosts a national children's television series and enjoys spending time with his wife, Brenda, and his two daughters, Nicole and MacKenzie. He may also be found speaking at colleges, church retreats, and writing seminars and working with the youth at his local church.

PROFESSIONAL

Education

B.A. in stage directing, University of Washington; Italian State Institute of Cinema and Television, Rome, filmmaking

Career

Actor; director; fiction writer; filmmaker

Awards

Winner of more than forty national and international awards for films directed, including New York International Film Festivals (three times); U.S.

Silver Screen Award; ITA Platinum Video Award (nine times); C.I.N.E. Golden Eagle (two times); Crown Best Youth Film; Crown Best Evangelistic Film, Best Director, Best Picture; Best Children's Film (two times); Youth in Film International: The President's Award; and Silver Angel Award (fourteen times); each McGee and Me! video has gone platinum (selling over 2.5 million units)

PUBLICATIONS

Adult Fiction

Blood of Heaven, 1996
Threshold, 1997
Fire of Heaven, 1999

Juvenile Fiction

McGee and Me! Series
The Not So Great Escape, 1982
The Big Lie, 1989
A Star in the Breaking, 1989
Skate Expectations, 1989
Twister and Shout, 1989
Back to the Drawing Board, 1990
Do the Bright Thing, 1990
Take Me out of the Ball Game, 1990
'Twas the Fight before Christmas, 1990
In the Nick of Time, 1992
The Blunder Years, 1993
Beauty in the Least, 1993
Bloodhounds, Inc. Series
The Ghost of KRZY, 1997
Mystery of the Invisible Knight, 1997
Phantom of the Haunted Church, 1997
Invasion of the UFOs, 1998
Fangs for the Memories, 1998
The Case of the Missing Minds, 1999
Journeys to Fayrah Series
The Portal, 1991
The Experiment, 1991
The Whirlwind, 1992
The Tablet, 1992

The Incredible Worlds of Wally McDoogle Series
My Life as a Smashed Burrito with Extra Hot Sauce, 1993
My Life as Alien Monster Bait, 1993
My Life as a Broken Bungee Cord, 1993
My Life as Crocodile Junk Food, 1993
My Life as Dinosaur Dental Floss, 1994
My Life as a Torpedo Test Target, 1994
My Life as a Human Hockey Puck, 1994
My Life as an Afterthought Astronaut, 1995
My Life as Reindeer Road Kill, 1995
My Life as a Toasted Time Traveler, 1996
My Life as Polluted Pond Scum, 1996
My Life as a Big Foot Breath Mint, 1997
My Life as a Blundering Ballerina, 1997
My Life as a Screaming Skydiver, 1998
My Life as a Human Hair Ball, 1998
My Life as a Walrus Whoopee Cushion, 1999
Forbidden Doors Series
The Society, 1994
The Deceived, 1994
The Spell, 1995
The Haunting, 1995
The Guardian, 1995
The Encounter, 1995
The Curse, 1997
The Undead, 1997
The Scream, 1998
The Ancients, 1998

Adult Nonfiction

Dr. Luke Examines Jesus (commentary on Luke), 1979
Faith Workout (commentary on James), 1986
Jesus: An Eyewitness Account (commentary on John), 1988
Nikolai, 1989
Christ, B.C. (devotional), 1990
Dark Side of the Supernatural, 1999

Juvenile Nonfiction

Hot Topics, Tough Questions (re-release), 1996
More Hot Topics, 1989
Faith Encounter, 1998

Films

McGee and Me! Children's Series (1989–1996)
The Weight
A Cry for Freedom
Bamboo in Winter
Fast Forward (video series based on *Hot Topics, Tough Questions*)

Cassettes

Blood of Heaven, 1996
Threshold, 1997

CD-ROMs

The Gospels, 1994
Prayer Bear with Steve Green, 1997
The Choice Is Yours, 1997

PERSONAL

On returning to the United States after completing his film studies in Rome, Bill Myers took acting jobs on stage and in film. Today, however, writing and directing claim his full attention. Much of his time is spent abroad directing films. He has written or directed film projects in Venezuela, Peru, Bolivia, Mexico, Great Britain, Germany, France, Switzerland, Hong Kong, Japan, China, Nepal, India, Sri Lanka, Zaire, the Central African Republic, and the former Soviet Union.

A documentary film that Myers made for young people, *A Cry for Freedom,* has received more than 18,000 requests for bookings from high school audiences. *The Weight* is his own favorite drama for youth. He recently completed *The Choice Is Yours,* featuring extensive interviews from prison with serial killer David Berkowitz ("Son of Sam").

Myers's books and films have led him to work with numerous ministries, including Child Evangelism Fellowship, Josh McDowell, Dawson McAllister, Teen Challenge, Open Doors, SIMS, World Missionary Press, Foursquare International, Assembly of God, and Evangelical Free Church Missions.

Perhaps Myers is currently best known for the series he developed for Focus on the Family called McGee and Me!, which can claim to be the best-selling children's Christian video series in the world, selling over 2.5 million units. These videos were run as ABC Weekend Specials three times and are now airing on the British Broadcasting Company (BBC) and eleven other international networks. Focus on the Family and Sparrow Records have also paired Myers with Steve Green to produce a preschool series on prayer titled Prayer Bear.

Expanding into the information age with CD-ROM programs, Myers plays the voice of Jesus on a CD-ROM titled *The Gospels,* published by a subsidiary of Collier's Encyclopedia.

Myers is active in radio, writing, producing, and directing radio plays for Washington State Radio for the Blind. He is also a voice-over talent for various radio spots. He writes, directs, and acts for Focus on the Family's Adventures in Odyssey radio series and has adapted a number of his own books into radio dramas. His two recent adult suspense novels have been produced on cassette tape, with Myers playing one of the characters on each edition.

Myers's interest in writing was sparked when he saw that it had the power to help change people's lives. Following Christ's example in using parables to teach solid principles, he uses stories to draw people closer to God. His research is exhaustive and his style engaging. Naming prayer as the greatest influence on his writing, Myers's plots center on the redemptive work of Christ.

SUMMARY: *BLOOD OF HEAVEN*

Michael Coleman, death-row inmate and hardened criminal, is given the opportunity to become a "guinea pig" in experiments involving genetically controlled behavior. Scientists want to see whether blood that allegedly was found on a twig from Jesus' crown of thorns can affect a person's genetic makeup.

As Coleman responds dramatically to the blood transfusions, he is transferred from prison to private life and given a whole new identity. However, other forces have a sinister interest in the experiments, and Coleman plays a pivotal role in the ensuing contest between good and evil.

THE BLUNDER YEARS (MCGEE AND ME! SERIES), REVIEWED BY TREVOR RASPBERRY, FOURTH GRADE

A new kid named Rex comes to school. He's really cool. Then one day he comes to Nick's house. Nick joins Rex's club, and all his old friends hate him. In the end, he makes up with them. I liked it when Nick did the right thing.

MY LIFE AS A BROKEN BUNGEE CORD (THE INCREDIBLE WORLDS OF WALLY MCDOOGLE SERIES), REVIEWED BY JENA WEST, FOURTH GRADE

Wally and his friends go for a balloon ride, but not all of them make it on—only Wally and Miguel. Soon they find out that something bad, a bull, is right on their tails. Out of all the books in this series, I think that *My Life as a Broken Bungee Cord* is the best, and I want you to think about reading it.

MY LIFE AS A HUMAN HOCKEY PUCK (THE INCREDIBLE WORLDS OF WALLY MCDOOGLE SERIES), REVIEWED BY STUART SMITH, FOURTH GRADE

This book is about a character who tries to be a hockey player but ends up as a hilarious guy in a chicken suit. This book is funny, unusual, and adventurous.

MY LIFE AS A TOASTED TIME TRAVELER (THE INCREDIBLE WORLDS OF WALLY MCDOOGLE SERIES), REVIEWED BY STUART SMITH, FOURTH GRADE

This book is about a character named Wally McDoogle who gets sucked into the future. Wally discovers what happens when he does not change the past from fame-and-fortune to dark-oid and weirdness. This book is funny and weird. If you like weird things, this book is for you to read.

MY LIFE AS CROCODILE JUNK FOOD (THE INCREDIBLE WORLDS OF WALLY MCDOOGLE SERIES), REVIEWED BY JANELLE VAUGHAN, FOURTH GRADE

Wally goes to the mission field. Through his adventures, he realizes he will be back again. I liked the story because it is very exciting. It gets you on the edge of your seat.

NOTE FROM THE AUTHOR REGARDING *THRESHOLD*

Those of you who know me know my dedication to teaching. Whether it is with my teen Bible devotions some twenty years ago; the McGee and Me!,

Forbidden Doors, or Journeys to Fayrah series; or even the children's comedy series The Incredible Worlds of Wally McDoogle, my purpose is always to instruct. (You can imagine how thrilled I was when a Bible professor from Concordia Seminary said that he was making *Blood of Heaven* required reading for all his theology students next year.)

Although I write to teach, I am also dedicated to making sure that there is enough entertainment in the story that the reader does not feel that he or she is sitting through a 300-page sermon. That is the case with *Threshold*.

Research: As I say in the foreword to *Threshold*, "If I've learned anything in writing this book, it's that truth can indeed be stranger than fiction.' I have tried to make the science as accurate as possible—including the research into the paranormal currently being conducted in laboratories around the world. The same can be said for many of the supernatural experiences described in the novel. When it comes to these two areas, I am afraid what fiction I have added only pales by comparison.

My research was extensive, starting as early as 1976, when Keith Green and I were involved in delivering a famous west coast psychic from intense demonic activity. It was then that the story began to take shape. I wanted to show how crafty and deceptive our adversary can be and yet how pure and powerful the Lord is.

But that was only the beginning of the research. I learned more while directing numerous missions films around the world. The spiritual warfare that some of these men and women are waging could fill a book.

Then there was my lengthy on-camera interview with David Berkowitz, a serial killer known as the Son of Sam—an ex-demoniac who was charged with shooting thirteen people and who is now a committed brother in Christ.

There were extensive and gracious conversations with leading psychic researchers, including Dr. Edwin May, who for twenty years headed the CIA's secret psychic research program and who also provided information on current Russian progress in this field.

There was also a lengthy visit to a leading psychic research lab as well as to a medical research facility at the University of California, Los Angeles, along with conversations with many pastors, physicists, professors, a medical researcher, and followers of Eastern mysticism. Their stories and research were both encouraging and chilling—encouraging in that ongoing scientific studies are clearly showing the presence of a supernatural world and the power of faith and chilling in that many of these well-meaning men and women are exploring the occult without even knowing it.

Teaching Elements: There are three areas I want to tackle in this book:

1. To explore what real faith in Christ is.
2. To demonstrate spiritual warfare and our authority as believers in Christ Jesus.
3. To expose the occult elements in New Age, Eastern mysticism, and contemporary psychic research.

If I can accomplish these goals, then I feel that the book is, as they say, "worth its tree." In any case, the prayer I sent out with this, as with all my work, is that you the reader will be drawn more closely and intimately toward the heart of the Lord Jesus Christ.

Janette Oke

Born on February 18, 1935, in Alberta, Manitoba, Canada, Janette Oke has far exceeded what her parents, Fred and Amy Steeves, might have expected. No doubt this farm family valued hard work, perseverance, and productivity, character qualities that are demonstrated in their successful daughter's career as a Christian writer.

Oke is not only a prolific writer but also the wife of Edward Oke, academic dean of Rocky Mountain College in Calgary, Alberta. Their family includes Terry, Lorne, Lavon, and Laurel, all born within a five-year period. Oke is a member of the Alberta Christian Writer's Group and enjoys gardening and being a grandmother to her nine grandchildren.

PROFESSIONAL

Education

Mountain View Bible College, Didsbury, Alberta, Canada; Honorary Doctor of Humanities, Bethel College, Mishawaka, Indiana

Career

Banker; office worker; bookkeeper

Awards

Gold Medallion Book Award, *Love's Long Journey,* 1983; Award of Merit-Fiction, *Love's Unending Legacy,* 1985; Final Nominee, Fiction, *Spring's Gentle Promise,* 1990; Final Nominee, Fiction, *Julia's Last Hope,* 1991; President's Award, 1992; Final Nominee, Fiction, *A Woman Called Damaris,* 1992; Angel Awards: *A Woman Called Damaris,* 1992; *They Called Her Mrs. Doc,* 1993; *A Bride for Donnigan,* 1994; *Reflections on the Christmas Story,* 1995; *The Red Geranium,* 1996; *Nana's Gift, Return to Harmony,* and *Drums of Change,* 1997; Honorary Alumnus Award for Personal Achievement, Bethel College, 1993; Final Nominee, Fiction, *The Measure of a Heart,* 1993; Final Nominee, Fiction, Evangelical Christian Publishers Association, *Heart of the Wilderness,* 1994

PUBLICATIONS

Adult Fiction

Hey, Teacher, 1982
The Red Geranium, 1995
Nana's Gift, 1996
The Matchmakers, 1997
Love Comes Softly Series
  Love Comes Softly, 1979
  Love's Enduring Promise, 1980
  Love's Long Journey, 1982
  Love's Abiding Joy, 1983
  Love's Unending Legacy, 1984
  Love's Unfolding Dream, 1987
  Love Takes Wing, 1988
  Love Finds a Home, 1989
Seasons of the Heart Series
  Once upon a Summer, 1981
  The Winds of Autumn, 1987
  Winter Is Not Forever, 1988
  Spring's Gentle Promise, 1989
Canadian West Series
  When Calls the Heart, 1983
  When Comes the Spring, 1985
  When Breaks the Dawn, 1986
  When Hope Springs New, 1986

Women of the West Series

Julia's Last Hope, 1990
A Woman Called Damaris, 1991
Roses for Mama, 1991
Calling of Emily Evans, 1992
Measure of a Heart, 1992
They Called Her Mrs. Doc, 1992
Bride for Donnigan, 1993
Heart of the Wilderness, 1993
Too Long a Stranger, 1994
The Bluebird and the Sparrow, 1994
A Gown of Spanish Lace, 1995
Drums of Change, 1996

A Prairie Legacy Series

The Tender Years, 1997
Quiet Strength, 1998
A Searching Heart, 1999

Coauthored with T. Davis Bunn

Return to Harmony, 1996
Another Homecoming, 1997
Tomorrow's Dream, 1998

Adult Nonfiction

Quiet Places, Warm Thoughts, 1983
Reflections on the Christmas Story, 1995
The Meeting Place, 1999

Juvenile Fiction

Spunky's Diary, 1982
New Kid in Town, 1983
The Prodigal Cat, 1984
Ducktails, 1985
The Impatient Turtle, 1986
A Cote of Many Colors, 1987
Prairie Dog Town, 1988
Maury Had a Little Lamb, 1989
Trouble in a Fur Coat, 1990
This Little Pig, 1991
Pordy's Prickly Problem, 1993
Who's New at the Zoo, 1994

Devotionals

My Favorite Verse, 1987
Father Who Calls, 1988
Father of Love, 1989
Father of My Heart, 1990
Faithful Father, 1993

PERSONAL

Janette Oke reveals that even as a child she had the desire to become a writer. Because her faith is vital to her life, she states that "writing is such a wonderful way to be able to share it [faith] with others, anything I write will be 'Christian.'"

Just as her characters are often pioneers in either the Canadian or the American West, Oke has been somewhat of a pioneer in Christian fiction writing. Most readers of the genre would agree that when Oke began putting pen to her thoughts, few other writers of Christian fiction were being published. Using that medium as a means to share her faith in fairly uncharted territory was a motivating factor for Oke to try her hand at the trade.

Having grown up in the Canadian West, Oke writes out of her own experience as well as from stories remembered from others. She has also amassed an extensive research library that helps her provide factual information that is essential to the historical accuracy of her novels. Her creativity is nourished in a quiet mountain condo where she retreats to initiate the writing process and to work with her characters without interruption. After drafting as quickly as inspiration will allow, she then heads home to complete her editing and rewriting stages. Her return gives treasured time with her family and distance enough from her original manuscript to edit objectively.

Such a process is, for Oke at least, the formula for success. Her thousands of readers must agree. "I write for young women, but I find that the readership is from eight to eighty, male as well as female." Perhaps the universal appeal of her work lies in both her plots and her themes. Plots are character driven, as demonstrated by the spunky Marty in *Love Comes Softly* or the prodigal Rebecca in *Too Long a Stranger.* The recurring theme is love. Oke states emphatically that the thread holding all her plots together is "not romance but love. It is first and foremost God's love, then love of family and love for others. Each book has a different theme, but it works out from that hub."

Being an avid reader since childhood, Oke states that many authors have contributed to her knowledge and "stretched her interest." However, her favorites were Louisa May Alcott, L. M. Montgomery, and Catherine Marshall. It was Marshall's *Christy* that created the love affair between Oke and Christian fiction that has resulted in blessings multiplied for her many fans.

Oke states that she "has no personal goals" that she hopes to achieve in her writing but that her "desire would be for a reader to find Christ as Savior through the prompting of the Holy Spirit as they read one of the stories. A very close second would be for those who already know Christ to think, to grow, and to understand more about their relationship with God and what it means in everyday living."

SUMMARY: *THE BLUEBIRD AND THE SPARROW* (WOMEN OF THE WEST SERIES)

When three-year-old Berta is presented with her new baby sister, Glenna, she is not nearly as charmed as all the adults seem to be. As the girls grow, Glenna's admiration for Berta is evident but is not returned, at least not with equal intensity. Throughout childhood, Berta continues to feel jealousy toward the beautiful, loving younger sister.

As the girls reach adulthood, their lives take vastly different directions. Berta chooses a career as a librarian, whereas Glenna becomes a contented wife and mother. Still the barrier created by jealousy threatens to ruin Berta's opportunity for a fulfilling life. Through the patient counsel of a minister, Berta arrives at self-acceptance, and Glenna reveals the surprising motives behind her near-perfect facade as well.

This is a story that speaks to the need in many families for brothers and sisters to take the risk of sharing their feelings openly, for parents to create an environment fertile to self-acceptance, and for all to reap the harvest of support and encouragement that God intended to take place in that haven called home.

PORDY'S PRICKLY PROBLEM

Dealing with shyness and overcoming the fear of new things are themes on which this story for young children is based. Pordy Porcupine fears anything new, whether it is climbing trees or making new friends. With acceptance and wisdom, Mother Porcupine encourages Pordy to develop confidence while demonstrating courage in facing the unknown.

Whether it is in the genre of devotional books, children's literature, or historical fiction, there is no question that Oke will always hold a special place in the hearts of her vast and devoted readership. She has demonstrated that she is a true pioneer, staking her claim in the world of Christian fiction.

Carole Gift Page

Observing the beautiful smile of the popular conference speaker, one would never guess that the original dream of this shy girl was to be left alone—really alone—to be allowed the privilege of writing without the intrusion of people into her private world. As a teenager, Carole Gift Page found that she could freely express feelings in poetry or prose that she could not verbalize. One might say that God allowed her years of privacy so that she might later reveal publicly the sensitive spirit to which many have responded through her conferences, her many books, or the more than 800 articles she has penned. Published in over 100 Christian periodicals, Page well represents the growing number of inspirational fiction writers.

Cofounder of Inland Empire Christian Writers Guild with Page is her husband, Bill. The Pages are presently reorganizing their creation to serve with the American Christian Writers Organization. Bill is also an aerospace engineer/checker. The Pages have four children: Kimberle Carole Page Bunch, David Aldon Page, Heather Gift Page, and Misty Lynne, who is in heaven and whose story is poignantly told in *Misty: Our Momentary Child*. Bill and Carole live in Moreno Valley, California.

PROFESSIONAL

Education

B.S. in art education (major) and English and Spanish (minors), Bob Jones University

Career

Biola University, adjunct teacher of creative writing; conference speaker and teacher of writing for twenty-four years; professional writer for twenty-eight years

Awards

C. S. Lewis Honor Book Award, Teen Novel, *Hallie's Secret,* 1987; Pacesetter Award, Biola University Writers Institute, 1990; Pacesetter Award, Mount Hermon Christian Writers Conference, 1991

PUBLICATIONS

Adult Fiction

Rachel's Hope, 1979, 1986
To Chase a Dark Shadow, 1985
Family Reunion, 1988
In Search of Her Own (rewritten version of *To Chase a Dark Shadow*), 1997
Decidedly Married, 1998
A Rose for Jenny, 1999
Heartland Memories Series
  The House on Honeysuckle Lane, 1994
  Home to Willowbrook, 1995
  The Hope of Herrick House, 1996
  Storms over Willowbrook, 1998

Coauthored with Doris Elaine Fell

Contemporary Romance Suspense Series
  Mist over Morro Bay, 1985
  Secret of the East Wind, 1986
  Storm Clouds over Paradise, 1986
  Beyond the Windswept Sea, 1987

Juvenile Fiction

Two Worlds of Tracy Corbett, 1980

Kara, 1980, 1994
Heather's Choice, 1982, 1991
Carrie, 1984, 1994
Neeley Never Said Goodbye, 1984, 1991
Maria: A Story of Loneliness, 1985; reissued as *Maria's Search,* 1991
Never Ashamed, 1986
Hallie's Secret, 1991
Kasey Carlone Series
Song for Kasey, 1992
Summer of a Stranger, 1992
Taste of Fame, 1992
Change of Plans, 1992
Bouquet of Goodbyes, 1992

Fiction: Short Stories

Petals in the Storm: A Collection of Short Stories about Women Making Life-Changing Decisions, 1991

Adult Nonfiction

Ms. Mystique or Mistake?, 1974
Let Not Money Put Asunder What God Has Joined Together, 1974
How to Failure-Proof Your Family, 1975
The Down Way Up (the Roy Comstock story), 1979
The Surgeon's Family (with David Hernandez), 1980
Misty: Our Momentary Child, 1987
The Child in Each of Us (with Dr. Richard Dickinson), 1989
The Pursuit of Intimacy (with David and Teresa Ferguson and Chris and Holly Thurman), 1993
Intimate Encounters (with David and Teresa Ferguson and Chris and Holly Thurman), 1994
Complete Guide to Christian Writing and Speaking (with other Christian writers), 1994
She Stays (the Ricky Van Shelton story, with Bettye Shelton and Andy Landis), 1995

PERSONAL

Strange as it might seem, a mosquito might have changed the course of author Carole Gift Page's life. At three years of age, little Carole Gift contracted encephalitis from an infected mosquito and was in a coma for three days.

When informed that if her tiny daughter did survive this deadly disease, the toddler would probably be "a vegetable," Millie Gift, Carole's mother, promised God, "If you'll heal my daughter, Lord, I'll give her life to you." She was miraculously healed. At twelve, sharing her mother's commitment, Carole surrendered her life and talents to God.

Although her lifelong dream had been to be a cartoonist for Walt Disney, near the end of her college career Carole was encouraged by English professor John Mays to use her gift of writing to honor the Lord. Having already written her first (unpublished) novel in high school, it was a natural step to consider the field of inspirational fiction. Page states that the desire to write came to her "as strong as any missionary call. . . . I had a profound sense that God was calling me to be a writer."

Therefore, after graduating, Carole and a roommate shared a "starving artists" existence, with cheap food and little money. A job as a secretary allowed Carole the coveted opportunity to write in the evenings unencumbered by the responsibilities of being a teacher, the job for which she had been prepared. However, her status as a young career woman changed when she met Bill Page, whom she married eleven months later. As children joined their home, writing plans had to be relegated to a less important place, but they were not forsaken. When *High,* a newsletter for teens published by the Baptist General Conference, accepted one of her stories, Page's professional writing career was born.

Along with her writing ministry, Page speaks at many conferences, with her most recent theme being "Becoming a Woman of Passion." Her seminars are designed for women "desiring to discover or rediscover their passion for life, their loved ones, and the Lover of their souls."

Page shares, "When I was growing up, I never felt accepted by my peer group (although I was always the class artist and found some recognition in my drawings). But I was extremely shy and had a hard time communicating with others. Part of the problem was that I had the worst set of buckteeth my orthodontist had ever seen (he even took the 'before' and 'after' plaster molds of my teeth around to his orthodontic conventions to show off his handiwork). As I became a teenager, I discovered that I enjoyed writing stories and poems, and others seemed to enjoy them as well. I found that I could communicate through my writing the thoughts and feelings I'd bottled up all my life. I could share myself with others by letting them read my stories and poems, and I didn't even have to face them or look them in the eye if I didn't wish to. I thought for sure that God had given me a talent for writing so that I would never have to face people and try to communicate; I could write alone in my little attic garret and never have to confront the world at large. However, God has a great sense of humor because it has been through writing that He has pushed me out into the world to speak and teach, and now I speak often to audiences of hundreds around the country."

When asked why she chose to write Christian fiction, Page responded, "I didn't choose it; it chose me; or, more accurately, God called me to write Christian fiction. During my last year of college at Bob Jones University, as I was about to receive my B.S. degree in art education, I happened to show some of my stories to an English instructor who was enthusiastic about my writing. He told me that I could be a good writer, perhaps a great one. He encouraged me not to teach but to get a bread-and-butter job and spend my time writing, writing, writing. I remember that I went back to the prayer room in my dormitory and sought God's will regarding this incredible possibility. Was it possible that God was calling me to do the very thing I loved doing with all my heart? I spent that day in prayer, and it was the closest I've ever come to experiencing a 'vision' of what God was calling me to do with my life. He impressed upon my heart that He was calling me to write for Him—to write novels and stories that would communicate His truths; He wanted me to be a Christian fiction writer. I wasn't even sure what that meant because I knew no one anywhere who was such a being; nor were there classes that I knew of to teach one such an occupation; nor did I have the slightest idea how to ever get my writing published. I had no answers to any of these questions, but I knew beyond a doubt I had received the calling as surely as any minister or missionary is called. It took several years of 'wandering in the wilderness,' so to speak, before I was finally published and actually launched my writing career. Now, after twenty-eight years of professional writing, I still feel the flame and passion for the ministry of writing that God ignited in that prayer room over thirty years ago."

Page's next response dealt with what themes appear in her work. "One of my favorite themes is this: Christ, the Lover of our Soul, interacts with us on a moment-by-moment basis as we respond to His Holy Spirit in our hearts. When I fall in love with Jesus with all my heart, mind, soul, and strength, my life is transformed, and I have the potential of living each day in His abundance. My goal in my fiction is always to show God at work in the lives of human beings and to make Christ real to the reader. Just as Jesus used parables to teach His precepts, I try to show in my stories how Christ woos and wins people to Himself as well as how He works in the ordinary day-to-day events of our lives. My favorite theme is of Christ as our constant, loving Friend, seeing us through life's hardships, obstacles, and traumas. To echo a passage from my book *Misty,* I want readers to catch a glimpse of how abundantly Christ loves them—'You are loved. You are so loved!' I feel I've accomplished my goal as a Christian fiction writer if I can help my readers know Jesus a little better in their own lives."

Finally, when asked to express her view of the future of inspirational novels, Page responded, "I think the future for Christian fiction is very bright. When I began writing Christian novels over twenty-five years ago, almost every publisher I talked with told me there was no market for Christian fiction because Christians wouldn't read it. I struggled for years to convince publishers to take a chance on Christian novels and eventually, thanks to Peretti, Oke, and others, the tide turned, and today almost every Christian publisher has a line of fiction titles. The quality of Christian literature has risen greatly, I believe, in recent years, and of course the competition has increased tremendously as well. One of the most encouraging trends I see today is the interest of secular publishers in Christian fiction. Harlequin-Silhouette Books, perhaps the largest publisher of novels in the world, did a study that showed that the fastest-growing market in the publishing industry is that of Christian novels. As a result, Harlequin has formed an imprint called Steeple Hill, which is publishing a line of Christian romance novels under the title of 'Love Inspired.' I was asked to write for the line and have contracted for four books, two of which—*In Search of Her Own* and *Decidedly Married*—have been recently released. I feel encouraged that my editor for this line is conscientiously attempting to produce quality, family-oriented, uplifting books, and she has given me complete freedom to explore spiritual issues as I feel led. I feel as if I have stepped into a brand-new mission field and the possibilities are endless. These books are not being relegated to the 'religious ghetto' of the secular bookstore along with theology books and so on; rather, they are appearing on bookstore shelves along with all the other fiction titles. That means many more people are likely to pick them up, read them, and come face to face with the God of the Bible who loves them. As we as Christian authors approach the year 2000, we should feel an even greater urgency to spread the 'Good News' to a hurting world. For me, at least, there is no greater vehicle to accomplish this than Christian fiction."

SUMMARY: *KARA*

As Kara Strickland is approaching high school graduation, she appears to have everything a girl could want. Her father is a successful and respected physician, and her beautiful mother, Anna, is devoted to her family. Although Kara has no brothers or sisters, she is content with her parents, especially her devoted father, with whom she spends as much time as possible. Although busy, Dr. Strickland finds time to spend with his daughter every day, listening to her concerns, talking about his interests, and in general sharing life with her.

In one night, all this security is shattered. For no apparent reason, Ben Strickland storms out of his house in the early morning hours and shortly thereafter is involved in a fatal car crash. Devastated by his accident, wife and daughter respond in vastly different ways. Kara stoically presses on to complete her senior studies. Anna seeks escape through alcohol, which is the undoing of all the two have left.

Through a series of tragedies, Kara discovers that her beloved father was not her biological parent, and suddenly she seems separated from her own self. As she sets about to establish an identity, she finds both faithful friends and formidable foes. At the conclusion, although she has suffered much, Kara discovers that her heart has not been broken by deception but, rather, enlarged to encompass more love than she ever thought possible.

Page has created a story that deals with many pertinent issues, including the death of a parent, alcoholism, coping with a burn victim, adoption, feelings of isolation, developing independence, the effects of drugs, and the true meaning of Christian forgiveness. In Kara, she has created a strong, sensitive, determined young lady who responds realistically to rejection, religion, and finally to faith.

THE HOPE OF HERRICK HOUSE (HEARTLAND MEMORIES SERIES)

While Bethany Rose Henry and her brother Luke have helped their work-worn, widowed mother, Laura, eke out an existence on their small farm, their half-brother and sister live in near luxury as influential members of another community. The common denominator of both families, Tom Herrick is the reason for the disparity in lifestyles.

Unhappy with his marital relationship when he met Laura, Tom soon fell in love with this country woman who accepted him as he was, on his own terms. Creating the family name of "Henry," Tom had fathered two children by Laura before he was free to share even that identity with her. For years, and with deception, this sometime-father attempted to spend time with both families. At his death, the two families meet, and the wealthy Herricks offer to help the less fortunate Henrys. Being "poor but proud," neither Luke nor Bethany ever intends to accept what they consider to be charity. However, in one tragic night, all of their lives are changed forever. The Herricks and Henrys become intertwined in a way that no one could ever have predicted.

In *The Hope of Herrick House*, Page has created a novel of intrigue, mystery, love, Christian responses to adversity, and enough variety in character and action to entertain the most jaded reader. Included in the plot are the issues of illegitimacy, extended families, dealing with grief, developing trust, blended families, alcoholism, codependency, and ultimate dependence on God. With all these aspects of life to juggle, Page still manages to create a memorable character in Bethany Rose and her supporting cast.

Gary Parker

A veteran of twenty years as pastor in five different churches across the southern United States, Gary Parker presently holds the position of coordinator for Baptist principles. Born in Spartanburg, South Carolina, in June 1953, he now resides in Georgia with his wife, Melody, and daughters, Andrea and Ashley. Beginning in the field of nonfiction, since 1994 he has moved into writing fiction for adults. To relax from this busy schedule of full-time job and part-time writing, he finds pleasure in playing a round of golf or bicycling long distances.

PROFESSIONAL

Education

Ph.D., Baylor University; M.Div., Southwestern University; B.A., Furman University

Career

Coordinator for Baptist Principles, 1996 to present; instructor, Eden Theological Seminary, 1994; pastor, First Baptist Church of Jefferson City, 1990–1996; pastor, Grace Baptist Church, 1985–1990; pastor, Warrenton Baptist Church, 1982–1985; pastor, Hilltop Lakes Chapel, 1979–1982; associate pastor, Denton Baptist Church, 1976–1979

PUBLICATIONS

Adult Fiction

Beyond a Reasonable Doubt, 1994
Desert Water, 1995
Death Stalks a Holiday, 1996
Dark Road to Daylight, 1997
A Capitol Offense, 1998
The Ephesus Fragment, 1999

Adult Nonfiction

The Gift of Doubt, 1990
Principles Worth Protecting, 1991
Creative Tensions, 1991
The Guilt Trip, 1993

PERSONAL

Gary Parker's interest in writing stems from the extensive reading he did as a child as well as the encouragement he received from his teachers. His sixth-grade teacher and his eleventh-grade English teacher were especially supportive, suggesting that he do more writing. Parker credits *The Robe,* one of the books he read in elementary school, with influencing his decision to turn his writing talents to producing Christian fiction. He states that this fictional account of what happened to the robe of Jesus after His crucifixion "moved me in a deep, spiritual way. So, as a believer, I naturally felt motivated by the desire to write stories that might touch someone. That led me to fiction and to Christian fiction."

Parker's research is done in two major ways: "I talk to experts in the field when I need information on a particular area, and I read (books, encyclopedias, and so on) when I need specific facts or data." Although he writes mainly about places with which he is familiar, he is free to use other people as resources when necessary. "If I don't know the place, I find someone who does and let them describe it for me."

Parker characterizes his writing style as "fairly simple. I describe only what is necessary to keep the action moving. My characters are real people—people with values but not syrupy sweet and always perfect." They are "composites of all the people I know and everything that I have experienced." Plots are mainly action centered, "with characters driven by what is happening around them." Parker designs his plots to have more than one layer, using "the intersecting pieces to keep the story interesting."

Weaving the theme of redemption through all his stories, Parker writes "for two main audiences: first, the Christian audience that wants to read a good story but one without the violence and sex usually associated with fiction, and, second, people who are not believers but who might find through a novel some spiritual truth that could make a difference in their lives."

When asked which writers he enjoys reading who have influenced his own writing career, Parker replied, "Writers I admire include historical greats such as John Steinbeck, Ernest Hemingway, Thomas Costain, and Charles Dickens. Modern writers I like to read include John Irving, Ken Follett, and Pat Conroy. I believe that every writer I've read influenced and influences me."

Beyond his basic goal of telling a good story, Parker wants his readers to feel close to his characters. He desires to communicate a message of God's grace and states (tongue-in-cheek, honestly, openly, and humorously) that one object is to be rich and famous. "Isn't that every writer's goal?"

Parker believes that Christian fiction will continue to grow as a segment of the reading market but that "we currently have far more books out than the market can absorb. In the future, I think fewer books will get published, but the books will be better. Right now, I see too many books that don't have enough quality. So, the market will 'shake out,' and the books that are published will be the best available. We are already seeing this happen as companies slim down their lists." Having begun to contribute his own line of mystery and adventure stories to this volume of material, Parker hopes to be one of those who remain.

SUMMARY: *DARK ROAD TO DAYLIGHT*

Bethany Chapman has faced many difficulties in life. The daughter of an alcoholic father who abandoned his family, Bethany is recently divorced from a manipulative, abusive husband. Just as she is pulling her life together with the help of her mother and therapist Burke Anderson, her ex-husband threatens to fight for custody of their beautiful little girl Stacy. When Stacy suddenly disappears, evidence points to Bethany as the possible kidnapper. With her mother in the hospital as the victim of a stroke and no other friends or family to help, Bethany turns to Burke Anderson for help. After the pressures of all that Bethany has experienced, it seems possible that she really could be guilty. Burke must decide whether to risk his reputation and the safety of his own family to help his patient prove her innocence.

Judith Pella

It is no wonder that the little girl who "adored history" and "loved all kinds of stories, especially if they weren't true," grew up to become the author of books with settings as widespread as California in the 1850s, modern Russia, Cheyenne Indian encampments, and Scotland.

The daughter of a truck driver and a factory worker, Judith Pella has had vocational experiences as varied as being a pickle packer, sales clerk, nurse, teacher's aide, church secretary, and Tupperware saleslady. It is no wonder that she can write with such authority about a range of occupations, social classes, and lifestyles. Her passion for reading and creating gives wings to her imagination while her heritage holds her with secure roots.

Pella currently lives in Eureka, California, with her husband, Paul, and family. Although she and Paul enjoy sailing together, Pella shares that her private pleasures also include activities as divergent as being a *Star Trek* fan, quilting, and collecting items for her dollhouse.

PROFESSIONAL

Education

Nursing degree, St. Francis Memorial Hospital, San Francisco; B.A. in social sciences, California State University at Humboldt

Career
Nurse; teacher

Memberships
Romance Writers of America

PUBLICATIONS

Adult Fiction

Blind Faith, 1996
Beloved Stranger, 1998
Texas Angel, 1999
Lone Star Legacy Series
- *Frontier Lady,* 1993
- *Stoner's Crossing,* 1994
- *Warrior's Song,* 1996

Coauthored with Michael Phillips

The Stonewycke Trilogy
- *The Heather Hills of Stonewycke,* 1985
- *Flight from Stonewycke,* 1985
- *Lady of Stonewycke,* 1986

The Stonewyke Legacy
- *Stranger at Stonewycke,* 1987
- *Shadows over Stonewycke,* 1988
- *Treasure of Stonewycke,* 1988

Journals of Corrie Belle Hollister Series
- *My Father's World,* 1990
- *Daughter of Grace,* 1991
- *On the Trail of Truth,* 1991
- *A Place in the Sun,* 1991
- The series continues with other books written by Michael Phillips (see his entry in this book).

The Highland Collection
- *Jamie MacLeod: Highland Lass,* 1987
- *Robbie Taggart: Highland Sailor,* 1987

The Russians Series
- *The Crown and the Crucible,* 1991
- *A House Divided,* 1992

Travail and Triumph, 1992
Heirs of the Motherland (written alone), 1993
Dawning of Deliverance (written alone), 1994
White Nights, Red Morning (written alone), 1996
Passage into Light (written alone), 1998

Coauthored with Tracie Peterson

Ribbons of Steel Series
Distant Dreams, 1996
A Hope Beyond, 1997
A Promise for Tomorrow, 1998
Westward the Dream, 1998
Ribbons West Series
Separate Roads, 1999

PERSONAL

Although Judith Pella began writing at an early age (creating a Civil War spy epic at age eleven), she took a somewhat circuitous route to being published. She gave attention to both nursing and teaching earlier in her career. During a difficult time in her life, she would take up the pen or sit at the typewriter and write to release tension. It was one of these pages that Michael Phillips, her longtime friend, happened to see and asked whether she had written it. Her reply was that she was "just fooling around." Phillips, having had publications already on the market, recognized talent when he saw it and asked whether she would be interested in collaborating on a Scottish novel that he wanted to write but felt that he would not have time to properly research. The rest is history, both literally and figuratively, as the writing team of Phillips and Pella have produced five very successful historical fiction series, with sales totaling more than two million.

Since that happy evening in 1985, Pella has firmly established herself as a team writer, collaborating with both Phillips and Tracie Peterson. She is also recognized for her own successful novels: those that stand alone, those that complete a series, and those that form their own set. Judith and Michael began the Journals of Corrie Belle Hollister books as a result of Pella's inspiration, with Phillips completing the series and even creating a spin-off continuation. In contrast, Phillips had the idea for the Russians series, which they began in tandem and Pella concluded on her own. The two remain friends and pay tribute to each other for joint contributions that have given both their careers a boost.

When asked about her research process, Pella shared that she begins by reading "general literature" on the topic to get an overview. Having been a history buff since childhood, much that she writes about has been hidden away until she needed it simply because she has always loved to read. As she writes, she researches whatever facts are necessary to give authenticity to her setting and her characters. The technology of writing is not as joyous to Pella as is the research. She shares that the word processor "uses" her. "I don't particularly like this computer age, but I have to admit it is too efficient to ignore." Writing in her home office, Pella takes advantage of the time when her children are in school. Reporting herself to be a "night person," she states, "I often don't really catch my stride until late afternoon."

Pella views her audience as mainly female, and her books focus on issues that are important to her readers, including such timeless problems as self-identity, spousal abuse, dealing with the death of a spouse, and the importance of family and heritage. Plots are intriguing, and characterization is realistic enough to convince the contemporary reader that on visiting the setting, one would surely find those who people her stories, even though they may have lived more than a century ago.

When asked who has had the greatest impact on her writing, it is no surprise that Pella responds with praise for Michael Phillips. "He has been most influential to me as a writer and as a person. He was instrumental in instilling confidence in me with his praise and his gentle criticism. I doubt that I would have finished those first books without his nudging, and I know that I wouldn't have had the nerve to actually send them to a publisher."

In considering the literary elements of her work, Pella relates that they are "for the most part action and character driven." She shares that she never writes with a specific theme in mind. "It's the story that usually sets any theme in my books. However, if there is any recurring theme, it has to be tolerance. There is simply no place in Christ for all the petty rules and legalism that unfortunately crop up in the Church."

Authors other than Phillips who have impressed Pella range from Carole Ryrie Brink and her beloved *Caddie Woodlawn,* which was a childhood favorite, to C. S. Lewis, J. R. R. Tolkien, and Stephen R. Donaldson. She credits Lewis and Tolkien for helping her "define beliefs or ideas" and setting a standard for "sheer beauty" of language. Donaldson's Thomas Covenant the Unbeliever series "is so marvelously written, and his use of language is astounding. It taught me how to write with passion and depth."

When asked about goals for her readers, Pella responded candidly, "I dislike goals." She adds that she wants her audience to "just enjoy" her work.

For herself and other authors of inspirational writing, Pella did set some objectives. She wants to see Christian fiction competing "on an equal field with general fiction. Wouldn't it be great to see novels with spiritual, evangelical content to be accorded the same respect and acceptance as secular novels rather than shunted to a single shelf in a bookstore with the ominous label 'Religion,' sandwiched in-between Charles Finney and the writings of Buddha?" With talent, versatility, and professionalism, Pella is making contributions to the quality of inspirational novels that puts such a goal within reach.

SUMMARY: *THE HEATHER HILLS OF STONEWYCKE* (THE STONEWYCKE TRILOGY)

Ian Duncan, second son and therefore not the favorite of the earl of Landsbury, is sent out of London to virtual exile at the home of a distant cousin in northeastern Scotland. With skills limited to drinking and being, for the most part, sociable, he anticipates little pleasure or satisfaction on the large, lonely estate. Margaret, Ian's country cousin, will one day be lady of the castle of Stonewycke and its vast holdings. Her love of the crofters, the land, and the sprawling castle itself provides contentment in her rather solitary existence.

When the two cousins meet, neither has high expectations for the other because their maturing years have taken them on such vastly different paths. However, as they forge a friendship based on common concerns that they never hoped to discover in each other, Ian and Margaret survive violence, intrigue, and even a murder.

This first novel in the long-popular Stonewycke Trilogy will whet the reader's appetite for both *Flight from Stonewycke* and *The Lady of Stonewycke,* the completing volumes of the set.

DISTANT DREAMS (RIBBONS OF STEEL SERIES)

Carolina Adams just does not fit in anywhere. As a fifteen-year-old growing up during the 1830s, her mother, her sister, and her peers expect her to be concerned only with appearance, attending parties, and catching the eye of a prospective husband. The common belief of Carolina's day is that too much education may "cause insanity" in the decidedly weaker sex. Some believe that it might already be too late for the precocious teen. Thankfully, her father not only understands his daughter's hunger for things technical and mechanical but also encourages her to investigate, read, and learn all she can. He even provides her with a tutor, much to the chagrin of her mother.

At the root of the controversy is the newly developed and much-debated rail system. Carolina is fascinated by everything about the iron monster: The sights, the sounds and even the smells of the rail yard draw her like a garden party does her older sister, Virginia. The only peer who shares Carolina's delight in the excitement of the railroad is Virginia's fiancé, James Baldwin, who has been hired to instruct the younger Adams in the higher education she so craves.

Pella and Peterson have created a lively, viable character in Carolina Adams, a young lady who attempts to harness her insatiable appetite for learning so as not to anger her convention-bound mother. She also wrestles with sibling rivalry and gender bias and is often caught in a power struggle between her beloved parents—all timeless issues as frustrating at the turn of the twenty-first century as in the early nineteenth. Relationships explored in this novel present insightful messages to both parents and their teens.

HEIRS OF THE MOTHERLAND (THE RUSSIANS SERIES)

Countess Mariana Remizov has been reared from birth to age eighteen by her uncle and aunt as a peasant while her father has been in exile. On his return, she is faced with the dilemma of becoming a part of the shallow, self-serving, elite society with which she has little in common except the nobility of her birth or of finding something useful to do with her life. To further complicate matters, Mariana finds herself being drawn to a brash, ambitious American newspaper reporter, Daniel Trent.

Spanning the years from 1896 to 1900, this novel plunges the reader into the vastly different segments of Russian society from which sprang the revolution that would forever change the Motherland. Hero and villain, rich and poor, czar and laborer all come alive in these pages.

THE DAWNING OF DELIVERANCE (THE RUSSIANS SERIES)

Mariana Remizov has forged a place for herself in the field of medicine since the reader last saw her. She is headed to Manchuria, straight into the war zone, to lend her hands of healing as Russia battles Japan. As a nurse, Mariana is competent and courageous, even facing down her past foe, Karl Vlasenko, who is now an influential doctor. While her noble birthright provides confidence, the hardships born out of growing up in poverty create strength—both equally important mainstays for a frontline nurse.

Although she is dedicated to doing service for her country and for those who are wounded, Mariana has a longing that can be fulfilled only by one special relationship. Perhaps Daniel Trent, who is now a war correspondent, is just the person to bring completion to her life. However, when Mariana and Daniel were last together, she felt betrayed when she discovered that he had used their friendship as the foundation for a news story. Why should she trust him this time?

From Manchuria to St. Petersburg, by rail and by boat, the reader moves swiftly through perilous territory in the final days of the reign of Nicholas and Alexandra, entering even into their royal estate. The zeal of laborers, coupled with the intrigue of the politically corrupt, propels the reader right into the heart of the revolution while never losing touch with the soul of the Russian people played out in hero and villain alike. Mariana, Sergei, Anna, and even Cyril Vlasenk are characters not quickly forgotten. What a satisfying way to live and learn Russian history.

FRONTIER LADY (LONE STAR LEGACY SERIES)

Embittered and grief-stricken, nineteen-year-old Deborah Martin impulsively agrees to leave her expansive home in Virginia and travel to Texas to marry her distant cousin, Leonard Stoner. Recently bereft of her beloved father and brother, who bravely surrendered their lives to the Confederate cause, and having no other family, Deborah simply wants to get away from everything that reminds her of sorrow and loss.

Her only personal contact with the prospective groom has been a fleeting visit when he suggested that the Union would offer her solace and a new start in life. Without a backward glance, Deborah flees her memories and accepts the challenge to become the wife of a man she hardly knows. Almost immediately, the new bride realizes not only that she has made a terrible mistake but also that she is practically a prisoner in a house controlled by her abusive husband, and his power-driven father, who feels threatened by anyone who displays spirit, especially a woman.

An unsolved murder, an abduction, bank robbers, Indian tribes (both friendly and hostile), and an ex-Texas-Ranger-turned-circuit-riding-preacher add to the action of the story as Pella unfolds a life to which many women can, unfortunately, relate. As Deborah Stoner discovers just how strong she is and how her weakness finds a home only in a Providential place, the message is clear for all women, from the happily married to those who cry from the shame of hidden blows.

One reader shared that *Frontier Lady* would always be memorable for her not only because of the compelling plot but also because for the first time she began to understand what her own mother had suffered at the hands of an abusive husband. As a survivor, Deborah provides a role model for all who suffer from similar circumstances.

Michael Phillips

Although psychologists and educators report that a person is generally either math/science oriented or has strong verbal skills, Michael Phillips seems to have been blessed with both. Majoring in physics and math in college should have led him to pursue a career in research or teaching—and it has, only not in the expected fields. He researches people, places, and issues. Through the medium of inspirational writing, he challenges his readers to think, to examine, and to have a ready defense for their faith in God. How did a physics student become an editor, a publisher, a bookseller, and an author of fiction? Phillips's succinct explanation for the direction of his life is "I love books."

Married in 1971, Michael and Judy Phillips are the parents of three sons: twins Patrick and Robin and the youngest, Gregory. While keeping two bookstores afloat, editing the works of George MacDonald and others into more readable English, and writing both fiction and nonfiction alone and with Judith Pella, Phillips has also assisted his wife in home schooling their sons. They both share as well in corresponding with the large number of readers who write in response to his books. It is not difficult to understand how Phillips writes so convincingly of marital partnership in his novels, as it seems that he and Judy live it.

PROFESSIONAL

Education
B.S. in physics (major) and math and history (minors), Humboldt State University (graduated magna cum laude)

Career
Bookstore owner; teacher

Awards
Gold Medallion Finalist for sixteen books

PUBLICATIONS

Adult Fiction

Jackson Maxwell Chronicles
Pinnacles of Power, 1991
Depths of Destiny, 1992
Secret of the Rose Series
The Eleventh Hour, 1993
A Rose Remembered, 1994
Escape to Freedom, 1994
Dawn of Liberty, 1995
Mercy and Eagleflight Series
Mercy and Eagleflight, 1996
A Dangerous Love, 1997
Rift in Time Series
A Rift in Time, 1998
Hidden in Time, 1999
Secrets of Heathersleigh Hall Series
Wild Grows the Heather in Devon, 1998
Wayward Winds, 1999
Journals of Corrie Belle Hollister Series
My Father's World (with Judith Pella), 1990
Daughter of Grace (with Judith Pella), 1991
On the Trail of Truth (with Judith Pella), 1991
A Place in the Sun (with Judith Pella), 1991

Sea to Shining Sea, 1992
Into the Long Dark Night, 1992
Land of the Brave and Free, 1993
Grayfox, 1993
A Home for the Heart, 1994

The Braxtons of Miracle Springs Series
The Journals of Corrie and Christopher, 1996
A New Beginning, 1997

Caldonia Series
Legend of the Celtic Stone, 1999

Coauthored with Judith Pella

The Peacemaker (written under the pseudonym of Mark J. Livingstone), 1990

The Stonewycke Trilogy
The Heather Hills of Stonewycke, 1985
Flight from Stonewycke, 1985
Lady of Stonewycke, 1986

The Stonewycke Legacy
Stranger at Stonewycke, 1987
Shadows over Stonewycke, 1988
Treasure of Stonewycke, 1988

The Highland Collection
Jamie MacLeod: Highland Lass, 1987
Robbie Taggart: Highland Sailor, 1987

The Russians Series
The Crown and the Crucible, 1991
A House Divided, 1992
Travail and Triumph, 1992
(See the remaining volumes in Judith Pella's entry in this book.)

Fantasy/Allegory

The Garden at the Edge of Beyond, 1998

Adult Nonfiction

A Christian Family in Action, 1977
Growth of a Vision, 1977
Does Christianity Make Sense?, 1978
Blueprint for Raising a Child, 1978
A Survival Guide for Tough Times, 1979
Control through Planned Budgeting, 1979

Building Respect, Responsibility, and Spiritual Values in Your Child, 1981
A Vision for the Church, 1981
Getting More Done in Less Time, 1982
In Quest of Gold (biography of Jim Ryun), 1984
George MacDonald, Scotland's Beloved Storyteller, 1987
Good Things to Know, 1992
Good Things to Remember, 1994
A God to Call Father, 1994
Best Friends for Life (with Judy Phillips), 1997
Raise up a Standard: A Challenge to Christian Writers, 1998

Edited Works of George MacDonald (1824–1905)

The Fisherman's Lady, 1982
The Marquis' Secret, 1982
The Baronet's Song, 1983
The Shepherd's Castle, 1983
The Tutor's First Love, 1984
The Musician's Quest, 1984
The Maiden's Bequest, 1985
The Curate's Awakening, 1985
The Lady's Confession, 1986
The Baron's Apprenticeship, 1986
The Highlander's Last Song, 1986
The Gentlewoman's Choice, 1987
The Laird's Inheritance, 1987
The Minister's Restoration, 1988
A Daughter's Devotion, 1988
The Peasant Girl's Dream, 1989
The Landlady's Master, 1989
The Poet's Homecoming, 1990

Edited Young Readers' Works of George MacDonald

Wee Sir Gibbie of the Highlands, 1990
Alec Forbes and His Friend Annie, 1990
At the Back of the North Wind, 1991
Adventures of Ranald Bannerman, 1991

Edited Nonfiction and Devotionals of George MacDonald

Discovering the Character of God, 1990
Knowing the Heart of God, 1990

A Time to Grow, 1991
A Time to Harvest, 1991

Edited Works of Harold Bell Wright (1872–1944)

The Shepherd of the Hills, 1988
The Least of These My Brothers, 1989
A Higher Call, 1990

Edited Works of Ralph Conner (1860–1937)

Jim Craig's Battle for Black Rock, 1988
Thomas Skyler, Foothills Preacher, 1988

PERSONAL

To discover how Michael Phillips began writing is to look into the heart of the man and to find both commitment to God and a generous spirit. Seeds of his original "store" were sown while he was still a college student. After reading *A Testament of Devotion* by Thomas Kelly, Phillips was so impressed that he began giving copies away. After investigating a less expensive way to purchase the books, he discovered that the most practical option was to get a retail license. The result was a small part-time bookstore, the One Way Book Shop, opened in a corner of a room. From its humble beginnings in his student apartment, the enterprise has become the One Way, Ltd., and Sunrise Books, housing one of the largest Christian bookstores in northern California. This ministry of literature plays an integral part in the Humbolt County Christian community. Recognizing that the secret of his success lies in sharing, Phillips continues to encourage his staff to give away a book a week. "I want my employees to pray that they can fill the needs of those God brings into the store."

As the bookstore was growing, Phillips also was expanding his talents. Although most authors of fiction would consider their craft a totally creative act, Phillips was introduced to the art of writing by making one of the past masters more readable for contemporary audiences. Impressed by the message in the novels by the Scottish pastor/author George MacDonald, he began editing the works while still serving customers in his bookstore. As can be seen in the listing, MacDonald provided a rich field, and apparently Phillips had just the touch for translation. He has performed a great service by making these deeply spiritual novels, with their timeless truths, available for modern readers.

Family members, as well as those authors whose works hold a place of honor in his extensive library, are those who have most influenced Phillips's writing and his philosophy of life. As would be expected, George MacDonald leads the list, followed by C. S. Lewis, Francis Schaeffer, Richard Foster, and, of course, Thomas Kelly. Phillips claims MacDonald as his "spiritual mentor" and his literary mentor as well. "*The Fisherman's Lady* is the finest crafted novel" that he has ever read. The other writers have added encouragement, exhortation, and insight throughout his life. Phillips also treasures the teamwork that exists with his wife, Judy. They were together at the inception of the bookstore, both taught school to assist in getting the business started, and currently she adds her special touch in the tremendous volume of correspondence resulting from Phillips's multiplied thousands in book sales. Recently, Judy has also joined him by coauthoring *Best Friends for Life*. Acknowledging the immeasurable impact of his father, Denver Phillips, Phillips pays this tribute to him in the dedication and foreword of *A Rift in Time*. "He lived the Proverbs, plain and simple. . . . Quiet, unseen faithfulness does not merely go to the grave and die. Faithfulness always lives on."

Readers may wonder how a man can manage bookstores full-time and write with the quality and quantity that Phillips has. It seems to be a matter of calling, creativity, determination, discipline, and teamwork. Phillips states that he is a morning writer, usually working from six or seven until noon or one. Exercise helps keep him healthy, and he runs from four to six miles a day after his morning writing. A "cool-down" for him is working outside "for perhaps an hour or two," then he writes again until about 6:00. Explaining how he is alert enough to be creative early in the morning, Phillips shares, "I am usually in bed by 9:00. I am not an evening person."

Phillips says that his routine, which is shaped around writing, has not always been so simple. "This schedule has varied through the years. When the children were young, . . . life fitted largely around them. In the early years of my writing, I was also the primary person operating our bookstore, while my wife, Judy, home schooled our three sons. In those days, I wrote at the bookstore (even at the counter, with my typewriter next to the cash register), then came home and wrote in the evenings on the kitchen table. Gradually, as the writing became a little more successful, I set up an office at the store so I could get away from the hubbub and write for a few hours a day. Over the years, I distanced myself more and more from the daily affairs of the business. Over the last ten years, we have been gradually scaling back our involvement in the bookstore business, selling all our stores (there were five), except the original one in Eureka. For the past five years, I have been writing in an office across town completely separate from the bookstore, a house surrounded by redwoods that we purchased just so that I would have a place to get away (after almost thirty years in the bookstore business, I needed it—the creative demands of writing just don't mix very well in retail!). We call the new place *Lebenshaus,* named after the Baron von Dortmann's estate in the Secret of the Rose series. I spend very little time in the store now. Judy manages it on a daily basis, now that our boys are all grown."

However, with his demanding life, Phillips does find time to enrich both his personal life and his writing by traveling. "I travel more to see and to drink in a locale than to conduct specific 'research' as such. But that firsthand knowing of a place, just from being there—feeling it, sensing it, smelling it, walking the streets and fields and paths, and so on in the early morning—is in another sense the most important research of all. I don't really do all that much travel. I can't afford to fly off to every place I write about. Practically speaking, I just can't. It's expensive and tiring. I do know Scotland, England, and Germany pretty well; those are the main countries abroad that I've visited more than once."

Phillips's other research is carried out through books (which is no surprise), studying maps, atlases, and most of all the history of the setting. He also has an extensive library of his own, enriched through his more than thirty-year love affair with books. He also utilizes the nearby university library, which he describes as having "almost anything anyone could ever want."

Phillips reveals that in creating his characters, he has to work harder to make heroes than villains. He reasons that readers are more easily drawn to dramatic events, such as fights and arguments, or to physical actions, such as chases, and those are the responses of the "bad guys." However, his goal for writing lends itself more to the people of stature and character, as he seeks to provide role models for his readers and for himself as well. The main reason he uses antagonists is to provide a contrast for the central character, who exemplifies the theme of the work. "My characters are not usually based on people I know. I do consider myself a student of human nature, as it were. I'm always watching, observing, analyzing . . . bits of this, bits of that help to create characters. Generally, I make up characters to be interesting composites of real human struggles and tensions and dilemmas. If they are anybody, I suppose most of my characters have some of me in them. I don't do that on purpose, but it cannot be helped. Yet . . . once I've got a living, breathing character, they can wind up impacting me, too. I started growing roses because of Baron von Dortmann, not the other way around. I just made it up and wrote about it and then followed suit myself. Now I have a fairly large rose garden, too."

Phillips acknowledges the challenge in his role as a writer of Christian fiction. He takes his task seriously and believes that he has the mission, along with his colleagues, to "change the way people think." Writing mainly to a Christian audience, Phillips is responding to the call God issued to him. He quotes that call: "I want you to speak to and write to and minister to *my* people, *my* body. . . . Others can tell of the Savior; you tell of the Father. I have thousands I am leading to tell the world about my salvation. . . . I want *you* to communicate what I give you to my people, to help them grow in wisdom and maturity as my sons and daughters." For this reason, Phillips says, "I try faithfully to do that. I do not try to write evangelical books because evangelism is something God has given other men and women to focus on. He has given me the job of helping people learn to grow in their faith."

Phillips observes that just as there are writers who include a salvation message in every book, many other writers have chosen to use the methods and priorities of secular writing and are not emphasizing those ideals that should set inspirational fiction apart. It is his desire to provide a balance between plots and themes designed for the new Christian or the not-yet-Christian and those that are barely inspirational. He sees the medium as more than entertainment. He views his writing as a means by which readers "might look up and behold the face of their Father."

Phillips emphasizes that writers of inspirational works need prayer support. He reminds his readers that authors have good and bad days, discouragements and temptations, just as do those who are uplifted, encouraged, and exhorted by their books. He reveals that often a letter of encouragement has come at just the time when he needed it. Those notes serve as bonds joining both reader and writer in a grand fellowship that spans time and is worldwide. Such support strengthens and gives the courage needed to continue with the ministry of creativity. He states that he visualizes the readers as he writes. This gives him the sense that he is writing to people instead of just writing a book. He prays for his audience, and it gives him great comfort to know that they are doing the same for him. "When prayers and letters later flow from readers to me, a peaceful sense comes to me in knowing that the Spirit of God is continually completing an invisible circle of relationship between His people in what to me is nothing short of a quietly miraculous way."

SUMMARY: *STRANGER AT STONEWYCKE* (THE STONEWYCKE LEGACY)

Allison MacNeil, age seventeen, faces each day with the realization that one day she will take her place as the Lady of Stonewycke. She will be following in the footsteps of gracious, courageous Christian ladies who have gained the respect of crofter and laird alike across northeastern Scotland. Inwardly intimidated by the reputation of her ancestors, Allison attempts to distance herself from the common people and constantly competes with her peers. Therefore, she sets about to win respect in her own way.

Logan Macintyre has grown up independent of any heritage that he would want to claim. At twenty-two, he has nearly perfected the art of being a cardsharp. In his eyes, respect is deserved by anyone who is successful in making money, whatever the method. His father figure, Skittles, has taught him the tricks of the trade, and they often work together to dupe unsuspecting tavern patrons out of cash. When Skittles is fatally injured by a rival, more powerful con man, Logan seeks revenge. Although he is successful in his attempt at restitution, he must then flee for his life.

Street-hardened fugitive and cynical young lady are brought face to face by circumstances that seem directed by fate. However, seen through the eyes of faith, the unlikely pair is on a collision course to serve a higher purpose and to learn eternal lessons in humility, self-acceptance, and trust.

Phillips and Pella use the vehicle of story to demonstrate the imperative of dependence on God and the infinite importance of the daily choices made by His children. In this first volume of the companion series to the Stonewycke Trilogy, loyalty, honesty, recognition, submission of pride, the burden and bounty of carrying on the family heritage, the impact of making choices, and God's sovereignty are interwoven through an intriguing plot. When finishing this introductory work, readers will want to have available *Shadows over Stonewycke* and *Treasure of Stonewycke* to continue the series.

MY FATHER'S WORLD (JOURNALS OF CORRIE BELLE HOLLISTER)

When fifteen-year-old Cornelia Hollister, better known as Corrie Belle, headed west with her mother and four younger brothers and sisters to find her delinquent uncle and perhaps her father, her plans never included becoming a writer. She kept a diary only because her Ma had told her that she should. Ma had said that she was not "the marryin' sort" and that since she had her "nose in a book" all the time, she should put her thoughts on paper, too. Neither could have guessed what doors Corrie's writing would open in her future—amazing opportunities for a woman in the 1860s.

Written in first-person format, this introductory book in the series reveals with intimate detail what life was like for women and children in the gold camps of the 1850s as seen through the eyes and from the heart of a teenage girl. Phillips and Pella have captured the sights, sounds, and smells of this boisterous time in American history when often the law was whatever the most powerful man said it was.

Dialogue flows freely with its "homespun flavor" retained in both conversation and introspection. Corrie and her siblings—Zack, Becky, Emily, and Tad—each develop their unique personalities as the series progresses. Pa,

Uncle Nick, and a number of others introduced in the first book have become old friends by the last. Lessons in life and death, expressions of heartbreak and joy, and adventures with friends and foes alike unfold at a realistic pace, framed in historical accuracy and colored with a colloquial sense of humor. As Corrie matures, her adventures and assessments of life make delightful reading for all, whether or not they are "the marryin' sort."

THE ELEVENTH HOUR (SECRET OF THE ROSE SERIES)

Using the metaphors of roses, gardens, seasons, home, family, and a father's sacrificial love, Phillips plants, prunes, tends, and harvests a powerful story. Opening in the peaceful rose garden of *Lebenshaus,* an estate beloved and maintained by the Prussian von Dortmann family for more than a century, the tale moves rapidly moves into the winds of war that swept throughout Europe.

Characters include American and European, military and civilian, soldier and spy, Christian and Jew—each following a course to which he or she has sworn allegiance or holds loyalty by birth or by choice. Baron Heinrich von Dortmann and his cherished wife and daughter choose to risk their lives to offer refuge to the hunted, American Ambassador McCallum and his visiting teenage son struggle with just what role their country is to play in the European unrest of 1937, and Count von Schmundt, his wife, and his son, as Nazi sympathizers, scramble to be a part of the elite yet sinister force that will change history.

In this first novel of this epic series, Phillips introduces characters, both good and evil, who will carve a niche in the reader's memory as surely as World War II scarred the face of Europe. A more personal involvement in the panorama of the times would be difficult to imagine. This is not a fairy tale, and everyone does not live happily ever after, but the reader will know what it was like to endure the trying times that led to the erection and eventually to the destruction of the Berlin Wall. Each novel in the set has its own purpose and pace. However, one note of caution: When beginning to read volume 3, *Escape to Freedom,* the reader should plan to do nothing else until the riveting conclusion is reached. Everything less important will wait.

WILD GROWS THE HEATHER IN DEVON (SECRETS OF HEATHERSLEIGH HALL SERIES)

When Charles Rutherford, loved by his wife and children, respected by those who care for his estate, and esteemed by his associates in Parliament, arrives in London to be knighted by Queen Victoria, he deems it to be the high point of his life. Little does he suspect that a "chance" encounter in the street on his way to the palace will alter his life for eternity.

As a student of Charles Darwin and a thoroughly liberated man, Sir Charles and his adoring wife, Jocelyn, are attempting to prepare their children, George and Amanda, to be intellectually active and to question everything. Both delight in dialogue with their young offspring, dialogue that leads to doubt, query, and pondering anything in the universe. Faith has no part in their existence. Spiritual beliefs are for the lazy of mind who want only easy solutions. Challenge is the thing, and protesting until a plausible reason is given is an action worthy of praise.

What happens in such a household when one member of the family is suddenly confronted by the Lord of life? What happens to the lively discussions that lead to more questions but rarely to permanent answers? Who becomes the outsider when faith and doubt meet face to face?

Phillips has created characters who are attempting to answer questions that baffled this early twentieth-century husband and wife and that still block faith in the dawn of the twenty-first. In a writing style that is reminiscent of C. S. Lewis, Phillips walks with readers back to a time when the beauty of nature was more available than it is to many modern city dwellers and shares delightful insights, both natural and spiritual, that would make both Lewis and George MacDonald proud.

Jos van Manen Pieters

For one who lists her education simply as high school and her career experiences as mother and housewife, Jos van Manen Pieters has an impressive list of accomplishments. Born in the Netherlands, Pieters states that even as a child she was "fascinated . . . that just those twenty-six tokens could, in combination, convey every message imaginable." Since her birth on March 21, 1930, to the present, she has published over thirty books in Dutch, with the Warbler Cottage Romances having been translated into English. Her love of language and her desire "to explore and master it" has been realized.

Pieters is the mother of Nelleke and Bert. She still resides in the Netherlands, where she is recognized as one of that country's most beloved writers of domestic novels. Her Warbler Cottage Romances have sold hundreds of thousands of copies across Europe.

As might be guessed from the content of her novels, Pieters's hobbies include gardening and taking long nature walks. She also enjoys photography and reading.

PROFESSIONAL

Education

High school

Career
Mother and housewife

Awards
The ATHOS Prize, Dutch Library Society, 1968; knighted in the Order of Orange-Nassau by Her Majesty Queen Juliana, 1980

PUBLICATIONS

Although all Pieters's books were originally published in Dutch, the English titles are listed here, with the exception of the first, a book of poetry, written before Pieters began her first novel. Her work spans forty years, and she considers her latter works to be of higher quality than her former ones. However, Pieters's Warbler Cottage Romances, some of her earlier works, might rank as the best written in the United States.

Adult Fiction

Because most of Pieters's books were printed in the Netherlands, many publication dates are not available.
Hart in het zoeklicht
The Discerning Heart, 1955, 1992
Calling in the Wind
God's Cryptography
Journey with No Voyage Home
A Gleam of Dawn, 1992
Rosemarie
There Will Be No Miracle
A Longing Fulfilled, 1992
This Lovely, Hazardous Life
This Is My Haven
Let Us Forget
In Excess of Happiness
Love Incognito
Give Me a Sign of Life
Dreams Will Not Die
By Hear-Say Only
Sometimes Happiness Comes with a New Face
A Path through the Wilderness
Footmarks on the Water
The Comforting Bird

Every Desert Has Its Well
Along Green Banks of Hope
Someone on Your Side
A Paper Ship
The Telescope
Like a Leaf in the Wind
Destined to Live
Lane of Refuge
A Hinge in Time
Eyes from Across, 1995

PERSONAL

Jos van Manen Pieters states that she did not choose to write Christian fiction but, rather, that it chose her. "This you do not choose. You write what you are, and what is in must come out." Her writing does reflect the qualities of the Dutch culture, with its values of determination, cheerfulness, and loyalty to family even at the loss of personal satisfaction and fulfillment.

However, Pieters's characters are anything but dull or too perfect to be believable. Tempers flare, impulsive decisions bring regret, and evidence of God's grace is demonstrated. One consistent characteristic of Pieters's work is the realism portrayed in her character development.

Pieters reports that research for her work is relationship oriented. She expresses her philosophy this way: "I am very thorough in this aspect. I read up on the subject, of course. But I really need to talk to people who have experienced multiple sclerosis, if my main character has MS—the things that you experience if you are the wife or husband of an MS patient. . . . This is not in any book or brochure. Only people can tell you what their life is like."

The intended theme throughout Pieters's novels is love. "That is, love in all the ways it manifests. The love of God for mankind, yes. A man and a women, romantically involved, yes. But there is much more. I write about love in all the shapes and forms and faces I see it in. I see it between a parent and a child, between a friend and a friend. I see it between an artist and a painting, if he is sincere about his art. Between a mechanic and a car, if he loves his craft. Between a man and his dog, a nurse and her patient. This love with its many faces, and the fact that I believe that people will always be helped by people, not miracles, is the recurring theme in my work."

Although most of her characters are created and not based on people known to her, Pieters relates that in *God's Cryptography* she is sharing "the story of my daughter's medical history as an infant. The parents, however, are totally different from her father and me."

When asked about what goals she has for her writing, Pieters related that she hopes that her readers will "enjoy the reading. If they think about the issues, if they learn anything, that is a bonus. I do not preach. In fact, I do not even like books that do." Certainly, her books are not sermons, but they do give the reader food for thought as characters learn or do not learn lessons about love and life.

When asked about the future of inspirational fiction, Pieters spoke with guarded skepticism but with hope. "I am pessimistic about the future of fiction, period. Television screens and computer screens are taking up more and more of the limited reading energy the new generation has to invest. I think books and newspapers and magazines are up for a hard battle against that endless offering of moving pictures. But I do not think the exquisite beauty of the written word will ever be without an audience."

SUMMARY: *THE DISCERNING HEART* (WARBLER COTTAGE ROMANCES)

Dealing with the pain of a wife who is dying of cancer and with a marriage that is already dead is a daily burden for Baron Reinier Van Herewaarden. Simultaneously trying to keep life happy for his lively four-year-old daughter, Ingeborg, creates a nearly impossible load to balance. When about at his wit's end, he reads an intriguing advertisement in the newspaper. It simply states, "Who is willing to entrust their children to my care? Twenty-one years old. No experience with children, but lots of goodwill." The nobleman-turned-factory-owner, drawn by the straightforward statement of lack of credentials but expressed desire to meet a need, responds to the ad and contacts young Marion Verkerk. Neither the baron nor the innocent Christian young lady can foretell how their lives will be altered, nor can they foretell what each will learn in the process.

What the reader discovers is how God can work to bring light to the darkest corners of life through the sincere and determined pursuit of His will. As Pieters has stated, she does not write books that preach at her readers, but, through the honest struggles for finding answers that make life livable and even delightful, she demonstrates how God touches and moves in His own time and in His own way.

A Longing Fulfilled and *A Gleam of Dawn* continue the saga of the Van Herewaarden children as they become adults, to complete the Warbler Cottage Romances. They are equally well written and will leave the reader with the assurance that even though these are works of fiction, the baron and his family must surely reside in Borg and that, if one were to travel in the Netherlands, visiting them would be a priority.

All three volumes of the Warbler Cottage Romances are published in the United States by Revell, a division of Baker Book House, Grand Rapids, Michigan.

Noreen Riols

When one reads the brief biographical sketch of Noreen Riols and finds that she lives with her husband in a French village, it would be tempting to think that anyone might be able to write novels in such a peaceful setting. On further investigation, however, one discovers that she has also worked for the British Broadcasting Company (BBC) and reared five children and yet has served as an international speaker and has had books published in France, Germany, Norway, the Netherlands, the United States, and her native England.

PROFESSIONAL

Education
Lycée Français de Londres

Career
BBC World Service, London; nurse's training, St. Thomas's Hospital, London

Memberships
Romantic Novelists Association; Association of Women Writers and Journalists; Society of Authors; Fellowship of Christian Writers

PUBLICATIONS

Adult Fiction

Laura, 1992
Katharine, 1994

The House of Annanbrae Series (also in British, Dutch, and German editions)
Where Hope Shines Through, 1994
To Live Again, 1995
Before the Dawn, 1996
Where Love Endures, 1997

Adult Nonfiction

Eye of the Storm (also in German, French and Norwegian editions; to be reissued in the United Kingdom in 1998)
My Unknown Child (first published in 1986 as *Abortion: A Woman's Birthright?;* reissued under *My Unborn Child* in 1995, French and German editions)
Only the Best, 1987
When Suffering Comes, 1990

PERSONAL

Noreen Riols states that she has been interested in putting her thoughts on paper since she was a child but began writing professionally at the request of a publisher. She writes inspirational fiction because she is a committed Christian, and this is her way of reaching out to non-Christians. Describing her work as both character and action driven, Riols shares that her goal from book to book is to share Jesus through the medium of story.

Research takes a minimal amount of Riols's writing schedule because she writes about things she is already familiar with and frequently bases her characters on her family and the people she knows. She states that most of the characters in her House of Annanbrae series are real people.

Reporting herself to be an avid reader, Riols relates that she learned her technique from many authors. She identifies Catherine Marshall as the most influential in her life.

Describing her view of the future of Christian fiction, Riols sees it as "rosy." She supports this by adding, "People are tired of kitchen-sink dramas, bad language and lurid sex scenes. Christian fiction gives them an ideal and a hope without preaching or judging."

SUMMARY: *WHEN HOPE SHINES THROUGH* (HOUSE OF ANNANBRAE SERIES)

When Katharine de Montval loses her mother, Rowena, and their London home in a German air raid, she feels bereft of all that has meaning in her life.

She has no idea how to begin looking for her father, who deserted her mother years ago. Shadowing her grief is the mystery that her mother seemed to be calling out with love to her father as she lay dying. Not only is that an enigma to Katharine, but with her last breath, as though it were of imminent importance, her mother pled with her to seek out some old trunks stored in her great aunt's attic.

Discovery of letters at the bottom of the last trunk gives Katharine hope that her father's choice to leave her mother was the result of a terrible misunderstanding and that he has tried in vain to return but has been hampered by the scourge of war wreaking its carnage all across Europe. Feeling that she has someone, somewhere, who truly loves her brings comfort, and Katharine begins to respond to the kindness offered by friends and relatives. While searching for direction, she is given the opportunity to attack her new life through training in the French Resistance.

Finding purpose for her life through the danger and drudgery of the underground inadvertently takes Katharine closer to finding her father and unraveling the mystery of his disappearance. Amid the air raids, near loss of life, and necessary deception of being part of military espionage, Katharine also finds love.

The author takes readers into the ranks of those nameless heroes who daily, often hourly, endured unbelievable danger to assist in freeing Europe from forces that would rule at any cost and without mercy. Capturing the breathless adventure of the men and women who share secret lives and care deeply for one another as they bravely attempt to outguess the enemy, Riols pays tribute to those who survived to celebrate victory and to those who fell unmourned.

Riols sparks the interest of readers with this quick peek at volume 2 in the series: "*To Live Again* takes Katharine to Paris, where she encounters a series of unexpected events and revelations regarding her father's family—an eccentric aristocratic collection of aunts, uncles, cousins, and the presiding great-grandmother living in an old chateau near the Spanish border."

Lee Roddy

Born on August 22, 1921, Lee Roddy lived his earliest years in Marion County, Illinois. His father, Thomas, was a laborer, and his mother, Neva, was kept busy rearing ten children. At the age of twenty-two, Roddy moved to Hollywood to begin a writing career. Five years later, on October 17, 1947, he married Cicely Price. A former radio, stage, and television commercial actress, Cicely currently works at editing her husband's books and attends to the details of his writing career. Their two children, Steven and Susan, are both schoolteachers and have sons of their own.

Although Roddy wrote for many years before publishing his first book in 1974, to date he has written or coauthored more than sixty books. He has made the *New York Times* Best-Seller List, and at least five of his novels have received the Silver Angel Award for Excellence in Quality Moral Literature from Religion in Media. His books for children have sold over 1.5 million copies and are available in seventeen countries. Among his best-known titles are *Grizzly Adams* (which was made into a popular television series), *The Lincoln Conspiracy* (which was produced as a motion picture), and *Jesus* (a film presently available in 300 languages).

PROFESSIONAL

Education

Los Angeles City College (graduated first in class); Modesto (California) Junior College; Oakdale (California) High School

Career

Writer for a Los Angeles advertising agency; writer for radio network dramas on NBC, CBS, and the Blue Radio Network (now ABC); staff novelist and researcher for a motion picture and television production company; advertising agency promotion director; general manager for radio stations in Honolulu, Hawaii; Hollywood, California, and the Disneyland Hotel, Anaheim, California; reporter for *Turlock Journal,* Turlock, California; reporter for *Modesto Bee,* Modesto, California; editor and publisher of four community newspapers; travel columnist; lecturer for *Writer's Digest Magazine;* seminar leader and speaker at writers' conferences across the United States; full-time professional author and speaker since 1980; newspaper columnist; wrote and narrated *Your American Heritage,* a daily radio program

Memberships

Author's League; Author's Guild of America

Awards

Pacesetter Award, Mount Hermon Christian Writers Conference, 1982; Silver Angel Award, *The Hair-Pulling Dog, The Bear Cub Disaster, Dooger, The Grasshopper Hound,* and *The Ghost Dog of Stoney Ridge,* 1985; International Angel Award, D. J. Dillon Adventures series, 1986; Silver Angel Award, *High Country Ambush,* 1992; named as one of fifteen distinguished alumni of the past 100 years by Oakdale (California) High School, 1993; Listed in *Who's Who in California, International Authors and Writers Who's Who, Contemporary Authors, Who's Who in Professional Speaking,* and *Notable Americans*

PUBLICATIONS

Adult Fiction

The Life and Times of Grizzly Adams (with Charles E. Sellier Jr.), 1977
The Taming of Cheetah, 1979
Search for the Avenger, 1980
The Mystery of Aloha House, 1981

Love's Far Horizon, 1981
The Impatient Blossom (with Cicely Roddy), 1985
Giants on the Hill, 1994
Cinnabar, 1995
Shiloh's Choice, 1996
Lady Pinkerton Chronicles
Days of Deception, 1998
Yesterday's Shadow, 1999

Juvenile Fiction

The Ladd Family Adventures
Secret of the Shark Pit, 1988
The Legend of Fire, 1988
Mystery of the Island Jungle, 1989
The Dangerous Canoe Race, 1990
Secret of the Sunken Submarine, 1990
Mystery of the Wild Surfer, 1990
Peril at Pirate's Point, 1993
Terror at Forbidden Falls, 1993
Eye of the Hurricane, 1994
Night of the Vanishing Lights, 1994
Case of the Dangerous Cruise, 1995
Panic in the Wild Waters, 1995
Tracked by the Wolf Pack, 1997
Stranded on Terror Island, 1997
Hunted in the Alaskan Wilderness, 1997
An American Adventure Series
The Overland Escape, 1989
The Desperate Search, 1989
Danger on Thunder Mountain, 1989
Secret of the Howling Cave, 1990
The Flaming Trap, 1990
Terror in the Sky, 1991
Mystery of the Phantom Gold, 1991
The Gold Train Bandits, 1992
High Country Ambush, 1992
D. J. Dillon Adventures Series
The Hair-Pulling Bear Dog, 1985
The Bear Cub Disaster, 1985
Dooger, the Grasshopper Hound, 1985
The Ghost Dog of Stoney Ridge, 1985

The Mad Dog of Lobo Mountain, 1986
Legend of the White Raccoon, 1986
Mystery of the Black Hole Mine, 1987
Ghost of the Moaning Mansion, 1987
The Secret of Mad River, 1988
Escape Down the Raging Rapids, 1989

Between Two Flags Series
Cry of Courage, 1998
Where Bugles Call, 1998
Burden of Honor, 1999

Juvenile Nonfiction

Robert E. Lee: Christian General and Gentleman, 1977

Ghostwritten, Edited, or Collaborated Nonfiction

On Eagle's Wings (with Tom Claus), 1976
Word of Fire (by George B. Derkatch with Lee Roddy; film edition published by World Christian Ministries), 1977
The Lincoln Conspiracy (with two listed authors; also a motion picture), 1977
In Search of Historic Jesus (with Charles E. Sellier Jr.), 1979
Jesus (released as a film by the Campus Crusade for Christ in 300 languages), 1979
Intimate Portraits of Women in the Bible, 1980
On Wings of Love, 1981
Making the Most of Your Mind, 1983
Writing to Inspire (by William Gentz and other prominent inspirational writers), 1992
The Complete Guide to Christian Writing and Speaking (with other Christian writers), 1994

PERSONAL

Lee Roddy shares, "A shoe with a three-and-a-half-inch cork sole made a writer out of me. I was born sick and handicapped. My left leg was three and a half inches shorter than the right. Health prevented me from leading a normal boy's life for ten years. During my confinement to bed or chair, I became an avid reader. Then surgeries corrected my problems, and my leg grew to match the other. By about age twelve, I knew I wanted to be an author." Influential authors for Roddy during this time were Jack London, Albert Payson Terhune, and Ernest Thompson Seton.

Contrary to what his great success might indicate, Roddy did not set out to become a writer of Christian fiction. "I didn't really choose it. The field opened to me after beginning in the secular area. I've pretty much stayed with the inspirational line." Roddy has identified his audience through the sales of his books. "From meeting thousands of people at personal appearances, I know that Christian parents, teachers, and middle-school children have bought more than 1.5 million copies of my books." Seeking to expand that group, his current objective is "to reach all public schools and public libraries with my writing without losing my concept."

Although Roddy reads widely as an adult, he does not feel that there is any one author who currently influences his writing. He does like stories that move the reader and claims that this preference helps direct his reading and consequently his own writing. He identifies his own style as popular, consisting of "easy-reading, lots of dialogue, and story movement to keep readers turning pages. My plots are action driven to hold the reader's attention, although theme and character are also important in all of my stories."

Roddy plans his story first and fits the necessary setting into the plot. "In order to make the story work right, I choose the setting and then travel or do whatever is necessary to authenticate that setting. . . . Knowing that research can be a trap that keeps an author from writing, I plan my story, then find the material needed to give authenticity to the finished project."

Unlike some authors, Roddy does not base his stories or characters on his personal experiences or on people he has known. "None of my characters are based on people I know. I can't think of a single story incident in my works that came out of my own experiences."

Besides holding a reader's attention, each of Roddy's stories has "an underlying focus of helping readers understand something about the Lord. . . . I know readers must be entertained to keep them turning pages. My lasting goal is to help them learn more about God so they will move closer to him through the story's content."

Optimistic about the future of Christian fiction, Roddy states, "Like anything else, fiction changes with readers' interests, but I believe a good story will always find an audience. At present, I'm told that about fifty percent of all Christian books are fiction, so I see a future in writing stories that quietly inform while entertaining." Roddy's three major goals are that "everything I write honors God, that my works become as popular in public schools as they are in Christian and home schools, and that I author at least one classic that lives on to be read by generations yet unborn."

SUMMARY: *GIANTS ON THE HILL*

Although captivated by her husband's love for the young California territory and his ambitious visions for its future, Shiloh is appalled by the crudity of life in this land, where explosive growth is fueled by gold fever. Standing by her husband's side as their ship sails into San Francisco harbor, her first view of their new home is a bay full of abandoned ships and rotting garbage. Drawn by the promise of easy gold, the population of the area is growing faster than order can be maintained.

Determined to overcome her dismay at the danger of life in this city, where women are vastly outnumbered, Shiloh clings to her husband's love, his visions of unlimited opportunities, and the dreams that he has for building a transportation system to tie California to the rest of the nation.

When tragedy strikes, Shiloh's life is shattered by the loss of the husband whom she has looked to for affirmation and direction. She finds herself penniless in a frightening world where she is being stalked by an unknown foe. Who is this man who watches her every move? Who wanted her husband's death?

Crushed with grief and torn in two directions, Shiloh must return to her family in the East or learn to survive in this wild and savage land, finding dreams to make her own.

MAD DOG OF LOBO MOUNTAIN (D. J. DILLON ADVENTURES SERIES)

Letting his dog Hero loose for just a few minutes at Devil's Point Public Campground, D. J. Dillon sets in motion a disastrous chain of events. As he seeks to recover the runaway pet, D. J. discovers that a rabid dog is also running in the mountains and that one of the animals has bitten a little boy who, as a result, has disappeared from the campsite. Because D. J. had not made the time to have Hero vaccinated, his pet's life hangs in the balance, as does that of the little boy. With the child's angry father threatening to shoot whatever dog he finds, D. J. desperately tries to find Hero first. Through his adventures, he discovers the importance of being responsible and making the right choices.

DANGER ON THUNDER MOUNTAIN (AN AMERICAN ADVENTURE SERIES), REVIEWED BY SARAH BARNETT, AGE THIRTEEN

Danger on Thunder Mountain is the third book in the American Adventure series. Set in the year of 1934, this book is packed full of action and suspense. Hildy Corrigan and Ruby Konning team up with various family members and friends in a search for Ruby's long-lost father. Along the way, the dedicated group runs into many challenges. Problems ranging from a missing raccoon to an exploding mountain are used to teach everyone important lessons about faith in God.

This book is great for any young teens who enjoy adventure stories. Roddy does a wonderful job of maintaining an exciting story line while teaching good moral values. I recommend *Danger on the Mountain* to everyone.

Gayle Roper

What a delightful paradox exists in one who has earned a certificate in pastoral counseling and has membership in an organization with the ominous name Sisters in Crime. Only among Christian fiction writers is such a person likely to be found, and Gayle Roper holds that distinction. When she is not counseling or creating crime scenes, Roper enjoys such normal pleasures as gardening, traveling with her husband, and dining out. The marriage partner of this unique individual is Dr. Charles Roper, a research engineer. Charles and Gayle make their home in Coatesville, Pennsylvania. They are the parents of two sons, Charles III and Jeffrey; two daughters-in-law, Audrey and Cindy; and "three beautiful granddaughters," Ashley, Brianne, and Abigail.

PROFESSIONAL

Education

B.A., Ursinus College; graduate work, Lehigh University; certificate in pastoral counseling, Christian counseling, and educational foundation, Laverock, Pennsylvania; Dallas Theological Seminary

Career

Director, Sandy Cove Christian Writers Conference, six years; staff member, CLASS (Christian Leaders, Authors and Speakers Services); board member

(1975–1994) and director (five years), St. Davids Christian Writers Association; chapter president, vice president, and secretary, National League of American Pen Women, Chester County Branch; faculty at numerous Christian writers' conferences across the country; speaker and retreat leader at several hundred church women's groups since 1972; approved speaker, Christian Women's Clubs.

Awards

Special Recognition Award, Mount Hermon Christian Writers Conference, 1987; Lois Henderson Memorial Award, St. Davids Christian Writers Conference, 1989; Honorary Member, Delta Kappa Gamma, 1990; Professional Contribution Award, Florida Christian Writers Conference, 1991; Special Recognition Award, Greater Philadelphia Christian Writers Fellowship, 1993

Articles

Articles in the following publications: *The Christian Communicator, Christian Reader, Discipleship Journal, The Lookout, Moody Monthly, The Pentecostal Evangel, Today's Christian Woman, Virtue,* and *Young Ambassador*

PUBLICATIONS

Adult Fiction

Fear Haunts the Summer, 1971
Death on an Island, 1980
The Midnight Intruder, 1987
Enough!, 1997
The Key, 1998
An Amhearst Mystery Series
  Caught in the Middle, 1997
  Caught in the Act, 1998
Palisades Series
  The Document, 1998
  The Decision, 1999

Juvenile Fiction

A Race to the Finish, 1991
Discovery at Denny's Deli, 1992
The Secret of the Burning House, 1992
Mystery at Harmony Hill, 1993

The Case of the Missing Melody, 1993
The Puzzle of the Poison Pen, 1994
Here Boy!, 1995
Cat Burglars, 1995
Manda's Mystery, 1996
Whoo Done It?, 1996
Bear Scare, 1996
Seventh Grade Soccer Star, 1998

Adult Nonfiction

A Mother's World, 1975
Wife: Mate, Mother, Me!, 1975
Mom, My Tummy's Nervous, 1977
New Program Ideas for Women's Groups, 1978
Time of Storm, 1981
Who Cares?, 1992
Balancing Your Emotions, 1992
Into Africa, 1995

PERSONAL

Gayle Roper reports that she has always been an avid reader and that, in her case, taking in words and ideas led to giving them back as well. "When I was a young mom staying at home with my little boys, it was natural to move from reading words to writing them. I had never planned to be a writer. I had taught junior high English and social studies and assumed that some day I'd return to the classroom. But God had other ideas, and soon I was immersed in writing and the publishing business. I have never looked back.

"I have chosen to write Christian fiction for several reasons. First, I am enamored with story. I love to read, watch, tell, or write stories. That I can take something I love so much and embed Christian values and principles into it is nothing short of wonderful."

Although the creative act of being an author is a delight, research is the aspect of Roper's profession that she likes the least. "I do what is necessary for accuracy, but I do not get pleasure out of finding facts for facts' sake. I am an auditory learner and a hands-on person, neither quality necessarily good for researching. My preferred method of research is to seek out people who know what I need to learn or who do what I need to write about and then interview them. My brother, the volunteer fireman, has come in handy any number of times. I find that in interviews I learn things I wouldn't otherwise, like the fact that in a house fire, the fish in the fish tank are boiled to death, a neat little piece of trivia that can add veracity."

When asked about the process of writing, Roper stated, "I write on a computer using Word for Windows. I'm a poor typist and have found the quick corrections possible through word processing a true boon. I am not a morning person, and I do my best work late in the afternoon. I would work more at night but for two problems: I can't get to sleep if I do (my mind won't shut down), and my husband tends to get cranky when I don't go to bed at what he considers a normal hour."

In reply to questions about the role of literary elements in her works, Roper reiterated what her loyal readers already know—that romance and "lots of humor" are trademarks in her mystery stories. However, she focuses on character development to build her theme. "I hope that my books are character driven, though all mysteries have strong plot lines, too. One of the challenges of Christian fiction is to let the Christian principles and truths discussed come from the characters themselves and their struggles instead of sounding tacked on. Finesse here requires character-driven books, I think."

Revealing that her recurring theme is that of characters making choices, Roper shares her philosophy: "In many ways everything boils down to choice. We choose to move ahead. We choose to do it God's way. We learn to choose from strength. We choose to risk rather than play it safe. We choose emotional family ties over genetic family ties. God chooses to work in spite of us."

Asked whether her characters are based on people she knows or are completely her own creations, Roper stated, "My characters are usually based on someone I know for their physical characteristics. That way I can remember what they look like. Otherwise, I tend to forget what color eyes I gave them, how long their hair is, and so on. As far as personality is concerned, I don't use friends. I try to develop characters who will each have a unique personality and disposition. For instance, in *The Document,* which I am now writing, Cara comes from a long line of strong personalities and has coped by keeping her head low and doing what she wanted in a quiet way—every bit as willful as the rest, just with fewer decibels. In the course of the book, she will come to learn she's as strong as the rest of her family; she just never had any cause to act on that strength before. She also hates change, and it's only the discovery of the document of the title that gives her a strong enough motivation to choose to make changes. One common characteristic I give all my lead characters is humor."

In response to a question about influential people and books that have touched her writing, Roper shared that there has been no single individual writer but rather "a rich amalgam of writers through years of reading and through personal friendships. My involvement over the years in Christian writers' conferences has provided some of the most delightful, encouraging, and challenging influences and opportunities a writer could ever want." She states that her personal reading habits have made an impact on her writing. "I tend to write what I like to read, fiction that touches the heart in an uplifting, entertaining, and thoughtful way. Among my earliest memories is my mother sitting with a book, always a book. I learned to love good fiction from her."

Roper's spiritual beliefs deeply affect her writing. "I find it impossible to imagine writing without my faith touching the pages. How can I write of anything substantive without talking about how God is involved? How can I write without talking about the necessity of Jesus, the reality of sin and its effects? I am a highly practical person who tends to kernel truths. Because of this, I constantly pray that God will give me the insight I need to write with depth. I pray He will enable me to peel the layers of pop truth to get to real truth, like peeling an onion. I'm always working on seeing the layers, the ramifications, the complexities."

When asked about her personal goals, Roper acknowledged that "the Lord and I have been down the personal goals road many times, and it always comes down to choosing not my will but His. My goal for my writing is that I will produce the very best I am capable of and that I will leave the rest to Him. Because I would love to write best-sellers and be the darling of Christian publishing (wouldn't we all?), I constantly have to go back to these basics. My personal mission statement has two points: to write quality material that points to the fullness of life in Christ and to teach others to do and find the same.

"As far as my readers are concerned, I pray over each book that they will find some truth in it to turn their hearts more fully to God. If they actually enjoy the story and laugh a little bit in the process, those are wonderful pluses."

Roper shared her view of the future of inspirational fiction: "I am encouraged as I look at Christian fiction. I see a wide variety of styles, a broadening variety of genres. I see the quality of the writing increasing all the time. As long as books are published because the story is worth telling and is well told, Christian fiction will continue to flourish. I count it a privilege and a high calling to be part of the train of writers God is using today."

SUMMARY: *CAUGHT IN THE MIDDLE* (AN AMHEARST MYSTERY SERIES)

When Merrileigh Kramer chooses to leave home and strike out for independence and the excitement of the fast-moving world of newspaper reporting, she could not have anticipated just how unpredictable her new life would be.

First, there is the harrowing ride home in the sleet on a "dark and stormy night" when she is almost run down by a reckless, speeding motorist. Then, almost immediately, as her car is spinning out of control, Merry nearly collides with a pedestrian. Arriving safe at home and in desperate need of a diet soft drink and a warm, cozy evening with her cat, Merry opens the trunk of her car to retrieve her drinks and discovers a dead body.

Later, as the blossoming young reporter is attempting to solve the mystery, she realizes that all her narrow escapes of that memorable evening were connected to the corpse that she had been carrying in her car. At that crucial point, however, she wonders whether she will survive to share her knowledge with the police.

This first novel in the Amhearst Mystery series sets a fast pace in action, character development, and relationships. Merry has a quick sense of humor that is at its best when she is laughing at herself. Her response to danger, her own vulnerability, and her desire to be strong are tempered realistically with her dependence on God. She is a believable protagonist and manages to find enough trouble to dabble in to entice the reader to be ready to delve quickly into the next installment of her adventures.

Nancy Rue

Perhaps it is the sense of humor bubbling up when she explains her method of choosing a husband that provides a clue to the popularity of writer Nancy Rue. A great fan of Nancy Drew, she says, "I couldn't find a nice guy with the last name Drew and settled for the next best thing." Perhaps it is the active life she chooses when not writing, raising three black Labrador retrievers and sailing on the family pontoon boat, that lends credibility to the action intrinsic in her writing style. Or maybe it is her joy in the basics of life, indicated by her decision to list reading and eating among her hobbies, that makes her such a realistic and delightful author to follow. Whatever the reason, Rue has created substantial competition for her childhood idol among juvenile readers of Christian fiction and made significant contributions to nonfiction writing as well.

A child of the 1950s, Nancy was born to Bill and Jean Naylor in Riverside, New Jersey. She lives in Lebanon, Tennessee, with her husband, Jim, who is a project/account manager for Stagecraft Set Design and Fabrication. The Rues are the parents of one daughter: Marijean.

PROFESSIONAL

Education

M.A. in education, College of William and Mary; B.A. in theater, University of Nevada, Reno; B.A. in English, Stetson University

Career

High school English teacher, eleven years; high school theater teacher, five years; artistic director, Nevada Children's Theater, five years

Memberships

Society of Children's Book Writers and Illustrators

Awards

Seven Evangelical Press Association Awards; Campus Life Book Award of Merit; C. S. Lewis Honor Book Award

PUBLICATIONS

Juvenile Fiction

Row This Boat Ashore, 1986
Stop in the Name of Love (Holly)/Stop in the Name of Love (Kyle) (Flipside Fiction), 1988
The Janis Project, 1988
Home by Another Way, 1991
The Lucas Secret and Other Stories by Nancy Rue (published in French), 1994
Retreat to Love, 1996
Christian Heritage Series
- The Salem Years
  - *The Rescue,* 1995
  - *The Stowaway,* 1995
  - *The Guardian,* 1995
  - *The Accused,* 1995
  - *The Samaritan,* 1996
  - *The Secret,* 1996
- The Williamsburg Years
  - *The Rebel,* 1996
  - *The Thief,* 1996
  - *The Burden,* 1997
  - *The Battle,* 1997
  - *The Invasion,* 1997
  - *The Prisoner,* 1997
  - *The Bridge,* 1997
  - *The Victory,* 1997
- The Charleston Years
  - *The Misfit,* 1997
  - *The Ally,* 1997

The Threat, 1998
The Trap, 1998
The Hostage, 1999
The Escape, 1999
Chicago Years Series
The Trick, 1999
The Chase, 1999
The Capture, 1999
The Stunt, 1999
Raise the Flag Series
Don't Count on Homecoming Queen, 1998
B Is for Bad at Getting into Harvard, 1998
I Only Binge on Holy Hungers, 1998
Right up There with Braces, 1998
Daughters of Courage Series
Stephanie, 1993

Adult Nonfiction

Handling the Heartbreak of Miscarriage, 1987

Young-Adult Nonfiction

Home Love It and Leave It (with David J. Wayne), 1983
Coping with Dating Violence, 1989
Coping with an Illiterate Parent, 1990
"The Value of Compassion" (*Encyclopedia of Ethical Behavior*), 1991
Choosing a Career in Hotels, Motels and Resorts, 1997
Guys and Other Things That Fry Your Brains, 1999
The Need to Know Library
Everything You Need to Know about Getting Your Period, 1995
Everything You Need to Know about Abusive Relationships, 1996
Everything You Need to Know about Peer Mediation, 1997

Plays, Articles, and Short Stories

Nine plays and about 200 articles and short stories

PERSONAL

Nancy Rue credits her "namesake," the well-known formula fiction heroine Nancy Drew, for her interest in reading and later in writing. She shares that when she was a child, she read two of the popular mystery series each day in the summer. After a time, she thought, "I can do that. I can make up my own Nancy Drews."

Rue says, "It certainly wasn't encouragement from others" that brought her to try writing. She remembers that the most frequent response when she said that she wanted to write was, "Yeah, but what are you going to do for a *living?*" However, Rue acknowledges, "primary was the fact that I was born to write. Bottom line? God initiated my interest in writing."

Rue's choice to write Christian fiction arose from the fact that there was a need for it. She observed that the quantity of secular fiction far outweighed the inspirational. Her wish is to "bulge our Christian bookstore shelves with high-quality writing because Christians and yet-to-become Christians can never get enough of seeing how God can work in people's lives."

Rue describes her research process as being "almost the most fun part of writing! I love to go to the local library and read everything I can find on my subject first, just to get a good background. Then I try to find a way to see it, smell it, touch it, hear it, and, of course, taste it firsthand. In writing the Christian Heritage series, I go to the town where the stories are going to be set and spend time hiking around, seeing it all, experiencing as many audience-participation demonstrations as I can (I've set off a cannon in Williamsburg, had my arm 'amputated' in Yorktown, put my head in the stocks at Salem, and so on). I eat the food, smell the air, listen to the way my feet sound when I walk on cobblestones or wooden sidewalks, that kind of thing. That tells me what I still need to know, so then I go to the library, bookstores, and museums there and read, read, read some more. One of the best ways to gather even more information is to talk to the people who have made it their life's work to know about the place or the time period. They know the really good stuff that you can't find in books, like what kinds of games the kids played or where they went to the bathroom."

Although Rue recognizes the importance of relating her facts with both accuracy and ambience, she writes with the vocabulary, action, and plot aimed at a certain age-group. "Whenever I start a project, I always begin with a specific audience in mind. The Christian Heritage series is written for kids eight to twelve years old, or kids six and seven if their parents read to them; teachers who want to find interesting ways to teach American history; adults who get a kick out of children's books; and people who can never get enough of historical fiction no matter what their age. Well, you see what happens. My audience is anyone who is interested in what I'm interested in: how God works in people's lives."

In describing the role of literary elements in her work, Rue characterizes her style as "conversational. . . . At least that's how I feel when I'm writing—as if I'm carrying on a conversation with my reader, only I'm doing all the talking, which is probably true of me in real life, too!" However, she sees the imperative of balancing all elements—plot, theme, and characterization—in her novels. "You have to have all of those to make a story work. I do select my theme first, though, because if a story doesn't have something important to say, if it doesn't make people, even little people, think or help them learn or clear something up for them or at least put a question in their minds, then it's just a nice story. But I don't believe in preaching in a story. Once I know what my theme is, then the characters and their actions have to show that theme in a realistic way, or it isn't even a nice story—it's a sermon!"

The recurring theme in Rue's work is that "God works in people's lives if they let Him in." She says that she tries to make each book, story, and play different in the way this idea is portrayed but sums up that "in spite of me—and because of the Lord—they all come out whispering the same basic thing. But there are so many layers to that, and so many sides, and so many facets, and so many—well you get the idea."

Because setting is integral to historical fiction, Rue states that her choice of place must be based on her interest. She believes that if she does not care about the place, that if she is not "intrigued by it or horrified by it or inspired by it or amused by it," neither will be her readers. Location lends great variety to her work because she is interested in "all kinds of places, the ones I've lived in (and there have been many), the ones I visit on purpose, the ones I come upon by accident. However I choose it, I think it is important to have a specific setting rather than trying to plunk a story in Anywhere, U.S.A. If someone is going to take the time to read what I write, I think that I owe it to them to take them somewhere they may never have been before."

Rue states that in creating characters for her books, she often starts out basing them on someone she knows but that as the story progresses they become their own people. For example, she shares that Josiah, in *The Salem Years* in the Christian Heritage series, "began as a reflection of a student I used to have, but by the end of the first book in the six-book series, he was someone else entirely. The same thing happened in *Retreat to Love,* in which Alexis was originally my daughter, Marijean, and in *The Williamsburg Years,* where Samuel was Brad Pitt! I'll tell you a secret, too: Almost every main character in every book I've written was, in some small way, me."

In reflecting on what has influenced her writing, Rue recounted that "there have been so many that if I started to list them. I would sound like somebody accepting an Academy Award. God is first. Then the authors whose work I've read and re-read, like F. Scott Fitzgerald, John Grisham, Emily Dickinson, Arthur Miller, Katherine Paterson, and Erma Bombeck (now there's a mix for you!). Then there have been the people directly involved in my writing career, all my editors and publishers, and my agent. But the people who have influenced my writing the most are the people who have influenced my life the most—because a writer's life experiences are so tightly entwined with the things she writes. So here we go with the Oscar acceptance speech—my parents, my husband, my daughter, my students—there isn't anyone who hasn't influenced my writing. Except maybe the IRS: I try not to think about them at all."

Rue's personal goals are expressed this way: "I want to travel with my fellow Christians toward the goal of seeing God more and more in our lives every day. I want to open doors to my yet-to-be-Christian brothers and sisters, make Jesus more accessible to them. Sure, I'd love to have a best-seller, be in demand as a speaker, show up on the *Today* show. But those aren't goals. Those are just treats to be picked up along the road toward my ultimate aim."

Through her books, Rue wants her readers "to see God more clearly in their own lives. I want my yet-to-be-Christian readers to know that you don't have to be perfect and wear sensible shoes to know the Lord. Through my writing, I want anyone who picks up my work to know that God works, and I want them to see concrete ways to have a relationship with Him so He can work for them."

As one would expect from the tone of Rue's other responses, she has a positive outlook for the future of inspirational novels. "I think it is going to get better and better. We're going to see more realistic, high-quality literature, more artistic and creative writing. Christian fiction is going to become part of our cultural heritage, just as secular works are—and I want to be part of that."

If the past is any indication of what is to be in the future, this talented and versatile writer will be remembered as a significant, realistic, and joyful contributor to the field of inspirational fiction and the special place that it holds in contemporary culture.

SUMMARY: *ROW THIS BOAT ASHORE*

Felix Parks is wealthy, somewhat pampered, and restless with a life that she feels is meaningless. Suddenly, as she enters her senior year in high school, cheerleading, competing for homecoming queen, and even the comfortable chatter with her longtime pal Annie seem shallow. When she is sent to the guidance counselor following a rather abrupt outbreak in class, her whole life begins to change.

Mr. Gillespie, the counselor, suggests that Felicia (commonly known as Felix) take some introductory-level courses at the local community college. Change comes not by the classes she takes but rather by a handsome upperclassman, Michael Barrineau, who is confined to a wheelchair. "Confined" is not a realistic term for Michael—"somewhat hampered" would be more accurate.

Michael opens new worlds to Felix through his enthusiasm for life, his invitation to her to accompany him on his regular visits to a children's hospital as a volunteer, and his vibrant Christian testimony. Everything about this young man crackles with life and joy—until he loses his independence. When Michael's specially designed van is stolen and Felix offers to become his chauffeur, he responds with a coldness bordering on resentment.

Readers who might have felt that Michael is almost saintly in his response to his disability begin to see the human side when he is forced to become dependent on others. His behavior leaves Felix feeling rejected and isolated, as she has withdrawn from her high school friends to adjust to Michael's world. The only event that holds any joy for the formerly self-centered young lady are her continued visits to the children's hospital, but even those are marred by a bitter teenage girl who resents Felix's presence and creates a real physical threat.

Resolution comes in renewed understanding between Felix and her family. Her recognition that there is a God who has His children in His care opens a new door of communication with her mother, and she establishes feelings of mutual respect with her father as well.

A fairytale ending to this complex story would not be realistic and is not forthcoming. However, the author does conclude with compassion and hope. She presents to the nonhandicapped reader a view of life from the wheelchair while injecting the sense of humor and bright turn of a phrase characteristic of her style. Character development, plot, and theme blend to create a "must read" kind of story.

THE RESCUE (CHRISTIAN HERITAGE SERIES), REVIEWED BY JOSHUA STONE, AGE TWELVE

This book is set in 1689 in Massachusetts. It is about a boy named Josiah Hutcherson, who, through an outcast friend, learns how to trust God in hard times, even when it seems that his sister might die. I liked this book because it shows that God can work all things out for good.

Patricia Rushford

Reporting that she began writing as a means of therapy, Patricia Rushford now creates with the printed word as a vocation and even considers it among her hobbies. For her many readers, it is rewarding to know that what is entertainment for them is a joy for her. Perhaps her pleasure in the creative act is what has given her book sales of over half a million and international exposure as an author and a speaker.

Born to Dagny and Hjalmar Anderson on December 4, 1943, in Rugby, North Dakota, Rushford has enjoyed a variety of vocations, all of which add authenticity to her writing. She and her husband, Ronald, currently are residents of Vancouver, Washington, where he is an investor and is actively involved in his wife's career. The Rushfords have two children: David Warren and Caryl Elaine.

PROFESSIONAL

Education

Masters degree in counseling, Western Evangelical Seminary; associate degree in nursing, Clark College

Career

Freelance writer, consultant, and writing instructor; speaker for various workshops, seminars, and retreats, including major conferences and school classrooms, 1983 to present; numerous appearances on radio and television talk shows across the United States and Canada; codirector, "Writers Weekend on the Beach" writers' conference; contributing editor, *Christian Parenting Today;* director, Annual Coaching Conference for the Oregon Association of Christian Writers; adjunct professor and writer in residence (part time), Western Evangelical Seminary, 1991–1993; teaching assistant, 1989–1990; counseling practicum, Columbia River Mental Health; research scholar, 1988–1989; pediatric nurse, Kaiser Permanente, 1975; nurse, team leader, and instructor, Veterans Administration Hospital; registered nurse, 1972–1990; secretary/bookkeeper, 1961–1970

Awards

Distinguished Scholar Award, Western Evangelical Seminary, for 4.0 grade-point average; *Who's Who Among Students in American Universities and Colleges,* 1989–1990, 1990–1991; EDGAR Nominee, Mystery Writers of America, *Silent Witness,* 1994; Best Young Adult Novel for 1997 from *The Oregonian, Betrayed;* Silver Angel Award, Excellence in Media, *Silent Witness;* numerous writing awards, including Writer of the Year Award, Warner Pacific Writers Conference; Pacesetter Award, Mount Hermon Christian Writers Conference

Memberships

Mystery Writers of America; Sisters in Crime; Oregon Christian Writers

PUBLICATIONS

Adult Fiction

Morningsong, 1998
Forgotten, 2000
Helen Bradley Mysteries
- *Now I Lay Me Down to Sleep,* 1997
- *Red Sky in Mourning,* 1997
- *A Haunting Refrain,* 1998

Adult Nonfiction

Have You Hugged Your Teenager Today?, 1983, 1998
The Help, Hope, and Cope Book, 1984
Caring for Your Elderly Parents, 1985, 1993
What Kids Need Most in a Mom, 1986
Emotional Phases of a Woman's Life (with Jean Lush), 1987
Lost in the Money Maze, 1992

The Humpty Dumpty Syndrome: Putting Yourself Back Together Again, 1994
The Jack and Jill Syndrome: Healing for Broken Children, 1996

Juvenile Fiction

Jennie McGrady Mystery Series
Too Many Secrets, 1993
Silent Witness, 1993
Pursued, 1994
Deceived, 1994
Without a Trace, 1995
Dying to Win, 1995
Betrayed, 1996
In Too Deep, 1996
Over the Edge, 1997
From the Ashes, 1997
Desperate Measures, 1998
Abandoned, 1998

PERSONAL

Creative writing expressed through journaling and poetry met the needs of Patricia Rushford during difficult days in her personal life. Out of her own method of surviving, she began to write nonfiction books to assist others during their periods of crisis. Beyond the counseling works, she has branched out into mysteries for both the adult and the teen audience. In a way, she is helping to unravel the mysteries that all humans must solve at one time or another. Yet, in regard to her novels, she says that she does not write "Christian fiction" but rather that she is a believer and that some of her characters are Christian, some are not. She says, "I write novels."

Rushford describes her research process as "rather broad. . . . I utilize the Internet and, of course, the library. I do a lot of interviewing whether I'm writing fiction or nonfiction. With fiction, I usually visit the area where my novel is set. There is an old adage: Write what you know. I don't think we can afford to limit ourselves in that way. I write what I can learn. I do exciting things in researching books, like taking cruises, learning how to shoot a gun, visiting and interacting with dolphins, and visiting a working mink farm."

Working as both author and editor requires different modes of thinking and, in Rushford's approach, different environments as well. She describes her dual roles this way: "I have a desktop and a laptop [computer]. I usually try to write in the mornings when I'm freshest. Some days, though, I'm at it for eight to ten hours a day (with breaks). I find that for my creative writing it helps when I'm sitting on a sofa or recliner (or outside in good weather) and using my laptop. With editing, correspondence, and so on, I use my desktop. I do have an office, but prefer writing at my beach cabin, where it's quiet and I don't have interruptions."

Rushford envisions her audience as including both men and women and encompassing a wide age range. "With my series of mysteries for kids, I have letters from fans as young as ten and as old as eighty-two, both men and women. For the adult mysteries, my readers are often quite young. The Jennie McGrady fans also enjoy the adventures of Jennie's grandmother, Helen Bradley. The Bradley series, however, is primarily geared to adults. With my nonfiction, I also have a wide range as my topics cover many areas."

Viewing her novels as plot, theme, and character driven, Rushford favors characterization as the most important literary element of her writing style. "If I would list them in order, it would be character first (I tend to give a great deal of thought to a character's actions, motives, personality, and that sort of thing), then action, then theme. I think a good novel needs a balance, and it would be very difficult to separate them. I don't really start out with a specific theme as such because I'm afraid I would focus too much on what I wanted to say and become too preachy rather than let the story and theme develop naturally as the characters work out their problems. The characters and the subject matter create the underlying theme as I go along." She describes her underlying theme as "simply good versus evil, and good wins."

Readers will testify that Rushford's characters are realistic and that her attention to detail enhances the feeling of being right in the presence of the action. Perhaps this feeling of being a part of the setting is because she has visited the place, and sometimes her characters are based on real people or compilations of characteristics. Rushford has a unique method of determining character names. "I do often use real names, especially in my Jennie McGrady books, as my fans love the idea of having their name in a book. I'll often do school visits and have a name drawing to see who gets to be a character in my next book. It's fun. Often my main characters will have some of my own traits. For example, Helen Bradley carries around a leather backpack and drinks Earl Grey tea. So do I. She does karate. I don't."

Rushford's response to what type of reading has influenced her writing would come as no surprise to her many fans. "I greatly appreciate a good mystery. It's my favorite type of novel. I do like the occasional romance and often read devotionals for more serious thoughts. But when I want to unwind, I pick up a mystery."

Although Madeleine L'Engle is the author whom Rushford names as most influential in her life, she credits the Trixie Belden and Nancy Drew books from her childhood with influencing her career as a writer. "I really didn't start out wanting to be a writer and only learned after trial and error and about thirty-seven years of discovering where I fit."

Perhaps the unique role played by Rushford is best expressed in her own words: "As I mentioned before, I am a Christian. I believe that people are as much spiritual as they are emotional or physical—perhaps even more so. I try to develop characters who are well rounded. Unlike many non-Christian writers, I don't leave out the soul. While I don't feel it is my job to preach to people though my books, I do feel it is important to maintain my values and a sense of integrity. I care very much about the people I write for, especially the children who read my books. I won't write a book that I wouldn't allow my grandchildren to read. It's as simple as that."

When asked about her personal goals, Rushford shared, " I often think it would be wonderful to be rich and famous, and it would be nice to make a little more [money] than I do. But in all honesty, the rewards for writing come in the form of letters from kids and adults who are helped through something I wrote. My goal is to write as long as the Lord allows, to stay true to myself and to God. I think I have already achieved, at least in part, the most important goal. I have found that in writing, I am following God's plan for my life, and I am delighted."

Rushford does express definite goals for her readers. "For the kids, I pray they will come away knowing how to deal with difficult issues they face. I would like them to model Jennie McGrady and be strong, self-assured, and not tempted to follow the wrong crowds. For the adults, I hope that my books can help them to deal with their own sets of problems, particularly in my nonfiction. For all of my readers, I hope they will come away wanting more, not only of my mysteries but of the Divine Mystery. I hope that I can instill in them a hunger to know God more intimately."

Rushford sees the future of inspirational novels as rich with possibilities. "I think many people—Christian and non-Christian alike—are looking for books that contain values and a moral message. Many are tired of picking up a book and having to put it down because of the indiscriminate use of profanity and explicit sex. I would like to see more books from Christian publishers on the shelves of the large bookstore chains, where they are more accessible to the public. I do have concerns for the genre in that too many Christian bookstores relegate fiction to a few, sparse shelves in the back of their store. We're seeing more and better fiction coming from Christian publishing houses. I only hope that the market will continue to expand."

SUMMARY: *NOW I LAY ME DOWN TO SLEEP* (HELEN BRADLEY MYSTERIES)

"Retirement" would be the last word most people would select to describe the lifestyle of Helen Bradley, a former police officer, now a freelance travel writer and occasional investigator for the U.S. government. It is Helen's success in solving mysteries that leads widow Irene Kincaid to seek her out when she believes that her husband was murdered instead of succumbing to a heart attack, as was reported. Complicating matters is the fact that her husband was the director of the upscale convalescent home where he died, and his son, who has taken his place, is the number-one suspect.

Helen checks herself into the facility to investigate, believing that this is the only way to obtain accurate information about Irene's husband's death. Her daring approach goes against the better judgment of her son, Jason, who is a police officer, and he pledges to intensify his work from the outside so that the charade may soon be completed. With the help of her granddaughter, Jennie, who becomes a volunteer at the home, the senior citizen sleuth moves into Edgewood Manor.

Rushford introduces readers to a new breed of grandmother in this first volume of the series. Helen has remarried after having been a widow for ten years, and as a new wife she demonstrates that love and desire can be ageless emotions. Her zest for living, learning, and adventure may be eye opening for the twenty-something set but are completely realistic and delightful. Perhaps this series is the trailblazer for more stories that remind the modern reader that women over fifty are not yet ready for the rocking chair and have much to offer to their families, themselves, and society.

TOO MANY SECRETS (JENNIE MCGRADY MYSTERY SERIES)

Jennie McGrady is just an average sixteen-year-old girl who is eager to finish her school requirements so that she will have the summer free to spend with her grandmother in Florida—"average," that is, if being home schooled, having a father who disappeared while working for the FBI, and having a grandmother who travels all over the world writing magazine articles is considered normal. One common denominator with some other teenagers is her crush on Ryan, the boy next door, only Ryan is "next door" to her grandmother, who lives 150 miles away.

When Jennie cannot reach Gram by telephone but receives a mysterious note from her instead, she becomes quite concerned about her safety and decides to take matters into her own hands. Through a rather elaborate scheme of deception involving her cousin Lisa, a fake trip to camp, and other daring adventures, Jennie manages to get herself into a very precarious situation. Not only is she in danger, but so are Ryan and her grandmother.

Rushford initiates a series that is sure to be popular with middle schoolers as they read about spunky, sensitive Jennie, who, although fiercely independent, is grieving the loss of her father, missing now for five years. Not allowing herself to believe that he is dead, Jennie is angry with her mother, who wants to go on with her life, including dating. This is a fast-paced novel that involves adventure, humor, teen relationships, and the insightful views of a young woman who is a little girl one moment and a woman the next.

Lisa Samson

Born in Baltimore, Maryland, Lisa Samson is the daughter of the late Dr. William J. Ebauer, a doctor of optometry, and Joy Snider Ebauer, homemaker and pro-life activist. After graduating from Liberty University with a degree in telecommunications, she married and is now the mother of Elizabeth (better known as Tyler), Jacob (also known as Jake), and Gwynneth. Her husband, William, is employed in the computer industry.

PROFESSIONAL

Education
B.S. in communications, Liberty University

PUBLICATIONS

Adult Fiction

Shades of Eternity Series
  Vol. 1: *The Moment I Saw You,* 1998
  Vol. 2: *Indigo Waters,* 1999
The Highlander Series
  The Highlander and His Lady, 1994
  The Legend of Robin Brodie, 1995
  The Temptation of Aaron Campbell, 1996
The Abbey Series
  Conquered Heart, 1996
  Love's Ransom, 1997
  The Warrior's Bride, 1997

PERSONAL

Lisa Samson's interest in writing was sparked by her own love of reading. Christian fiction was a "good fit" for her as a vehicle of expression because it was an extension of her own beliefs. She never really considered writing in any other genre.

Research has been somewhat of a family affair for Samson with her first work, *The Highlander and His Lady*. Her interest in the country has developed in part because of her husband's Scottish heritage. Also, a visit to this historical country during her college years set the stage for her love affair with the land and the people. Scotland became a natural backdrop for her work. Since that first visit, being a full-time wife and mother has taken priority for the author, and intercontinental travel has been limited. As a result, Samson has turned to nonfiction, reference books, and the Internet for her research in creating settings and characters for her novels. Samson shares that she must have a strong interest in a particular time period in order to pursue research in that place and time. As she is drawn to strong historical personalities, she gains the inspiration to give life to her own compelling characters and story lines.

Samson describes her style of writing as "appreciative of the English language." She seeks out unusual situations to dramatize, as demonstrated in *The Legend of Robin Brodie* (reviewed here). Rich, descriptive scenes and realistic dialogue demonstrate her ability to use the language that she appreciates in a way that entertains her audience and compels them to continue reading. Fast-paced plots keep the action moving and enhance full character development. One consistent theme throughout Samson's work is sexual purity and the importance of the expression of love between husband and wife.

Because Samson did not plan to be a writer, the experience of being successfully published has been a great delight. She believes that God has used this opportunity to allow her to fulfill her desire to be a stay-at-home mother while satisfying the creative desires that make her a whole person. Artistic fulfillment brings its own set of joys, as does being a homemaker. Her goal is to hold on to both. In speaking to university classes, Samson always tells those who feel strongly about being at home with their children to seek God's help. She believes that He can provide a way for that to happen.

To her readers, Samson would give the gifts of enjoyment and encouragement. *The Highlander and His Lady* addresses the need for self-acceptance. *The Legend of Robin Brodie* speaks to the therapy of forgiveness. *The Temptation of Aaron Campbell* deals with the age-old struggle of sibling rivalry as well as other issues. Although all her books can be read simply for pleasure, each one has a theme that may bring healing to those in need.

SUMMARY: *THE LEGEND OF ROBIN BRODIE* (THE HIGHLANDER SERIES)

Set during the British occupation of Scotland following the defeat of Bonnie Prince Charlie, this story opens in tumultuous times. Robin, an eleven-year-old boy, is returning from the war in which he has witnessed his father's death. As he wearily walks into the clearing of his family's cottage, he discovers British soldiers ravaging his mother and sisters. Filled with rage and hatred, he charges the men, who savagely slash him, leaving him scarred for life.

As his physical wounds heal, Robin struggles with his belief that each time his beloved mother and sisters look at him, they will be reminded of their degrading experience. To relieve them of this hardship, Robin chooses to become invisible by running deep into the forest, where he lives the life of a hermit.

For the next eighteen years of his life, Robin has no direct contact with other human beings. Although his mother grieves at his absence, she leaves food and clothing for him to find, and he remains a recluse. In time, somewhat of a legend grows up around the enigmatic Robin, encouraged by his wearing of the clan tartan, which has been outlawed by the British.

One day the young daughter of the laird, on whose land Robin has lived his entire life, is charged by a wild boar while wandering in the forest. Robin risks his anonymity by rescuing her, beginning a unique friendship. The lady is intrigued by his manner and mode of existence, and Robin finds acceptance with her despite his scarred face. The warmth of their relationship increases as the two establish trust and a mutual respect.

Resolution does not follow the expected route in this novel, and the reader will be held in suspense to the satisfying conclusion. There is enough action for the adventure fan and enough romance for the one who reads for relationships.

Elaine Schulte

Born and raised in Indiana, the daughter of Louise and Dietrich Young, Elaine was exposed to the storytelling skills of her grandmother at a young age. After graduating as valedictorian from Merrillville High School, she attended Purdue University. While in college, she realized her own talent for storytelling and graduated with a degree in creative writing. Later, she continued to hone her skills by taking a course in creative writing at a local community college.

Schulte's interests, in addition to her own writing, include history, archaeology, travel, cooking, language, and the teaching of writing.

PROFESSIONAL

Education

B.S. in creative writing, Purdue University

Career

Publication specialist for a research-and-development firm; inspirational novel panelist, Booklover's Conference; instructor at numerous writers' conferences; speaker at churches, colleges and schools, libraries, luncheons, and radio and television interview shows; books featured in book clubs, including Doubleday Crossings, Billy Graham's Grason Books, Guideposts, and Family Bookshelf

Awards

Who's Who of American Women, contemporary author; *World's Who's Who of Women; Dictionary of International Biography;* P.E.N. West Award Nominee, 1995; Christian Booksellers Association Gold Medallion Nominee on numerous occasions; Purdue University Distinguished Alumna Award; Writer of the Year, Book of the Year, and Short Story of the Year Awards, San Diego Christian Writer's Guild; featured on the cover of *The Christian Writer*

PUBLICATIONS

Juvenile Fiction

Zack and the Magic Factory, 1976 (adapted as an ABC-TV Weekend Special, 1981)
Johanna, 1995 (originally published as *Whither the Wind Bloweth,* 1982)
Twelve Candles Club Series
- *Becky's Brainstorm,* 1992
- *Jess and the Fireplug Caper,* 1993
- *Cara's Beach Party Disaster,* 1993
- *Tricia's Got T-R-O-U-B-L-E,* 1993
- *Melanie and the Modeling Mess,* 1994
- *Bridesmaid Blues for Becky,* 1994
- *Double Trouble for Jess McColl!,* 1995
- *Cara and the Terrible Teeners,* 1995
- *Tricia and the Money Mystery,* 1996
- *Melanie and the Cruise Caper,* 1996
- *Lily Vanessa and the Pet Panic,* 1997
- *Becky's Secret Surprise,* 1998

Colton Cousins Series
- *Suzannah and the Secret Coins,* 1992
- *Daniel Colton under Fire,* 1992
- *Suzannah Strikes Gold,* 1992
- *Daniel Colton Kidnapped,* 1993

Ginger Series
- *Here Comes Ginger!,* 1989
- *Off to a New Start,* 1989
- *A Job for an Angel,* 1989
- *Absolutely Green,* 1990
- *Go for It!,* 1991

Adult Fiction

Voyage, 1996
California Pioneer Series
Eternal Passage, 1989
Golden Dreams, 1989
The Journey West, 1989
With Wings as Eagles, 1990
Peace Like a River, 1993
Mercies So Tender, 1995; audio book, 1995
Serenade/Serenata/Saga Series
On Wings of Love, 1983; reprinted, 1996
Song of Joy, 1984; reprinted, 1990
Echoes of Love, 1985; reprinted, 1990
Westward, My Love, 1986
Dreams of Gold, 1986

Short Stories and Articles

Short stories in magazines such as *Good Housekeeping, Today's Christian Woman, Virtue, Jack & Jill,* and *Focus on the Family;* articles in magazines such as *Travel/Holiday, Woman's World, Parents, Look,* and *Bookstore Journal;* article "Writing the Inspirational Novel" in *Writer's Digest*

Newspaper Articles

Syndicated in the *San Diego Union, Denver Post, San Francisco Examiner, Boston Herald American, New York Newsday, Cleveland Plain Dealer,* and others

PERSONAL

Elaine Schulte's grandmother was a great storyteller, and Elaine herself always loved reading, but it was not until she attended college that she realized her own talent for storytelling. She earned a bachelors degree in creative writing at Purdue University and later enrolled in an advanced writer's class at a community college. Encouraged by her teacher to submit a story to *Good Housekeeping,* Schulte found her article accepted; thus began a successful period of writing articles for magazines such as *Travel/Holiday, Woman's World, Parents, Look, Bookstore Journal,* and

Jack and Jill. Her juvenile novel titled *Zack and the Magic Factory* became an ABC-TV Weekend Special.

In 1978 Schulte was converted to Christianity, and her thinking so changed that she began to pen novels for adults, teens, and preteens that were written with a Christian emphasis. The Twelve Candles Club series, written in response to her agent's request that she create books similar to the Baby-Sitter's Club series, presents preteen experiences from a Christian perspective. She now states her personal goals for writing in this way: "I want to please God, and I want to show the path to joy and a worthwhile life." Schulte's writing continues to be successful as she follows this new direction. Since its first release, the Twelve Candles Club series alone has sold over 300,000 copies.

Schulte's historically based series are researched on site whenever possible. "For *The Journey West,* my husband and I actually drove along parts of the covered-wagon trail to California. We took pictures, and I bought lots of postcards, brochures, and history books. One of my greatest . . . joys was the first time I researched at the Library of Congress. I also use museums, historical societies, and public libraries. Since my California Pioneer series deals with taking the gospel west, I was especially grateful to use a Christian college library.

"The process begins with prayer, then a leading about what I should write. My life seems to take me to all the right places for research. At the moment, I'm preparing for a trip to Ireland, Wales, and England. We're meeting my son's family there, as they live in Europe, but I know that my next series will also begin in those places. Being in the right places simply happens. I probably use only ten percent of my historical research in the stories, but the other ninety percent gives me a surer feel for the era. I also research for contemporary novels. For *Voyage,* I went with a church group on a holy lands trip 'in the footsteps of the Apostle Paul,' visiting Mars Hill, Corinth, Ephesus, Jerusalem, and far more.

"For my preteen Twelve Candles Club series, I recently researched such diverse subjects as goats, gymnastics, child modeling, being an American-born Chinese girl, being a black singer, and how to make pizza party invitations using real pepperoni slices. I've called . . . the police for information on how they'd try to stop a pack of dogs chasing a girl on a bike and the fire department for suggestions on teaching girls about babysitting. Finding just the right information is part of the adventure of writing stories."

When asked to characterize her style of writing, Schulte replied, "It's been described as 'compelling.' I try to grip the reader and never let go, something I learned as a short-story writer. For adults, my works are usually character and theme driven. For teens and preteens, I use more action, but the characters and theme remain of vital importance. My characters are never based on people I know. I use imaginary characters, give them limited freedom to act, and use human emotions. When they 'come alive,' I'm often surprised at what they do. In *Mercies So Tender,* which begins in 1860 on the Kansas-Missouri border, I needed border ruffians, but I didn't want to use swearing or vulgarities to depict them. Imagine my amazement when the first fellow yelled, 'Whooeee, Kate Talbot! Ah bet you're a right sassy gal under them infernal good manners! About time someone showed you how to cut loose. Whooeee!'"

Schulte says that her writing is most influenced by Scripture and her own observations. "I want to please God, and I want to show the path to joy and a worthwhile life." Her hope is that her readers "will recognize truth."

In answer to her view regarding the future of Christian fiction, Schulte responded, "The outlook is excellent for writers who are willing to invest their lives in their work. As time goes on, there will be fewer places for the writers who 'toss off' a book a month. Christian readers and editors will grow more and more savvy about what's well written and what isn't."

Schulte is not one to "toss off" a book. She writes for a broad spectrum of age levels and is well established in the genre. Her works show careful research, a strong awareness of human nature, and the ability to craft a story that will keep readers interested to the last page.

SUMMARY: *BRIDESMAID BLUES FOR BECKY* (TWELVE CANDLES CLUB SERIES)

Becky Hamilton is a strong-willed young lady whose father has died. Because she had been very close to her father, she feels betrayed by her mother's engagement to John Bradshaw, a widower with three boys. She misses the way her mother used to confide in her, and she does not wish to adapt to a new father and three new brothers.

Becky displays her anger in disagreeable ways and eventually recruits the help of Quinn, John Bradshaw's youngest son, to join in her efforts to undermine the wedding plans. Thinking that her friends in the Twelve Candles Club would understand her unhappiness at the coming events, Becky is surprised when they think that her new stepfather is wonderful.

Through Becky, Schulte accurately portrays an adolescent's feelings at having her world turned upside down. Preteens will love this story and would benefit from the message that circumstances that appear difficult and wrong can actually work for good in their lives.

GOLDEN DREAMS (CALIFORNIA PIONEER SERIES)

Rose is about to be married when a freak accident takes the life of her fiancé. Pressured by his twin brother to submit to a loveless marriage, Rose escapes with the help of handsome and mysterious Joshua Talbot. Boarding a clipper ship bound for California, she sets out to find her father, who has gone on ahead in search of gold and the promise of new opportunities. Rose must trust God to protect her from the dangers of the trip as well as from the greed and violence that characterized the Gold Rush in order to bring her into the fulfillment of her dreams.

Schulte does not avoid writing about the strong passions or difficult decisions of life. In *Golden Dreams,* also part of her California Pioneer series, Rose Wilmington meets potentially devastating circumstances with courage and honesty.

Beverly Bush Smith

Beverly Bush Smith began her life in Omaha, Nebraska, in 1927, as the daughter of Martin and Zoe Bush. Her father was a professor, university department head, pianist, and organist. Her husband, Robert, is currently a semiretired aerospace engineer. They have two sons. Smith loves skiing, swimming, and classical music. Even with her writing schedule, she finds time to lead Bible studies at her church and serves as a senior mentor to MOPS (Mother of Preschool Children).

PROFESSIONAL

Education
B.A., University of Nebraska at Omaha (graduated magna cum laude)

Career
Advertising copywriter; freelance writer

Memberships
Southern California Restaurant Writers; Christian Writer's Guild of Orange County (California)

Awards

Henrietta Mears Award for Excellence in Christian Literature, 1986

PUBLICATIONS

Adult Fiction

Zoe Journals Series
Wings of a Dove, 1996
Evidence of Things Unseen, 1997

Adult Nonfiction

Uniquely You, 1984
Change for the Better, 1986
Caught in the Middle, 1988

PERSONAL

Beverly Bush Smith credits the newspaper columns that her father wrote as a music critic with initiating her own interest in writing. However, as for choosing fiction, she states, "I think it chose me! The transition from nonfiction to fiction had a huge learning curve. But I realized that Jesus taught by telling stories, and I could 'get across' difficult material better and help women to identify better in a fiction format."

When researching for a story, Smith finds "people who have 'been there,' experienced what I'm writing about. Interview, interview . . . check with the experts: sheriff, police, prison officials." She checks with all her sources to ensure accuracy. When necessary, she goes to where the action happens. Her writing then is done "in my office at home and at our second home in Mammoth Lakes, using a laptop." She writes at "all hours, though I'm not a night person and write at night only when on deadline."

Several people have influenced Smith's writing, urging her to continue. "Anne Ortland encouraged my first book, and we continue to cheer for, commiserate with, and pray for one another." In fiction, "Ernie Own, former CEO and now acquisitions editor of Word Publishing, has believed in me, serving as my advocate, shepherding my books personally from proposal to publication."

Other writers have influenced Smith as well. "There is nothing like reading good writing to make me a better writer. Frankly, I need to make time for more; I tend to use the time to write. I love C. S. Lewis's mind, Madeleine L'Engle's enormous creativity, Max Lucado's elegant and economical prose,

Anne Tyler's characters. Currently, I'm enjoying Pat Conroy's beautiful writing. Childhood favorites are Kipling and Milne."

Smith describes her characters as being based on people whom she knows. "My heroine in *Wings of a Dove* is a composite of many abused women I've met through the years. They taught me how this woman thinks." She sees her audience mainly as Christian women and would like to "hold a mirror up to women, so they'll ask, 'Is this me? Is this someone I know? What can I learn?'" The overall theme she desires to convey to these readers is that "God's way is best; trust and stay close to Him."

Smith plans to keep making contributions to the field of Christian fiction. "I don't know yet how many books will comprise the Zoe Journals series, but I hope at least two more after *Evidence of Things Unseen*. In response to the field in general, she comments, "How it has grown. I think it will continue. A Christian bookstore owner told me that ten years ago she had no requests for fiction. What a difference today."

SUMMARY: *WINGS OF A DOVE* (ZOE JOURNALS SERIES)

Leslie Harper has spent years proceeding with caution, trying not to trigger her husband Charles's anger, determined to do better in order to please him. Somehow, there is always reason for his displeasure. Somehow, she always fails. In desperation, Leslie faces the truth about her painful marriage and begins to confront the problems she has been trying to ignore. With the prayers of her mother, Zoe, and the encouragement of a small group of women struggling with similar issues, she begins to realize her true worth as a person. When Charles's anger increases, endangering her own life and the welfare of their children, Leslie realizes that she must act to protect them all.

EVIDENCE OF THINGS UNSEEN, SUMMARY BY THE AUTHOR

Andrea Lang is a woman in a hurry, an achiever with a house in Malibu, a thriving career, and two adorable children. But when her daughter disappears and God seems to default on her "bargain" with Him, she bitterly renounces Him. With her focus fixed on finding her daughter, "whatever it takes," her marriage falters, and her son struggles with loneliness and guilt. While her mother-in-law, Zoe, ministers to the family and wages prayer warfare, Andrea, in her agitation for answers, willingly opens the door to evil. A chilling climax points the way to resolution.

Michael Waite

Michael Waite lives in Eugene, Oregon, with his wife, two cats, and an Old English sheepdog. His career includes both the technical and the traditional as he designs computer games and write children's books for a living. When not writing or designing, he might be found fly-fishing, canoeing, or skiing in the Northwest backcountry.

PROFESSIONAL

Career

Art teacher in public schools; special effects artist in the film industry; producer of animated films; professor of English at the University of Oregon and Oregon State University

PUBLICATIONS

Juvenile Fiction

Jojofu, 1996

Building Christian Character Series

- *Handy-Dandy Helpful Hal: A Book about Helpfulness*, 1987
- *Suzy Swoof*, 1987
- *Buzzle Billy*, 1987
- *Miggy and Tiggy*, 1987
- *Max and the Big Fat Lie*, 1988
- *Casey the Greedy Young Cowboy*, 1988
- *Sir Maggie the Mighty*, 1988
- *Boggin, Blizzy, and Sleeter the Cheater*, 1988
- *Sammy's Gadget Galaxy*, 1992
- *Gilly's Gift for Granny*, 1992
- *Sylvester the Jester*, 1992
- *The Hollyhonk Gardens of Gneedle and Gnibb*, 1993

Camp Windy Woods Series

Digger's Marvelous Moleberry Bush, 1995

Shelby the Magnificent, 1995

Bartholomew Beaver and the Stupendous Splash, 1995

Daisy Doodlepaws and the Windy Woods Treasure, 1996

Board Books

Lady Bug Island, 1995

Butterflies for Two, 1995

Middle Grade Novels

Hoomania, 1987

Emma Wimble, Accidental Astronaut, 1988

Eddy and the Rude Green Grood, 1988

PERSONAL

A very private person, Michael Waite does not publicize a great deal about his personal life or religious viewpoints except through his published works for children. However, there are two things that one might surmise about the author from his stories. One is that building Christian character traits into children is important, as each of his series books is based on a trait, such as helpfulness, honesty, or being a friend. The other is that this process can be fun. Using rhyme and cartoon characters, Waite creates stories that both delight and instruct.

SUMMARY: *HANDY-DANDY HELPFUL HAL: A BOOK ABOUT HELPFULNESS* (BUILDING CHRISTIAN CHARACTER SERIES)

Mom and Dad are worn out trying to do all the household chores when a funny fellow named Handy-Dandy Helpful Hal comes their way. Pulling a wagon full of tools, mops, and gadgets of every sort, he miraculously convinces Sam and Sue to help their parents accomplish all the needed tasks. With cartoon characters and rhyming lines, Waite helps make the task of building Christian character a little easier.

JOJOFU

Tracking wild boar and stag, Takumi ventures into the dangerous mountains with his favorite dog, Jojofu, and the rest of his pack of hunting dogs. Allowing Jojofu to lead the way, he is confused when she veers from the path into the woods. As he follows her, Takumi is saved from being buried beneath a violent landslide of rock. In this and other adventures, Jojofu's continued bravery brings honor to her owner and makes her a legend throughout the province.

Departing from his usual style, Waite has created a classic retelling of a Japanese folktale. Waite's prose is greatly enhanced by the stunning illustrations of Yoriko Ito.

John White

When you have lived almost three-fourths of a century on two continents and served in at least three major career fields, it is difficult to imagine what you might fantasize about. John White, born in England, married in the United States, and now residing in Canada, has been a surgeon, a missionary, and a professor of psychiatry, yet he can enter quite smoothly into the fantasy world and write stories that young adults have enjoyed for more than a decade.

On the other hand, it seems that White's life has been the stuff of which stories are spun. Born in Liverpool, England, on March 5, 1924, to a car salesman, Harold White, and his "home keeper" wife, Mary Ellen, White went off to defend his country in the Fleet Air Arm of the Royal Navy during World War II. After the war, he studied medicine at the University of Manchester, and during that time served as chairman of the executive committee of British InterVarsity Fellowship (now renamed University and Colleges Christian Union). He then trained as a surgeon before volunteering for missionary service.

In 1955, White married Loretta O'Hara. They have five children (to whom he has dedicated some of his fantasy series): Scott, Kevin, Liana, Leith, and Miles, the last two being twins. The Whites served as missionaries in Latin America until 1964. During the last five years there, White held the post of associate general secretary of the International Fellowship of Evangelical Students (IFES), coordinating the work in Latin American countries.

On leaving the Latin American field in 1965, the Whites moved to Canada, where White studied psychiatry, completing his specialization in 1969. A year later, he began to serve on the faculty of the University of Manitoba, occupying a number of hospital and university positions. Later he functioned as associate professor of psychiatry.

John and Loretta have nine grandchildren. He continues to write and dedicate books to the second generation, who, no doubt, have given him inspiration. For a number of years, he has traveled throughout the world giving lectures and addresses on university campuses and conferences sharing the gospel. More recently, he has traveled on overseas tours. It has been quite a journey for the son of a car salesman from Liverpool.

PROFESSIONAL

Education
Medicine; psychiatry

Career
Medical missionary; professor of psychiatry

PUBLICATIONS

Juvenile Fiction

Archives of Anthropos Series
The Tower of Geburah, 1978
The Iron Sceptre, 1981
The Sword Bearer, 1986
Gaal the Conqueror, 1990
Quest for the King, 1995

Adult Nonfiction

The Cost of Commitment, 1976
The Fight, 1976
Eros Defiled, 1977
Daring to Draw Near, 1977
The Golden Cow, 1979
Flirting with the World, 1982
The Masks of Melancholy, 1982
The Race, 1984

Excellence in Leadership, 1986
Putting the Soul Back in Psychology, 1987
When the Spirit Comes with Power, 1988
Magnificent Obsession, 1990
Changing on the Inside, 1991
Greater Than Riches, 1992
Church Discipline That Heals, 1992
Money Isn't God, 1993
Eros Redeemed, 1993
Money Isn't God: So Why Does the Church Worship It? (new edition of *The Golden Cow*), 1994
The Pathway of Holiness, 1995

PERSONAL

John White states that his interest in reading initiated his interest to write and that he chose the Christian worldview because it is the only one that seemed sensible to him. "As I explore the world of spirit—for God is spirit—I add to the knowledge I have. Life is a journey of exploration."

In describing his writing process, White is spanning more than twenty years. "I began to write by dictating, and now I use a computer." He writes at "any time of day or night. Sometimes I wake with themes on my mind, write, then go back to bed, but the process goes on endlessly. At times, I write all night long. Early mornings are for prayer and meditation in Scripture. But yes, I do sleep!"

A glance at the list of White's publications reveals that his reading audience varies in both age and interest. He sees his nonfiction, adult readers as the "whole church and Messianic Jews" who are concerned about "serious Christian issues." However, when he writes fiction, his readers are "children between seven and seventy."

In explaining how a writer for adults came to write for children, White states, "My children 'ganged up' on me one day and said, 'You write adult stuff for Christians. Write a book that we can read!'" Thus came about *The Tower of Geburah*. He reports that the senior editor at InterVarsity Press "incited" him to go on writing. He shares that the characters in the Archives of Anthropos series are "very loosely" based on his first three children.

Other influences in White's writing are as varied as Dr. Martyn Lloyd-Jones, C. S. Lewis, Charles Kingsley, Kenneth Graham, and E. Nesbitt. He relates that Lloyd-Jones "greatly influenced my view of what Christianity was and was a member of a committee I once chaired. He still stands as a rock in my thinking." The others were childhood favorites. He says of Lewis's books,

"I read every one as they came out in England, fiction and nonfiction, children's books and adult books—all as soon as they came out."

In describing the literary elements found in his young-adult books, he states, "They are theme and character controlled. A constant theme is the sorcerer/prophet theme—their similarities and differences. I use fiction as allegory."

When asked about goals for his work, White replied, "It is impossible for me to separate my personal goals in writing from my personal goal in life, which is to know Christ and to know the Father. If I influence people, I do so in that direction."

White states that the role of Christian fiction is to "mirror real life exactly as it is in a sinful world and our struggles against dark powers. Any other fiction can only appeal to our carnality. We need good fiction, and I hope it will abound in the future."

SUMMARY: *THE TOWER OF GEBURAH* (ARCHIVES OF ANTHROPOS SERIES)

While Wesley, Kurt, and Lisa are visiting with their Uncle John, they go exploring in his mysterious attic. Without really intending to do so, they are drawn into a strange land of talking wolves, sorcerers, and flying horses.

When Lisa feels betrayed and deserted by her brothers, she succumbs to the temptation of revenge. It is only through trusting Gaal, the high emperor, that she can be redeemed. Kurt also is deceived. His downfall is the result of a desire for power, and he jeopardizes the lives of his brother and sister because he trusts the wrong beings. His encounter with Gaal is quite different from Lisa's. Through their adventures, both children learn a very personal lesson in trust and obedience.

Readers of C. S. Lewis will find delightful parallels running between *The Lion, the Witch and the Wardrobe* and *The Tower of Geburah*. Both are rich in symbolism and powerful figures of speech. Like Lewis, White has begun a memorable series. What a beautiful way for elementary readers to learn important lessons about good and evil while being enthrallingly entertained.

Lori Wick

Born on October 11, 1958, to Harland and Pearl Hays, Lori Wick has accomplished more with her high school diploma and three semesters of Bible school than many who have a lengthier set of credentials. Having published her first novel in 1990, by 1996 she had sales of nearly one million. Since she began publishing, it is unusual to read the Christian Fiction Top 20 List and not find a title by Wick. Currently, her sales total more than 1,400,000.

An avid reader of her works would not be surprised that Wick lists her hobbies as counted-cross-stitch and watching musicals and old movies. Those leisure activities just seem to fit with the coziness of her novels. Involvement with her children's school as a weekly volunteer and attending Bible studies in her church round out her busy schedule.

Wick's husband, Bob, is also her agent. They have three children—Timothy, Matthew, and Abigail—who their mother enthusiastically qualifies as "the most wonderful children in the world." Bob also works for a large manufactured-housing firm that is owned and operated by his family.

PROFESSIONAL

Education

High school; three semesters of Bible school

Awards

Finalist, ECPA Gold Medallion, Evangelical Christian Publishers Association, *A Place Called Home,* 1991; *Sophie's Heart,* 1996; *Where the Wild Rose Blooms,* 1997; and *Whispers of Moonlight,* 1997

PUBLICATIONS

Adult Fiction

Sophie's Heart, 1995
Beyond the Picket Fence (short stories), 1998
Pretense, 1998
The Princess, 1999
A Place Called Home Series
  A Place Called Home, 1990
  A Song for Silas, 1990
  The Long Road Home, 1991
  A Gathering of Memories, 1991
The Californians Series
  Whatever Tomorrow Brings, 1992
  As Time Goes By, 1992
  Sean Donovan, 1993
  Donovan's Daughter, 1994
Kensington Chronicles
  The Hawk and the Jewel, 1993
  Wings of the Morning, 1994
  Who Brings Forth the Wind, 1994
  The Knight and the Dove, 1995
Rocky Mountain Memories Series
  Where the Wild Rose Blooms, 1996
  Whispers of Moonlight, 1996
  To Know Her by Name, 1997
  Promise Me Tomorrow, 1997
The Yellow Rose Trilogy
  Every Little Thing about You, 1999

PERSONAL

Lori Wick states that she first began writing because she "had a story in her head." Being an avid reader, she was often left with a feeling of "vague dissatisfaction" by the ending of many books. "I love a love story, and I think the greatest love story is that God's perfect Son came to earth to die for sinful man. I love romance and a happy ending, but unless there is more—a personal relationship with Christ—something will always be missing. I've been married to a man for seventeen years who shares my beliefs. I can't imagine a sweeter marriage than one joined in Christ."

Wick describes her research process as "period based." She surrounds herself with information on the time and place of her current work. If possible, she visits her setting. She subscribes to magazines that will help her become a part of the era about which she writes. She also utilizes her public library. She relates that she is "very visual." When visiting England, she did not record any images on paper, but if she closes her eyes, she is transported back and can capture the scene to put on paper.

Wick uses her creative powers to the fullest. "One of the main points to remember with my writing is that I take the word 'fiction' in its most literal sense. If I need a church on the corner of Fifth and Vine in 1872, and there wasn't one there, I'll just put it in."

Wick envisions her audience as mostly adult women. However, she also hears from men and teen readers. She feels that her themes are serious and therefore more suitable for adults. When asked which of her books would be appropriate for teens and younger children, she advised the adult to choose a book, read it, and then decide whether to recommend it to a younger reader.

Wick classifies her books as "definitely character driven." She includes her own brand of conflict and suspense, stating, "Most books also have a mystery of some sort, if nothing more than the mystery of how the man and woman will get together. My goal is romance, but not only romance; it's also to show that characters are whole in and of themselves. I include the gospel message . . . in every book." Wick credits her spiritual beliefs for her writing. "Jesus Christ is the basis for all, and without Him nothing can have full meaning."

When asked about character creation and its relation to actual people, Wick stated that she does not plan to include people she knows in her books but that it is almost impossible not to include some aspects of her own life or some of her acquaintances. For example, she reveals that she and Bob have participated in many of the activities that her characters, Sophie and Alec of *Sophie's Heart,* enjoyed.

It seems that Bob Wick has had a great impact on all his wife's works. Lori states, "My husband is the greatest influence on my writing since I talk over all the plots with him. If he is very busy while I'm writing, it is harder for me to get into a book."

One goal that Wick has for the future is to win a Gold Medallion, which she describes as "the highest award in Christian publishing." She would also like to see all her books published in other languages. Finally, she says that she would like for every book to "be the best I've ever written." Goals for her audience include "delight" and "entertainment." She hopes that her readers will take "real truth into their own world." It is her prayer that her characters would be those that her readers can "relate to and learn from."

Wick sees the standard for Christian fiction rising. With the recent bombardment of the market, publishers are "sifting through manuscripts with a more critical eye, and the cream is coming to the top." She is pleased with this phenomenon because it challenges her not to "rest on past successes but to strive to be the best each time."

The following is a special message from Wick to her readers: "I would love to tell you that I have a college degree in English or journalism, but I can't. I'm a small-town girl with a high school diploma and a few semesters of Bible school under my belt. However, my lack of training gives me a tremendous opportunity to glorify God. It's because of Him that I write. I have learned that He can do amazing things with vessels that are willing to be filled.

"Above is a quote from a speech I gave several years ago. I was asked to come and share my testimony about becoming a writer. My family is young, so as a rule I do not accept invitations for speaking engagements, but the statement still stands.

"I started writing in March of 1988. I had a story to tell, and I simply began to put it on paper. Were it not for the encouragement of my husband, Bob, I would not have kept on, but he liked what I wrote, and I pushed forward. I wrote throughout the summer that year and was well along with the plot by fall.

"Mine is not a story of years and years of writing and rejection notices. I first submitted to Harvest House Publishers a few sample chapters of *A Place Called Home*. It was rejected, so I gained permission from Bethany House Publishers to send the entire manuscript. They enjoyed it but couldn't use it. They recommended that I go to Harvest House. I didn't tell them that I'd already tried that arena but did as they suggested, and in February of 1989, after seeing the entire manuscript, Harvest House called and said they wanted to publish the book. I have done two books a year with them ever since.

"I didn't always want to be a writer, but my imagination has always been huge. Even as a child, I had to embellish everything. One of my favorite quotes, and I wish I knew the originator, is 'As a child, you're a liar; as an adult, you're a fiction writer.' I never recite this without a smile on my face because it so perfectly depicts my life as a child and then an author.

"The question I am asked most often is where do I get my ideas. It's not an easy question to answer, and for many years I said, 'I don't know.' But in time I remembered how 'people centered' my books are. You don't come to Lori Wick for a history lesson. My books focus on interpersonal relationships, and since there are billions of people in the world, the ideas are legion.

"I am also asked if I have plans to continue. The last count on the storyboard in my mind was more than fifteen other book ideas, and I think of new ones to add to that list all the time. By the way, that doesn't include short stories.

"As brief as I want to keep this story about myself, I must not forget to tell you that the basis of all of this is my relationship to Jesus Christ, my husband, and three children. These will always come first in my life, but as long as my Lord gives me stories and my husband and I agree that I should carry on, I will strive to write for Christ's glory alone."

SUMMARY: *WHERE THE WILD ROSE BLOOMS* (ROCKY MOUNTAIN MEMORIES SERIES)

A household of five daughters is certain to be lively, especially if the young ladies have been encouraged to be independent and to take the place of sons. Such is the Fontaine family, consisting of Eddie, Jackie, Danny, Alex, and Sammy.

When Morgan Fontaine is invited to move west to Colorado and become partners with his brother in running a successful general store, he quickly agrees, realizing that merchandising is one vocation in which girls can be as useful as boys. Each daughter has her responsibilities at home as well as in the store.

Life is not all work and no play, however, and the mercantile is a logical place to make new friends. When handsome, mischievous Clayton Taggart becomes a regular customer, all the sisters become his friends, and he eventually proposes marriage to Jackie. Two tragedies separate the perfectly matched pair, and both must adjust to very different lifestyles before God directs their paths to cross again.

Wick has created characters about which the reader will genuinely care as they experience joy and pain as well as birth and death. She successfully weaves the theme of salvation by grace throughout the story line without overriding the plot. Learning to live with a handicap is also integral to her characterization in this novel.

Where the Wild Rose Blooms is the first in Wick's Rocky Mountain Memories series. Just a hint of the plot for volume 2 is suggested in the closing pages. The avid reader might want to have that volume, *Whispers of Moonlight,* close at hand after completing volume 1.

Robert L. Wise

Forty years of counseling "pastorally and as a psychotherapist" have provided Robert Wise with a rich background for his works, both fiction and nonfiction. With a strong respect for the ability of story to convey truth and "as a priest of the church and preacher of the Word," he has chosen Christian fiction as a means for presenting the Christian message. Wise has found that his audience "fairly well covers the age spectrum, depending on the subject. Most of my readers are Christians or people seeking the Christian perspective. Many of my nonfiction books have been for hurting people. My fiction works also draw from this audience."

Born in Kansas City, Missouri, Wise now resides in Oklahoma with his wife, Margueritte, who shares his interest and training in the pastorate and in psychotherapy. Children are the Reverend Robert Todd Wise, Ph.D.; Christopher Matthew Wise, Ph.D.; Matthew Tate Wise; and Mrs. Traci Miller.

PROFESSIONAL

Education

Ph.D., California Graduate School of Theology; M.Div., Phillips Graduate Seminary; B.A., Central Oklahoma University; B.A., Phillips University; postgraduate work, Jung Institute of Zurich (Switzerland)

Career
Social worker; president, General Synod of the Reformed Episcopal Church in America; bishop in the Communion of Evangelical Episcopal Churches

Memberships
The Writers Guild of New York City

Awards
Angel Award for Religion in the Media, 1987

PUBLICATIONS

Adult Fiction

The Dawning, 1991
The Exiles, 1993
The Fall of Jerusalem, 1994
All That Remains, 1995

Coauthored with Paul Meier

The Third Millennium, 1993
The Fourth Millennium, 1996
Beyond the Millennium, 1997
The Code, 1998

Adult Nonfiction

Your Churning Place, 1977
When There Is No Miracle, 1977
How to Not Go Crazy, 1980
You Bet Your Life, 1984
The Church Divided, 1986
The Pastor's Barracks, 1986
When the Night Is Too Long, 1990
The Other Victims, 1990
A Deeper Walk, 1994
Windows of the Soul, 1995
Quest for the Soul, 1996
Nicht Ein Stein auf Dem Andern, 1996
Traiime Fenster der Seel, 1996

PERSONAL

The decision of Robert Wise to contribute to the field of literature stemmed from his own reading experience. "Reading the great classic literature shaped and molded my interest in writing. I found that truth could be conveyed through the form of story more effectively than other more didactic means. I also came to respect the form of imagination. Nothing can take the place of a 'good read.' My favorite childhood works were those of Robert Louis Stevenson. *A Child's Garden of Verses* remains a favorite. In junior high, I read everything written by Shakespeare and was highly intrigued by historic novels. In addition, my teen years were shaped by reading the major classic American writers." Today, Wise attempts "to read a novel a week. By reading a wide range of authors, I find new voices emerge as I write. I do not believe anyone can successfully write fiction without significant time spent reading."

A disciplined writer, Wise states that he starts "writing every morning at 6:30 and continues to 9:00 regardless of the demands of the day. Generally, I spend one entire day each week at the computer. Late evenings are spent in editing." Research, according to Wise, "reflects a lifetime of study and a rather substantial library that I know like the back of my hand. Of course, I use the Internet resources that are current bill of fare."

Influences on Wise's work are Lloyd C. Douglas, A. J. Cronin, Charles Dickens, and Victor Hugo. Also, "Susan Howatch is a great inspiration and encouragement. As of late, I am taken with the brilliant contemporary style of Elmore Leonard."

Wise's novels tend to be theme driven, and if there is any one recurring theme, he believes that it would be "the integrity or veracity of the Christian faith. . . . Since my spiritual beliefs are central to my personal meaning in life, they are central to what I write." For those who open his books, he hopes "to write something that will have enduring significance in guiding readers toward what is both eternal and timely for the moment in which we live."

Wise's view of the future of Christian fiction is that the field "is wide open if the publishing industry can get beyond being mired into a reactionary fear of offending the conservative Christian community. Much fiction is not realistic either in language or content because of concern for a fundamentalist backlash. The result is literature that often sounds more like propaganda than life. Christian readers generally want their worldview affirmed, not challenged. This tendency reduces the scope of what writers can say and have published in the Christian market. The great Christian literature of the past was not fettered with such prejudice. Examples of a wide-open approach would be Charles Dickens and Sinclair Lewis assaulting social evil. Once the

Christian community learns to read to be challenged and not soothed, a significant literature will follow."

SUMMARY: *THE EXILES* (PEOPLE OF THE COVENANT SERIES)

Sixty years after the death and resurrection of Yeshua, the world is in chaos. Conflict between rebel and conqueror increases in the streets of Jerusalem while Nero rules the Roman world with increasing madness. Brutality and treachery abound.

Drawn from their beloved Jerusalem to the imperial city of Rome, the family of Jairus Ben Aaron finds itself in the midst of political storm. Determined to carry the message of hope in Yeshua to all who will listen, they become instrumental in the burgeoning growth of believers. Under the patronage of Gaius Honorius Piso, head of the Praetorian Guard, they share the peace that they have found with all who will listen. While others teach, Miriam works diligently to commit to writing the words and acts of their beloved Messiah so that Christians everywhere will have the benefit of the Master's teachings.

Fearing the explosive growth of followers of this new religion and seeking a scapegoat for his evil schemes, Nero launches a savage persecution of all who carry the name of Christ. Not even the power of General Piso is enough to protect them. Only the power of the God they follow can carry them through.

Steven Wise

Any teacher reading the inspirational novels of Steven Wise should take encouragement. Here is a role model for those in the field of education who always hope that the knowledge they share will make a significant impact on some student who will become successful and perhaps recognize that a bit of his or her achievement might be credited to what took place in the classroom. In his case, Wise pays tribute to both a grade-school teacher, Miss Lillian Allen, and a high school English teacher, Miss Florence Hudson. Whatever they taught, he must have been a receptive student, and now his readers are reaping the rewards.

Wise was born on July 15, 1948, in California, Missouri, to Floyd and Norma Wise. He and his wife, Cathy, who is a registered nurse, live in Columbia, Missouri, with their two children: Travis and Stacee. He lists his hobbies as "occasional golf and hunting" but states that writing, attempting to keep up with two active children, and his involvement in the activities of his church occupy most of his nonvocational time. His participation in a church service provided the inspiration for his first novel.

PROFESSIONAL

Education

B.A. in economics, University of Missouri

Career
Missouri state general certified real estate appraiser

Memberships
Appraisal Institute, National Professional Appraiser's Organization

PUBLICATIONS

Adult Fiction

Midnight, 1993
Chambers, 1994
Long Train Passing, 1996

PERSONAL

It is obvious from his career experiences that Steven Wise did not set out to write inspirational fiction. However, he does relate that his interest in writing began in high school. He credits the late Miss Florence Hudson, his English teacher, with "instilling [in him] a love for literature and a realization of the power of the written word. . . . She possessed nearly mystical power in recognizing the ability level of her students and then drawing out everything that those abilities were capable of producing. Admittedly, this process was not always pleasant, and it was not until I was a college student that I began to recognize what she had done for me. Through the years, I became an avid reader and began to take great care with the assemblage of words—in my vocation as well as in my personal life. About eight years ago, following a short personal testimony given in my church, the pastor's wife asked me if I had ever considered writing anything down. Her words of encouragement spurred me to begin work on my first novel manuscript." Wise states that it was "quite natural" that Christian fiction would be his choice of writing style, given his "upbringing in the church and continued involvement."

In describing his writing style and process, Wise says that his books are character driven and that settings are "largely based on residence." He explains the importance of those who people his works this way: "I believe that strong characters are much more important than theme or plot. Good characters may very well sustain an unremarkable plot, but the opposite is not true. I believe that the primary responsibility of the writer is to give the reader people to care strongly about. The feelings evoked may be positive or negative, but they must be strong enough to make the reader turn the pages to find out what happens with the characters."

Perhaps a part of that page-turning response results from the fact that Wise frequently bases his characters on people he knows or on those who have crossed his path in the past. "An excellent example would be Miss Annabelle in *Long Train Passing*. She is based on a former grade-school teacher, the late Miss Lillian Allen, who made an indelible impression on me as a youngster. This lady was the embodiment of the finest qualities of the teaching profession. We remained friends for many years beyond school."

Wise states that research is a limited factor in his writing because his plots arise from his own experience or are compilations of readings he has enjoyed over the years. Characterizing himself as "a storyteller," he states that his writing "has been greatly influenced by observing 'small town' or 'ordinary' heroes—people who have been engaged in 'in-the-trenches' Christianity and who go unrecognized by the world."

Wise says that his goal in writing Christian fiction is to focus on those unsung heroes who have made a difference. "I hope to present these people in my novels in a fashion that draws my readers to them. I hope that my characters will enrich the lives of my readers, leaving them with something worthwhile and lasting."

Wise reflects a positive view of the future of Christian fiction. He predicts "a growing awareness among Christians and many others as well that high-quality fiction, sans gratuitous violence and sex, is available. . . . I hope to play a part in this continuing trend."

SUMMARY: *LONG TRAIN PASSING*

To the reader, Miss Annabelle Allen's handicap seems almost a holy thing, blessing her with wisdom and compassion. Injured by a fall while still an infant, diminutive Miss Annabelle is no stranger to the emotional isolation of being "different." When faced by the challenge of teaching Jewell Cole, the withdrawn and uncooperative teenage son of an alcoholic, Miss Annabelle establishes communication by extending both empathy and respect to the young man.

The future holds bright promise for Jewell as his teacher discovers his well-hidden abilities, both intellectual and artistic. School becomes the only joy in his dreary life until Jewell's father, Jubal, feels betrayed by his son's success. The elder Cole decides that he can control his son only when the little schoolteacher no longer exists. However, the villainy plotted by Jubal Cole's wasted mind is foiled by raw courage, loyalty, and the power of love, but not without leaving behind scars of revenge.

Rare is the novel that combines the charm of small-town characters speaking in dialogue so realistic that the reader feels guilty for eavesdropping with a suspenseful, page-turning plot, but Wise has created just such a mix. It would be safe to say that in this story, he is "right on track."

Lance Wubbels

It might seem to be a gigantic leap from editing the theological works of Charles Spurgeon and the historical treatises of F. B. Meyer to writing family stories set on farms in Minnesota, but Lance Wubbels has managed it gracefully. Readers are richer for this longtime editor's efforts at preserving for posterity the stories that he remembers from his childhood and his choice to pay tribute to his father's memory by committing them to paper in novel form.

Born in 1952 in Preston, Minnesota, to Gerald and Marjorie Wubbels, a machinist and a housewife, Wubbels went on to earn a bachelors degree from Bethany College. He and his wife, Karen, an office manager at Bethany House Publishers, are the parents of two children, Ingerlisa and Nils, to whom book 3 in The Gentle Hills series, *Keeper of the Harvest*, is lovingly dedicated.

PROFESSIONAL

Education

B.A. in Bible and missions, Bethany College of Missions

Career

Managing editor, Bethany House Publishers; instructor, Bethany College of Missions

Awards

Angel Award, *One Small Miracle,* 1996

PUBLICATIONS

Adult Fiction

One Small Miracle, 1995
The Bridge over Flatwillow Creek, 1998
The Gentle Hills Series
Far from the Dream, 1994
Whispers in the Valley, 1995
Keeper of the Harvest, 1995
Some Things Last Forever, 1996
In the Shadow of a Secret, 1999

Nonfiction, Compiler/Editor

Christian Living Classics by Charles Spurgeon (written under the pseudonym Robert Hall)
The Power of Prayer in a Believer's Life, 1993
Spiritual Warfare in a Believer's Life, 1993
What the Holy Spirit Does in a Believer's Life, 1993
Grace Abounding in a Believer's Life, 1994
The Triumph of Faith in a Believer's Life, 1994
A Passion for Holiness in a Believer's Life (as Lance Wubbels), 1994
The Power of Christ's Miracles, 1995
The Power of Christ's Prayer Life, 1995
The Power of the Cross of Christ, 1995
The Power of Christ's Tears, 1996
The Power of Christ the Warrior, 1996
The Power of Christ's Second Coming, 1996

Edited and Updated Works of F. B. Meyer

The Life of Paul, 1995
The Life of David, 1995
The Life of Joseph, 1995
The Life of Abraham, 1996
The Life of Moses, 1996
The Life of Peter, 1996

Thirty-Day Devotional Treasury
Charles Finney on Spiritual Power, 1998
George Muller on Faith, 1998
Andrew Murray on Holiness, 1998
Hudson Taylor on Spiritual Secrets, 1998
Charles Spurgeon on Prayer, 1998
R. A. Torrey on the Holy Spirit, 1998

PERSONAL

Having worked as an editor at Bethany House Publishers for ten years, Lance Wubbels viewed himself mainly as an editor and a college Bible instructor. Two events, neither of which was pleasant, "pushed him out of the nest" and challenged him to try his wings as a fiction writer. The first was the choice to leave his post as college teacher as a result of changes in his institution, which he could not support. The second was the death of his father.

Wubbels describes his father, Gerald, as "a simple, quiet, loving, caring, poor, gentle man from a rural background." Gerald had served in World War II and had shared his experiences with his family. His son realized that when his parents died, many wonderful stories would perish with them unless someone recorded them so that they could become a part of a precious heritage. Wubbels even chose to use his parents' names for characters in his series. "I thought it would be fun to at least attempt weaving some of my father's wartime experiences into a fiction story, sprinkle in some of my mother's stories, and splash on some of our family stories as well. I had no idea if I could pull it off, but why not try, right? I didn't consider myself a writer, so to be rejected couldn't damage an ego that wasn't there. The result was my first series of four books with Bethany House Publishers, The Gentle Hills."

Explaining why he chose to write Christian fiction, Wubbels states, "Having trained in an evangelical college with a strong emphasis in missions and then having taught biblical courses for ten years and working even longer as an editor for a major Christian publisher, for the past twenty-five years my work has primarily revolved around Christian themes. That's really the world from which I derive my stories. Besides, as a believer, I can't see writing a fiction story that would not bear something of the spiritual imprint the gospel has made on my life."

Regarding the amount and type of research supporting his novels, Wubbels says, "Before I do much research, I first spend a lot of time allowing the story to begin to percolate in my mind. I am not following a romance formula, so, knowing what the story is going to be about and where it will head, what the characters are going to be like and what they'll do, and so on, is what takes most of the time. Once I have a feel for that, I am able to read and search for the background I'll need to complete the picture."

Still employed as an editor with Bethany House, Wubbels must arrange his writing schedule around his "day job," his family, and his hobbies—fishing, movies, books, and sports. He describes the process this way: "I write in the evenings, weekends, and some vacation days—juggling that around my family commitments. I write in the den at home. My current method of writing is to sit in a rocking chair with my laptop on my knees and plunk away. I try to write every night and as long as I can without burning out. Occasionally, I grab shorter time blocks, but I prefer to work a couple hours in a row without breaking my concentration."

Describing his style as "simple, country, homey, charming, and touching all the human emotions," Wubbels shares that even though marketing experts profile the Christian fiction reader as "primarily forty-year-old women," it is his desire to write "a beautiful story that men, women, and young people all could enjoy." He attempts to accomplish this feat by focusing on themes of "personal growth and character development as characters face adversity and challenge." Certainly, these are aspects relevant across age and gender lines.

As has been stated, the characters in The Gentle Hills series were based on stories from Wubbels's past and those recounted by his father, so, naturally, they were framed on people already familiar to the author. The award-winning *One Small Miracle* is a reflection of Wubbels's own teaching experience, although the teacher is a female and the classroom is fifth grade rather than college. So, to this point, character creation has been a matter of depicting known persons realistically. However, "*The Bridge over Flatwillow Creek* has characters I did not know, so it took longer for us to get to know one another—and more rewriting!"

When asked who, other than those of his heritage, has influenced his writing, Wubbels named J. R. R. Tolkien and George MacDonald as well as the many writers with whom he has worked at Bethany House. "I truly don't know how this reading has shaped my writing. Perhaps it has helped me to see what I like and what I don't, but I truly believe that I have to write with my own voice and that it's foolish to try to emulate another writer's style."

In a more concrete way, Wubbels credits Carol Johnson and Anne Buchanan as helping him advance as a writer. "Carol Johnson, the editorial director at Bethany House, was the first person to whom I showed my first chapter. She is the best fiction editor I know, and her 'Keep writing, I like it' encouraged me to continue. Anne Buchanan, who edited my first four books, showed me some of my weaknesses as a writer and has shaped me in a better mold. And I would say that hearing from readers has been a terrific motivator. Their responses have kept me going."

When asked how his own beliefs affect his writing, Wubbels responded, "They stand behind and underneath everything I write. My purpose in writing is not to force my spiritual beliefs into the story or upon my readers, but they will be there, woven into the fabric of every story."

Expressing his goal for his readers, Wubbels also reveals the effect his audience has on him. "It is my greatest joy to hear from readers who say something is different in their lives because of something they read in my story. I want the reader to enjoy his read, to be entertained, but I also want the lives of my characters and the truth in the story to touch and inspire."

Assessing the place of inspirational novels in the culture of the future from his vantage point as an editor, Wubbels observes, "I believe there will always be room for a well-told Christian story. At present, the limited size of the Christian bookseller market makes it very tough for new writers to break in. It is my hope that new avenues for book sales will open up to Christian publishers and widen the playing field, touching millions more readers and providing more writers a sufficient financial remuneration that allows them to write full time."

SUMMARY: *FAR FROM THE DREAM* (THE GENTLE HILLS SERIES)

For Marjie Livingstone, Jerry Macmillan, and their friends, the Depression was the specter spoken of and still felt by their parents in the winter of 1941. However, a new enemy loomed on the horizon, this one bent on ravaging Europe as well as North America, and Asia had just played her trump card with the Japanese attack on Pearl Harbor. The spirit of patriotism was moving through the Minnesota farmland, sweeping up all the able-bodied young men who could possibly leave their parents, wives, or sweethearts.

When his best friend for life suffers devastating wounds as the battleship *Arizona* is hit and sunk in Pearl Harbor, the only honorable action for Jerry Macmillan to take is to enlist in the Navy and seek retribution for his buddy's injuries. Leaving his widowed father to care for the farm is not easy, especially when the relationship between father and son is already somewhat strained. Leaving Marjie as his sweetheart is unthinkable, so the two choose to part as husband and wife instead.

Using the vehicle of young love and the hardship of separation by war, Wubbels demonstrates how friendship can draw lives to the Lord. Throughout the book, ordinary people who are not really adept at presenting "the plan of salvation" still are used effectively to attract loved ones and friends within an arm's reach of God.

Following the hardships and victories of Marjie on the home front and of Jerry in battle, the reader gains an appreciation of what parents or grandparents experienced to help keep America free. Inclusion of authentic foods, music, technology, vocabulary, and the values representative of the time gives the contemporary reader, poised on the brink of the twenty-first century, a realistic view of what life was like during the war. Perhaps this story will even ignite a spark of courage to once again stand up for what one believes is right.

Appendix

WRITERS' RESOURCES

How to Write (and Sell) a Christian Novel: Proven and Practical Advice from a Best-Selling Author, by Gilbert Morris. ASIN: 0892838787.

The Complete Guide to Writing and Selling the Christian Novel, by Penelope J. Stokes. Published by Writers Digest Books, 1998. ISBN 8098798108.

Christian Writer's Market Guide, by Sally E. Stuart. Published by Harold Shaw Publishers, 1998. ISBN 0877881685.

PUBLISHERS' ADDRESSES

Baker Book House
Box 6287
Grand Rapids, MI 49516

Bethany House Publishers
11300 Hampshire Ave. S.
Minneapolis, MN 55438

Chariot Victor Publishing
4050 Lee Vance View
Colorado Springs, CO 80918

Crossway Books
1300 Crescent St.
Wheaton, IL 60187

Doubleday Publications, Inc.
245 Park Ave.
New York, NY 10017

Fleming Revell/Chosen Books
Divisions of Baker Book House
P.O. Box 6287
Grand Rapids, MI 49516-6287

Focus on the Family, Publishing
8605 Explorer Dr.
Colorado Springs, CO 80920

Harvest House Publishers
1075 Arrowsmith
Eugene, OR 97402-9197

InterVarsity Press
P.O. Box 1400
Downers Grove, IL 60515

Moody Press
820 N. LaSalle Blvd.
Chicago, IL 60610

NavPress Publishing Group
P.O. Box 35001
Colorado Springs, CO 80935

Questar Publishers, Inc.
P.O. Box 1720
Sisters, OR 97759

Random House Publishing
201 E. Fiftieth St.
22nd Floor
New York, NY 10022

Thomas Nelson Publishers
596 Nelson Place
Nashville, TN 37214

Tyndale House Publisher
351 Executive Drive
Box 80
Wheaton, IL 60187

Word Publishers
1501 LBJ Freeway, #650
Dallas, TX 75234-6052

YWAM Publishing
P.O. Box 55787
Seattle, WA 98155

Zondervan Publishing House
5300 Patterson Ave. S.E.
Grand Rapids, MI 49530

INTERNET RESOURCES

Articles can be found on the World Wide Web with the key words "Christian fiction" or by looking for individual author names. Some authors have Web sites that have been set up by their publishing companies. The following Web sites have proven to be fruitful resources. For convenience, they are arranged by their particular focus.

Sites that list best-sellers or special types of Christian fiction:

http://www.polyweb.com/bookbowers/inspirational/inspirational.htm
http://www.cba-intl.org/publications/marketplace/isbnfict.htm
http://www.ingrambook.com/ecpa/fiction.html
http://harvest.reapernet.com/bo/top20.html
http://www.ingrambook.com/TITLEWAVE...CATEGORY_INFO/category_files/files/fi.html
http://www.tyndale.com/journal/bestsellers/

Sites that address issues related to Christian fiction:

http://pwp.usa.pipeline.com/~jeriwho/meremora.html

Sites that give reviews of Christian fiction:

http://www.revel8.com/books/fiction/fiction.html
http://www.netcentral.net/acl/9708acl/fiction/atimeofwar.html

http://www.tyndale.com/journal/fiction/
http://www.wpl.lib.oh.us/library/services/adult/2wv_chf.html
http://www.whidbey.com/hisplace/booksrev.htm
http://www.ala.org/booklist/christ.html
http://www.acloserlook.com/ecpa/fiction.html

Sites that list Christian publishing companies:

http://www.crosssearch.com/Publishing/
http://www.bookwire.com/index/Religious_Publishers.html
http://www.christianretailing.com/phonebook/listings/152.htm
http://wwwgospelcom.net/

Sites for individual publishers that include submission guidelines for manuscripts:

http://www.zondervan.com/mail.htm
http://www.thomasnelson.com/Pagx
http://www.doubleday.com/backyard/contact.html

Cross-Index of Titles and Authors

The following is a comprehensive list of only the fiction titles written by the authors profiled in this book. Since the focus of the book is writers of fiction, nonfiction titles have intentionally been omitted from the index. Coauthors are listed where necessary, although coauthors without an entry in the book have also been omitted. Pseudonyms are contained in parentheses.

Title	Author
Aaron's Christmas Donkey	Johnson, L. W.
Abandoned	Rushford
Abandoned on the Wild Frontier	Jackson, D. and N.
Above All Else	Crow
Absolutely Green	Schulte
The Accused	Rue
The Adversaries	Cavanaugh
Afton of Margate Castle	Hunt
Alabaster's Song	Lucado
Alex's Triple Threat	Levene
All That Glitters	Morris, G.
All That Remains	Wise, R.
All the Children of the World	Mezek
All the Days Were Summer	Funderburk
All the Shining Young Men	Funderburk and Morris, G.
All Things New	Crow
The Allies	Cavanaugh
The Ally	Rue
Allyson	Jenkins
Along Green Banks of Hope	Pieters
Always in September	Fell
The Amazon Stranger	Gustaveson
The Amber Room	Bunn
Ambushed in Africa	Doyle
Ambushed in Jaguar Swamp	Jackson, D. and N.
Among the Gods	Austin
Among the King's Soldiers	Morris, G.
The Ancients	Myers
Andy	Borntrager
The Angry Gymnast	Jenkins
Anna Apple	Carlson
Annie	Borntrager
Another Homecoming	Bunn and Oke
Apollyon	Jenkins
Apple-Turnover Treasure	Levene
April Is Forever	Fell
Arabian Winds	Chaikin
The Arizona Longhorn Adventure	Dengler
Arrow of the Almighty	Morris, G.
As Time Goes By	Wick
Assassins	Jenkins
Assassins in the Cathedral	Jackson, D. and N.
At Home in Mitford	Karon
Attack in the Rye Grass	Jackson, D. and N.
Attack of the Amazons	Morris, G.

Title	Author
Autumn Secrets	Carlson
Awakening Heart	Carlson
B is for Bad at Getting into Harvard	Rue
Back to the Drawing Board	Myers
Backfire	Kritlow
Backwater Blues	Herndon
Balancing Act	Brinkerhoff
The Bandit of Ashley Downs	Jackson, D. and N.
The Banks of the Boyne: The Generations of Northern Ireland	Crow
Bartholomew Beaver and the Stupendous Splash	Waite
A Basket of Roses	Hunt
The Battle	Rue
Battle of Lookout Mountain	Morris, G.
A Battle of the Weeds	Carlson
The Bear Cub Disaster	Roddy
Bear Scare	Roper
Beauty in the Least	Myers
Because I Love You	Lucado
Becky's Brainstorm	Schulte
Becky's Secret Surprise	Schulte
Before Night Falls	Minatra
Before the Dawn	Riols
Before the Judge	Jenkins
Before Winter Comes	Fell
The Beginning of Sorrows	Morris, A., G., and L.
Behind the Locked Door	McCusker
Behind the Veil	Chaikin
Beloved Stranger	Pella
Beneath a Dakota Cross	Bly
Benjamin's Box	Carlson
Berlin Encounter	Bunn
Betrayal	Arthur
Betrayed	Rushford
The Betrayer's Fortune	Jackson, D. and N.
Between Earth and Sky	Morris, A.
Beyond a Reasonable Doubt	Parker
Beyond the Millennium	Wise, R.
Beyond the Picket Fence	Wick
Beyond the Quiet Hills	Morris, G.
Beyond the River	Elmer
Beyond the River	Morris, G., and Funderburk
Beyond the Windswept Sea	Fell and Page
The Big Lie	Myers
Billy 'n' Bear Go to a Birthday Party	Gunn
Billy 'n' Bear Go to Sunday School	Gunn
Billy 'n' Bear Go to the Doctor's	Gunn
Billy 'n' Bear Go to the Grocery Store	Gunn
Billy 'n' Bear Visit Grandpa and Grandma	Gunn
The Bizarre Hockey Tournament	Jenkins
Black Dragon	Davis
Blackberry Bart	Carlson
Blind Faith	Pella
Blind Trust	Blackstock
Blizzard	Jenkins
Blockade Runner	Morris, G.
Blood Money	Kritlow
Blood of Heaven	Myers
Blue Mist on the Danube	Fell
The Bluebird and the Sparrow	Oke
The Blunder Years	Myers
Boggin, Blizzy, and Sleeter the Cheater	Waite
Boomtown	Morris, G.
Bouquet of Goodbyes	Page
Bride for Donnigan	Oke
The Bridge	Rue
Bridge over Flatwillow Creek	Wubbels
Bright Sword of Justice	Morris, A.
Bring the Boys Home	Morris, G.
Broken Wings	Blackstock
Brothers	Hunt
Bucks of Goober Holler	Morris, G.
The Burden	Rue
Burden of Honor	Roddy
Butterflies for Two	Waite
Buzzle Billy	Waite
By Dawn's Early Light	Hunt
By Hear-Say Only	Pieters
By Honor Bound	Morris, A.
Cain	Huggins

Title	Author
Calico Bear	Hunt
A Call to Honor	Funderburk and Morris, G.
The Calling	Jenkins
Calling in the Wind	Pieters
Calling of Emily Evans	Oke
The Camping Caper	Davoll
A Capitol Offense	Parker
Captive at Kangaroo Springs	Elmer
The Captive Bride	Morris, G.
Captive Heart	Chaikin
The Capture	Rue
Cara's Beach Party Disaster	Schulte
Cari's Secret	Coyle
Carnival of Secrets	McCusker
Carrie	Page
The Case of the Birthday Bracelet	Hunt
The Case of the Counterfeit Cash	Hunt
Case of the Dangerous Cruise	Roddy
The Case of the Haunting of Lowell Lanes	Hunt
The Case of the Missing Melody	Roper
The Case of the Missing Minds	Myers
The Case of the Mystery Mark	Hunt
The Case of the Phantom Friend	Hunt
The Case of the Teenage Terminator	Hunt
The Case of the Terrified Track Star	Hunt
Casey the Greedy Young Cowboy	Waite
The Castle of Dreams	Crow
Cat Burglars	Roper
Cat Killer	Dengler
The Cat Who Smelled Like Cabbage	Jackson, N.
Catacombs	McCusker
Caught in the Act	Roper
Caught in the Middle	Roper
The Caves That Time Forgot	Morris, G.
Chain Five Mystery	Dengler
The Chairman	Kraus
Chambers	Wise, S.
The Chance of a Lifetime	Hunt
Change of Plans	Page
Chariots in the Smoke	Morris, G.
Charles Towne	Hunt
The Chase	Rue
Chased by the Jewel Thieves	Doyle
Chasing the Wind	Elmer
Cherished Wish	Carlson
Cherry Blossom Princess	Holmes
Cherry Cola Champions	Levene
The Children of the King	Lucado
The Chimney Sweep's Ransom	Jackson, D. and N.
Choice Summer	Brinkerhoff
Christmas at Rumpole Mansion	Mezek
Christmas by the Hearth	Hunt
The Christmas Treasure Hunt	Carlson
Christopher Churchmouse Birthday Collection	Davoll
Christopher Churchmouse Classic Treasury	Davoll
A Churchmouse Birthday	Davoll
A Churchmouse Christmas	Davoll
A Churchmouse Musical Book	Davoll
Cinnabar	Roddy
Citadel and the Lamb	Herr
A City Not Forsaken	Morris, G. and L.
Close to a Father's Heart	Coyle
Close Your Eyes	Gunn
Closer Than Ever	Gunn
Clouds	Gunn
The Clubhouse Mystery	Jenkins
The Code	Wise, R.
Code of Honor	Dengler
The Colonists	Cavanaugh
The Color of the Star	Funderburk and Morris, G.
Columbia Falls	Bly
Come As You Are	Johnson, L. W.
A Comedy of Errors	Johnson, L. H.

Title	Author
The Comforting Bird	Pieters
Conquered Heart	Samson
Copper Hill	Bly
Cosmic Christmas	Lucado
A Cote of Many Colors	Oke
Courtney	Jenkins
A Covenant of Love	Morris, G.
Coyote True	Bly
Crash in Cannibal Valley	Jenkins
The Creeping Shadows	Johnson, L. W.
Crimson Snow	Kritlow
The Crimson Tapestry	Joens
The Crippled Lamb	Lucado
Crocodile Meatloaf	Levene
The Crossed Sabres	Morris, G.
The Crown and the Crucible	Pella and Phillips
Cry of Courage	Roddy
Crystal's Blizzard Trek	Bly
Crystal's Grand Entry	Bly
Crystal's Mill Town Mystery	Bly
Crystal's Perilous Ride	Bly
Crystal's Rodeo Debut	Bly
Crystal's Solid Gold Discovery	Bly
The Curse	Myers
Daisy Doodlepaws and the Windy Woods Treasure	Waite
Danger at Deception Pass	Bly
Danger Lies Ahead	McCusker
Danger on the Flying Trapeze	Jackson, D. and N.
Danger on Thunder Mountain	Roddy
The Dangerous Canoe Race	Roddy
Dangerous Devices	Bunn
A Dangerous Love	Phillips
The Dangerous Voyage	Gustaveson
The Dangerous Voyage	Morris, G.
The Dangerous Zone	Gustaveson
Dangers of the Rainbow Nebula	Morris, G.
Daniel	Borntrager
Daniel and the Lions' Den	Carlson
Daniel Colton Kidnapped	Schulte
Daniel Colton Under Fire	Schulte
Daniel's Big Decision	Jenkins
Daniel's Big Surprise	Jenkins
Dark Passage	McCusker
Dark Road to Daylight	Parker
Dark Spell over Morlandria	Morris, G.
A Darkness before Dawn	Minatra
Daughter of Grace	Pella and Phillips
Dawn of Liberty	Phillips
The Dawn of Mercy	Joens
The Dawning	Wise, R.
Dawning of Deliverance	Pella
Days of Deception	Roddy
The Deacon's Woman	Jenkins
Deadline	Alcorn
The Deadly Chase	Hunt
Deadly Deception	Morris, G.
The Deadly Maze	Kritlow
Death Bird of Paradise	Herndon
Death on an Island	Roper
Death Stalks a Holiday	Parker
Death Valley	Dengler
Deceived	Rushford
The Deceived	Myers
Decidedly Married	Page
The Decision	Roper
Defeat of the Ghost Riders	Jackson, D. and N.
Delta Factor	Bunn (Locke)
Depths of Destiny	Phillips
The Depths of Malice	Morris, A. and G.
Desert Water	Parker
The Desires of Your Heart	Crow
Desperate Measures	Rushford
The Desperate Search	Roddy
Destined to Live	Pieters
Digger's Marvelous Moleberry Bush	Waite
Dingo Creek Challenge	Elmer
The Disappearing Stranger	Johnson, L. W.
Disaster at Windy Hill	Johnson, L. W.
Disaster in the Yukon	Jenkins
The Discerning Heart	Pieters
Discovery at Denny's Deli	Roper
Distant Dreams	Pella
Dixie and Bandit	Morris, G.

Title	Author
Dixie and Champ	Morris, G.
Dixie and Dolly	Morris, G.
Dixie and Iran	Morris, G.
Dixie and Jumbo	Morris, G.
Dixie and Perry	Morris, G.
Dixie and Sandy	Morris, G.
Dixie and Stripes	Morris, G.
The Dixie Widow	Morris, G.
Do the Bright Thing	Myers
The Document	Roper
The Dog Who Loved to Race	Jackson, N.
The Dog Who Would Not Smile	Bly
Dominion	Alcorn
Donovan's Daughter	Wick
Don't Count on Homecoming Queen	Rue
Don't You Wish	Gunn
Dooger, The Grasshopper Hound	Roddy
A Door of Hope	Coyle
Double-Crossed in Gator Country	Herndon
The Dove and the Rose	Herr
Drastic Park	Davis
A Dream to Cherish	Hunt
Dream Voyager	Bunn (Locke)
Dreamers	Hunt
Dreams of Gold	Schulte
Dreams of Promise	Carlson
Dreams Will Not Die	Pieters
Driving Lessons	Kritlow
Drummer Boy at Bull Run	Morris, G.
The Drummer Boy's Battle	Jackson, D. and N.
Drums of Change	Oke
Drums of War	Doyle
Dublin Crossing	Dengler
Ducktails	Oke
Dusty Mole—Private Eye	Davoll
Dying to Win	Rushford
East of Outback	Dengler
The East Side Bullies	Jenkins
Echoes	Gunn
Echoes of Love	Schulte
Eddie and the Rude Green Grood	Waite
Edge of Eternity	Alcorn
The Eleventh Hour	Phillips
Elizabeth: Days of Loss and Hope	Crow

Title	Author
Ellie	Borntrager
The Emerald Isle	Hunt
Emerald Sea	Dengler
Emma Wimble, Accidental Astronaut	Waite
Empire Builders	Chaikin
Empress of the Underworld	Morris, G.
The Encounter	Myers
Encounter at Cold Harbor	Morris, G.
Encounter the Light	Crow
The End of Glory	Funderburk and Morris, G.
Endangered!	Chaikin
Enough!	Roper
The Ephesus Fragment	Parker
Erin	Jenkins
The Escape	Rue
Escape Down the Raging Rapids	Roddy
Escape from Black Forest	Doyle
Escape from the Red Comet	Morris, G.
Escape from the Slave Traders	Jackson, D. and N.
Escape into the Night	Johnson, L. W.
Escape to Freedom	Phillips
Escape to Murray River	Elmer
Escape with the Dream Maker	Morris, G.
Eternal Passage	Schulte
The Everlasting Flame	Chaikin
Every Desert Has Its Well	Pieters
Every Little Thing about You	Wick
Eve's Daughter	Austin
Evidence of Mercy	Blackstock
Evidence of Things Unseen	Smith
The Evil Plot of Doctor Zarnof	Crow
The Exiles	Wise, R.
The Experiment	Myers
Eye of the Hurricane	Roddy
Eyes from Across	Pieters
Facing the Future	Jenkins
The Fall of Jerusalem	Wise, R.
False Claims at the Little Stephen Mine	Bly
Family Reunion	Page

Title	Author
Fangs for the Memories	Myers
Far from the Dream	Wubbels
Far from the Storm	Elmer
The Fastest Car in the County	Levene
Fate of the Yellow Woodbee	Jackson, D. and N.
Fated Genes	Kraus
Fear Haunts the Summer	Roper
The Fiddler's Secret	Johnson, L. W.
The Fields of Bannockburn	Crow
The Fields of Glory	Morris, G.
The Final Adversary	Morris, G.
The Final Chapter of Chance McCall	Bly
The Final Curtain	Morris, G.
Final Justice at Adobe Wells	Bly
The Final Kingdom	Morris, G.
Fire in the Bramblewood	Davoll
Fire of Heaven	Myers
Fire on the Lake	Kritlow
Fire over Atlanta	Morris, G.
The Fires of Autumn	Funderburk
Firestorm at Kookaburra Station	Elmer
The Flames of Rome	Maier
The Flaming Trap	Roddy
Flee the Darkness	Hunt
Flight from Stonewycke	Pella and Phillips
Flight of the Eagles	Morris, G.
Flight of the Fugitives	Jackson, D. and N.
A Flood of Friends	Davoll
Florian's Gate	Bunn
Fly Away	Austin
The Flying Cavalier	Morris, G.
Follow the Star	Elmer
Follow Your Dream	Holmes
Footmarks on the Water	Pieters
For Whom the Stars Shine	Chaikin
The Forbidden Road	Gustaveson
A Forever Friend	Hunt
Forgotten	Rushford
Foul Play at Moler Park	Davoll
Fourteen Days to Midnight	Jenkins
The Fourth Millennium	Wise, R.
Fox Island	Bly
Freedom Run	McCusker
French Fry Forgiveness	Levene
From the Ashes	Rushford
From the Secret Place in My Heart: The Diary of Christina Juliet Miller	Gunn
Frontier Lady	Pella
Gaal the Conqueror	White
The Gallant Boys of Gettysburg	Morris, G.
The Gallant Outlaw	Morris, G.
The Garden at the Edge of Beyond	Phillips
Gate of His Enemies	Morris, G.
The Gates of Neptune	Morris, G.
Gateway	Jenkins
A Gathering of Eagles	Morris, G.
A Gathering of Memories	Wick
The Gathering Storm	Davis
General Kempthorne's Victory Tour	Crow
A Gentle Calling	Crow
The Gentle Rebel	Morris, G.
Gentle Touch	Hunt
The Ghost Dog of Stoney Ridge	Roddy
The Ghost of KRZY	Myers
Ghost of the Moaning Mansion	Roddy
Giants on the Hill	Roddy
Gibraltar Passage	Bunn
The Gift	Bunn
A Gift for Grandpa	Hunt
Gila Monster	Dengler
Gilly's Gift for Granny	Waite
Give Me a Sign of Life	Pieters
Gladys Grape	Carlson
Glastonbury: The Novel of Christian England	Crow
A Gleam of Dawn	Pieters
Glimpses of Truth	Cavanaugh
The Glory of Love	Hunt
Go for It!	Schulte
God Lives in My House	Carlson
God's Cryptography	Pieters
The Gold Miners' Rescue	Jackson, D. and N.
The Gold Train Bandits	Roddy

Title	Author
The Golden Cross	Hunt
Golden Dreams	Schulte
Golden Palaces	Chaikin
Good Sport/ Bad Sport	Jenkins
Goodnight Blessings	Mezek
A Gown of Spanish Lace	Oke
Grandpa's Secret	Davoll
Grandpa's Stolen Treasure	Johnson, L. W.
Grapefruit Basket Upset	Levene
Grave Matters	Crow
Grayfox	Phillips
Greengold Autumn	Crow
The Guardian	Myers
The Guardian	Rue
Guilt by Association	Morris, G.
The Gypsies' Secret	Davoll
The Hair-Pulling Bear Dog	Roddy
Hallie's Secret	Page
The Hamster Who Got Himself Stuck	Jackson, N.
Handy-Dandy Helpful Hal	Waite
Hard Winter at Broken Arrow Crossing	Bly
The Hare-Brained Habit	Davoll
Hartford	Hunt
The Haunting	Myers
Hawk and the Jewel	Wick
Hawks Don't Say Good-Bye	Bly
Hazards of the Half-Court Press	Bly
Heart and Soul	Funderburk
Heart Chaser	Bunn (Locke)
A Heart Full of Hope	Gunn
Heart of the Wilderness	Oke
Heart of Valor	Morris, A.
Heartbeat	Jenkins
Heartland Skies	Carlson
The Heather Hills of Stonewycke	Pella and Phillips
Heather's Choice	Page
The Heirloom	Minatra
Heirs of the Motherland	Pella
Hello, God!	Johnson, L. W.
Here Boy!	Roper
Here Comes Ginger!	Schulte
Hero for a Season	Levene
Hey, Teacher	Oke
Hidden in Time	Phillips
The Hidden Jewel	Jackson, D. and N.
The Hidden Message	Johnson, L. W.
High Country Ambush	Roddy
High Flyer with a Flat Tire	McCusker
The Highlander and His Lady	Samson
Hillary	Jenkins
A Hinge in Time	Pieters
Hobo Holiday	Davoll
Hold on Tight	Gunn
Hollyhock Gardens of Gneedle and Gnibb	Waite
The Holy Warrior	Morris, G.
Home by Another Way	Rue
A Home for the Heart	Phillips
Home to Willowbrook	Page
Homeward	Carlson
Homeward Heart	Johnson, L. H.
The Honorable Imposter	Morris, G.
Hoomania	Waite
A Hope Beyond	Pella
The Hope of Herrick House	Page
The Horse Who Loved Picnics	Dengler
The Hostage	Rue
Hot Chocolate Friendship	Levene
Hot Pursuit on the High Seas	Doyle
A House Divided	Pella and Phillips
The House of Tunnels	Jenkins
The House on Honeysuckle Lane	Page
Howie Hugemouth	Hunt
Hunted along the Rhine	Doyle
Hunted in the Alaskan Wilderness	Roddy
Hyaenas	Dengler
I Can Count on God	Carlson
I Only Binge on Holy Hungers	Rue
The Ice Queen	Johnson, L. H.
If I Had Long, Long Hair	Hunt
I'm Off to Montana for to Throw the Hoolihan	Bly

Title	Author
The Impatient Blossom	Roddy
The Impatient Turtle	Oke
Imperial Intrigue	Morris, A. and G.
Imprisoned in the Golden City	Jackson, D. and N.
In Deep Water	Jenkins
In Excess of Happiness	Pieters
In Search of Her Own	Page
In the Nick of Time	Myers
In the Presence of the Holy	Crow
In the Shadow of a Secret	Wubbels
In the Shadow of Victory	Bunn
In the Twilight, in the Evening	Morris, G. and L.
In Too Deep	Rushford
In Your Dreams	Gunn
The Indentured Heart	Morris, G.
Independence	Doyle
Indigo Waters	Samson
Ingram of the Irish	Hunt
Inside the Privet Hedge	Coyle
Into the Flames	Elmer
Into the Long Dark Night	Phillips
Intrigue at the Rafter B Ranch	Bly
The Invasion	Rue
Invasion of the UFOs	Myers
The Iron Lady	Morris, G.
The Iron Sceptre	White
Island Bride	Chaikin
Island Dreamer	Gunn
Island of the Innocent	Morris, G. and L.
Island Quarry	Herndon
Istanbul Express	Bunn
It Happened at the Sunset Grille	Cunningham
It's Your Misfortune and None of My Own	Bly
Jacob's Gift	Lucado
Jamaican Sunset	Chaikin
Jamestown	Hunt
Jamie MacLeod: Highland Lass	Pella and Phillips
Janell	Jenkins
The Janis Project	Rue
Jed Rivers: Rock of Ages	Bly
The Jennifer Grey Mysteries	Jenkins

Title	Author
Jen's Pride and Joy	Coyle
Jess and the Fire Plug Caper	Schulte
Jessica	Carlson
The Jeweled Spurs	Morris, G.
A Job for an Angel	Schulte
Jojofu	Waite
Jonah and the Big Fish	Carlson
Jordan's Crossing	Arthur
The Journals of Corrie and Christopher	Phillips
The Journey West	Schulte
Journey	Hunt
Journey with No Voyage Home	Pieters
Julia's Last Hope	Oke
Jungle Gold	Dengler
Just in Case You Ever Wonder	Lucado
Just Like Ice Cream	Johnson, L. H.
Justifiable Means	Blackstock
Kara	Page
Karlyn	Jenkins
Katharine	Riols
Kathryn: Days of Struggle and Triumph	Crow
Katie and the Amazon Mystery	Mezek
Katie Goes to New York	Mezek
Katie Lost in the South Seas	Mezek
Katie Sails the Nile	Mezek
Katie's Russian Holiday	Mezek
Katie's Swiss Adventure	Mezek
Keeper of the Harvest	Wubbels
The Key	Roper
Kidnapped by River Rats	Jackson, D. and N.
Kidnapped in Rome	Doyle
The Kidnapping	Jenkins
The Kill Fee of Miss Cindy Lacoste	Bly
Kimberly and the Captives	Hunt
King of the Stars	Dengler
The King's Quest	McCusker
Kingscote	Chaikin
The Knight and the Dove	Wick
Koala Beach Outbreak	Elmer
Lady Bug Island	Waite

Title	Author
Lady of Stonewycke	Pella and Phillips
Lambs of the Lie	Johnson, L. H.
Land of the Brave and Free	Phillips
Land of the Shadow	Morris, G.
Lane of Refuge	Pieters
The Last Confederate	Morris, G.
Last Dinosaur	Dengler
Last Hanging at Paradise Meadow	Bly
The Last Stubborn Buffalo in Nevada	Bly
Launched from the Castle	Doyle
Laura	Riols
Left Behind	Jenkins
The Legend of Fire	Roddy
The Legend of Robin Brodie	Samson
Legend of the Celtic Stone	Phillips
Legend of the White Raccoon	Roddy
Let Us Forget	Pieters
Lethal Mercy	Kraus
Letters from the Other Side	Cunningham
Leviathan	Huggins
The Life and Times of Grizzly Adams	Roddy
Light and Shadow	Bunn
A Light in the Castle	Elmer
A Light in the Window	Karon
Light Weaver	Bunn (Locke)
Lights Out at Camp What-a-Nut	McCusker
Like a Leaf in the Wind	Pieters
Lily Vanessa and the Pet Panic	Schulte
Lindsey	Jenkins
Lions of the Desert	Chaikin
Listen for the Whippoorwill	Jackson, D. and N.
Little People of the Lost Coast	Herndon
A Load of Trouble	Davoll
Lone Wolf	Morris, G.
The Long Road Home	Wick
Long Train Passing	Wise, S.
The Longing Fulfilled	Pieters
Lord Foulgrin's Letters	Alcorn
The Lord Is My Salvation	Austin
The Lord Is My Song	Austin
The Lord Is My Strength	Austin
The Lost Diary	Gustaveson
Lost in the Secret Cave	Doyle
The Lost Manuscript of Martin Taylor Harrison	Bly
The Lost Princess	Mezek
The Lost Swan in Sacramento	Bly
Love and Glory	Funderburk
Love Burning Bright	Hunt
Love Comes Softly	Oke
Love Embraces Destiny	Crow
Love Finds a Home	Oke
Love Incognito	Pieters
Love Is a Hopscotch Thing	Holmes
Love Takes Wing	Oke
Love Unmerited	Crow
Love's Abiding Joy	Oke
Love's Enduring Promise	Oke
Love's Far Horizon	Roddy
Love's Long Journey	Oke
Love's Ransom	Samson
Love's Unending Legacy	Oke
Love's Unfolding Dream	Oke
Loving One Another	Jackson, N.
The Lucas Secret and Other Stories	Rue
Lyle Lemon	Carlson
Lyssa	Jenkins
The Mad Dog of Lobo Mountain	Roddy
The Maestro	Bunn
The Maiden's Sword	Herr
The Man with the Terrible Secret	Jenkins
Manda's Mystery	Roper
Mandy	Borntrager
Margo	Jenkins
Margo Mysteries, Volume I	Jenkins
Margo Mysteries, Volume II	Jenkins
Margo's Reunion	Jenkins
Maria's Search	Page
The Marquesa	Bly
Marty's Secret	Jenkins
Mask of the Wolf Boy	Jackson, D. and N.
Master of Disaster	Levene
The Masterpiece	Minatra

Title	Author
The Matchmakers	Oke
Maury Had a Little Lamb	Oke
Max and the Big Fat Lie	Waite
The Mayflower Secret	Jackson, D. and N.
Meaghan	Jenkins
Measure of a Heart	Oke
The Meeting Place	Bunn and Oke
Megan's Promise	Coyle
Melanie and the Modeling Mess	Schulte
Melon Hound	Dengler
Memory's Gate	McCusker
Mercy and Eagleflight	Phillips
Mercy So Tender	Schulte
The Messenger	Bunn
The Messiah	Holmes
Midnight	Wise, S.
The Midnight Intruder	Roper
Midnight Rescue	Johnson, L. W.
Miggy and Tiggy	Waite
Mint Cookie Miracles	Levene
The Misfit	Rue
Miss Fannie's Hat	Karon
Miss Fontenot	Bly
The Missing Video	Gustaveson
Mist over Morro Bay	Fell and Page
A Model Murder	Dengler
The Moment I Saw You	Samson
Monday's Child	Chaikin
Morning, Morning True	Herndon
Morningsong	Rushford
Mortal Intent	Massie
Moses in the Bulrushes	Carlson
A Most Inconvenient Death	Crow
Mouse Trapped	Dengler
Mr. Zanthu's Golden Scheme	Crow
Mrs. Rosey-Posey and the Chocolate Cherry Treat	Gunn
Mrs. Rosey-Posey and the Empty Nest	Gunn
Mrs. Rosey-Posey and the Treasure Hunt	Gunn
The Much-Adored Sandy Shore	Hunt
Murder on the Mount	Dengler
The Music Box	Bunn
My Church	Davoll
My Father's God	Austin
My Father's World	Pella and Phillips
My Foot's in the Stirrup, My Pony Won't Stand	Bly
My Friends	Davoll
My Grandparents	Davoll
My Helpers	Davoll
My Home and Family	Davoll
My Life as a Blundering Ballerina	Myers
My Life as a Broken Bungee Cord	Myers
My Life as a Human Hair Ball	Myers
My Life as a Human Hockey Puck	Myers
My Life as a Screaming Skydiver	Myers
My Life as a Smashed Burrito with Extra Hot Sauce	Myers
My Life as a Toasted Time Traveler	Myers
My Life as a Torpedo Test Target	Myers
My Life as a Walrus Whoopee Cushion	Myers
My Life as Alien Monster Bait	Myers
My Life as an Afterthought Astronaut	Myers
My Life as Big Foot Breath Mint	Myers
My Life as Crocodile Junk Food	Myers
My Life as Dinosaur Dental Floss	Myers
My Life as Polluted Pond Scum	Myers
My Life as Reindeer Road Kill	Myers
My World	Davoll
The Mysterious Case	Gustaveson
The Mysterious Football Team	Jenkins
Mysterious Hideaway	Johnson, L. W.
Mysterious Love	Brinkerhoff
Mysterious Signal	Johnson, L. W.
Mystery at Harmony Hill	Roper
Mystery at McGehan Ranch	Dengler
Mystery at Raider Stadium	Jenkins
Mystery at Smokey Mountain	Gustaveson
Mystery of Aloha House	Roddy

Title	Author
Mystery of the Black Hole Mine	Roddy
Mystery of the Golden Palomino	Jenkins
Mystery of the Invisible Knight	Myers
Mystery of the Island Jungle	Roddy
Mystery of the Kidnapped Kid	Jenkins
Mystery of the Missing Map	Johnson, L. W.
Mystery of the Missing Sister	Jenkins
Mystery of the Mixed-Up Teacher	Jenkins
Mystery of the Phantom Gold	Roddy
Mystery of the Phony Murder	Jenkins
Mystery of the Scorpion Threat	Jenkins
Mystery of the Skinny Sophomore	Jenkins
Mystery of the Wild Surfer	Roddy
Mystery on the Midway	Jenkins
Nana's Gift	Oke
Narrow Walk	Brinkerhoff
Neeley Never Said Goodbye	Page
The Neighborhood's Scariest Woman	Jenkins
Never Again Good-Bye	Blackstock
Never Ashamed	Page
Never Dance with a Bobcat	Bly
The Never Ending Day	Johnson, L. H.
A New Beginning	Phillips
New Kid in Town	Oke
New Song	Karon
Nicolae	Jenkins
Nicolae High	Jenkins
Night of the Jungle Cat	Herndon
Night of the Vanishing Lights	Roddy
Nightmare in Branco Grande	Jenkins
No More Broken Promises	Hunt
No Other Choice	Johnson, L. H.
Noah and the Ark	Carlson
The Not So Great Escape	Myers
Now I Lay Me Down to Sleep	Rushford
Now Picture This	Gunn
Off to a New Start	Schulte
Old Familiar Places	Funderburk
Omega Network	Bunn (Locke)
On Hope's Wings	Carlson
On the Trail of Truth	Pella and Phillips
On Wings of Love	Schulte
Once Upon a Summer	Oke
One False Move	Bunn
One Shenandoah Winter	Bunn
One Small Miracle	Wubbels
One Went to Denver and the Other Went Wrong	Bly
Only You Sierra	Gunn
Opal Fire	Dengler
Open Your Heart	Gunn
Operation Cemetery	Jenkins
The Operative	Jenkins
The Other Brother	Carlson
Out of the Whirlwind	Morris, G.
Out to Canaan	Karon
Over the Edge	Rushford
Over the Misty Mountains	Morris, G.
The Overland Escape	Roddy
A Pack of Lies	Davoll
Paige	Jenkins
Panic at Emu Flat	Elmer
Panic in the Wild Waters	Roddy
A Paper Ship	Pieters
The Parrot Who Talked Too Much	Jackson, N.
Passage into Light	Pella
A Passage through Darkness	Bunn
Path Finder	Bunn (Locke)
A Path through the Wilderness	Pieters
The Patriots	Cavanaugh
Peace Like a River	Schulte
The Peacemaker	Phillips (Livingstone) and Pella
The Peacemakers	Cavanaugh
Peach Pit Popularity	Levene
Peachy Pete	Carlson
Peanut Butter and Jelly Secrets	Levene
Penny Pear	Carlson
Peril at Pirate's Point	Roddy
The Pet That Never Was	Levene
Phantom of the Circus	Morris, G.

Title	Author
Phantom of the Haunted Church	Myers
A Picnic with the Barleys	Mezek
Pineapple Paul	Carlson
Pinnacles of Power	Phillips
The Pioneers	Cavanaugh
The Pirate and His Lady	Chaikin
A Place Called Home	Wick
A Place in the Sun	Pella and Phillips
A Place to Come Home To	Carlson
Point of No Return	McCusker
Polly	Borntrager
Pontius Pilate	Maier
Pordy's Prickly Problem	Oke
Port Royal	Chaikin
The Portal	Myers
The Potluck Supper	Davoll
Power of Pinjarra	Dengler
Prairie Dog Town	Oke
The Presence	Bunn
The President's Stuck in the Mud	Bly
Presumption of Guilt	Blackstock
Pretense	Wick
The Pride and the Passion	Cavanaugh
The Princess	Wick
Princess Bella and the Red Velvet Hat	Bunn
The Prisoner	Rue
Private Justice	Blackstock
The Problem with Prickles	Davoll
The Prodigal Cat	Oke
Professor Q's Mysterious Machine	Crow
Project Black Bear	Johnson, L. H.
A Promise for Tomorrow	Pella
A Promise Is Forever	Gunn
Promise Me Tomorrow	Wick
The Promise of Peace	Grant
The Promise of the Harvest	Grant
The Promise of the Willows	Grant
The Promise of Victory	Grant
Promises to Keep	Bunn
The Proposal	Hunt
The Proving Ground	Davis
The Puritans	Cavanaugh

Title	Author
Pursued	Rushford
The Puzzle of the Poison Pen	Roper
The Quality of Mercy	Morris, G.
The Queen's Smuggler	Jackson, D. and N.
Quest for the King	White
Quest for the Lost Prince	Jackson, D. and N.
Quest for the Promised Land	Cavanaugh
The Quick and the Dead	Dengler
Quiet Strength	Oke
The Quilt	Bunn
Race against Time	Morris, G.
A Race against Time	Kritlow
The Race for Autumn's Glory	Fell
Race for Freedom	Johnson, L. W.
Race for the Record	Jackson, D. and N.
A Race to the Finish	Roper
Race to Wallaby Bay	Elmer
Race with Death	Morris, G.
Rachel	Borntrager
Rachel's Hope	Page
The Rainbow's End	Funderburk
Rainy Day Rescue	Davoll
The Ramparts of Heaven	Morris, G.
Rebecca	Borntrager
The Rebel	Rue
The Reckoning	Huggins
Red Dove of Monterey	Bly
Red Geranium, The	Oke
Red Sky in Morning	Rushford
The Refining Fire	Davis
Rehoboth	Hunt
The Reluctant Bridegroom	Morris, G.
The Remnant	Morris, G., and Funderburk
Reno	Morris, G.
The Rescue	Rue
Rescue at Boomerang Bend	Elmer
Rescue in the Desert	Dengler
Retreat to Love	Rue
Return to Harmony	Bunn and Oke
Reuben	Borntrager
The Revelation	Grant
Revenge at the Rodeo	Morris, G.
Revenge of the Space Pirate	Morris, G.
Revenge on Eagle Island	Bly
Rhineland Inheritance	Bunn
The Riddle of Baby Rosalind	Hunt

Title	Author
Ride the Wild River	Morris, G.
Riders of the Pale Horse	Bunn
A Rift in Time	Phillips
The Right Hand of God	Morris, G.
Right up There with Graces	Rue
Rimrock	Morris, G.
"Rivers" of Arizona	Bly
Roanoke: The Lost Colony	Hunt
Robbie Taggart: Highland Sailor	Pella and Phillips
Rookie	Jenkins
A Rose for Jenny	Page
A Rose Remembered	Phillips
Rosemarie	Pieters
Roses for Mama	Oke
Roses in Autumn	Crow
The Rough Rider	Morris, G.
Row This Boat Ashore	Rue
The Rumpoles and the Barleys	Mezek
The Runaway Clown	Johnson, L. W.
Runaway Dreams	Johnson, L. H.
The Runaway's Revenge	Jackson, D. and N.
Rustlers of Panther Gap	Morris, G.
Sahara Crosswind	Bunn
The Saintly Buccaneer	Morris, G.
Salty Scarecrow Solution	Levene
The Samaritan	Rue
Sammy's Gadget Galaxy	Waite
Sarah	Borntrager
Saturday Night	Holmes
Saved by the Bell	Davoll
The Scary Basketball Player	Jenkins
Scattered Flowers	Jenkins
The Scream	Myers
The Sea Hag's Treasure	Carlson
Sea to Shining Sea	Phillips
Sean Donovan	Wick
Search for the Avenger	Roddy
A Searching Heart	Oke
Seasons under Heaven	Blackstock
Second Chance	Jenkins
The Secret	Rue
Secret at Mossy Roots Mansion	Davoll
The Secret Baseball Challenge	Jenkins
Secret Cave of Robin Wood	McCusker
The Secret Footage	Gustaveson
The Secret in the Kitchen	Johnson, L. H.
The Secret of Cravenhill Castle	Hunt
The Secret of Lizard Island	Herndon
The Secret of Mad River	Roddy
The Secret of Richmond Manor	Morris, G.
The Secret of the Burning House	Roper
Secret of the East Wind	Fell and Page
Secret of the Howling Cave	Roddy
The Secret of the Old Rifle	Bly
Secret of the Planet Makon	Morris, G.
Secret of the Shark Pit	Roddy
Secret of the Sunken Submarine	Roddy
Secret Place of Thunder	Morris, G. and L.
Secrets	Gunn
Senior Trip	Holmes
Separate Roads	Pella
Seventeen Wishes	Gunn
Seventh Grade Soccer Star	Roper
Shades of Light	Carlson
Shadow of Doubt	Blackstock
The Shadow of Eden	Joens
The Shadow of His Wings	Morris, G.
Shadow of the Mountains	Morris, G. and L.
The Shadow Portrait	Morris. G.
Shadows over Stonewycke	Pella and Phillips
The Shamrock Shore	Dengler
Shanghaied to China	Jackson, D. and N.
Shannon	Jenkins
Sharon's Hope	Coyle
Shelby the Magnificent	Waite
The Shield of Honor	Morris, G.
Shiloh's Choice	Roddy
A Shiny Red Sled	Davoll
Shoelaces and Brussels Sprouts	Levene
A Short Tail	Davoll
SHRUG, The Self-Doubting Thomas	Jackson, D. and N.

Title	Author
A Silence in Heaven	Funderburk and Morris, G.
The Silent Track Star	Jenkins
Silent Witness	Rushford
Silk	Chaikin
Silver Dreams	Chaikin
The Silver Star	Morris, G.
The Silver Sword	Hunt
The Singing Shepherd	Hunt
Sir Maggie the Mighty	Waite
Sisters of the Wolf	Herndon
Skate Expectations	Myers
A Skeleton in God's Closet	Maier
The Sleeping Rose	Hunt
Sliced Heather on Toast	Johnson, L. H.
SMASH, How to Survive Junior High by Really Trying	Jackson, D. and N.
Smugglers on Grizzly Mountain	Herndon
SNAG, "I'm Dreaming of a White Christmas"	Jackson, D. and N.
SNAP, How to Act Like a Responsible Almost-Adult	Jackson, D. and N.
The Society	Myers
Socorro Island Treasure	Dengler
The Soldier Boy Discovery	Morris, G.
Some Things Last Forever	Wubbels
Someone On Your Side	Pieters
Something to Live For	Johnson, L. H.
Sometimes Happiness Comes with a New Face	Pieters
Son of an Arizona Legend	Bly
Song for Kasey	Page
A Song for Silas	Wick
Song in a Strange Land	Morris, G.
The Song of Princes	Morris, G.
The Song of the King	Lucado
Song of the Nereids	Dengler
Songs of Joy	Schulte
Sophie's Heart	Wick
Soul Harvest	Jenkins
Sound the Trumpet	Morris, G.
The Spell	Myers
SPIN, Truth, Tubas, and George Washington	Jackson, D. and N.
The Spirit of Appalachia	Morris, G.
The Spring of Our Exile	Funderburk
Spring's Gentle Promise	Oke
Springtime Discovery	Jenkins
Spunky's Diary	Oke
Spy for the Night Riders	Jackson, D. and N.
The Stain	Kraus
Stainless Steal Hearts	Kraus
Stalked in the Catacombs	Doyle
Standoff at Sunrise Creek	Bly
A Star in the Breaking	Myers
Star Light, Star Bright	Hunt
Starry Night	Gunn
Stars for a Light	Morris, G. and L.
Stars in Their Courses	Morris, G.
Stay away from That City, They Call It Cheyenne	Bly
Stephanie	Rue
Stephanie: Days of Turmoil and Peace	Crow
A Sticky Mystery	Davoll
The Stolen Necklace	Gustaveson
Stoner's Crossing	Pella
Stop in the Name of Love (Holly)	Rue
Stop in the Name of Love (Kyle)	Rue
Storm Clouds over Paradise	Fell and Page
Storms over Willowbrook	Page
The Stowaway	Rue
Stranded on Terror Island	Roddy
Strange Journey Back	McCusker
The Strange Swimming Coach	Jenkins
Stranger at Stonewycke	Pella and Phillips
Stranger in the Mist	McCusker
Stranger's Message	McCusker
Strawberry Sam	Carlson
The Stunt	Rue
Sudden Switch	McCusker
Summer Is Coming	Fell

Title	Author
Summer of a Stranger	Page
Summer of the Wild Pig	Dengler
Summer Promise	Gunn
Summer Snow	Dengler
A Sunday Surprise	Davoll
Sunsets	Gunn
Surprise Endings	Gunn
Surrounded by Crossfire	Doyle
Suspended Animation	Davis
Suzannah and the Secret Coins	Schulte
Suzannah Strikes Gold	Schulte
Suzy Swoof	Waite
Sweet Carolina	Bly
Sweet Dreams	Gunn
The Swindler's Treasure	Johnson, L. W.
The Sword Bearer	White
The Sword of Camelot	Morris, G.
The Sword of Truth	Morris, G.
Swords and Scimitars	Chaikin
Sylvester the Jester	Waite
The Table	Myers
Take Me out of the Ball Game	Myers
Take My Hand	Gunn
The Tale of Three Trees	Hunt
A Tale of Two Houses	Carlson
The Taming of Cheetah	Roddy
Tammy Tangerine	Carlson
The Tapestry	Minatra
Taste of Fame	Page
Taste of Victory	Dengler
Tattletale Tongue	Davoll
T-Bone Trouble	Levene
The Telescope	Pieters
Tell Me the Secrets	Lucado
Tell Me the Story	Lucado
The Temptation of Aaron Campbell	Samson
Ten O'Clock Scholar	Holmes
The Tender Years	Oke
Tenderness and Fire	Funderburk
Terror at Forbidden Falls	Roddy
Terror in the Sky	Roddy
Texas Angel	Pella
There Will Be No Miracle	Pieters
These Golden Days	Funderburk
These High Green Hills	Karon
They Called Her Mrs. Doc	Oke
The Thief	Rue
The Thieves of Tyburn Square	Jackson, D. and N.
The Third Millennium	Wise, R.
This Is My Haven	Pieters
This Little Pig	Oke
This Lovely, Hazardous Life	Pieters
This Rolling Land	Dengler
The Threat	Rue
Three Days in Winter	Jenkins
Three from Galilee	Holmes
Threshold	Myers
Through the Flames	Jenkins
Tidings of Comfort and Joy	Bunn
A Time of War	Morris, G.
A Time to Be Born	Morris, G.
A Time to Build	Morris, G.
A Time to Cherish	Gunn
A Time to Die	Morris, G.
A Time to Heal	Funderburk and Morris, G.
Time to Tell	Jenkins
A Time to Weep	Morris, G.
Time Warp Tunnel	Bly
Time Will Tell	Gunn
To Be Worthy	Crow
To Catch the Summer Wind	Fell
To Chase a Dark Shadow	Page
To Die in the Queen of Cities	Dengler
To Dust You Shall Return	Crow
To Know Her by Name	Wick
To Live Again	Riols
To the Ends of the Earth	Bunn
Tomorrow's Dream	Bunn and Oke
Too Late to Tell	Jenkins
Too Long a Stranger	Oke
Too Many Secrets	Rushford
Touch the Sky	Elmer
Toward the Sunrising	Morris, G. and L.
The Tower of Geburah	White
Tracks of Deceit	Morris, A. and G.
Traitor in the Tower	Jackson, D. and N.
The Trap	Rue
Trapped by the Wolf Pack	Roddy
Trapped in Pharaoh's Tomb	Doyle
Travail and Triumph	Pella and Phillips
Treachery at the River Canyon	Bly

Title	Author
The White Trail	Davoll
Who Brings Forth the Wind	Wicke
Whoo Done It?	Roper
Who's New at the Zoo	Oke
Wild Grows the Heather in Devon	Phillips
Wind from the Wilderness	Morris, G.
Winds of Allegiance	Chaikin
The Winds of Autumn	Oke
The Winds of God	Morris, G.
Winged Raiders of the Desert	Morris, G.
Wings of a Dove	Smith
Wings of Healing	Morris, A.
Wings of the Morning	Wicke
Winter Is Not Forever	Oke
Winter of Grace	Funderburk
Winter Palace	Bunn
Winterspring	Dengler
Wisdom Hunter	Arthur
Wise Man's House	Carlson
Wishing Upon a Star	Johnson, L. H.
With This Ring	Gunn
With Wings as Eagles	Schulte
Without a Doubt	Gunn
Without a Trace	Rushford
Witness in Heaven	Morris, G.
Wizards of the Galaxy	Morris, G.
Wolf Story	Huggins
A Woman Called Damaris	Oke
The Wonder of Christmas: A Family Advent Journey	Carlson
Word of Honor	Blackstock
World by the Tail	Holmes
The Wounded Yankee	Morris, G.
Yankee Belles in Dixie	Morris, G.
Yesterday's Shadow	Roddy
You Are Special	Lucado
You Can Always Trust a Spotted Horse	Bly
You Say Tomato	McCusker
Yours Forever	Gunn
The Yukon Queen	Morris, G.

About Janice DeLong and Rachel Schwedt

Janice DeLong holds two master's degrees in education and has completed postgraduate hours in children's literature. She taught in both public and parochial schools for thirteen years prior to entering the collegiate system in 1985. Since that time, she has served on the education faculty at Liberty University in Lynchburg, Virginia. Janice is married to Robert DeLong, a member of the psychology faculty at Liberty University. They are the parents of Beth, Michael, Lynne, and Kara and share the hobbies of flower gardening, bird watching, and reading. Janice also enjoys working in the church nursery and singing in the choir.

Rachel Schwedt holds a master's degree in library science and has been a kindergarten teacher, English teacher, and librarian in both private and public schools. She presently supervises the curriculum library at Liberty University in Lynchburg, Virginia. Rachel is married to Ronald Schwedt, who teaches woodworking, drafting, and photojournalism. They have two grown children, Julie and Alan, and enjoy searching for antiques together.